CORPORATE PLANNING MODELS

CORPORATE PLANNING MODELS

Thomas H. Naylor

Duke University
and President Social Systems, Inc.
Chapel Hill, N.C.

ADDISON-WESLEY PUBLISHING COMPANY

Reading, Massachusetts · Menlo Park, California
London · Amsterdam · Don Mills, Ontario · Sydney

ISBN 0-201-05226-1
BCDEFGHIJ-MA-79

To Dawn

Preface

Although corporate planning models came into existence in the early 1960s, their use did not become widespread until the middle 1970s. The advent of computer-based planning models is a direct response to a series of very serious problems encountered by corporations throughout the world in the early 1970s including increasing energy costs, the 1974–1975 recession, double-digit inflation, environmental pollution, cash shortages, consumerism, and increased government regulation to mention only a few. These problems have placed enormous pressure on the senior management of large corporations. As it became increasingly apparent that manual planning systems were not adequate to meet the planning requirements of the future, corporate planning models have proven to be extremely powerful tools to enable management to cope more effectively with an uncertain future.

This book is concerned with the theory and practice of corporate planning modeling. It attempts to outline a systematic approach to the design, development, and implementation of corporate planning models. The methodology employed in this book has been tested in several hundred different companies. The orientation is pragmatic and focuses on the necessary steps required to achieve acceptance of computer-based planning models by top management.

For expository purposes the discussion is divided into three functional areas—finance, marketing, and production. In each case the methodology is developed and illustrated with example models. The treatment of time series forecasting models and econometric models assumes a minimal knowledge of basic statistics on the part of the reader. Otherwise, elementary algebra is the only mathematical prerequisite for the book. An integrated business planning model is presented in Chapter 9 that features a financial planning model that is driven by an econometric marketing model and a relatively unsophisticated production model.

Perhaps the most important chapter in the entire book is Chapter 10 entitled

"The Politics of Corporate Model Building." Special attention is devoted to the interface between the model builders and the model users, namely senior management. Some of the typical political conflicts surrounding corporate planning models are described. Questions of goals and objectives, organization, and implementation are also treated. The chapter also contains a list of common reasons why corporate models may fail.

Five corporate modeling case studies are included in the book. David F. Weigel and Lucy Quintilliano describe project planning for a corporate planning model developed by Hammermill Paper Company. The *New York Times* planning model, an integrated financial, marketing, and production planning model, is presented by Dr. Leonard Forman. Another integrated planning model, the Dresser planning model, has been summarized by its authors, Charles H. Hatfield, Jr., and Bryant K. Kershaw. The most advanced computer-based planning model in Europe, the CIBA–GEIGY model, is presented by Dr. Friedrich Rosenkranz. Finally, the integrated power system planning model of the Tennessee Valley Authority, probably the most sophisticated planning model in the United States, has been contributed by Dr. Douglas H. Walters and R. Taber Jenkins.

Chapters 4 through 7 and Chapter 9 make use of a special purpose planning and modeling computer language known as SIMPLAN. Given the English-like nature of SIMPLAN, the reader need not have previous knowledge of computer programming to follow the SIMPLAN examples included throughout the book. SIMPLAN has been installed on IBM computers throughout the United States as well as in Canada, Mexico, Europe, and the Middle East. In addition, it is available throughout the world on seven computer service bureaus: (1) Information Services Business Division of the General Electric Company (worldwide); (2) Data Services Division of Informatics, Inc. (United States); (3) Canada Systems Group, Ltd. (Canada and United States); (4) AVCO Data Services (Northeast); (5) A. O. Smith Data Systems Division (Midwest); (6) Martin Marietta Data Systems; and (7) McDonnell Douglas Automation.

Appendix A contains an introduction to SIMPLAN. However, the reader who wishes to obtain an in-depth knowledge of SIMPLAN should consult *Corporate Planning and Modeling with SIMPLAN* written by R. Britton Mayo and published by Addison-Wesley in 1978. Developed by Mr. Mayo, SIMPLAN is the property of Social Systems, Inc. (SSI). Mr. Mayo was assisted in the development of SIMPLAN by his colleagues Horst Schauland, William L. Lindley, Edmund Pettiss, Michael W. Sherrill, David L. Wilkerson, and Franklin W. Hecker – all members of the staff of SSI.

This book evolved over an eight-year period and many people contributed to its development. Terry G. Seaks and W. Corbett Rouse wrote portions of some of the chapters and have been acknowledged as co-authors. Mitchell S. Diamond, Daniel L. Blakely, and Malcolm B. Coate made numerous technical suggestions. Among those who helped with the preparation of the manuscript over the years were Gail Parks and Carol Hamlett.

I am grateful to the Literary Executor of the late Sir Ronald A. Fisher, F.R.S., to Dr. Frank Yates, F.R.S., and to the Longman Group Ltd., London, for permission to reprint Table III from their book *Statistical Tables for Biological, Agricultural, and Medical Research* (6th ed., 1974).

This book is dedicated to Dawn Naylor who, for five of the eight years in which this book was in progress, provided inspiration, support, and good cheer when they were needed most.

Chapel Hill, North Carolina   T.H.N
July 1978

Contents

1   Introduction to Corporate Planning Models

WHY CORPORATE PLANNING MODELS?

Nearly 2000 firms in the United States, Canada, and Mexico are either using, developing, or experimenting with some form of corporate planning model. Computer-based planning models represent an attempt to describe the complex interrelationships among a corporation's financial, marketing, and production activities in terms of a system of mathematical and logical relationships which have been programmed into a computer.

In 1969, George Gershefski was able to identify only 63 firms which were actually using corporate planning models.[1] Two questions emerge when we consider the aforementioned data. Why has the number of corporations employing computer-based planning models increased so dramatically? Why corporate planning models?

Lewis Young, editor-in-chief of *Business Week* has suggested that "Corporate planning models and management science are substitutes for good management." On the other hand, one of the advertisers in *Business Week*, the International Business Machines Corporation, frequently devotes the major portion of its two-page advertisements to only two words—"What if?" In the lower right-hand corner of these ads one reads:

> Planning will never become an exact science
> But it can now be less of a venture into the unknown.
> The Future is a moving target.
> Computers can improve your aim.

This book is about computer-based planning models and how these models can be used to "improve your aim."

The essence of corporate planning is to help corporate management face *risk* and *uncertainty*. If management knows (1) what its competitors are going to do; (2) what legislation will be passed by Congress or the state legislature; (3) what policies will be enacted by the Federal Reserve Board; (4) what the pricing and supply policies of the

Organization of Petroleum Exporting Countries (OPEC) will be; and (5) what the Chinese, Russians, Arabs, and Israelis are going to be doing, then planning is a technical exercise and management need not resort to the use of any computer-based planning model to plan its course of action. But rarely is management armed with even partial information about such important events. It is more likely that management will be confronted with a high degree of risk and uncertainty concerning major external events of this nature.

The rationale underlying the use of computer-based planning models is identical to the rationale underlying corporate planning. Corporate planning models cannot predict the future, but they can be used to help management get a handle on risk and uncertainty. Forecasts generated by corporate planning models are no better than the assumptions on which they are based, but corporate planning models can improve management's ability to cope with the impact a wide variety of problems and opportunities may have on a company that cause risk and uncertainty. In the following paragraphs, six sets of problems and opportunities are described that have caused corporate management to reevaluate the importance of formalized corporate planning and to turn to computer-based planning models.

Energy Crisis

In the fall of 1973, the OPEC signaled the beginning of the "energy crisis" by cutting off the supply of crude oil from the Middle East and by setting the price of crude oil at a level most people never dreamed possible. The price of gasoline doubled within a few weeks and gasoline shortages began to appear at the retail level. The energy crisis exposed the fact that the state of the art of planning in the United States and other parts of the world was abysmal. The federal government neither anticipated the timing nor the depth of the problem.

Ed Carlson, Chairman of United Air Lines (UAL), expressed the dilemma of the airline industry in the *New York Times*:

> The airline industry is faced with many problems, but the worst problem of them all is our government is unable to move toward a unified, workable, productive energy policy. It is our greatest concern.

The Treasurer of UAL was equally concerned about the recession spawned by the energy crisis and the fact that jet fuel prices at United would increase by 250 percent in 18 months. Specifically, the treasurer was troubled by questions such as: What will be the impact on UAL's cash flow of a leveling off in air traffic demand combined with substantial increases in jet fuel prices? Should UAL raise or lower fares, and what changes should be made in the fleet of jet aircraft? Should UAL follow Eastern and Braniff's lead in reducing and replacing the airline's fleet of DC-10s and 747s by stretched 727s? What will the impact be on the company's cash situation over the next two years? To be sure, all of these questions could have been answered manually by the accountants and financial analysts at United Air Lines. But every time the treasurer asked a different "What if?" question, it would literally take workdays to crank out the answers. In 1974, UAL developed a simple cash forecasting model to facilitate its financial planning process and help the treasurer answer some of these questions.

In 1974, companies such as Babcock and Wilcox, General Electric, and Westinghouse, which produce nuclear power generators, were suddenly confronted with a series of delays and cancellations of orders for nuclear generators. Within a few months, electric utilities, which buy nuclear power generators, encountered a sequence of severe problems. First, the prices of natural gas, oil, and coal increased substantially, thus increasing the cost of producing electricity. Second, consumer advocates were pressing for lower electric energy rates. Third, environmentalists expressed concern over the hazards of nuclear power. Fourth, the financial markets from which private utilities obtain funds temporarily ceased to exist. Faced with this array of problems, it was not surprising that electric utilities began hedging their bets on the future because the lead-time to install a nuclear power plant is nearly 15 years. Companies which produce nuclear power generators began asking themselves about the financial consequences of cancellations and delays in orders for nuclear power plants.

During 1974 through 1976, major shortages of natural gas in the textile industry in North and South Carolina were averted only by unusually mild winters. Unfortunately, the projected shortages materialized in the winter of 1977. What if there is sufficient natural gas to operate the mill for only two shifts a day for three days a week? The dearth of formal planning systems in the textile industry has made it difficult to answer questions of this type. Again the energy crisis exposed deficiencies in management's ability to plan for the future.

Finally, state and local governments and other institutions encountered similar problems in forecasting the energy crisis and planning for the consequences of energy shortages. The series of energy offices set up in each of the 50 states of the United States proved to be ineffective and powerless in coping with the problem.

But in places such as Houston, Texas, one does not refer to the energy crisis but to the energy opportunity. Indeed, many people in the oil and gas business in Houston were not even aware of the 1974–1975 recession. Companies such as ARCO, Phillips Petroleum, and Standard Oil of Ohio (SOHIO) stand to reap substantial profits from recently discovered oil fields which are now being developed. SOHIO and ARCO are the principals in the development of the North Slope of Alaska. The completion of the Alaskan pipeline is of great importance to each of them. Phillips, on the other hand, has a major interest in the North Sea. In each case, these oil companies will enjoy significant increases in profits and cash flow as a result of the completion of these projects. What should they do with the profits? First, they might simply increase their dividend payments to their stockholders. Second, they could reinvest their profits in new exploration projects in hopes of finding yet other sources of oil. Third, they may choose to hedge and put some of their profits into coal, shale oil, or nuclear power. Fourth, they may want to seek new investment alternatives completely removed from energy production. In any case, comprehensive planning will be a necessity if these companies are to exploit the full potential of their opportunities. Corporate planning models may make it easier to evaluate the alternatives available to the oil companies.

Shortages

In 1974, for the first time since the end of World War II, manufacturing industries encountered shortages in a wide variety of factor inputs in their production processes. Natural gas, coal, petroleum feedstocks, and a broad range of minerals were all in short supply. Indeed, the energy crisis was merely a special case of a more general problem. Although the 1975 recession brought temporary relief, this problem appears to be a long-run problem. An excessive rate of population growth throughout the world and increased per capita consumption among the more affluent nations are the causes of this problem. Our natural resources are being depleted at alarmingly high rates.

We have drilled the shallow oil wells and have developed the surface mines. The next time around, the oil wells will be much deeper and more expensive. Offshore wells will replace conventional wells. Our mines will also be deeper than they were in the past. We have skimmed off the cream and have taken the easy profits. Barring some major breakthrough in technology, which seems unlikely, shortages and rising factor input prices are likely to be with us for a long time.

Both the energy crisis and the more general problems of shortages have put enormous pressure on energy producing companies. Political opportunists and demagogues have proposed countless pieces of legislation, some of which would further aggravate our energy problems in the long run. Oil companies are confronted with irrational price controls and proposals to force them to divest themselves of many of their current activities and projects. The vice-president of a major oil company has suggested three alternative scenarios for planning for the future of the oil industry:

- Our problems will be overcome.
- The present momentum will continue.
- Socialism will triumph.

As a direct result of the energy crisis and shortages, increased attention is being given to the case for national economic planning in the United States. In *Time* magazine's feature article (June 14, 1975) entitled "Can Capitalism Survive?" Henry Ford II called for the creation of a highly visible and vocal federal planning body, "not because some wild radicals demand it but because businessmen will demand it to keep the system from sputtering to a halt." According to Mr. Ford, a national planning organization should analyze

> cost effectiveness and set timetables. It should take a look at population growth; usages of raw materials and their availability; what the price situation is going to be over a long period of time. We are going to need all kinds of plans.

Money

In the 1960s, inflation was not a major concern to most of us. It was something we read about that existed in faraway places like Brazil and Chile. By the early 1970s, inflation had become a fact of life in virtually every country in the western hemisphere. Corporate planners found that they had no real choice but to take inflation into consideration in evaluating future plans.

Inflation, tight money, the international liquidity crunch, high interest rates, and cash flow problems represent a set of interdependent problems which very few firms throughout the world managed to escape during the 1970s. Although we have all felt the impact of these problems, financial institutions (banks, savings and loan associations, and insurance companies) have been particularly influenced by these forces. The demise of the Penn Central, the Franklin National Bank, and W. T. Grant did not go unnoticed by financial institutions in the United States, nor the fact that there were 13 bank failures in 1975—the largest number in one year since the end of the Great Depression. Property–casualty insurance companies were particularly hard hit by inflation, a slow economic recovery, and premium levels inadequate to cover large underwriting losses from both property and accident-and-health insurance.

Banks, insurance companies, and others began asking themselves the question: "Do I have an adequate early warning system to enable me to anticipate liquidity problems before they become acute and while I still have a number of viable options available to me?" Many financial institutions, including some very large banks, were made to realize that their planning systems were inadequate to meet these challenges. Since 1974, banks in particular have shown increased interest in bank planning models, asset–liability models, cash flow models, and investment analysis models.

In 1973, a large regional bank in the United States (the largest in its region) based its 1974 plan on one and only one assumption—the prime rate of interest would go down in 1974. Unfortunately, the prime rate of interest did *not* go down in 1974. Instead, it reached 12 percent. As a result of *one-scenario planning*, that bank became the second largest bank in its region. Many firms engage in one-scenario planning because the cost of manually evaluating alternative scenarios is so high in terms of personnel time that management is frequently presented only one plan or one scenario. A simple financial planning model would have made it possible for the bank's management to compute the cost of being wrong in its assumption about the prime rate of interest. In other words, suppose that we bet that the prime would drop to 7 percent in 1974 and it actually went to 10 percent or possibly even 12 percent. What risks do we take by assuming the prime will go down, if, in fact, if goes up? Forecasting the prime is difficult business and econometric model builders are not noted for their success in attempting to predict this rate. Would the bank's management have made a different decision if it had known the cost of being wrong?

Computer-based planning models enable management to examine alternative futures and to look at multiple scenarios. Indeed, it can be argued that computer-based planning models make planning possible. Without the ability to look at alternative futures, planning is impossible.

Government Regulation

Increased government regulation has become a fact of life in the United States. No major industry has managed to escape the ever-extending arms of all levels of government in this country. Although many government regulations are well intended, their side effects are frequently extremely costly.

Consider the following examples. The requirement of pollution abatement devices on all automobiles sent prices sky high and contributed significantly to the 1974–1975 depression of the auto industry. Federal water pollution regulations drove many marginal producers of paper out of business and greatly increased the cost of building new paper mills. Artificially imposed price ceilings on natural gas and crude oil have had an adverse effect on exploration and drilling activity in the oil and gas industries at a time when we could ill afford reductions in the supply of these critical sources of energy.

For some industries, increased governmental activity may produce windfall gains. The pharmaceutical industry would reap substantial benefits from the passage of a national health insurance program by the Congress. Per capita drug consumption in the U.S. would probably double or triple. On the other hand, national health insurance may be accompanied by government-imposed price controls on drugs.

If one is planning for the future, one cannot avoid taking into consideration the likely impact of pending government legislation and programs. Although we do not know how to build models to predict the behavior of legislative bodies and governmental agencies, we can build planning models to monitor the possible impact of proposed programs on a particular company.

International Competition

In recent years, the United States has encountered some difficulty in keeping up with the rate of growth in productivity among the more highly industrialized countries of the world. During several years we have lagged significantly behind the rate of growth in productivity of the other ten most highly industrialized nations of the world. It goes without saying that this problem can result in severe competitive problems for companies based in the United States unless it is brought under control.

That part of this problem is attributed to attitudes of blue-collar workers toward work is well documented in the literature. This problem is sometimes referred to as worker alienation, blue-collar blues, and the Lordstown syndrome.

We would like to suggest that there may also be another problem—a management problem. For over 50 years the United States has led the world in technological innovation and the ability to manage large business enterprises. Yet there is increasing evidence that maybe the rest of the world is catching up with the United States. The gap between American corporations and certain Japanese, Swiss, West German, and Swedish corporations may even have a negative sign associated with it. In all too many cases, American business leaders and American business schools have become smug and complacent. In Europe in the 1960s, a number of large European multinational corporations managed to beat their American counterparts at their own game. West German corporations have successfully experimented with innovative programs involving worker participation in management and co-determination. Messerschmitt has introduced flextime work and Siemens pioneered in some exciting new programs in leadership development. Volvo's nontraditional production methods are now being emulated in other parts of Europe and even in the United States.

Economic Uncertainty

Many American corporations did not accurately forecast the timing or depth of the 1974–1975 recession. National econometric forecasters did not do very well either in forecasting the recession. Some forecasts were better than others. Forecasting the future is the single most difficult goal to achieve both with corporate planning models and econometric models.

Consider the case of the semiconductor manufacturer in New Jersey in 1975 that had built a new corporate office building but did not have sufficient cash to move into the building. Management had assumed that somehow the rate of growth of the semiconductor business would continue to grow forever at the same rate it had grown in the 1960s, but it didn't work out that way. The company was stuck with an eight-story, unoccupied building providing a constant reminder to its stockholders of its bad forecasting and poor planning.

In August of 1974, when there were clear signs on the horizon that the economy was headed toward a recession, the textile industry was accumulating inventories at a rapid rate at precisely the time when the prices of cotton and synthetic fibers were at record highs. The conspicuous absence of formalized planning in the industry left it extremely vulnerable to an unexpected economic downswing. When the crunch came, the industry was badly crippled and the rate of unemployment in the state of North Carolina went over 13 percent. For several months, only the state of South Dakota had a rate of growth in personal income that was less than that of North Carolina. Both the textile industry and the economies of North Carolina and South Carolina paid dearly for the textile industry's inept forecasting and planning.

As Michael J. Kami has pointed out in *Planning Review* (March, 1976), a number of corporate giants including Sears, Roebuck and General Motors were

mesmerized by constant growth and consequently dismissed the repetitive signals of discontinuity as unimportant wiggles on the charts. Some of the most astute corporate managements took the same blind trail. For example, Sears, Roebuck and Company, considered by many as the leading organization in its excellence of strategic and tactical planning, made this error. . . . But in 1974 the sales growth was far less than inflation growth, and profits slumped for the first time in 13 years. Sears missed several turning points and kept going in the wrong direction. Sears' stores were growing through the strategy of "upgrading"—increasing the value of their wares. Through extensive television advertising, Sears promoted its house brands as name brands, pushed its higher-quality and higher-priced lines. Soon higher markups meant that all prices crept up, and whole segments of lower-priced merchandise were surrendered to discounters and other competitors—even to Montgomery Ward.

The Sears strategy of "Trade Up America" was natural under the premise of a steadily increasing affluent society. With considerable foresight, in September 1974, *Forbes* compared this approach to the hypothetical situation of MacDonald's introducing the sirloin steak, raising the price of the Big Mac, and completely withdrawing its plain hamburger.

Sears chose to ignore the fact that the University of Michigan Consumer Confidence Index had reversed its long-term upward trend in 1965 and had zigzagged downward ever since to its lowest point in December 1974. . . .

Sears and many other consumer-dependent organizations ignored another significant advance warning signal: The per capita disposable personal income, converted to real dollars, had continued to move upward for the past 35 years, almost without a trace of hesitation, until the third quarter of 1973, when it reached $2952. It coasted through the fourth quarter of 1973 and then moved steadily downward to a low of $2775 before resuming a zigzag trend in 1975. The historic age of continuous growth of U.S. affluence and rise in standard of living ended in September 1973, but many still refused to believe it. Did Sears change its strategy, its policies, or its operations? Apparently not, since the "upgrading" continues and Sears increased its inventories. In September 1974, a full year after the beginning of the standard-of-living decline, Sears projected a highly optimistic rebound in the fourth quarter. It turned out to be one of the worst quarters and projections in Sears history. After 75 years of planning leadership, the giant had faltered by refusing to recognize change, because it was not to its liking.

Certainly, Sears was not an isolated case. As another example, the Chairman of the Board of General Motors confidently predicted in September 1974 a 10-million-car year for 1975. Any car owner in the country would have told him that the 9-million-car annual rate at that time was due to customer's buying defensively as a protection against 1975 price increases. The U.S. car industry has had the sharpest one-year sales decline in its entire history; its domestic production has been set back 20 years; the consumer has decided since the beginning of 1973 to end his love affair with the car as a status symbol by cutting his car budget as a percentage of his total expenditures by 27 percent over two years. But one of the highest-paid executives in the world has not yet discovered, and no planner has yet been able to convince him, that there may be a need for a new strategy at General Motors!

Summary

In summary, the major reason why corporate managers have turned to computer-based models during the past two or three years was the need to obtain answers to some of the difficult "What if?" questions which have arisen as a result of a series of problems and opportunities generated by (1) the energy crisis, (2) shortages, (3) international liquidity problems, (4) international competition, and (5) economic uncertainty: that is, top management has become increasingly aware that the old ways of "muddling through" are not adequate to meet the complex problems facing corporations in the future. The need for a more systematic approach for evaluating the consequences of alternative managerial policies and socioeconomic and political events on the future of the corporation has become self-evident. A change in pricing or advertising policies affects production operations, cash flow, and the profit-and-loss statement. Difficulty in borrowing additional funds to finance inventories leads to reverberations not only in the balance sheet but also in marketing strategies and production plans. The problem is that everything is related to everything else. Ad hoc plans which focus on only one functional area of the business are likely to be myopic and ineffective and can lead the firm into troubled waters. In order to survive during these turbulent days, corporate plans must be both comprehensive and systematic.

Computer-based planning models are an attractive, viable alternative to informal, ad hoc planning procedures. The uses of these models vary from company to company depending on managerial objectives. The Memorex Corporation used a financial planning model to negotiate a more favorable line of credit with a bank. A Swedish shipyard employs a corporate financial model to determine which currencies to use to buy raw materials when building ships and which currencies to use when the ships are sold. New venture decisions are evaluated by J. Ray McDermott with a planning model. Firms like Monsanto, Mobil, and United Air Lines use corporate planning models to forecast cash requirements. Advertising demand and circulation are forecast by the *New York Times* with an econometric planning model. Multidivision, consolidated financial plans are produced by Santa Fe Industries and Northwest Industries with financial planning models.

EXPERIENCE WITH CORPORATE PLANNING MODELS

In 1976 we published the results of a survey of 1,881 corporations which were thought to be either using, developing, or planning to develop a corporate planning model.[2] Of the 346 corporations which responded to the survey, 73 percent were either using or developing such a model. Another 15 percent were planning to develop a corporate planning model, and only 12 percent had no plans whatsoever to develop a corporate planning model.

We shall summarize the results of this survey and attempt to provide at least some tentative answers to some of the following questions. Who is using corporate planning models? Why are they used? How are they used? What resources are required? What political problems are involved? What are the benefits and limitations?

Who Is Using Corporate Models?

In our survey we asked those firms which are using corporate simulation models to indicate the actual users of the model. The results are tabulated in Table 1.1. The table shows the percentage of firms in our sample for which a particular person is receiving and using information produced by the corporate model.

Table 1.1 People receiving and using output from the model

User	Percentage
Vice-president of finance	55
President	46
Controller	46
Executive vice-president	32
Treasurer	30

These results are indeed encouraging for they indicate that in approximately half of the corporations which are using corporate simulation models, the right people are receiving and actually using the output generated by the models. There is abundant evidence available to support the hypothesis that it is crucial to the success of any corporate modeling project to have the active participation of top management in both the problem definition phase of the project and the implementation stage. The fact that the president and senior financial executives of half of the firms using corporate models are among the users of these models bodes well for the future corporate modeling.

Next we examine the relative size of the firms in our sample which are using corporate simulation models. Total sales are used as a measure of the size of these corporations (Table 1.2).

Table 1.2 Sales of firms using corporate models

Sales	Percentage
Under $50 million	7
$50 million to $100 million	3
Over $100 million to $250 million	8
Over $250 million to $500 million	16
Over $500 million to $1 billion	21
Over $1 billion	38
No response	7
Total	100

Although over half of the firms in our sample of corporate modeling users have sales in excess of $500 million, it is interesting to note that 10 percent of the users of corporate models have sales which are less than $100 million.

Why Are They Used?

Financial applications dominate the list of reasons corporations are using corporate planning models these days. Cash flow analysis, financial forecasting, balance sheet projections, financial analysis, pro forma financial reports, and profit planning are among the leading applications of corporate simulation models. Table 1.3 contains a summary list of existing applications of corporate models based on our survey results. The percentages denote the percentage of firms in our sample of users which make use of a particular applications.

How Are They Used?

Next we shall analyze the results of a series of questions in our survey aimed at determining how corporate models are used. Table 1.4 indicates that corporate simulation models were used most often (1) to evaluate alternative policies, (2) to provide financial projections, (3) to facilitate long-term planning, (4) to make decisions, and (5) to facilitate short-term planning.

Table 1.3 Applications of corporate models

Applications	Percentage
Cash flow analysis	65
Financial forecasting	65
Balance sheet projections	64
Financial analysis	60
Pro forma financial reports	55
Profit planning	53
Long-term forecasts	50
Budgeting	47
Sales forecasts	41
Investment analysis	35

Table 1.4 How corporate models are used

Use	Percentage
Evaluation of policy alternatives	79
Financial projections	75
Long-term planning	73
Decision making	58
Short-term planning	56
Preparation of reports	47
Corporate goal setting	46
Analysis	39
Confirmation of another analysis	35

Resource Requirements

Most (67 percent) of the existing corporate models were developed in-house without any outside assistance from consultants, 24 percent were developed with outside consulting, and 8 percent were purchased from an outside vendor.

Eighteen work-months was the average amount of effort required to develop models in-house without outside assistance. The average cost of these models was $82,752. For those models which were developed in-house with the help of outside consultants, the average elapsed time required to complete the model was ten months. The average cost for those models was $29,225.

In terms of computer hardware, 42 percent of the models were run on in-house computing equipment, 37 percent were run on an outside time-sharing bureau, and 19 percent were run both in-house and on a time-sharing bureau. Of the firms using corporate models in our sample, 62 percent ran their models in conversational mode while 56 percent utilized the batch mode of computation.

Political Support

To get some feeling for the political environment in the firms in which corporate modeling is being used, we asked a series of attitudinal questions concerning the interest of management in the corporate modeling activities of their firms. The findings displayed in Table 1.5 seem to imply that the corporate models included in our survey enjoy a relatively high degree of political support from management. In 60 percent of the firms which are using corporate models top management is "somewhat interested" in corporate modeling while another 30 percent is "very interested." On the other hand, the degree of interest in corporate modeling expressed by planning departments and finance is even higher.

In Chapter 10, we shall treat the politics of corporate model building in more detail.

Table 1.5 Attitudes of management toward corporate modeling

	Very interested	Somewhat interested	Indifferent	Not at all interested	No response
Top management	30%	60%	8%	1%	1%
Planning	67%	22%	4%	1%	6%
Finance	54%	37%	5%	3%	1%
Marketing	23%	39%	24%	8%	6%

Benefits

The primary benefits to be derived from the use of corporate simulation models stem from the ability to use these models to conduct "What if" experiments; that is, alternative scenarios can be generated reflecting a wide variety of different managerial policies and assumptions about the external environment in which the firm will operate. Scenarios can be produced almost as fast as the human mind can conceive of alternative policies and/or assumptions about economic, political, and social conditions confronting the firm.

Once one has developed an adequate database, formulated a set of mathematical and logical relationships describing the firm's functional activities, and expressed the relationships in the form of a computer program, then one automatically has the ability to answer two other equally important questions. We call these the "What is?" and "What has been?" questions; that is, if one has gone to the trouble to construct a corporate simulation model, then a natural by-product of such an undertaking is the capability to access the firm's database and ask questions about the current status of sales, cost of goods sold, cash, profitability, etc. In other words, a corporate simulation model can be used as the front-end of a management information system.

Not only can we answer the "What if?" type of questions but we can also answer the "What has been?" type of questions. Again, using the corporate model as the front-end of a total management information system, we can interrogate the database and produce instantaneous historical reports. We can also conduct experiments with the historical data to ascertain "What might have been?" In other words, we may want to evaluate the previous consequences of alternative strategies which have been used in the past as a means of providing guidance in developing long-range plans for the future.

According to our survey, the major benefits which present users of corporate models have derived include: (1) ability to explore more alternatives, (2) better quality decision making, (3) more effective planning, (4) better understanding of the business, and (5) faster decision making.

Table 1.6 Benefits of corporate models

Benefits	Percentage
Able to explore more alternatives	78
Better quality decision making	72
More effective planning	65
Better understanding of the business	50
Faster decision making	48
More timely information	44
More accurate forecasts	38
Cost savings	28
No benefits	4

Limitations

Opinions about the limitations of corporate models (Table 1.7) do not appear to be as intense or as well defined as opinions about the benefits of these models. The three shortcomings mentioned most often were: (1) lack of flexibility, (2) poor documentation, and (3) excessive input data requirements.

Table 1.7 Limitations of corporate models

Shortcomings	Percentage
Not flexible enough	25
Poorly documented	23
Requires too much input data	23
Output format is inflexible	11
Took too long to develop	11
Running cost is too high	9
Development cost was too high	8
Model users cannot understand model	8
No shortcomings	9

More will be said about the limitations of corporate planning models in Chapter 10.

NOTES

1. George Gershefski, 1969. Corporate planning models: the state of the art, *Managerial Planning*, (November–December).

2. Thomas H. Naylor, 1976. The future of corporate planning models, *Managerial Planning* (March–April); Thomas H. Naylor and Horst Schauland, 1976. A survey of users of corporate simulation models, *Management Science* (May); Thomas H. Naylor and Horst Schauland, 1976. Experience with corporate simulation models: a survey, *Long Range Planning* (April).

BIBLIOGRAPHY

Boulden, James B., 1975. *Computer assisted planning systems*. New York: McGraw-Hill.

Grinyer, Peter H., and Christopher D. Batt, 1975. Some corporate financial simulation models, *Operational Research Quarterly* 25.

————, and Jeff Wooller, 1975. *Corporate models today*. London: Institute of Chartered Accountants.

Hamilton, W. F., and M. A. Moses, 1972. An optimization model for corporate financial planning, *Operations Research* (May–June).

————, 1974. A computer-based corporate planning system, *Management Science* (October).

Mayo, R. Britton, 1978. *Corporate Planning and Modeling with SIMPLAN*. Reading, Mass.: Addison-Wesley.

Naylor, Thomas H., 1971. *Computer simulation experiments with models of economic systems*. New York: Wiley.

————, 1975. The politics of corporate model building, *Planning Review* (January).

————, 1976. The future of corporate planning models, *Managerial Planning* (March–April).

————, 1976. Elements of a planning and modeling system, *AFIPS Conference Proceedings* (National Computer Conference). Montvale, N.J.: AFIPS Press.

————, 1976. Corporate planning models: the state of the art, *California Management Review* (Summer).

————, 1976. A conceptual framework for corporate modeling and the results of a survey of current practice, *Operational Research Quarterly*.

————, 1977. A symposium on the future of corporate planning models, *Planning Review*.

————, Harold Glass, David Milstein, and John Wall, 1977. *SIMPLAN: a planning and modeling system for government*. Durham, N.C.: Duke University Press.

————, and M. James Mansfield, 1976. Corporate planning models: a survey, *Planning Review* (May).

————, and Horst Schauland, 1976. A survey of users of corporate simulation models, *Management Science* (May).

————, and Horst Schauland, 1976. Experience with corporate simulation models— a survey. *Long Range Planning* (April).

_____, and John M. Vernon, 1969. *Microeconomics and decision models of the firm*. New York: Harcourt, Brace and World.

Ogunsula, Oyekola, 1975. *An integrated theory of corporate simulation models: a case study of a hypothetical oil company*. Unpublished Ph.D dissertation, Duke University.

Pindyck, Robert S., and Daniel L. Rubinfield, 1976. *Econometric models and economic forecasts*. New York: McGraw-Hill.

Power, P. D., 1975. Computers and financial planning, *Long Range Planning* (December).

Schreiber, Albert N., (ed.) 1970. *Corporate simulation models*. Seattle: University of Washington.

Wheelwright, Steven C., and Spyros G. Madriadakis, 1972. *Computer-aided modeling for managers*. Reading, Mass.: Addison-Wesley.

2

The Design of Computer-Based Planning and Modeling Systems

INTRODUCTION[1]

In this chapter we shall describe a collection of elements which we believe to be of critical importance in designing a corporate planning model. Our objective is to develop a set of criteria that can be used not only for designing a planning and modeling system but also for facilitating the evaluation and comparison of alternative planning and modeling systems.

We believe there are eight basic elements which one must consider in designing a planning and modeling system:

- Planning system
- Management information system
- Modeling system
- Forecasting system

- Econometric modeling
- User orientation of the system
- System availability
- Software system

PLANNING SYSTEM

The point of departure for any corporate planning model is the planning system itself, that is, the design of the planning system for the organization should be set in place before any consideration is given to the modeling system.

As the most general case let us consider a large, decentralized company consisting of multiple divisions, groups, products, or strategic business units. For simplicity, we shall refer to any such subsystem of an integrated company as a *business unit*. Each business unit is assumed to be autonomous and is responsible for its own marketing and production activities. Although cash management and overall corporate financial planning are centralized at the corporate level, each business unit is responsible for its own income statement.

At the beginning of the planning cycle, global goals and objectives for the company are specified by top management and interpreted to the business units by the corporate planning department. These corporate goals may take the form of specific target objectives for the company as a whole or for individual business units. Typical target variables may include return on investment (ROI), market share, sales growth, and cash flow, as well as environmental, social, and political objectives.

The corporate planning department designs the report formats to be employed by the business units in formulating their business plans. Standarized reporting at the business unit level greatly facilitates the consolidation of plans across all business units. However, individual business units are permitted to make their own assumptions concerning marketing and production provided they are explicit about the external assumptions and policy assumptions underlying their business plans. Financial plans at the business unit level follow logically from given assumptions about revenues and costs.

Plans from the business units are transmitted to the corporate planning department for consolidation, review, and evaluation. In the initial stages of the planning process, the business plans will be returned to the business units for modification and reformulation in light of corporate goals. This iterative process will be replicated until all of the business plans have been approved and consolidated into the company's overall corporate plan.

In Chapter 3 we shall describe how business planning models can be integrated into the planning process.

Business Planning Models

Figure 2.1 contains a flowchart of a consolidated corporate planning model that is driven by a series of business planning models for the individual businesses of the company. These models may be used either on a stand-alone basis at the business unit level or consolidated and used by the corporate planning department, senior financial officers, or the chief executive officer. Each business unit model consists of a front-end financial model driven by a marketing model and a production model.

The objectives of the business unit models are to generate alternative scenarios and business plans based on varying assumptions about business unit policies and assumptions about the external environment of the businesses.

Financial planning models Each business planning model produces as output data a pro forma income statement for the business unit. In cases in which the business unit is actually a subsidiary of the parent company, pro forma balance sheets and sources-and-uses of funds statements may be produced as well. Basically, these business financial models can be used to simulate the effects on net profit of alternative business strategies for a given business unit. The validity of the results generated by a business unit financial model will be no better or worse than the assumptions underlying the revenue and production cost projections which feed the model.

Typically, the availability of financial data is not an obstacle to the development of a corporate planning model. Most firms, large and small alike, have sufficient financial data to build a financial planning model.

For example, an annual financial planning model for a corporation can be

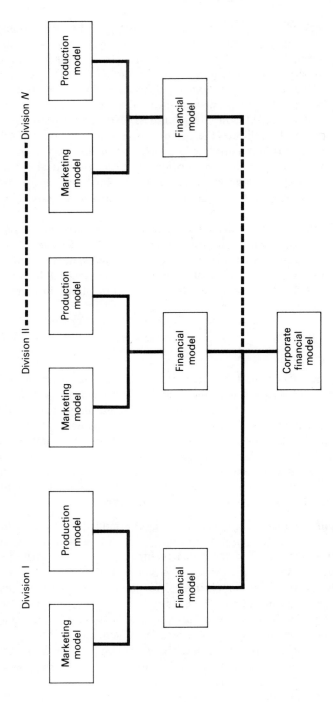

Fig. 2.1 A conceptual framework for corporate models.

developed with last year's balance sheet and annual report data for the previous three or four years. Stand-alone financial models simply do not require substantial amounts of historical data. The first corporate financial model developed by Hercules, Inc., was based entirely on annual report data from the preceding four years.

Of course, it is important to differentiate between a financial planning model and a model of the company's accounting structure. A model of the firm's accounting system may consist of thousands of equations, one for each accounting line item. Several electric utility companies have developed models of their accounting systems. These models produce hundreds of pages of output and are almost completely worthless as financial planning models. The human mind cannot comprehend that much information. A financial planning model should contain only that information which is essential to plan and control the organization.

Accountants frequently suggest that a financial planning model must be tied back to the company's general ledger. This is a completely ridiculous suggestion and represents gross statistical overkill. First, a financial planning model should contain a minimum number of variables or line items (usually fewer than 100). Second, it is not necessary for financial planning data to be accurate to the nearest dollar. Data rounded to thousands of dollars or even millions of dollars will usually suffice. Third, linking a financial planning model back to the general ledger may prove to be prohibitively expensive and require enormous amounts of computer time. If the credibility of the model depends on tying it back to the general ledger, then there is a serious educational problem on the part of management. This problem should be addressed and resolved before continuing.

In summary, one should differentiate between financial planning models and large detailed number crunchers. Beware of turning the control of a planning model over to the accountants, for the entire project may drown in a sea of unnecessary data.

Frequently, skeptics will use insufficient financial data as an excuse for delaying the implementation of financial modeling. Rarely is insufficient financial data the real reason for not developing such a model.

Financial models will be treated in more detail in Chapter 4.

Marketing planning models Marketing planning models provide the revenue projections which drive the business planning models. Two alternatives are available— forecasting models and econometric marketing models. Short-term forecasting models are naive, mechanistic models, devoid of explanatory power. They cannot be used to do "What if?" analysis. On the other hand, econometric models are rich in explanatory power and may be used to link sales to the national economy and to conduct marketing policy simulation experiments. With econometric marketing models, it is possible to simulate the effects on sales and market shares of alternative advertising, pricing, and promotional policies.

Marketing models provide the sales revenue forecasts which are required to drive both the financial and production models in Fig. 2.1. Marketing models are described in more detail in Chapters 5, 6, and 7.

Marketing data are much more serious problems in the development of a planning model than are financial data. Ideally, we would like to have at least 30 observations of historical data to build econometric marketing models. If the model is a monthly model, we would need even more observations. As a rule, we would like to have data on sales volume or market share by product or product group. Sales volume data are usually available, but market share data may not be easy to obtain for some industries. Explanatory variables might include price, advertising, competitive strategies, expenditures for technical support, and a number of national or regional economic indicators. Data for some of these variables are extremely difficult, if not impossible, to obtain.

Production planning models Given a sales forecast for a particular business unit, how much will it cost to produce at a level which will satisfy the demand forecast? That is the raison d'être for production planning models. A number of companies including Monsanto and Inland Steel use a type of activity analysis approach to production planning modeling which generates the cost-of-goods sold associated with a given demand forecast. A reasonable extension of this approach is for the production model to generate the minimum cost associated with a given level of demand for the products of the business unit. This latter alternative represents a logical interface between mathematical programming and other optimization techniques and corporate simulation models.

The ability to model the production activities of a company is entirely dependent on the quality of the cost accounting data generated by the company's production operations. Continuous process types of industries such as petroleum refineries and chemical plants usually have reasonably good production cost data. The same is true of steel mills and automobile assembly lines. But the closer the manufacturing operations of a plant come to being a "job shop" type of operation, the less likely the chances are of having adequate production cost data.

One of the reasons so few banks have attempted to model bank operations is the dearth of cost accounting data pertaining to banking operations. Many banks simply do not know how much it costs to make a $100,000, 90-day, commercial loan. Without this type of data, bank operations planning models are impossible to formulate.

Production planning models are covered in more detail in Chapter 8.

Integrated planning models It is important to be able to integrate marketing and production models into financial planning models at the business unit level as illustrated by Fig. 2.2. That is, revenue forecasts and operating costs are generated respectively by the marketing and production models. The integration of the latter two models into the former will greatly facilitate the use of the business planning model.

Of those firms which are using corporate planning models, our survey (cited in Chapter 1) indicates that 39 percent have modeled the "total company." We suspect that this figure overstates the case and may reflect differences in interpretation of what constitutes the "total company." In actual practice, relatively few firms have managed to integrate the financial, marketing, and production activities of the company into truly integrated corporate planning models. Two notable exceptions include

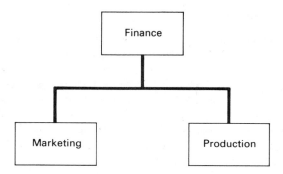

Fig. 2.2 An integrated business planning model.

the *New York Times* model and the Dresser Industries model (both described in Chapter 11).

Our survey also indicated that most (76 percent) of the corporate planning models in use today are "What if?" models, that is, models which simulate the effects of alternative managerial policies and assumptions about the firm's external environment. Only 4 percent of the models in our sample were optimization models in which the goal was to maximize or minimize a single objective function such as profit or cost, respectively. However, 14 percent of the models used both approaches.

Those firms which do use optimization techniques in conjunction with corporate planning models tend to use them for production planning rather than as global optimization models for an entire business or the corporation as a whole.

Although optimization models are widely used in certain process industries such as oil refineries, rarely are these production scheduling models integrated into a corporate planning model. Virtually every major oil refinery in the world uses mathematical programming to schedule its operations. At this time we are not aware of a single oil company which has a linear programming model linked to a corporate planning model.

The difficulty with using optimization techniques to develop optimal plans for a corporation as a whole is a problem of problem definition. Although top management is indeed interested in profits, ROI, discounted cash flow, or some equivalent measure of performance, these are by no means the only measures of effectiveness which management uses to evaluate corporate plans. Output of corporate planning models is a vector, not a single variable. If the company wants to survive, management must necessarily monitor a whole host of output variables—profit, ROI, market share, sales growth, cash flow, as well as all of the line items of the income statement and balance sheet.

Faced with a multiple output planning problem, optimization techniques with optimize with respect to a single output variable are of limited use to corporate planners. The use of *goal programming* and *utility theory* has been suggested as a means of quantifying trade-offs among conflicting corporate objectives. The track records of these two techniques as corporate planning tools are not impressive.

Consolidated Planning Models

As previously indicated, the individual business planning models may either be used as planning tools for the separate business units or consolidated at the corporate level to form consolidated corporate plans. The corporate planning department should have the option to perform "What if?" experiments with any of the business unit models on either a stand-alone basis or as part of a totally integrated planning and modeling system. The output reports of a consolidated corporate planning model typically include pro forma income statements, balance sheets, and sources-and-uses of funds statements. In the following paragraphs we shall outline several important features of consolidated planning models.

Horizontal consolidation With a multidivisional firm it is desirable to be able to consolidate financial reports, plans, or models over all divisions as illustrated in Fig. 2.3. This type of consolidation is known as horizontal consolidation. If the divisions are all independent, then the consolidation will be additive, but if the divisions are interdependent, then there may be transfer payments among the different divisions. Transfer payments are taken into consideration through accounting eliminations.

Vertical consolidation Sometimes multidivisional companies are subdivided into groups of divisions. Each division in turn may consist of several business units. Each business unit produces multiple products. This type of organization structure implies a hierarchy of databases, models, and reports. Obviously, one would want to be able to consolidate product plans into business unit plans, division plans into group plans, and group plans into corporate plans. Figure 2.4 illustrates this type of vertical consolidation.

Multidirectional consolidation The case for horizontal and vertical financial consolidations for multiple regions, groups, divisions, businesses, subsidiaries, profit centers, and products was made in the previous two paragraphs. The importance of bottom-up consolidation is obvious. Top-down consolidations may also be important for allocating overhead back-down to cost centers for reconsolidation at all levels. In other words, multidirectional consolidation is a useful feature of a planning and modeling system.

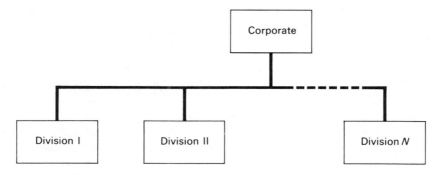

Fig. 2.3 Horizontal consolidation.

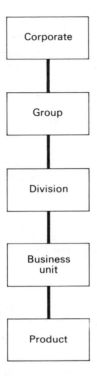

Fig. 2.4 Vertical consolidation.

Eliminations As previously indicated, interdependent divisions, business units, and profit centers require the use of financial eliminations to account for transfers among the respective divisions, business units, and profit centers.

Nonstandard chart of accounts Some banks and accounting firms market canned financial modeling packages which restrict the user to a limited number of standard accounts. Since the chart of accounts varies from firm to firm, this limitation is likely to be particularly inconvenient for most companies. A planning and modeling system should be flexible and be able to cope with any type of chart of accounts which may be employed by the user.

Postprocessing of consolidated data Postprocessing of consolidated financial data is necessary if we are to implement "What if?" experiments with consolidated corporate financial models. Although this feature seems rather obvious, not all planning and modeling systems have this capability.

Summary In summary, a corporate planning and modeling system should have the ability to integrate finance, marketing, and production at the business unit level and the ability to run the business unit models separately or as part of a consolidated corporate financial planning model. Whether the company engages in "top-down" or "bottom-up" planning is less important than whether or not the planning modeling system can be easily adapted to the planning system. Regardless of the type of planning system, two features are critical: (1) the ease with which financial, marketing, and production models can be integrated and (2) the ease with which financial consolidation can be achieved.

MANAGEMENT INFORMATION SYSTEM

Given a planning system, the next important element in the development of a corporate planning modeling system is the management information system. We shall define the term *management information system* to include the following elements: (1) database, (2) database system, (3) report generator, (4) graphics, and (5) security system.

Database

A decision to develop a corporate planning model is tantamount to a serious commitment to the maintenance of comprehensive internal and external databases. Our database requirements become quite explicit once we settle on the design for a corporate planning model.

Internal data   To develop an annual financial planning model we need at least three or four years of historical financial data. We require even more data if the model is a monthly or quarterly model. Econometric marketing models should have 25 to 30 observations of historical data.

External data   Most econometric marketing models attempt to link sales volumes and sales revenues to the national or regional economy in which a particular product is sold. A number of service bureaus offer national historical macroeconomic data and econometric forecasts to their clients.

Database System

Not only should a planning and modeling system have databases but it should also have a flexible, easy to use database management system for reading data into the system, storing them, and making them readily available for modeling and report generation. At least three different approaches to database management have emerged among the numerous planning and modeling software systems which are currently available: (1) matrix, (2) row–column, and (3) record-file.

Matrix   Several FORTRAN- and APL-based planning and modeling systems use matrices to read data into the system. Both database management and modeling functions are carried out using matrix manipulations. If the user is a scientific programmer, matrix manipulations should cause no problems. However, many corporate planners and financial analysts are neither mathematicians nor scientific programmers and may find matrix manipulations difficult, if not impossible, to use.

Row–column   Some planning and modeling systems make use of row numbers and column numbers to create databases, formulate models, and generate reports. While the row–column number approach may have some appeal to accountants who are accustomed to working with financial spread sheets, the user must keep track of the row and column numbers. Furthermore, econometric and production data do not necessarily lend themselves to this restricted notation.

Record-file   Other planning and modeling systems make use of records as the basic unit of data. A *record* is a time series variable such as SALES, COST, or PROFIT. A record has a name, an abbreviation, a value, units, and a security level that determines who has access to which records. A *file* is a cross section of records. Each business unit may have one or more files. For example, for a given business, one file may contain actual historical data. Another file may contain budgeted, projected, or simulated series. Variance reports and validation runs are particularly easy to implement with the multiple file concept.

Multiple files   As indicated in the preceding paragraph, multiple files provide the user with the ability to manage multiple division, groups, business units, products, etc. The data for each division's plan can be assigned to a separate file. Multiple files also permit the storing of the output of multiple scenarios generated by "What if?" experiments. Simulated results can easily be compared with actual historical values for validation purposes. Comparisons of budgeted values with actuals so as to compute variances are also facilitated with multiple files.

Multiple databases   If we define a database as a collection of files, the user of the planning system will no doubt find it useful to have multiple databases. Some of these databases may be internal; others may be external.

Cross file manipulations   If the planning and modeling system has multiple files, then it should be possible to access data across files and to carry out modeling procedures on data for any file in the database. Specifically, it should be possible to build models which employ records for any combination of files in the given database.

Hierarchical databases   The need for hierarchical databases was established previously in our discussion of vertical consolidations (Fig. 2.4).

Multiple time periods   The database should be designed in such a way that it can accommodate daily, weekly, monthly, quarterly, or annual data. It should be possible to process data from multiple time periods in planning models and reports.

Independence of data, models, and reports   In some planning and modeling systems, models and data are linked. In other systems, models and reports are locked together. In both cases, the flexibility of the planning and modeling system is likely to be greatly reduced.

Consider a situation in which management wants to see six financial scenarios. For the first and sixth scenarios, a complete income statement and balance sheet are required. However, for scenarios two through five, management is interested only in seeing net profit and cash. If models and reports are locked together, it is not trivial to suppress part of the output so as to generate net profit and cash without the entire income statement and balance sheet. If models, reports, and data are independent, then it would be quite straightforward to edit out of the income statement and balance sheet those line items which are required. The importance of this feature cannot be overemphasized.

Database limitations Not only must the user be aware of the attributes of a particular database system but the limitations of the database system should also be thoroughly understood. A checklist of database system limitations follows that one might consider:

- Number of variables
- Number of periods
- Number of files
- Number of databases
- Lengths of variable names

- Length of variable abbreviation
- Length of variable units
- Length of user identification number
- Number of digits of accuracy

Report Generator

The front-end of any planning system is a set of financial reports. Therefore, it follows that a report generator should be an integral part of any planning and modeling system. Basically, management should be able to have any type of report it desires; that is, the report generator should not impose any restrictions on the type of report which is produced by the system.

The report generator should be flexible and easy to use. Some report generators are so easy to use that typists with no previous programming experience can be taught to produce financial reports with little or no effort.

Of the planning and modeling software packages available today, over two-thirds are primarily report generators; that is, they can produce financial reports and do financial consolidations, but have very limited database management, modeling, and econometric features. Although financial report generation and financial consolidations are important elements in a planning and modeling system, there are other important elements to consider. Unfortunately, a number of users of systems which are primarily report generators have found themselves locked into expensive outside time-sharing charges only to realize, when it is too late, that they need additional database management, modeling, econometric, and forecasting features that are not available in their financial report generator. Although simple financial modeling and report generation are ideal starting points for those who are just beginning to develop a planning and modeling system, beware of dead-end systems which can do only report generation and are not available for installation on an in-house computer. In summary, in selecting a report generator, make sure that the planning and modeling system of which it is a part has the flexibility and features that will be needed in the future as well as in the present.

Choice of output report formats Some planning and modeling systems provide management with a limited number of output reports or report formats from which to choose. If the planning and modeling system is to be useful, management should be able to have any type of output report which is needed. Complete flexibility in output reporting is of critical importance in maintaining satisfied users of a corporate-based planning system.

User-specified reports To assure flexibility in output reporting, the planning and modeling system should offer the user the option of specifying his or her own reports. Furthermore, the report generator must also be easy to use.

Report limitations In evaluating a particular report generator, the user may want to consider the following limitations:

- Number of reports
- Number of characters per line
- Number of lines per report

Report definition editing It should also be easy to make changes in user-specified reports. The ability to edit reports will greatly facilitate changes in reports which may be required by management from time to time. Report definition editing will contribute substantially to the flexibility and power of the planning and modeling system.

Graphics

An increasing number of planning and modeling software packages now offer graphics as an alternative way of displaying output data and corporate plans. The graphical display of sales, cost, and profit trends can be an effective way to present planning data to top management.

Security System

There should also be some means of controlling who has access to which files, records, models, and reports within the planning and modeling system. Division managers should be able to access their own databases, models, and reports, but not those of other divisions or of the entire corporation. Corporate management should, on the other hand, be able to access the corporate database as well as all division databases, models, and reports. A built-in security system makes all of this possible. Among the security options, which one may want to consider, are the following:

- Individual database
- Individual file
- Individual variable
- Individual model
- Individual report definition
- Individual function

MODELING SYSTEM

This section defines some of the basic terminology used to develop corporate planning models including definition of variables and model specification. A number of features are then described that may prove to be useful in a planning and modeling system: (1) recursive models, (2) simultaneous-equation models, (3) logical models, and (4) risk analysis, as well as several other features.

Definition of Variables

Fundamental to the specification of a corporate model or some component thereof is the definition of the variables to be included in the model. This section describes the

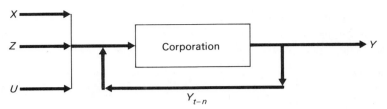

Fig. 2.5 Flowchart of variables in a corporate model.

different types of variables typically included in corporate models. Figure 2.5 provides a framework for classifying these different types of variables.

The "black box" in Fig. 2.5 may either represent the corporation or the financial, marketing, or production component of the firm. Our objective is to formulate a set of mathematical and logical relationships between a set of *output variables* given by Y and a set of *input variables $X, Z, U,$ and Y_{t-n}*.

Output variables We use the symbol Y to denote the *output variables* describing the behavior of a firm or one of its components. Depending on whether one is a mathematician, a statistician, or an econometrician, the Y's may be called either *dependent* variables, *response* variables, or *endogenous* variables, respectively.

The output variables of a corporate financial model are the line items of the income statement, balance sheet, cash flow statement, or sources-and-uses-of-funds statement. Marketing output variables include market share and sales by product. Units of output and cost of goods sold represent output variables in a production model.

The output variables of a corporate model are set in place when the goals and objectives of the model are defined. They basically represent the indicators by which management judges the performance of the firm or some subsystem of the firm.

External variables Certain variables affect the behavior of a company but are not affected by the behavior of that corporation. These variables are called *external* or *exogenous* variables. We use the symbol X to represent this class of variables that are too important to ignore. Causality is assumed to be unidirectional in the case of external variables; that is, X is assumed to influence Y, but Y has only a negligible effect on X. Furthermore, X is read into the model and is neither explained nor forecasted by the model.

The most obvious example of an external variable is the national economy of a country to which a corporation sells. Other external variables might include social and political events, strikes, and national disasters. Watergate is a good example of such an event. Wars, economic boycotts, and labor disputes are also examples of crucial external variables. Although variables of this type are difficult, if not impossible, to model and predict, it is indeed possible to model and predict the impact of such events on the future performance of the firm. This is an extremely important point.

Some corporate managers have argued that they face so many uncontrollable external variables that modeling would be impossible. These myopic managers have precisely missed the point of planning models.

Consider the case of Standard Oil of Ohio (SOHIO), which owns over 50 percent of the Alaskan oil field. The financial future of SOHIO was vitally dependent on the completion date of the Alaskan pipeline. SOHIO had no model to predict whether or not the United States Congress would approve the pipeline. They had no model to predict when the pipeline might be completed. But they did have a model to simulate the effects on SOHIO's financial structure of alternative (hypothesized) completion dates for the pipeline. They projected their cash requirements for alternative completion dates for the pipeline long before it was actually completed in 1977.

The interface between external events and corporate models is crucial. There must be someone on the corporate modeling team who is familiar with the global environment of the firm and who can anticipate the different types of external events which may affect the firm.

Policy variables The policy variables are the variables over which management can exercise some degree of control. Financial policy variables might include such variables as cash management policy, debt management policy, taxation policies, depreciation policies, and merger–acquisition decisions. Marketing policy variables include pricing decisions, advertising policies, promotional policies, and geographic location of sales personnel. Capital investment decisions, new product decisions, and plant location decisions are examples of production policy variables. The symbol Z is used to represent policy variables.

Random variables Frequently when we construct corporate planning models there may be considerable risk and uncertainty associated with particular forecasts. Suppose that our analysis indicates that sales are expected to increase by 5 percent next year. However, there is some chance that sales may increase by only 1 percent or even possibly decrease by 10 percent. There is a remote possibility that they will increase by over 15 percent. What can we say about the sensitivity of our model to random shocks or perturbations not only with regard to sales but to other external variables as well? In these circumstances, it may be appropriate to treat some of the external variables which drive the model as random variables U with given frequency distributions or assumed probability distributions such as uniform, normal, or triangular distributions. The inclusion of random variables in the model transforms it from a strictly *deterministic* model to a *risk analysis* model. Techniques for generating random variables from given frequency distributions and probability distributions are described in a book by Naylor *et al.*, entitled *Computer Simulation Techniques* (New York: Wiley, 1966).

With risk analysis it is possible to construct confidence intervals and test hypotheses concerning the impact of alternative managerial policies and assumptions about the firm's external environment.

Unfortunately, our survey indicated that of those companies in our sample which use computer-based planning models, only 6 percent employ risk analysis. There are at least two reasons why risk analysis is so seldom used with corporate simulation models. First, you should plan on multiplying the computer bill for your deterministic model by a factor of anywhere from 50 to 100. To reduce the effects of random error, a risk analysis model must be replicated, say, 50 to 100 times. These replications can become prohibitively expensive with very large models, particularly if they are run on time-sharing service bureaus. Second, risk analysis models are much more difficult to explain and interpret to management than are deterministic models.

Lagged output variables   To make the model dynamic and more realistic we also introduce lagged output variables Y_{t-n}. The rationale for including lagged output variables is that corporations are ongoing dynamic enterprises. For example, sales today depend in part on sales last month, the month before, and the month before that. We represent lagged output variables by sequences of the following type: Y_{t-1}, $Y_{t-2}, \ldots, Y_{t-n}$. Last year's balance sheet is an example of a set of lagged financial output variables.

Model Specification

Once we have defined the input and output variables for our model, we must then specify a set of mathematical and logical relationships linking the input variables to the output variables. The average number of equations in the models in our survey was 545. The range varied from 20 equations to several thousand equations. Most of the equations are definitional equations which take the form of accounting identities. The average number of definitional equations was 445. The average number of behavioral (empirical) equations was only 86. Behavioral equations take the form of theories or hypotheses about the behavior of certain economic phenomena. They must be tested empirically and validated before they are incorporated into the model.

Definitional equations   Definitional relationships are exactly what the term implies— mathematical or accounting definitions. Definitional relationships are encountered most often in the formulation of corporate financial models. They are typically defined by the firm's accountants and financial analysts. The following is an example of a definitional equation:

$$CASH = CASH(-1) + CAR + NDEBT - NASSET - PAP - LPAY \qquad (2.1)$$

Equation (2.1) is a typical cash equation in a corporate financial model. It states that beginning cash (CASH) is equal to previous period cash (CASH (−1)) plus collection of receivables (CAR) plus borrowing (NDEBT) minus the purchase of assets (NASSET) minus the payment of accounts payable (PAP) minus loan repayments (LPAY).

Equation (2.2) provides us with a second example of a definitional equation.

$$INV = INV(-1) + MAT + DL - CGS \qquad (2.2)$$

It may be interpreted as follows. Beginning inventory (INV) is equal to previous period inventory (INV(−1)) plus new material purchases (MAT) plus direct labor costs (DL) minus the cost of goods sold (CGS).

Some definitional equations are determined by government regulations such as tax laws, investment credit allowances, and depreciation rates.

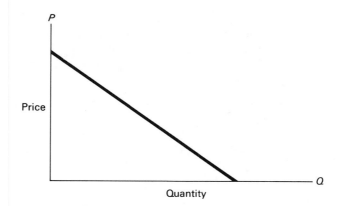

Fig. 2.6 A demand model.

Behavioral equations Behavioral relationships are hypotheses that are subject to empirical testing and validation. They are theories that reflect management's understanding of certain internal and external relationships affecting the firm.

A behavioral model well known to economists is

$$Q = a - bP. \tag{2.3}$$

The thrust of the specification of Eq. (2.3) is that higher prices (P) will be associated with reduced consumption of the commodity or product (Q) in question. Graphically, this demand theory can be expressed as shown in Fig. 2.6.

This demand theory can be tested empirically. We can collect some data on P and Q, estimate the parameters a and b, and determine whether or not there is a significant negative relationship between P and Q. (This is an oversimplification for there are certain well-known econometric problems in dealing with such a simplistic model.)

Equation (2.4) represents a more realistic example of a behavioral equation.

$$\text{SALES} = a + bP + c\text{ADV} + d\text{GNP} + e\text{RD} + f\text{P}_c + u. \tag{2.4}$$

This equation hypothesizes a linear relationship between the quantity sold of a given product and price (P), advertising expenditures (ADV), Gross National Product (GNP), research and development expenditures (RD), the price of the firm's leading competitor (P_c), and a random error term (u). If we have time series or cross sectional data on SALES, P, ADV, GNP, RD, and P_c, we can estimate the values of the parameters a, b, c, d, e, and f. We can test the statistical significance of the parameter estimates and evaluate the overall explanatory power of the model. Finally, we can simulate the effects on sales of alternative pricing, advertising, and research and development strategies. We can also experiment with alternative assumptions about the national economy as measured by GNP.

Recursive Models

Most of the financial planning models that have been developed to date are recursive, or causally ordered, models; that is, by replacing the equations of the model in the proper order, it is possible to solve each equation one at a time by substituting the solution values of previous equations into the right-hand side of each equation. Recursive models have the computational advantage that solution of the system of equations does not require matrix inversion or some other simultaneous equation technique. Below is an example of a recursive model.

(1) SALES   = A − B * PRICE
(2) REVENUE = PRICE * SALES
(3) CGS   = .60 * REVENUE
(4) PBT   = REVENUE − CGS
(5) TAX   = .50 * PBT
(6) NPR   = PBT − TAX

In this example, the selling PRICE is given. A and B are parameters and

SALES   = Sales volume (units)
REVENUE = Sales revenue
CGS   = Cost of goods sold
PBT   = Profit before taxes
TAX   = Taxes
NPR   = Net profit

In many financial models it is impossible to express the logic of the model as a series of recursive, causally ordered equations. It is for this reason that a corporate modeling system should include the capability to solve simultaneous equation models as well as recursive models.

Simultaneous Models

Consider the following five-equation financial model.

(1) INT   = .12 * DEBT
(2) PROFIT = REVENUE − CGS − INT − TAX
(3) DEBT   = DEBT(−1) + NDEBT
(4) CASH   = CASH(−1) + PROFIT + NDEBT
(5) NDEBT = MBAL − CASH

Profit (PROFIT) in equation (2) is defined as sales revenue (REVENUE) less cost of goods sold (CGS), interest (INT), and taxes (TAX). But INT depends on total indebtedness (DEBT) in equation (1). From the balance sheet total debt in equation (3) for this period is equal to last period's debt (DEBT(−1)) plus new debt (NDEBT). New debt is defined in equation (5) as the difference between the minimum cash balance (MBAL) and cash (CASH). CASH in equation (4) is the sum of last period's CASH, PROFIT, and NDEBT.

Although this model is quite simple, it is nevertheless a simultaneous equation model. It is impossible to solve the model recursively merely by placing the equations in the correct order. Solution of this model requires the use of a technique capable of solving simultaneous equations. This model may be solved either through matrix inversion techniques or some other generalized technique such as the Gauss–Seidel method, which is suitable for both linear and nonlinear simultaneous-equation models.

As can be seen from our example model, it is indeed quite likely that we will encounter simultaneity even in quite simple financial models. Very few of the financial modeling software packages have the ability to solve simultaneous systems of equations. (Simultaneous equation problems can also arise in econometric marketing models where two or more products are either complements or substitutes.)

Many banks have developed a special type of financial planning model known as an asset–liability model. Most of these models have been formulated as recursive models. Yet logically this is totally absurd, for the very nature of a bank's assets and liabilities is a simultaneous jointly determined structure. For example, demand deposits and time deposits are substitutes and both are likely to be correlated with various loan demand equations. Loan demand depends on interest rates and interest rates depend on the supply and demand for loans. Consumer loans and mortgage loans may be substitutes for one another. To attempt to model the asset–liability structure of a bank with a recursive model makes little or no sense. It is not surprising to find that a number of banks have encountered serious difficulties in attempting to validate recursive, bank planning models. The financial structure of a bank is simply not recursive.

Logical Models

The ability to check whether or not cash balances or inventory levels have dropped below some predetermined minimum level is another important element of a planning and modeling system. Logical commands such as an IF statement or a GO TO command are desirable features for a planning modeling system.

Risk Analysis

In spite of the limitations of risk analysis, a case can be made for treating some of the external variables in a corporate planning model as random or probabilistic variables with given hypothetical or empirical probability distributions. Risk analysis is useful in testing the sensitivity of the planning model to random shocks and perturbations, constructing confidence intervals, and testing hypotheses. Risk analysis is discussed in detail in the 1971 text by Naylor entitled *Computer Simulation Experiments with Models of Economic Systems*, New York: Wiley.

Given the limitations of risk analysis, some analysts use a type of pseudorisk analysis in which they experiment with "optimistic," "pessimistic," "most likely" values of external variables rather than treating them as random variables.

Other Modeling Features

Equation-type models   For anyone who is familiar with basic, high school algebra, models expressed as equations will have a certain degree of appeal. Most planning models consist of equations and logical operations. Modeling systems which employ modeling techniques other than equations are likely to be difficult to use and limited in scope.

Algebraic operators Some of the older planning and modeling systems employ numeric operators rather than algebraic operators to denote addition, subtraction, multiplication, division, and exponentiation. Algebraic operators are much easier to use than are numeric operators. More recent vintage planning and modeling systems all use arithmetic operators of the following type:

Operation	Arithmetic operator
Addition	+
Subtraction	−
Multiplication	*
Division	/
Exponentiation	**

Storing models It should be possible to save models which may be used repetitively in the future through the use of a SAVE or STORE command.

Storing results of a model Likewise it is desirable to be able to store the results of scenarios produced from model solutions. The multiple file feature described previously was designed to make it easy to store results of a model.

Storing equations from estimating techniques Once an acceptable equation has been estimated either by an econometric estimating technique or by a time series forecasting technique, it is useful to be able to store the estimated equation or integrate it into another model. Relatively few modeling systems provide this feature.

Storing projections from estimating techniques A corollary to the previous two modeling features is the ability to store projections from econometric and time series estimating techniques.

Model integration Repeatedly, we have stressed the importance of being able to integrate marketing and production models into financial models. Parameters estimated by econometric estimating techniques can be transferred directly into specific planning models without the user having to retype the estimated equation.

Line number independence In some modeling systems, equations are tied directly to row numbers or column numbers of financial reports or to specific line numbers. These systems are inflexible or cumbersome to use. Models whose equations are independent of line numbers are more flexible and easier to use.

Model editing Planning models must be both flexible and adaptable, since planning is a dynamic process. Models must frequently be respecified, reestimated, and re-solved. The modeling system should include an editor to facilitate changes in the model.

FORECASTING SYSTEM

The ability to generate short-term forecasts not only for market planning models but also for any external variable that appears to have a reasonably stable relationship with respect to time is another important element to be considered for inclusion in a planning modeling system. A variety of short-term, "naive," forecasting tools are available. Although short-term forecasting models have a definite role to play in corporate modeling, they have little or no explanatory power and cannot be used for "What if?" analysis.

Exponential Smoothing

Exponential smoothing techniques consist of a set of weighting schemes that assigns greater weight to more recent historical observations than to those from the more distant past. Again, the rationale is the same. To forecast the future all one needs to know is the correct relationship between past sales and future sales. The problem of exponential smoothing is one of selecting the appropriate weighting scheme.

Time Trends

Probably the most straightforward forecasting models are simple linear, quadratic, exponential, or logarithmic time trends which express volume, for example, as a function of time only. The parameters are estimated by ordinary least-squares (OLS) techniques.

Adaptive Forecasting

Adaptive forecasting models are a collection of techniques which have the ability to "self-correct" if the forecast is not tracking the actual behavior of the system. Adaptive forecasting techniques are much easier to use than are some more sophisticated techniques and have been known to perform equally well. Adaptive forecasting techniques as well as other time series techniques will be discussed in Chapter 5.

ECONOMETRIC MODELING SYSTEM

If the user wants to use computer simulation experiments to evaluate the effects on sales volume or market share of alternative pricing, advertising, and competitive strategies, then econometric models are the appropriate analytical tools. Econometric models can also be used to link market forecasts to national and regional economies. Formally, our understanding of the market behavior of specific products or groups of products can be considerably enhanced through the use of econometric marketing tools. But the forecasting accuracy of any econometric marketing model is no better than the accuracy of the policy assumptions and assumptions about the firm's external environment which underlie the model.

Econometric modeling involves a four-step methodology which will be summarized below. These steps include: (1) model specification, (2) parameter estimation, (3) validation, and (4) policy simulation. Given the present state of development of computer software, it is now possible to implement all four of these steps within the planning modeling system without having to go out of the system to FORTRAN, PL/1, or some other type of subroutines.

Specification

Unfortunately, most econometric textbooks are concerned only with the question of "Given an econometric model, how do we estimate the parameters of the model?"

In other words, the entire question of model specification has been assumed away by most textbooks and university courses on econometrics.

The specification of econometric marketing models requires: (1) considerable knowledge of the market of the product or group of products being modeled, (2) familiarity with econometric and statistical methods, and (3) some knowledge of microeconomics and the theory of markets.

Estimation

Ordinary least-squares Single-equation econometric models can be estimated using ordinary least-square regression techniques.

Two-stage least squares Simultaneous-equation models require the use of techniques like two-stage, least squares (TSLS) or other simultaneous-equation estimators. The application of OLS to simultaneous-equation models may yield biased, inconsistent estimates. Most of the planning and modeling software packages include OLS, but very few of them offer TSLS or other simultaneous equation estimators.

Non-linear regression Frequently econometric models take the form of polynomials, logarithmic functions, ratios, exponential functions, or other nonlinear relationships. For this reason, nonlinear regression techniques may also be useful!

Statistics Associated with each of the aforementioned econometric estimating techniques are a set of statistics that may be useful in screening data, model formulation, and model evaluation. These statistics include:

- Means
- Standard errors
- t-statistics
- F-statistic
- R^2s
- Durbin–Watson statistic

- Residuals
- Standard errors of the estimate
- Analysis of variance
- Correlation coefficients
- Partial correlation coefficients

Validation

The ultimate test of the validity of an econometric model is how well it forecasts the actual behavior of the system it was designed to emulate. This implies solving the model each period for the output variables in terms of given policy variables and external variables as well as lagged values of the output variables generated by the model in preceding time periods. In other words, the model is viewed as a closed-loop dynamic system which is driven by a set of starting values for the lagged output variables and given values for the policy and external variables.

Because econometric models may either be linear or nonlinear and either recursive or simultaneous, a technique like the Gauss–Seidel method is needed to solve the simultaneous equation models. Ideally, simple one-word commands like SOLVE and VALIDATE can be used to solve and validate econometric models. It is also desirable to produce a comparison of simulated and actual values and perhaps compute mean percent absolute errors for each output variable.

Policy Simulation

Finally, once we have specified, estimated, and validated an econometric model that we feel we can live with, we are then ready to conduct policy simulations with the model. We simply change the policy variables and external variables and solve for the output variables. Again we need a technique like the Gauss–Seidel method to solve the simultaneous equations.

Integrated Models

Although estimation, validation, and policy simulation are, in fact, three separate computer programs, it is possible to integrate each of these steps into a single system so that the user can move easily from one step to another. Commands like ESTIMATE and TSLS can be used to estimate the parameters with ordinary least squares and two-stage least squares, respectively. In addition, a set of test statistics for each equation will also be produced—R^2, t-statistics, F-statistic, standard errors, Durbin–Watson statistic, etc. VALIDATE and SOLVE commands generate the time paths of the output variables for validation purposes and policy simulation.

Some systems also contain a SAVE command which enables the user to save the structural specification and parameter estimates of an econometric marketing model and pass them on to a financial model without ever leaving the system. With this feature, it is quite easy to integrate financial, marketing, and production models. No longer is it necessary to develop econometric models on one system and then recode them for use on a different system if one wants to use the econometric results for planning. Econometric modeling as well as forecasting modeling can now be fully integrated into the planning modeling system.

National and Regional Econometric Models

It is also possible to link national econometric models and economic databases directly to a planning and modeling system. For example, Monsanto and Dresser Industries each have a national econometric model and database installed on their in-house computer and linked to their business planning models.

USER ORIENTATION OF THE SYSTEM

Up to this point we have described a number of basic elements which we believe to be worthy of serious consideration in the design of a planning and modeling system. Various subsets of each of these elements are available in the form of special purpose computer software packages. Many of these software packages are quite well suited for special purpose functional applications. But if our objective is comprehensive corporate planning and modeling, then we are likely to require (1) a database system, (2) a security system, (3) a report generator, (4) a simulation modeling system, (5) a forecasting system, and (6) an econometric modeling system. And, furthermore, it would be extremely convenient to have all of these features linked together as subsystems of a truly integrated planning and modeling system.

Free Format Input

Free format input greatly facilitates the reading of input data into the planning database. Most of the more powerful planning and modeling systems offer this feature. One of the real disadvantages of scientific programming languages like FORTRAN is the fact that FORTRAN requires the use of fixed format input data.

User Specified Subroutines

Although we have advocated a planning and modeling system which contains a substantial number of powerful built-in functions and subroutines, we recognize the impossibility of building a system which is all things to all people. There will always be a user who wants some special subroutine to satisfy his or her own unique needs. With this thought in mind, an integrated planning and modeling system should be sufficiently open-ended to permit the user to write his or her own subroutines in, for example, FORTRAN or PL/1. With this feature, the user never gets locked into a particular system.

Easy to Use

It is one thing to advocate an integrated planning and modeling system consisting of the six subsystems described three paragraphs ago, but what if the resulting system is an extremely cumbersome, difficult to use system which requires the user to be a senior programmer or computer scientist? Fortunately, recent breakthroughs in computer science and corporate modeling techniques have made it possible to design and implement an easy to use planning and modeling system which includes all six of the subsystems described in this book. More will be said concerning the ease of use of planning modeling systems when we discuss computer software systems.

SYSTEM AVAILABILITY

Corporate planning modeling systems may be run either interactively or in batch, either on the user's in-house computer or on an outside service bureau. Although computer service bureaus, particularly time-sharing bureaus, may provide a convenient vehicle for the development and testing of individual business unit planning models, putting an integrated comprehensive total corporate planning model and database up on an outside service bureau is likely to be prohibitively expensive. The disk charges for the corporate databases alone will be enormous. Over the long run, we believe that most of the really serious corporate planning and modeling systems for large companies will be implemented on in-house computers rather than on an outside bureau. However, smaller firms, which are equivalent to single business units like those depicted in Fig. 2.1, will still find service bureaus to be the most cost effective alternative for doing financial planning and modeling.

Interactive

All things being equal, it is difficult to argue against the merits of interactive computing for corporate planning and modeling. The benefits of conversational computing to planning are obvious and well documented in the literature. But interactive computing can be quite expensive even on in-house computers if one considers the opportunity cost of alternative uses of computer central processing units. Therefore, we recommend interactive computing during the model debugging stage and when the timeliness of alternative plans and scenarios justifies the premium charges for interactive computing.

Batch

Batch computing is more appropriate for creating large historical databases and doing multiscenario production runs when the user is not faced with an urgent deadline to make a decision.

Service Bureau

In the initial stages of the development of a corporate planning model, a computer service bureau may prove to be an extremely convenient way to begin the project. As previously indicated, time sharing can be very useful to the model builder during the early stages of model development and debugging. Basically what time sharing service bureaus have to offer is service. If the user is not satisfied with the level of service provided by the bureau, the contract with the bureau can be cancelled on short notice.

In-House Hardware

However, if one develops a truly integrated, consolidated corporate planning model of the type described in Fig. 2.1, then this type of modeling may become quite expensive on an outside service bureau. For this reason, many corporate modeling projects are begun on a service bureau and then are switched to the company's in-house computer when the outside time-sharing charges become excessive.

Before installing a particular planning and modeling system on one's in-house computer, several questions must be answered. What are the computer hardware requirements for the particular planning and modeling system? Is it available only on a time-sharing bureau or can it be installed in-house? What operating systems are required? What are the core (computer memory) requirements? Does the vendor of the system make the source code available to its clients or not? What kinds of service and support are provided by the vendor?

SOFTWARE SYSTEM

What about the task of programming a corporate planning and modeling system? Basically, two alternatives are available. The system can be programmed either in a general purpose scientific language like FORTRAN, PL/1, or APL, or it can be coded in a planning and modeling language like the one used throughout this text—SIMPLAN.

There are at least two major benefits associated with the use of one of the scientific programming languages. First, they are extremely flexible; that is, every feature that we have proposed for a planning and modeling system could be coded in FORTRAN, PL/1, or APL. Indeed, our survey showed that 50 percent of the corporate models in our sample had been written in FORTRAN. Second, these languages are quite well known, particularly FORTRAN.

But there are some very serious limitations to the use of scientific programming languages for corporate planning models. First, corporate planners and financial analysts may not be familiar with any of these languages since they may not have had previous computing experience. Second, database management and report generation are not the main strengths of FORTRAN and APL. (PL/1 has some features which facilitate file manipulation and report generation.) Third, these languages offer little assistance either in formulating or coding corporate planning models since they are general-purpose scientific languages. Fourth, it is the rule rather than the exception for top management to make frequent changes in their requirements in terms of report formats, policy assumptions, external assumptions types of consolidations, etc. Mergers and acquisitions occur, new products are introduced, and old products are dropped. These types of changes are not easy to implement with scientific programming languages. A major reason for the demise of most of the large-scale models developed in the 1960s was their lack of flexibility. Most of these models were programmed in FORTRAN. When Sun Oil merged with another oil company, the model was dropped rather than reprogramming it in FORTRAN. Fifth, even if the model builders are accomplished programmers, econometric modeling is very difficult with scientific programming languages.

Some have suggested that APL will be the wave of the future for corporate modeling. Although APL is one of the more powerful scientific languages available today, it has some unique disadvantages which are likely to render null and void the fantasy of corporate managers sitting at their APL terminals doing corporate planning. First, APL assumes the user is proficient at mathematics including matrix algebra. This assumption simply does not hold up in the real world. Very few managers have ever been exposed to matrix algebra. Second, the special characters and mathematical operators of APL are likely to be foreign to most managers, financial analysts, and corporate planners. In summary, APL is an excellent language for computer scientists and mathematicians, but its utility as a corporate planning tool is severely limited.

The alternative to scientific programming languages is to use one of the new planning and modeling languages designed specifically to facilitate the formulation and coding of corporate planning models. Among the benefits to be derived from using one of these planning and modeling systems are the following. First, they are easy to use. To do financial modeling with a system like SIMPLAN, the user must be familiar with high school algebra, accounting, and finance. The user need not be familiar with modeling or computer programming. Second, some of these systems provide a conceptual framework for planning and modeling which makes it much easier to develop the model in the first place. Third, with a select few of these systems, it is possible to have all six of the following subsystems integrated within the planning and modeling system: (1) database management, (2) security, (3) report generation, (4) simulation modeling, (5) forecasting, and (6) econometrics. Fourth, many of these planning and modeling systems are quite flexible. Changes in databases, models, and reports are easy to implement. Fifth, econometrics, forecasting, and risk analysis are much easier to implement with one of these systems than they are with a scientific language. Sixth, an efficient planning and modeling system should lead to reduced costs for the total project.

Of course, the advantages of these planning and modeling software systems must be weighed against their costs. First, these systems are not available free of charge to the user; that is, the user may pay a fee for the use of these planning and modeling systems. A limited number of systems can be licensed for use on in-house computers. Nearly all of these systems are available on a surcharge basis on various time-sharing service bureaus. Second, since the computer is doing the work of many programmers, the computer running costs will definitely be higher than, say, similar models programmed in FORTRAN, but the project costs should be considerably less. In the final analysis, it is the total project cost rather than the computer cost that is the most important consideration.

SUMMARY AND CONCLUSIONS

With the large number of companies now experimenting with some form of planning model, it is not surprising to observe that many of these companies began using a particular modeling system without giving much thought to the long-run implications of the system which was selected. It is not uncommon to find one division of a company using one system, another using a second system, and a third using a FORTRAN model running on yet a third service bureau's computer. At the same time, the corporation maintains a corporate database as well as databases for each division on the in-house computer. Corporate planning may also subscribe to one or more outside econometric forecasting services.

In other words, it is not unusual to find large companies subscribing to as many as six different modeling services with exact duplicates of the corporate database running on the in-house computer as well as on outside service bureaus.

With a little thought and careful planning, it is possible to design an integrated planning and modeling system which will satisfy corporate management as well as the management of all of the business units. Financial, marketing, and production planning models all can be developed within one system which is linked to a national econometric database. And, finally, the system can be implemented on the company's in-house computer thus eliminating outside time-sharing charges and the costly duplication of databases.

In summary, time spent on the design of a company's planning and modeling system may be time well spent. The following pages contain a checklist of important features to be considered in the design or evaluation of a computer based planning and modeling system.

In Chapter 3 we turn our attention to the difficult question of how to integrate a corporate planning model into the planning process.

ELEMENTS OF A PLANNING AND MODELING SYSTEM

I. **Planning System**

   A. Business planning models

      1. Financial planning models
      2. Marketing planning models
      3. Production planning models
      4. Integrated planning models

   B. Consolidated planning models

      1. Horizontal consolidation
      2. Vertical consolidation
      3. Multidirectional consolidation
      4. Number of levels
      5. Eliminations
      6. Nonstandard chart of accounts
      7. Postprocessing of consolidated data

II. **Management Information System**

   A. Databases

      1. Internal
      2. External

   B. Database System

      1. Matrix
      2. Row–column
      3. Record file
      4. Multiple files
      5. Multiple databases
      6. Cross file manipulations
      7. Hierarchical databases
      8. Multiple time periods
      9. Independence of data, models, and reports
      10. Database limitations
         a. Number of variables
         b. Number of periods
         c. Number of files
         d. Number of databases
         e. Length of variable name
         f. Length of variable abbreviation
         g. Length of variable units
         h. Length of userid
         i. Number of digits of accuracy

   C. Report Generator

      1. Choice of output report formats

   2. User-specified reports
   3. Report limitations
      a. Number of reports
      b. Number of characters per line
      c. Number of lines per report
   4. Report definition editing
D. Graphics
E. Security System
   1. Individual database
   2. Individual file
   3. Individual model
   4. Individual report definition
   5. Individual functions

III. Modeling System

A. Recursive models

B. Simultaneous-equation models

C. Logical models

D. Risk analysis

E. Other modeling features
   1. Equation-type models
   2. Algebraic operators
   3. Storing models
   4. Storing results of a model
   5. Storing equations from estimating techniques
   6. Storing projections from estimating techniques
   7. Model integration
   8. Line number independence
   9. Model editing

IV. Forecasting System

A. Exponential smoothing

B. Time trends

C. Adaptive forecasting

V. Econometric Modeling System

A. Specification

B. Estimation
   1. Ordinary least-squares
   2. Two-stage least-squares
   3. Nonlinear regression
   4. Statistics

   a. Means
   b. Standard errors
   c. *t*-statistics
   d. *F*-statistic
   e. R^2's
   f. Durbin–Watson statistics
   g. Residuals
   h. Standard error of the estimate
   i. Analysis of variance
   j. Correlation coefficients
   k. Partial correlation coefficients

C. Validation

   1. Simulation versus actual
   2. Mean percent absolute errors
   3. Theil's inequality coefficient

D. Policy simulation

E. Integrated models

F. National and regional econometric models

VI. User Orientation

A. Free format input

B. User specified subroutines

C. Easy to use

VII. System Availability

A. Interactive

B. Batch

C. Service bureau

D. In-house hardware requirements

   1. Hardware
   2. Operating systems
   3. Code size
   4. Source code

VIII. Software System

NOTE

1. This chapter is based on a paper by Thomas H. Naylor and M. James Mansfield entitled The design of computer-based planning and modeling systems, which was published in *Long Range Planning* (February, 1977).

3 The Integration of Corporate Planning Models into the Planning Process

Despite dramatic increases in the usage of computer-based planning models since 1970, relatively few corporations have successfully integrated their planning models into the planning process. In many cases, planning models are treated as though they were merely mathematical appendages to the planning process rather than tools to be integrated into the planning process. The failure to integrate planning models into the planning process has severely limited the usefulness of some models as planning tools. All too little attention has been given in the past to the problem of designing planning models to meet the specific planning requirements of a particular company.

A few organizations have been successful in their efforts to integrate business planning models into the planning process. They include Northwest Industries, Ross Laboratories, and the *New York Times*. Without exception, the goal of integrating the business planning model into the planning process was accomplished by each of these organizations only through a deliberate, well-planned effort to implement a truly integrated planning and modeling system. Such a goal is not easily reached.

Drawing heavily on the experiences of those companies that have integrated their planning models into the planning process (and some that have failed to do so), this chapter outlines a six-step approach for integrating a corporate planning model into the planning process:

1. Review of the planning environment
2. Specification of planning requirements
3. Definition of the goals and objectives for planning
4. Evaluation of existing planning resources
5. Design of an integrated planning and modeling system
6. Formulation of a strategy for integrating the planning model into the planning process.

STEP 1: REVIEW OF THE PLANNING ENVIRONMENT

The first four steps of the approach we are about to describe take the form of what some have called a "planning audit." In order to ensure objectivity, it may be desirable to have these four steps implemented by independent outside consultants who can step back and observe both the strengths and the weaknesses of the present business environment, planning process, and planning tools.

The initial step in this process involves a review of the overall environment in which planning takes place within the company. Such a review must necessarily include: (1) organizational structure, (2) management philosophy and style, (3) business environment, and (4) planning process.

Organizational Structure

Fundamental to a review of a company's planning process is the company's organizational structure. How is the company organized? Is it decentralized or highly centralized? How much autonomy is given to individual divisions, groups, profit centers, or business units? How many production locations does the firm have? What is the geographic spread of its production facilities and sales offices? Does the company do business in foreign countries? The answers to these questions are critical to the evaluation of the company's planning requirements and the design of a suitable planning and modeling system.

Management Philosophy and Style

The next major consideration in reviewing the planning environment is the philosophy and style of management of the company. What type of management does the company have? Can management be described as authoritarian, permissive, passive, aggressive, or entrepreneurial? Does the chief executive officer behave either as the ceremonial head of the company or the corporate planner or does he or she delegate the planning function?

Does management subscribe to the so-called Theory X approach to management in which unilateral decisions on the part of top management are forced on subordinates or does it adhere to the Theory Y approach in which top management, middle management, and staff members work together to define and implement common goals and objectives.

Does management carry out its functions of planning, organizing, motivating, and controlling the behavior of the company in a rigid, formal fashion or does it rely on less formal methods? What is the age distribution of top management? What kind of educational background does management have? What is management's attitude toward formal planning and the use of quantitative tools such as corporate planning models? Is management in tune with the realities of its external environment? Does management appreciate the benefits of multiscenario planning? How flexible is management? The persons doing the planning audit must have a very good grasp of the answers to these questions before proceeding to the next step.

Business Environment

The company's business environment will play an important role in determining the planning requirements. What are the major problems facing the company during the next five years? Is the company vulnerable to energy shortages or substantial increases in the price of fuels, petroleum feedstocks, electricity, etc.? Are other inputs into the production process likely to become in short supply? Will the firm encounter liquidity problems? What does the competitive environment look like? Is the company strongly influenced by cyclical swings in the national economy? Does the company have problems with environmental pollution? Are there any changes in government policies and pending regulations that may affect the company's performance? The answers to these questions will strongly influence management's commitment to formal planning and the use of computer-based planning models.

Other factors which may influence the company's planning requirements include its size, the nature of its markets, and its production processes. Whether the company is small or large, growing or stagnating, prosperous or financially insecure, or mature or unstable can have a significant effect on the company's planning requirements. Among the market factors which may serve as determinants of the company's planning requirements are: (1) the extent of the company's product lines, (2) the accuracy of market forecasts, (3) market stability, (4) the degree of competition, and (5) the number of customers. On the production side, the capital–labor ratio, production technology, and degree of integration may also play an important role in defining the planning requirements.

Consider the case of the cigarette industry in the United States. Until recently the cigarette industry was one of the most profitable industries in the country. Except in R. J. Reynolds Industries, formal planning still does not exist in most tobacco companies today. However, there is increasing evidence that this situation is likely to change very soon. Increased antismoking campaigns by the government and proposed new taxes based on the tar and nicotine content of cigarettes have had a sobering influence on the tobacco companies. Already the tobacco companies are taking steps to beef up their planning departments.

A complete knowledge and understanding of the company's business environment is vital to anyone who wants to evaluate the firm's planning requirements. Although planning requirements may be influenced by opportunities and problems which arise in the external environment of the firm, managers seem to respond more quickly to problems than to opportunities in defining their planning requirements.

Planning Process

The final step in the review of the organization's planning environment is the review of the planning process itself. Among the basic questions to be answered are: What kind of planning process does the company have—bottom-up, top-down, or inside-out? Who does planning in the company? Does the company have centralized corporate planning? What is the interface between division planning and corporate planning? What level of detail is supported by the present planning system? What is the length of the planning cycle?

There are also a number of important political questions that must be answered. What is top management's attitude towards planning? Is planning taken seriously by management? Who controls the planning function? What has been the track record of corporate planning in the company? Who is likely to feel threatened by changes in the planning process? What planning tools are employed?

In summary, this step of the planning audit involves a very careful evaluation of the details of the existing planning process as well as its political support.

STEP 2: SPECIFICATION OF THE PLANNING REQUIREMENTS

During the second step of this approach, it is desirable to have outside consultants interview key executives who are involved in the planning process in order to determine their planning requirements. Corporate officers down through the vice-presidential level should be interviewed. Directors and managers who are directly involved in planning should also be interviewed. The in-depth interviews should last for about two hours and should focus on questions of the following types:

· What are the specific planning requirements of the individual managers? What are the corporate planning requirements? What are the division planning requirements?
· What data are required for planning and forecasting? What data are available internally? What external data may be required?
· What types of external events (economic, governmental policy, competitive, and political) may affect the company during the next five years?
· What are the major business strategies to be considered over the next few years?
· What type of "What if?" questions would the individual managers like to have answered?
· What kind of reports are needed? What level of detail is required for these reports?

Armed with the information gleaned from the management interviews, it becomes possible to formalize the planning and modeling requirements of the company. (A sample questionnaire is included at the end of this chapter to illustrate the kinds of questions typically included in a planning audit of the type summarized in this chapter.)

STEP 3: DEFINITION OF THE GOALS AND OBJECTIVES FOR PLANNING

Once the planning requirements have been finalized based on the interviews in Step 2, the goals and objectives for planning can be defined. The results of the interviews with management must be summarized and presented to those managers who have participated in the project as a tentative statement of their goals and objectives. Among the questions to be answered at this stage are the following: Have we accurately captured management's perceptions of the planning process? Is management in agreement with the summary statement of their goals and objectives for planning? Given this feedback from management, it is then possible to finalize the goals and objectives for planning and modeling.

Only after the completion of Steps 2 and 3 of this process do we have sufficient information to evaluate the company's existing planning resources and to design an integrated planning and modeling system.

The importance of evaluating existing planning resources in light of planning requirements was dramatically portrayed in one of Naylor's consulting assignments with a large manufacturing company based in New York. For convenience, we shall call the company the Oriental Company.

At the time of the consulting assignment, three financial analysts at Oriental were spending full time maintaining, documenting, and enhancing a financial planning model. The computer time-sharing charges for the model amounted to $200,000 a year. The model was primarily a giant number cruncher in which financial plans from 60 divisions were read into the model as input data and consolidated to produce a corporate "strategic plan." The model was very detailed and included financial forecasting for five-, ten-, and fifteen-year planning horizons. The documentation of the model was excellent and quite easy to use. Technically speaking, the model was analytically sound.

Interviews with several of the users of the model at the division level revealed that they had no idea why they were being asked to use the model. No "What if?" experiments were being conducted, either at the division level or at the corporate level. Corporate management did not even check consolidated corporate plans for financial feasibility. Division plans were simply added up and presented to corporate management.

Corporate plans produced by the Oriental financial planning model consisted of one and only one scenario. There were no linkages to the marketplace or the national economy. In no sense was the model integrated into the planning process.

In summary, Oriental was spending close to $350,000 per year on a financial planning model that was producing absolutely no benefits for anyone. Unfortunately, there are a lot of companies that have developed financial planning models similar to the Oriental model. Frequently a model of this type will go unnoticed until some executive starts asking questions about the outside time-sharing charges. By the time the absurdity has been exposed by management, successful corporate planning modeling may be set back at least five years.

The moral to the Oriental story is quite obvious. It simply makes no sense whatever to begin developing a corporate planning model until the goals and objectives for planning and modeling have been carefully spelled out.

STEP 4: EVALUATION OF EXISTING PLANNING RESOURCES

Having defined the planning and modeling requirements for the company as well as the goals and objectives for planning, we must turn our attention to the existing planning resources of the company. Specifically, we must evaluate the following resources in light of given planning requirements: (1) databases, (2) forecasts, (3) models, (4) reports, (5) computer software, and (6) human resources.

Databases

What types of internal databases are available? Are these databases in machine-readable form? Are they adequate to meet the company's planning requirements? Which external databases are available? Is it possible to supplement existing data with market survey data?

Although insufficient data may prove to be a limiting factor in the development of business planning models, frequently data limitations are used as a strawman. An imaginative corporate planner can frequently circumvent data problems. An important by-product of corporate planning models is to give specificity to the company's data requirements.

Forecasts

Although forecasting is only one element of corporate planning, it is nevertheless an important element. What can be said about the historical track record of the company's forecasts? Have previous forecasts been accurate? If not, what have been the consequences of the inaccurate forecasts? What forecasting tools are available? Does the company use econometric forecasting models? What type of forecasting expertise exists within the company?

Models

Although most companies with sales over $100 million now have some kind of computer-based planning model, many of these models are ill-conceived and have only limited usefulness. Does the model provide timely answers to the right "What if?" questions? Is the model flexible enough? Does the model include too much detail or insufficient detail? Is the model expensive to run? Is the company locked into some outside time-sharing vendor? To what extent is the model integrated into the planning process? Does management have confidence in the model?

These are challenging questions and very few of the existing corporate planning models have successfully passed the tests implied by these questions. All too many corporate planning models have been designed by corporate time-sharing addicts who have little or no knowledge of planning, budgeting, or even modeling.

Reports

More often than not, the reports included in corporate plans have represented an excessive amount of detail—far more than anyone in management can possibly comprehend. This phenomenon seems to be a carry-over from the days when the only corporate planning which was done in many companies was financial planning. If the financial planning function was in the hands of an accountant, the corporate plans and forecasting frequently took the form of volumes of computer printout.

Corporate plans should be concise and to the point. The number and scope of reports included in corporate plans should be kept to reasonable proportions. The output reports of corporate plans should be closely tied to the company's actual planning needs. If management drowns in a sea of computer printout produced by the corporate planning model, corporate planning and modeling may soon meet a similar fate.

Software

Although there are nearly 50 planning and modeling software packages available, relatively few of these systems offer sufficient power, flexibility, or ease of use to be effective planning tools. Many of the existing software packages are little more than financial report generators and provide few benefits as planning tools. Sometimes the limitations of these software systems do not become obvious until they have been in use for six months or a year. Switching from one system to another may involve a costly process.

Unfortunately, most of the planning and modeling software systems are marketed exclusively by computer service bureaus whose primary objective is to sell computer time. There are very few time-sharing bureaus that have expertise in planning and modeling. Indeed, it can be argued that time-sharing representatives who are involved in the sale of planning and modeling software in which the client is charged in proportion to usage are actually involved in a conflict of interest. Consultants on planning and modeling should have as their primary concern the most efficient way of meeting the client's planning requirements, not whether the client is spending enough each month on time-sharing charges.

Corporate planners should devote more attention to selecting planning software than they have in the past. They should not delegate this responsibility to the systems analysts or managment scientists. Furthermore, the selection of software should be made only after the goals and objectives for planning have been defined explicitly.

Human Resources

A decision to develop an integrated planning and modeling system is tantamount to a commitment to invest in the human resources required to design, implement, and support such a system. A corporate planning model should not be developed on a shoe-string budget insufficient to support the people required to implement such a project. If the planning model is to be credible, it should be developed primarily with the use of in-house human resources. Model specification, data collection, parameter estimation, and computer coding should all be done in-house. However, outside consultants are likely to be necessary in most companies to assist in: (1) the specification of planning requirements, (2) the definition of the goals and objectives for planning, (3) the evaluation of planning resources, (4) the design of the planning model, and (5) the formulation of a strategy for integrating the model into the planning process.

Successful corporate modeling requires a variety of talents including financial analysis, econometrics, economics, systems analysis, management science, mathematics, statistics, and data processing. Perhaps the weakest link in most corporate modeling efforts is the system design. Just because a financial analyst can develop a simple pro forma financial planning model or a cash management model, it does not follow that such a person can successfully design an integrated planning and modeling system. More attention needs to be given to this problem and to the human resources necessary for successful corporate planning models.

STEP 5: DESIGN OF AN INTEGRATED PLANNING AND MODELING SYSTEM

Having reviewed the planning environment, having specified the planning requirements, and having evaluated the existing planning resources, we can now turn our attention to the design of an integrated planning and modeling system. The elements of a planning and modeling system were previously defined in Chapter 2.

Because these elements have been discussed in Chapter 2, we need not repeat descriptions of them here. Suffice it to say that the exact design of an integrated planning and modeling system is totally dependent on the planning environment, the planning requirements, and the resources which can be committed to planning.

STEP 6: FORMULATION OF A STRATEGY FOR INTEGRATING THE PLANNING MODEL INTO THE PLANNING PROCESS

Step 6 in the approach outlined in this chapter involves the formulation of a gameplan for implementing the planning and modeling system designed in Step 5. The strategy involves seven major elements.

First, the strategy must necessarily include an *organizational framework* for developing, implementing, and maintaining the model and integrating it into the planning process. Of course, any organizational changes which might be proposed must be politically feasible.

Second, it may be necessary to make certain changes in the existing *planning process* as a result of information obtained in Steps 2 and 3 of this methodology; that is, the present planning system may simply not be fulfilling the planning requirements of the company and may need to be altered.

Third, it may also be desirable to modify or enhance existing *databases, forecasts, models, reports,* and *computer software* to make these planning tools more compatible with the company's planning needs. Indeed, it is possible that the entire planning and modeling system may have to be completely redesigned.

Fourth, the *human and technical resource requirements* for an integrated planning and modeling system must be specified. It may be necessary to recruit additional staff members to implement and support the planning and modeling system. In addition to using more powerful computer software, it may also become important to upgrade the company's in-house computer hardware.

Fifth, an *educational program* to familiarize management with the use of the planning and modeling system must be designed. Ignorance on the part of management of the merits of modern planning tools is still one of the greatest impediments to successful corporate planning modeling today. A strong educational program may be the single most important factor in determining whether or not a planning model is integrated into the planning process.

Sixth, a *schedule* for implementing the corporate modeling gameplan must be drawn up. We strongly recommend a modular, stepwise approach with tangible benchmarks and results tied to specific dates in a timetable. Above all, the leader of any corporate modeling effort must be warned not to bite off too much at once.

Seventh, management will want to see a *budget* for the proposed corporate modeling project. Assessing whether or not the benefits of a proposed corporate planning model will exceed the costs is frequently a difficult task. The benefits of a corporate planning model are related to more complete, more accurate, and more timely information on which to plan the future of the business. Unfortunately, quantifying these benefits is not a trivial process. Although cost justifications of corporate planning models may be difficult to produce, they are not impossible and do represent an important factor in convincing management of the payoff of computer-based models.

A SAMPLE PLANNING AUDIT QUESTIONNAIRE

1. Name _____

2. Title _____

3. Date _____

4. What is your opinion of the Monthly Operating Plan?

   _____

   _____

   _____

   _____

Strengths

   a. _____

   b. _____

   c. _____

   d. _____

Limitations

   a. _____

   b. _____

   c. _____

   d. _____

5. What would you like to see changed about the Operating Plan?

   _____

   _____

   _____

   _____

6. What kinds of "What if?" questions would you like to have answered with the Operating Plan?

_____

_____

_____

_____

7. What kinds of *external assumptions* would you like to be able to evaluate in conjunction with the Operating Plan?

_____

_____

_____

_____

8. What kinds of *business strategies* would you like to be able to evaluate in conjunction with the Operating Plan?

_____

_____

_____

_____

9. What is your opinion of the reports included in the Operating Plan? Are they adequate to meet your needs?

_____

_____

_____

_____

10. What can you say about the forecasting accuracy of the Operating Plan?

_____

_____

_____

_____

11. What is your opinion of the Long-Range Plan?

_____

_____

_____

_____

Strengths

a. _____

b. _____

c. _____

d. _____

Limitations

a. _____

b. _____

c. _____

d. _____

12. What would you like to see changed about the Long-Range Plan?

_____

_____

_____

_____

13. What kinds of strategic "What if?" questions would you like to have answered in conjunction with the Long-Range Plan?

_____

_____

_____

_____

14. What kinds of *external assumptions* would you like to be able to evaluate with the aid of an annual five-year planning model?

   _____

   _____

   _____

   _____

15. What kind of *business strategies* would you like to be able to evaluate with an annual five-year planning model?

   _____

   _____

   _____

   _____

16. Are you satisfied with reports produced by the Long-Range Plan?

   _____

   _____

   _____

   _____

17. Is the planning system adequate to meet your needs?

   _____

   _____

   _____

   _____

18. Do you have any experience with computer-based planning and forecasting systems? Was your experience favorable or not?

   _____

   _____

   _____

   _____

19. Do you feel that the company's revenues and profits are strongly influenced by external factors such as the national economy, government regulations, or foreign competition? Explain your reasons for feeling as you do.

_____

_____

_____

_____

20. What do you feel are the major opportunities available to the company over the next five or ten years?

_____

_____

_____

_____

21. What are the major problems facing the company?

_____

_____

_____

_____

22. What are the most important goals and objectives for the company?

_____

_____

_____

_____

23. What obstacles do you see to the achievement of these goals?

_____

_____

_____

_____

24. If the company develops its own computer-based planning model, how would you like to relate to the model? Please be as specific as possible.

_____

_____

_____

_____

25. If the company develops its own planning model, what type of output reports would you like to have available? Be as specific as possible. List the line items you would like to see included.

_____

_____

_____

_____

26. What type of "What if?" questions would you like to be able to answer with a planning model?

_____

_____

_____

_____

External assumptions:

1. _____

2. _____

3. _____

Business strategy assumptions:

1. _____

2. _____

3. _____

27. Would you like to be able to manipulate the model at a terminal? Would you prefer to work through an analyst?

_____

_____

_____

_____

28. Should the model be interactive or batch? _____

29. How often would you use the model?

   a. Weekly _____

   b. Monthly _____

   c. Quarterly _____

   d. Annually _____

   e. Ad hoc _____

30. Please write any other suggestions concerning the development of a computer-based planning and modeling system.

_____

_____

_____

_____

_____

_____

_____

_____

_____

_____

4　Financial Planning Models

INTRODUCTION

This chapter describes a process for developing financial planning models. Although there is a variety of different types of financial planning models, the underlying structure of these models is very similar whether the model be a financial model for a division, profit center, product group, or the entire corporation.

Financial models are used to produce pro forma financial reports and financial ratios. A typical corporate financial model generates as output some combination of the following financial forecasts: balance sheet, income statement, sources-and-uses of funds statement, and various financial ratios. In this chapter sales revenue forecasts and production cost projections are treated as given data; that is, no model is developed to forecast either of these two driving inputs of the financial model. In other words, we are considering stand-alone financial models in this chapter. In Chapters 5, 6, and 7 we discuss marketing models. Production models are treated in Chapter 8. Chapter 9 contains an integrated business planning model in which marketing and production models are linked directly to the financial model.

Financial planning models may be used for many different purposes. Among the more important applications of these models are:

- Cash forecasting
- Cash management
- Financial forecasting
- New venture analysis
- Merger–acquisition analysis

- Divestiture analysis
- Tax planning
- Budgeting
- Profit planning
- Capital budgeting

To illustrate the process for developing and using a financial planning model, we shall describe a typical financial planning model. Although the model is relatively simple, it is representative of a broad class of financial planning models.

OBJECTIVE

The objective of this model is to provide the vice-president of finance with the capability to simulate the effects of alternative financial policies and assumptions about the firm's external environment on the financial structure of the firm. Specifically, management wants to conduct "What if?" experiments to evaluate the impact of different cash management, debt, equity, and materials-purchasing policies on the corporation's profit and loss statement, balance sheet, and sources-and-uses-of-funds statement. Management also desires the facility to do financial projections based on alternative assumptions about sales, revenue, materials, costs, interest rates, etc.—factors that cannot be controlled by the firm. The model will also be used for tax planning.

Management has expressed an interest in having a relatively flexible financial model so that changes in policy assumptions and market conditions can easily be evaluated through the use of the model. The planning horizon is 1975 through 1979.

COLLECTION OF FINANCIAL DATA

Our model is based on annual data for the preceding three years. Historical data are available for the following financial reports: (1) profit and loss statement, (2) balance sheet, (3) sources-and-uses of funds statement, and (4) balance sheet changes.

MODEL SPECIFICATION

Output Reports

Four different financial reports are required by the vice-president of finance over the period 1975 through 1979. These reports are displayed in Tables 4.4 through 4.7.

The entries and formats of these reports have been specified by management; that is, management has indicated that it wants to have reports which are identical to those which are currently produced by manual procedures.

Input Requirements

Our model is driven by three different sets of inputs—(1) an initial balance sheet, (2) external assumptions, and (3) policy assumptions.

Initial balance sheet   The point of departure for our financial projections is the firm's 1974 balance sheet which is given in Table 4.1.

External assumptions   Since the firm is selling in a competitive market, it is a price taker; that is, the market sets the price for its product. The first two rows of Table 4.2 contain management's assumptions for dollar sales and price for the 1975–1979 period. Price is expressed as an index in which the base year 1974 is equal to 1.0. Projected cost indices (with 1974 equal to 1.0) for materials, production, and administration and sales are given in the next three rows of Table 4.2.

Materials, production, and administrative and sales expenses are projected on the basis of their relationship to the 1974 selling price on the firm's product. These fractions of the 1974 selling price are projected in the next three rows of Table 4.2.

The last two rows contain projections for the long-term and short-term interest rates which the firm is likely to face.

The letters in parentheses in Table 4.2 denote the SIMPLAN record abbreviations (variables) which will be used in the specification of our SIMPLAN model.

Since this is a relatively simple financial planning model, all of the external assumptions are treated as given data. After management has acquired some experience with the use of the model, it may want to consider the use of either forecasting techniques or econometric methods to project sales, price, costs, and interest rates.

Table 4.1 Balance sheet 1974 (in millions)

	1974
Cash	$204.0
Accounts receivable	200.0
Materials	200.0
Tax overpayment	0.0
Total current assets	$604.0
Buildings	900.0
Furniture	12.0
Machinery	114.0
Less accumulated depreciation	(100.0)
Net fixed assets	$926.0
Total assets	$1,530.0
Accounts payable	$120.0
Short-term debt	0.0
Retirement of long-term debt	0.0
Tax payment	0.0
Total current liabilities	$120.0
Long-term debt	400.0
Deferred taxes	10.0
Stock	1,000.0
Retained earnings	0.0
Total liabilities	$1,530.0

Policy Assumptions The first two rows of Table 4.3 represent the materials purchasing policy for the firm over the next five years. The line item *materials-purchasing policy* denotes the minimum amount which will be purchased each year. The second row represents annual replacement purchases.

New stock, new long-term debt, retirement of long-term debt, and short-term debt are all policy variables related to the company's capital structure. Investment

Table 4.2 External assumptions

	1975	1976	1977	1978	1979
Sales (SALESD3)	2100.00	3600.00	4400.00	5000.00	5500.00
Price (PRICE)	1.12	1.15	1.15	1.35	1.45
Materials cost (MATCOST)	1.10	1.22	1.40	1.70	1.90
Production cost (PROCOST)	1.10	1.20	1.25	1.36	1.46
Administration and sales (SELCOST)	1.10	1.20	1.25	1.36	1.46
Materials fraction (MPERCENT)	0.37	0.36	0.35	0.35	0.35
Production fraction (PPERCENT)	0.33	0.33	0.31	0.31	0.28
Administration and sales fraction (SPERCENT)	0.20	0.20	0.19	0.19	0.17
Long-term interest rate (LTIRATE)	0.10	0.10	0.10	0.10	0.10
Short-term interest rate (STIRATE)	0.15	0.15	0.15	0.15	0.15

Table 4.3 Policy assumptions (dollars in millions)

	1975	1976	1977	1978	1979
Materials-purchasing policy (MATPURCH)	0.00	0.00	0.00	0.00	0.00
Purchase of materials (MATBUY)	733.91	1507.01	1949.04	2185.50	2537.28
New stock (NEWSTOCK)	0.00	0.00	0.00	0.00	0.00
New long-term debt (NEWLTD)	0.00	0.00	0.00	0.00	300.00
Retirement of long-term debt (RETIRE)	40.00	40.00	40.00	40.00	40.00
Short-term debt (STDEBT)	0.00	19.08	244.81	163.99	132.57
New building (BUILD)	0.00	0.00	0.00	0.00	200.00
Purchase of furniture (FURN)	2.00	2.00	2.00	2.00	8.00
Purchase of machinery (MACH)	8.00	4.00	2.00	7.00	107.00
Depreciation policy (DEPCHOIC)	2.00	2.00	2.00	2.00	2.00
Dividend policy (DIVPAY)	0.07	0.07	0.07	0.07	0.07
Minimum cash level (CASHLOW)	100.00	100.00	100.00	100.00	100.00

policies are also projected for new buildings, purchase of furniture, and purchase of machinery. There are two depreciation options—straight line and declining balance. The last two policy variables in Table 4.3 are dividend policy and minimum cash level.

Equations

Given the set of assumptions and input data of Tables 4.1 through 4.3, we must now specify a set of mathematical and logical relationships which will enable us to "explain" and project each of the line items of Tables 4.4 through 4.7. Each line item will require its own SIMPLAN equation. We shall now describe the development of the model.

Accounts receivable   Accounts receivable are assumed to be equal to 11 percent of sales in equation 260.

> 260 ACCREC=.11 * SALESD3   (receivables are a percentage of sales)

Cost calculations   Materials, production, and administrative and selling costs are calculated in equations 310 through 330.

> 310 MATPERCENT = MPERCENT * MATCOST / PRICE
> 320 PROPERCENT = PPERCENT * PROCOST / PRICE
> 330 SELPERCENT = SPERCENT * SELCOST / PRICE

Materials purchase   Materials used and inventory adjustments are computed in equations 370 through 390.

> 370 MATUSED = MATPERCENT * SALESD3   (dollar value of materials used)
> 380 MAT = MAT(−1)+(MATPURCH−MATUSED)/MATCOST
> (volume of current inventory)
> 390 MAT$ = MAT * MATCOST   (value of current inventory)

The minimum inventory level or reorder point has been set equal to three months' supply of raw materials. If inventories fall below the reorder point (MATMIN), then the supply of raw materials is replenished.

> 430 MATMIN = MATUSED/4   (determine inventory minimum at current prices)
> 440 IF MAT$ < MATMIN   (is inventory below policy minimum?)
> 450 MATBUY = MATPURCH+(MATMIN−MAT$)
> (buy purchasing minimum + inventory deficit)
> 460 MAT=MAT+(MATMIN−MAT$)/MATCOST (add purchase volume to inventory)
> 470 MAT$=MATMIN   (inventory deficit is made up)
> 480 ELSE   (inventory is at least at minimum level)

490 MATBUY = MATPURCH   (buy purchasing minimum only)

500 END

Straight-line depreciation[1] There are two depreciation options in our model–straight-line and accelerated depreciation. For straight-line depreciation the useful lives for furniture, machinery, and buildings are assumed to be 10 years, 15 years, and 33 years, respectively. Salvage value is assumed to be equal to zero. The straight-line depreciation calculations are defined as follows:

550 SLFURN = FURN/20+(FURN(−1)+FURN(−2)+FURN(−3)−
555   +FURN(−4)+FURN(−5))/10   (sum of purchase/10)
560 SLMACH = MACH/30+(MACH(−1)+MACH(−2)+MACH(−3)−
565   +MACH(−4)+MACH(−5))/15
570 SLBUILD = BUILD/66+(BUILD(−1)+BUILD(−2)+BUILD(−3)−
575   +BUILD(−4)+BUILD(−5))/33

If straight-line depreciation is the policy option chosen, then the depreciation values are set equal to the values computed in equations 550 through 580, respectively.

680 IF DEPCHOIC = 1   (straight-line depreciation policy code)

690 DEPFURN = SLFURN
700 DEPMACH = SLMACH
710 DEPBUILD = SLBUILD
720 END

Accelerated depreciation If accelerated depreciation is selected as the policy option, then depreciation is calculated according to the following equations:

740 IF DEPCHOIC = 2   (accelerated depreciation policy code)
820 DEPFURN = FURN ∗ .2+FURN(−1) ∗ .16+FURN(−2) ∗ .128−
825   +FURN(−3) ∗ .102+FURN(−4) ∗ .082+FURN(−5) ∗ .066
          (double declining balance, 10-year life)
870 DEPMACH = MACH ∗ .13+MACH(−1) ∗ .11+MACH(−2) ∗ .099−
875   +MACH(−3) ∗ .086+MACH(−4) ∗ .075+MACH(−5) ∗ .065
          (double declining balance, 15-year life)
920 DEPBUILD = BUILD ∗ .045+BUILD(−1) ∗ .043+BUILD(−2) ∗ .041 −
930   +BUILD(−3) ∗ .039+BUILD(−4) ∗ .037+BUILD(−5) ∗ .036
          (1.5 declining balance, 33-year life)
940 END

Depreciation is calculated for the five-year span of the model.

Net fixed assets Net fixed assets are calculated by equations 1020 through 1090. This completes the balance sheet except for cash and tax overpayment. Cash is the line item which balances the balance sheet. Tax overpayment will be calculated in a separate income tax routine.

1020 ACCFURN = ACCFURN(−1)+FURN   (add purchases to furniture account)

1030 ACCMACH = ACCMACH(−1)+MACH   (add purchases to machinery account)

1040 ACCBUILD = ACCBUILD(−1)+BUILD   (add purchases to building account)

1050 NEWFA = FURN + MACH + BUILD   (subtotal fixed asset purchases)

1060 DEPREC = DEPFURN + DEPMACH + DEPBUILD
    (total depreciation for the year)

1070 SLDEPREC = SLFURN + SLMACH + SLBUILD
    (total straight line depreciation for the year)

1080 ACCUMDEP = ACCUMDEP(−1)+DEPREC   (update depreciation contra-asset item)

1090 NETFA = ACCFURN+ACCMACH+ACCBUILD−ACCUMDEP
    (net fixed assets)

Income before taxes Total expenses and income before taxes are computed in equations 1140–1180.

1140 COSTGS = (MATPERCENT+PROPERCENT) ∗ SALESD3
    (cost of goods sold)

1150 SELLEXP = SELPERCENT ∗ SALESD3   (selling expenses)

1160 INTEREST = STIRATE ∗ STDEBT+LTIRATE ∗ LTDEBT
    (total interest expense)

1170 TOTALEXP = COSTGS+SELLEXP+INTEREST+SLDEPREC
    (total expense)

1180 INCOMEBT = SALESD3−TOTALEXP   (income before taxes)

Liability accounts Accounts payable and long-term debt are calculated by equations 1190 and 1200, respectively.

1190 ACCPAY = .08 ∗ COSTGS+.05 ∗ SELLEXP (payables are assumed to be percentages of operating and selling expenses)

1200 LTDEBT = LTDEBT(−1)+NEWLTD−RETIRE
    (current level of long-term debt)

Income tax initialization Income tax calculations are initialized by storing taxable income for the previous five years in temporary fields for convenient reference while net taxable income is being calculated. This initialization is achieved in equations 1260 through 1300. Taxable income for the current year is computed by equation 1310.

1260 Y5 = Y4(−1)   (amount from sixth preceding year is dropped and last five taxable income figures are "pushed down" to allow computation for the current year)

1270 Y4 = Y3(−1)
1280 Y3 = Y2(−1)
1290 Y2 = Y1(−1)
1300 Y1 = TAXINCOME(−1)
1310 TAXINCOME = INCOMEBT + SLDEPREC − DEPREC

Current profit   If the company has a profit during the current year, then the previous five years are searched for an offsetting loss for tax purposes:

1350 IF TAXINCOME > 0   (bypass unless a profit was made this year)

1360 IF Y5 < 0   (a loss was sustained in the fifth prior year)

1370 TAXINCOME = TAXINCOME + Y5   (algebraic addition deducts loss)

1380 IF TAXINCOME < 0   (loss was greater than current profit)

1390 TAXINCOME = 0
1400 END
1410 END
1420 IF TAXINCOME > 0 & Y4 < 0   (some current profit remains after fifth year offset, and another loss was incurred in the fourth prior year)

1430 TAXINCOME = TAXINCOME + Y4
1440 IF TAXINCOME < 0   (if fourth year loss was greater than remaining profit)

1450 Y4 = TAXINCOME   (portion not deductible is saved for next year)

1460 TAXINCOME = 0
1470 ELSE   (all of fourth year loss has been applied)

1480 Y4 = 0
1490 END
1500 END
1510 END

Current loss   A current loss requires a search of the past three years for offsetting profits before storing the loss value to be carried forward. Coding for both profit and loss effects are combined in blocks for the three years prior to the current year.

1550 IF TAXINCOME * Y3 < 0   (bypass unless income values for current and third prior years have opposite signs and will offset)

1560 TAXINCOME = TAXINCOME + Y3
1570 IF TAXINCOME * Y3 > 0   (bypass unless after offset the current and the prior value have like signs)

1580 Y3 = TAXINCOME
1590 TAXINCOME = 0
1600 ELSE
1610 Y3 = 0
1620 END
1630 END
1650 IF TAXINCOME * Y2 < 0   (bypass unless current and second prior year taxable incomes will offset)

1660 TAXINCOME = TAXINCOME + Y2   (repeat offset calculations for second prior year)

1670 IF TAXINCOME * Y2 > 0
1680 Y2 = TAXINCOME
1690 TAXINCOME = 0
1700 ELSE
1710 Y2 = 0
1720 END
1730 END
1750 IF TAXINCOME * Y1 < 0   (bypass unless current and last year taxable incomes will offset)

1760 TAXINCOME = TAXINCOME + Y1   (repeat offset calculations for last year)

1770 IF TAXINCOME * Y1 > 0
1780 Y1 = TAXINCOME
1790 TAXINCOME = 0
1800 ELSE
1810 Y1 = 0
1820 END
1830 END

Tax liability   Once the effects of previous profits and losses on current taxable income have been computed, the tax liability can be calculated. A tax rate of 50 percent is assumed. It is also assumed that regular tax payments are made in the current year for taxes accrued last year and that the tax payments are made at year end.

1880 IF TAXINCOME > 0   (bypass unless positive taxable income exists)

1890 TAXES = .5 * TAXINCOME
1900 ELSE
1910 TAXES = .5 * (INCOMEBT—TAXINCOME)
1920 END
1960 IF TAXES(—1) > 0   (tax liability was accrued last year)

1970 PAID = TAXES(—1)
1980 ELSE   (no taxes accrued last year)
1990 PAID = 0
2000 END
2040 IF TAXES < PAID   (account for tax overpayment, if any)

2050 TAXOVERPAY = PAID — TAXES
2060 TAXPAY = 0
2070 ELSE   (account for tax payments, if due)

2080 TAXPAY = TAXES — PAID
2090 TAXOVERPAY = 0
2100 END

The tax provision and net income values are stored to complete the profit and loss statement. The balance sheet item, deferred taxes, is also computed and stored.

2150 DDT = .5 * (DEPREC—SLDEPREC)   (computes change in deferred tax value for sources and uses statement)

2160 DEFTAXES = DEFTAXES(—1)+DDT
2170 TAXPROV = TAXES + DDT
2180 NETINCOME = INCOMEBT — TAXPROV

Dividends and retained earnings Dividends and the change in retained earnings are computed next. Also, any new stock which may have been issued is posted to complete the equity portion of the balance sheet.

2230 STOCK = STOCK(—1) + NEWSTOCK
2240 IF NETINCOME > DIVPAY * STOCK   (if net income exceeds dividend requirement . . . .)

2250 DIVIDENDS = DIVPAY * STOCK   (pay full dividend)
2260 ELSE   (if net income does not exceed dividend requirements . . . .)

2270 IF NETINCOME > 0
2280 DIVIDENDS = NETINCOME   (pay out all net income, if any)

2290 ELSE
2300 DIVIDENDS = 0
2310 END
2320 END
2330 RE = RE(−1)+NETINCOME−DIVIDENDS

Cash balance   The balance sheet is balanced with the cash account. The cash balance is assumed to be the sum of liabilities and equity less all assets other than cash. If cash is less than the required minimum cash balance, additional short-term debt equal to 1.25 times the cash deficit is generated.

2380 CASHD3 = ACCPAY+STDEBT+RETIRE+TAXPAY+LTDEBT−
2385   +DEFTAXES+STOCK+RE −
2390   −(ACCREC+MAT$+TAXOVERPAY+ACCBUILD−
2395   +ACCFURN+ACCMACH−ACCUMDEP)
2430 IF CASHD3 < CASHLOW
2440 STDEBT = STDEBT+1.25(CASHLOW−CASHD3)
2450 END

Change in financial position   Finally, subtotals for the balance sheet (Table 4.5) sources and uses of funds statement (Table 4.6) and the balance sheet changes statement (Table 4.7) are calculated.

2510 TOTCA = CASD3+ACCREC+MAT$+TAXOVERPAY
                                    (current assets)
2520 TOTAS = TOTCA+NETFA   (total assets)
2530 TOTCL = ACCPAY+STDEBT+RETIRE+TAXPAY
                                    (current liabilities)
2540 CHANGEWC = NETINCOME+DEPREC+DDT+NEWLTD+NEWSTOCK−
2545   −NEWFA−RETIRE−
2550   − DIVIDENDS   (sources and uses of funds as reflected in profit and loss statement items and noncurrent balance sheet items)
2560 WORKCAP = TOTCA−TOTCL   (net working capital)
2570 END   (end of one pass through the model)

POLICY SIMULATIONS

Tables 4.4 through 4.7 contain the output generated by the model for 1975 through 1979 for the scenario based on the information given by Tables 4.1 through 4.3. The report generation commands have not been included in this write up.

It is now quite easy for management to conduct a wide variety of "What if?" experiments by changing such policies as materials purchases, debt managment, equity, depreciation, cash management, and dividends. Alternatively, management may want to experiment with various assumptions about sales revenue, operating costs, and interest rates.

For each set of policy assumptions and/or external assumptions the model will generate a new set of financial reports similar to those displayed in Tables 4.4 through 4.7.

Table 4.4 Profit and loss statement (in millions)

	1975	1976	1977	1978	1979
Sales	$2,100.0	$3,600.0	$4,400.0	$5,000.0	$5,500.0
Cost and expenses					
Cost of goods sold	1,425.6	2,599.7	3.346.2	3,757.0	4,050.3
Selling expenses	412.5	751.3	908.7	957.0	941.4
Depreciation	54.6	51.8	48.6	46.2	68.0
Interest	36.0	34.9	64.7	48.6	69.9
Total expenses	$1,928.7	$3,437.7	$4,368.2	$4,808.8	$5,129.6
Income before taxes	$171.3	$162.3	$31.8	$191.2	$370.4
Tax provision	85.6	81.2	15.9	95.6	185.2
Net income	$85.7	$81.1	$15.9	$95.6	$185.2

NOTE

1. The actual SIMPLAN statements for statements 550, 560, and 570 require only one line. Page size limitations necessitate the use of two lines per statement. The (—) at the end of the first line of each statement indicates that it is to be continued on the next line.

Table 4.5 Balance sheet (in millions)

ASSETS	1975	1976	1977	1978	1979
Current assets					
Cash	$344.3	$101.0	$130.6	$108.2	$106.6
Accounts Receivable	231.0	396.0	484.0	550.0	605.0
Materials	190.8	343.7	468.7	550.9	630.6
Tax overpayment	0.0	2.8	63.4	0.0	0.0
Total current assets	$766.1	$843.5	$1,146.7	$1,209.1	$1,342.2
Plant, Property and equipment					
Buildings	900.0	900.0	900.0	900.0	1,100.0
Furniture	14.0	16.0	18.0	20.0	28.0
Machinery	122.0	126.0	128.0	135.0	242.0
Less accumulated depreciation	(154.6)	(206.4)	(255.0)	(301.3)	(369.2)
Net fixed assets	$881.4	$835.6	$791.0	$753.7	$1,000.8
Total assets	$1,647.5	$1,679.1	$1,937.7	$1,962.8	$2,343.0
LIABILITIES					
Current liabilities					
Accounts payable	$136.1	$246.7	$314.0	$349.1	$372.9
Short-term debt	0.0	19.1	244.8	164.0	132.6
Maturity of long-term debt	40.0	40.0	40.0	40.0	40.0
Income tax	76.6	0.0	0.0	81.2	82.4
Total current liabilities	$252.7	$305.8	$598.8	$634.3	$627.9
Long-term debt	$360.0	$320.0	$280.0	$240.0	$500.0
Deferred taxes	$19.1	$26.5	$32.1	$36.1	$47.5
Shareholders equity					
Stock	1,000.0	1,000.0	1,000.0	1,000.0	1,000.0
Retained Earnings	15.7	26.8	26.8	52.4	167.6
Total shareholders equity	$1,015.7	$1,026.8	$1,026.8	$1,052.4	$1,167.6
Total liabilities	$1,647.5	$1,679.1	$1,937.7	$1,962.8	$2,343.0

Table 4.6 Balance sheet changes (in millions)

	1975	1976	1977	1978	1979
Current assets					
Cash	$140.3	($243.3)	$29.6	($22.4)	($1.6)
Accounts receivable	31.0	165.0	88.0	66.0	55.0
Materials	(9.2)	152.9	125.0	82.2	79.7
Tax overpayment	0.0	2.8	60.6	(63.4)	0.0
Total current assets	$162.1	$77.4	$303.2	$62.4	$133.1
Current liabilities					
Accounts payable	16.1	110.6	67.3	35.0	23.8
Short-term debt	0.0	19.1	225.7	(80.8)	(31.4)
Current maturity long-term debt	40.0	0.0	0.0	0.0	0.0
Tax payment	76.6	(76.6)	0.0	81.2	1.2
Total current liabilities	$132.7	$53.1	$293.0	$35.4	($6.4)
Change in working capital	$29.4	$24.3	$10.2	$27.0	$139.5

Table 4.7 Sources-and-uses-of-funds statement (in millions)

	1975	1976	1977	1978	1979
Sources of working capital					
Net income	$85.7	$81.1	$15.9	$95.6	$185.2
Depreciation	54.6	51.8	48.6	46.2	68.0
Deferred tax	9.1	7.4	5.6	4.2	11.3
New long-term debt	0.0	0.0	0.0	0.0	300.0
New stock	0.0	0.0	0.0	0.0	0.0
Total sources	$149.4	$140.3	$70.1	$146.0	$564.5
Uses of working capital					
New fixed assets	10.0	6.0	4.0	9.0	315.0
Retirement of long-term debt	40.0	40.0	40.0	40.0	40.0
Dividends	70.0	70.0	15.9	70.0	70.0
Total uses	$120.0	$116.0	$59.9	$119.0	$425.0
Change in working capital	$29.4	$24.3	$10.2	$27.0	$139.5

5 Marketing Forecasting Models

TERRY G. SEAKS AND
THOMAS H. NAYLOR

INTRODUCTION

This chapter discusses forecasting models in which the variable to be forecast is modeled as a function of time. Such models are naive or mechanistic in the sense that the forecasts depend only on past values and the particular function of time that is used. Despite their simplicity, they often yield reasonably good forecasts for short time periods. And although these models are presented within the context of market planning models, these models are much more general in nature and are by no means restricted to marketing applications.

The general approach of the chapter will be to start with the simplest possible models, and gradually introduce more complex models. Thus we begin by considering the problem of modeling a process in which a variable fluctuates about a fixed mean and equal weight is given to all observations. From this we proceed to the case of a changing level of the variable, and next a changing level with seasonal patterns is considered. Then the assumption of giving equal weight to all observations is modified so that less weight is given to older observations. By the end of the chapter we have explored a broad class of time series models. SIMPLAN is used to illustrate most of the time series modeling techniques.

The emphasis in this chapter and in the following chapter is on the application of market forecasting and econometric models, respectively. Although the only prerequisite for these two chapters is a knowledge of high school algebra, it is desirable for the reader to have some knowledge of basic statistics. Unfortunately, it is impossible to avoid the inclusion of a minimum amount of algebra in the development of these models. However, the reader who is uncomfortable with algebra may choose to skip over the algebraic details and concentrate on the applications.

TIME SERIES FORECASTING MODELS

The fundamental assumption underlying time series forecasting models is that it is possible to model the dynamic structure of a time series variable by incorporating no other information than the historical values of the particular time series. In other words, with forecasting models we assume that what happens tomorrow and the day after depends only on what happened yesterday, the day before, and the day before that. Forecasting models have little or no "explanatory power," for they are based on neither economic nor marketing theory. They represent a somewhat mechanistic approach to marketing modeling but may yield accurate forecasts for short periods of time. In addition, they are less expensive to build and require less knowledge of economics and marketing than is the case with marketing policy models.

Such models are sometimes called naive models, extrapolation models, or mechanical models. They are naive in the sense that they do not take into account any changing external factors in trying to forecast the future; they simply parrot the past. They involve extrapolation or some mechanical method in the sense that some mathematical formula is used to convert the past data into a future forecast.

Although such forecasting models are obviously not very sophisticated, they often produce reasonably good forecasts for the short term, hence their name. And although the philosophical basis for such models does not seem to be very complicated, the mathematical basis for such short-term forecasting models sometimes becomes quite complicated (as in the Box–Jenkins models discussed later in this chapter). A carefully chosen short-term forecasting model can pick up very subtle and complicated patterns in a time series.

Although there is no reason why mechanical or extrapolation methods must be used *only* for forecasting the near term, they obviously produce less reliable forecasts when the past is blindly extrapolated far into the future. When looking far into the future, conditions which held in the past are less and less likely to continue to hold and the mechanical forecasts tend to become less and less reliable since they do not take into account that external conditions may be changing. To apply a mechanical extrapolation method to a series and project it ten years into the future is certainly mathematically possible, but it is not likely to produce very good forecasts because many forecasts that can be assumed constant in the short run are likely to change considerably over such a long period.

In other words, if all that is required is a short-term forecast and nothing else, then some of the forecasting models described in this section may be appropriate. However, if something goes wrong with a particular forecasting model, it is sometimes very difficult to ascertain the source of the problem. Not only are mechanistic forecasting models devoid of explanatory power but they are also of limited usefulness for evaluating alternative marketing policies and strategies. With the exception of Box–Jenkins models, it is impossible to include marketing policy variables or external variables in forecasting models.

To summarize, if one wants mechanistic, short-run forecasts and is willing to forgo explanatory power and policy analysis, then the models described in this section may be of interest. We shall describe five different types of forecasting models: moving averages, time trends, exponential smoothing, adaptive forecasting, and Box–Jenkins.

Moving Averages

The moving average is a very simple and very often used technique for deriving a forecast. It is appropriate for use in forecasting a time series that fluctuates around a constant mean. A moving average is not useful in situations where a strong time trend is present in a series. Figure 5.1 shows two types of time series behavior; in (a) a moving average is appropriate for forecasting, in (b) it is not appropriate due to the strong trend.

The idea of the moving average is to forecast the next value of a data series by taking the mean of the n most recent values. Typically values of n are chosen in the range of 4 to 8. The larger the value of n, the more weight that is given to older observations. The smaller the value of n, the less weight there is given to older observations and the more weight there is placed on the relatively recent values in a time series.

As an example, suppose we had the following observations on sales volume per week: 7, 10, 4, 6, 3, 5, 7. The moving average forecast of sales for the next week would be given simply by the sum of the most recent n values, divided by n. If we chose n to be 4, our estimate of downtime next week would be given by

$$\frac{6 + 3 + 5 + 7}{4} = 5.25. \tag{5.1}$$

If instead we had chosen n to be 6, our estimate would be

$$\frac{10 + 4 + 6 + 3 + 5 + 7}{6} = 5.83. \tag{5.2}$$

From the foregoing, it is apparent that we are simply taking an average. How does the notion of "moving" come into the picture? To answer this, suppose that another week elapses, and the actual sales for this week are observed to be eight hours. What is our forecast for the next period?

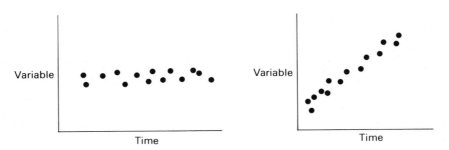

Fig. 5.1 (a) Moving average is appropriate for forecasting, (b) moving average is not appropriate for forecasting.

The solution is to *move* the average forward one time period by dropping off one old observation and adding in the newest observation. For the case of $n = 4$, the old estimate was

$$\frac{6 + 3 + 5 + 7}{4} = 5.25. \tag{5.3}$$

The new estimate would be

$$\frac{3 + 5 + 7 + 8}{4} = 5.75. \tag{5.4}$$

Actually the arithmetic can be simplified if we compute

$$\text{new avg.} = \text{old avg.} + \frac{(\text{new observation} - \text{oldest observation})}{n}. \tag{5.5}$$

For the foregoing example, this would give:

$$\text{new avg.} = 5.25 + \frac{(8 - 6)}{4} \tag{5.6}$$

$$= 5.25 + 0.5$$

$$= 5.75.$$

Aside from being easier for calculator applications than re-adding all the numbers the above computations indicate that the average is increased by $\frac{1}{n}$ times the new value and the average is decreased by $\frac{1}{n}$ times the old value being dropped out. Thus old values have their influence removed, while new values have their influence added, both receiving the same weight of $\frac{1}{n}$.

An obvious improvement over the simple moving average would be some type of scheme that does not give equal weight to the oldest value and the newest value. Intuitively, it would make much more sense to give relatively more weight to the most recent values, and rather little weight to the oldest values. This notion leads to the process known as exponential smoothing.

For forecasting purposes, only the most recent moving average is required and this value is taken as the forecast for the next time period and all subsequent time periods in the future. However, it is often useful to compute not only the single moving average forecast but also the moving average of the whole data series. The moving average series gives a new series which is smoother. Its values exhibit less fluctuation due to random variation than do the values of the original data series. While forecasting with moving averages requires that a time series be stationary and devoid of any time trend, it is often useful to compute a moving average of a non-stationary series—not for forecasting, but to smooth the series so that it can be used to reflect more reliably the movements of the variable under study. This is often the case when working with quarterly data that display some seasonal pattern. Then a four-period moving average will smooth out the fluctuations in the data series that are due only to seasonality. If working with monthly data, a twelve-month moving average would be appropriate.

Time Trends

In the previous section a moving average was described as inappropriate for forecasting a time series with a strong trend. Models for series with trends can be developed as simple extensions of moving average models. Such time trend models can be easily estimated by the methods of least squares. To explore this more fully, let us reconsider the moving average as a least-squares estimator, and then explore how simply a time trend can be incorporated.

Suppose we have a time series $Y_1, Y_2, \ldots, Y_n$ that we wish to forecast. If it is stationary, it can be forecast by a moving average, as we have seen. But suppose we wished to approach the forecasting problem by asking, "What is the forecast value that will minimize the sum of the squared errors for my available data?" That is, we seek a single value to be our estimate of all future time periods, and we require of this value $\hat{Y}$ that the sum of squared deviations from it be a minimum; that is, we wish

$$s = \sum_{i=1}^{n} (Y_i - \hat{Y})^2 \tag{5.7}$$

to be a minimum by an appropriate choice of $\hat{Y}$. We can accomplish this by differentiating the above equation with respect to $\hat{Y}$, setting the resulting equation equal to zero, and solving for $\hat{Y}$. The solution is:

$$\hat{Y} = \frac{\sum_{i=1}^{n} Y_i}{n} \tag{5.8}$$

It is apparent that this is simply saying that an n period moving average of the series gives the estimate with the minimum sum of squared deviations.

Linear Now in the case of a time trend, we would not wish to minimize the sum of squared deviations about a single value $\hat{Y}$ since we know that $\hat{Y}$ must be rising or falling through time in order to accurately forecast the time series; that is, $\hat{Y}$ must be of the form $\hat{Y}_i = a + bt$ in the case of a linear time trend, and a more complicated function of time (t) can be used for cases in which a linear trend is inadequate. Here $t = 1, 2, \ldots, n$, and a and b are values to be determined such that

$$\sum_{i=1}^{n} (Y_i - \hat{Y}_i)^2 = \Sigma(Y_i - a - bt)^2$$

is a minimum. Note that now $\hat{Y}$ contains a subscript i to indicate that its value is not a constant as it was in the case of the moving average.

If we apply standard rules of differential calculus to this expression, we can obtain the values of a and b such that the sum of the squared errors is minimized. Because this proof appears in every basic econometrics book, it will be omitted here. Instead, we display the main result that states that estimates of the intercept and slope

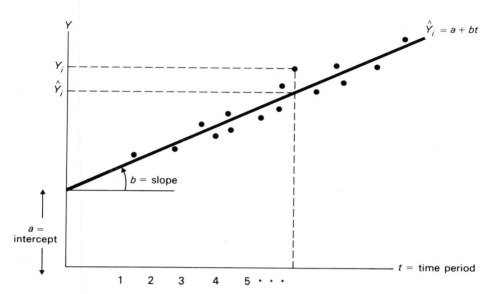

Fig. 5.2 Linear time trend model $\hat{Y}_i = a + bt$.

b for the time trend model $\hat{Y}_i = a + bt$ can be obtained by solving the following two equations. (Subscripts are omitted for notational simplicity.)

$$\Sigma Y = na + b\Sigma t \tag{5.9}$$

$$\Sigma t Y = a\Sigma t + b\Sigma t^2 \tag{5.10}$$

where there are n different observations $Y_1, Y_2, \ldots, Y_n$, and corresponding to these values are values of t, assumed to be $1, 2, \ldots, n$. Because the two equations contain two unknowns a and b, it is a straightforward process to solve for a and b.

The values of a and b provided by solving the two equations above give the intercept and slope, respectively, of the line picture in Fig. 5.2. This line has the property that the sum of the squared deviations from the trend line is at a minimum; that is, if any other values of a and b are used, the sum of squared deviations associated with these other values must be greater than the sum of squared deviations associated with the least-squares estimators of a and b. Figure 5.2 also shows a typical error, the distance from $\hat{Y}_i$ to Y_i.

To illustrate the procedure for fitting a linear trend line to a time series, consider the sales revenue data shown in Table 5.1.

We define the variable SALES to denote sales revenue. Employing the SIMPLAN command TLINE we obtain the following estimates of the parameters for a linear time trend equation.

$$\widehat{\text{SALES}} = 121 + 2.6t \tag{5.11}$$

Table 5.2 contains the SIMPLAN output from applying the TLINE command to the

Table 5.1 Sales revenue (millions of dollars)

Year	Sales (Y)	Time Period (t)
1961	122.7	1
1962	127.4	2
1963	128.8	3
1964	132.3	4
1965	135.2	5
1966	136.9	6
1967	135.9	7
1968	141.1	8
1969	144.7	9
1970	148.7	10

data in Table 5.1. For the moment we shall concern ourselves only with the coefficient estimates of the constant term a and the slope of the time trend b. These are marked in the Table 5.2. In Chapter 6 we will define and interpret other statistical measures associated with least squares that may aid the analyst.

Table 5.2 Output for SIMPLAN TLINE command: a linear trend

```
ANALYSIS.

TLINE SALES 11-13

LINEAR TREND
```

ESTIMATED EQUATION IS: SALES=121.067+2.6006*TIME			
INDEPENDENT VARIABLES	ESTIMATED COEFFICIENT	STANDARD ERROR	T-TEST
CONSTANT	121.0666	1.0500	115.2985
TIME	2.6006	0.1692	15.3675

```
    TIME GOES FROM     1 TO    10
    R-SQUARED=   0.9672                   F-STATISTIC(  1,  8)=    236.1669
    ADJUSTED R-SQUARED=   0.9631          DURBIN-WATSON STATISTIC=    1.5997
    STANDARD ERROR=         1.5371        DEGREES OF FREEDOM FOR T-TEST=   8
    SUM OF SQUARED ERRORS=          18.9010
```

FORECASTS FOR 11 TO 13	
PERIOD	FORECAST
11	149.6732
12	152.2738
13	154.8744

```
ANALYSIS.
```

The estimated time trend is plotted in Fig. 5.3 along with the actual observed values of SALES. Equation (5.11) may be used to forecast SALES in any period by

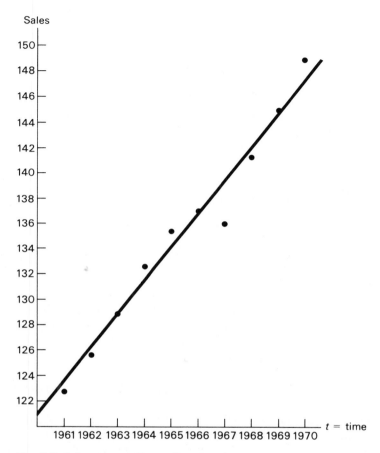

Fig. 5.3 Sales revenue linear time trend.

letting $t = 1$ in 1961, $t = 2$ in 1962, etc. and solving for SALES. Sales projections based on the estimated model appear in Table 5.3. They were taken from the computer printout shown in Table 5.2.

Table 5.3 Sales revenue forecasts

Year	Projected sales	Time
1971	149.7	11
1972	152.3	12
1973	154.9	13

Quadratic Thus far time trends have been discussed for the case in which the trend is a linear function of time. That is, $\hat{Y}$ is assumed to be of the form $\hat{Y} = a + bt$. This

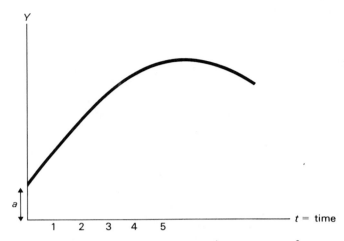

Fig. 5.4 Quadratic time trend model $\hat{Y} = a + bt + ct^2$.

is the simplest form of trend line, but there is no reason why the function $\hat{Y} = f(t)$ must necessarily be linear. Two other functional forms that have frequent use in forecasting are the quadratic model and the semilogarithmic model. Just as the linear trend was a generalization of the moving average model, the quadratic model may be viewed as a generalization of the linear trend line model.

When the linear trend line model is employed, the coefficient b estimates the constant amount by which the series grows (or decays if b is negative) each time period. In the sales revenue example of Table 5.1, it was found that $b = 2.6$, implying that with each passing year sales will grow by \$2.6 million. But it might seem more reasonable to assume that not only was sales revenue changing but perhaps its rate of change was also changing. A model that would permit a sales figure to change with time, as well as allowing for a change in the rate of change, would be the quadratic model $\hat{Y} = a + bt + ct^2$. Such a curve can be obtained by the usual least-squares method of selecting values of a, b, and c such that the sum of squared errors between the actual values and the quadratic trend line are at a minimum. (Note that the estimated a and b of the linear trend line will not in general be the same as the estimated a and b of the quadratic model if both models are fitted to a time series.)

Figure 5.4 displays a graph of the model $\hat{Y} = a + bt + ct^2$. The figure indicates that the curve rises to a peak and then declines. The curve can also be fitted to data that fall to a low point and then rise. In either case, the curve is symmetric, rising and falling at the same rate at points equidistant from the high or low point.

In order to obtain the estimates of a, b, and c that yield a minimum sum of squared errors for the expression $\Sigma(Y - \hat{Y})^2 = \Sigma(Y - a - bt - ct^2)^2$, calculus can again be applied to this expression. The result is a set of three simultaneous Eqs. (5.12) which may be solved for the coefficients a, b, and c.

$$\Sigma Y = na + b\Sigma t + c\Sigma t^2 \tag{5.12}$$

$$\Sigma t Y = a\Sigma t + b\Sigma t^2 + c\Sigma t^3$$

$$\Sigma t^2 Y = a\Sigma t^2 + b\Sigma t^3 + c\Sigma t^4.$$

When the quadratic model is fitted to the sales revenue data in Table 5.1, the SIMPLAN TQUAD command produces the following results:

$$\text{SALES} = 121.88 + 2.20t + 0.037t^2, \tag{5.13}$$

where $a = 121.88$, $b = 2.20$, and $c = 0.037$. Again t is measured as $t = 1$ for 1961, etc. The complete SIMPLAN output for the TQUAD command appears in Table 5.4.

Table 5.4 Output from TQUAD command: a quadratic time trend

```
ANALYSIS.

TQUAD SALES 11-13

QUADRATIC TREND
```

ESTIMATED EQUATION IS: SALES=121.875+2.19643*TIME+0.03674*TIME**2			
INDEPENDENT VARIABLES	ESTIMATED COEFFICIENT	STANDARD ERROR	T- TEST
CONSTANT	121.8749	1.8959	64.2844
TIME	2.1964	0.7918	2.7740
TIME**2	0.0367	0.0702	0.5238

```
 TIME GOES FROM    1 TO    10
R-SQUARED=   0.9685                F-STATISTIC(  2,  7)=    107.5098
ADJUSTED R-SQUARED=   0.9595       DURBIN-WATSON STATISTIC=   1.6536
STANDARD ERROR=        1.6119      DEGREES OF FREEDOM FOR T-TEST=  7
SUM OF SQUARED ERRORS=       18.1881

    FORECASTS FOR     11 TO    13


    PERIOD              FORECAST
     11                 150.4815
     12                 153.5230
     13                 156.6380

ANALYSIS.
```

Forecasts for 1971, 1972, and 1973 may be obtained by using values of 11, 12, and 13 for t in Eq. (5.13). The forecasts from the linear and quadratic models are compared in Table 5.5.

Table 5.5 Sales revenue forecasts

Year	Linear model	Quadratic model	Time
1971	149.7	150.5	11
1972	152.3	153.5	12
1973	154.9	156.6	13

While the linear trend line showed that sales grew by a constant amount, $2.6 million each year, the quadratic model allows the amount of change to be variable through time. The annual rate of change implied by the quadratic model is given by the expression

$$\frac{d\hat{Y}}{dt} = 2.20 + .073t. \tag{5.14}$$

The quadratic model implies that sales are growing by $2.27 million per year in 1961, but by 1970 the annual growth rate implied by the model is $2.93 million per year. Thus the quadratic model says that sales are increasing at an increasing rate. This could have been determined at once from the original model by observing that both b and c were positive.

Exponential While the quadratic time trend model is an improvement over the linear time trend model in that the rate of growth is no longer a fixed amount each time period, neither model takes into account a very common growth process: that of a variable that grows in proportion to its own size. Such behavior is basic to population, compound interest, and a number of other demographic processes in which a variable grows by a certain percentage each time period.

Mathematically, such a process may be described by the following equation

$$\hat{Y} = Ae^{rt}, \tag{5.15}$$

where r is the growth rate, t is the time period, e is the base of the natural logarithm (2.718), and A is a scale constant. To estimate such a model, one gathers data on Y and t, and then attempts to estimate A and r. However, since rt appears as an exponent, this model cannot conveniently be estimated by ordinary least squares in its present form. By taking natural logarithms of both sides of Eq. (5.15), it can be transformed into a model that can be easily estimated by simple least squares. Taking logs we have:

$$\log_e \hat{Y} = \log_e A + rt \log_e e \tag{5.16}$$

$$= \log_e A + rt.$$

Such a model is now linear in that it is of the form

$$\hat{Y}* = a + bt, \tag{5.17}$$

where $Y* = \log_e \hat{Y}$, $a = \log_e A$, and $b = r$.

To estimate the semilog model for our sales data we employ the TLOG command of SIMPLAN to the equation

$$\text{SALES}* = a + bt, \tag{5.18}$$

where $\text{SALES}* = \log_e \text{SALES}$. As we see from the SIMPLAN output in Table 5.6 the coefficient estimates are given by

$$\text{SALES}* = 4.80 + 0.019t, \tag{5.19}$$

where $a = 4.80$ and $b = r = .019$. The meaning of Eq. (5.19) is that the natural log-arithm of SALES can be predicted at any point in time by the expression $4.80 + .019t$. The estimate of $\log_e$ SALES can be transformed into an estimate of SALES simply by taking antilogs.

Table 5.6 Output of TLOG command: a semilog (exponential) time trend ANALYSIS.

```
TLOG SALES 11-13

SEMI-LOG TREND
```

ESTIMATED EQUATION IS: SALES=EXP(4.80077+0.01921*TIME)			
INDEPENDENT VARIABLES	ESTIMATED COEFFICIENT	STANDARD ERROR	T- TEST
CONSTANT	4.8008	0.0076	632.4785
TIME	0.0192	0.0012	15.7056

```
TIME GOES FROM    1 TO   10
R-SQUARED=  0.9687                    F-STATISTIC(  1,  8)=    247.7155
ADJUSTED R-SQUARED=  0.9648          DURBIN-WATSON STATISTIC=   1.6774
STANDARD ERROR=        0.0111        DEGREES OF FREEDOM FOR T-TEST=  8
SUM OF SQUARED ERRORS=        0.0010

INTERPRETATION WITH DEPENDENT VARIABLE NOT IN LOG FORM
THE % GROWTH RATE IS     1.9399
```

FORECASTS FOR 11 TO 13	
PERIOD	FORECAST
11	150.2212
12	153.1353
13	156.1058

ANALYSIS.

Table 5.7 contains the forecast values of SALES* and SALES for the period 1971 through 1973.

Table 5.7 Sales revenue forecasts semilog time trend

Year	SALES*	SALES	t
1971	4.82	150.2	11
1972	4.84	153.1	12
1973	4.86	156.1	13

It was mentioned above that an advantage of the semilog time trend model is that the rate of growth appears directly as the estimated value of b. We found that the growth rate in the case of sales revenue was .0192, or 1.92 percent. It is worth noting that this is actually the *instantaneous* growth rate, assuming continuous growth and compounding. If it is desired to transform this rate into a percentage growth rate per time period (which would be a per annum rate in the case of our sales data), we must take the antilog of .0192, which yields 1.0194. This implies that for each time period, sales are 1.0194 times the value during the previous time period. Or, the annual percentage growth rate is 1.94 percent. In general, if the instantaneous growth rate associated with the semilog model is not too large (less than 10 percent roughly), there will be rather little difference between the instantaneous growth rate and the per-period growth rate.

Given that we have developed three different time trend forecasting models, a question that naturally arises is: "How does one choose the appropriate one?" Occasionally the nature of the process generating the data will provide a key (a semilog trend is appropriate for sales growth forecasting models which are closely tied to population, for example), but many times the analyst will not have any clear guidelines concerning the appropriate model. In such cases, the R^2 statistic, which appeared in Tables 5.2, 5.4, and 5.6, is frequently helpful in choosing an appropriate forecasting model. It is not a foolproof or infallible guide, but it is a very useful statistic for a thumbnail sketch.

R^2 is simply the square of the correlation coefficient between the Y values and the $\hat{Y}$ values. (This is discussed further in Chapter 6.) By defining the time series e to be the difference between each actual Y value and the time trend value $\hat{Y}$, we may compute R^2 as

$$R^2 = 1.0 - \frac{\Sigma e^2}{\Sigma(Y - \bar{Y})^2}. \tag{5.20}$$

In the case of a perfectly fitting trend line, all the e terms are zero, hence Σe^2 is also zero, and R^2 assumes the value of 1.0. In the opposite case of a very poor trend line, the deviations from the trend line are just as large as the deviations of the Y's from their mean $\bar{Y}$, thus $\Sigma e^2/(Y - \bar{Y})^2$ is 1, and R^2 is equal to 0. In other cases, the value of R^2 will range between 0 and 1, being closer to 0 as the line fits poorly, and being closer to 1 as the line fits better.

R^2 is useful for giving a summary indication of how well a trend line fits the data, but for comparing, say, a linear trend line with a quadratic trend line, the R^2 is not as useful. This is because the R^2 for a quadratic trend line will always be larger (closer to 1) than the R^2 for the linear trend line. To see why this is so, it is necessary only to note that the least-squares method deliberately minimizes the quantity Σe^2, and this quantity can always be made smaller when estimating the three parameters of the quadratic model instead of the two parameters of the linear model. (Theoretically, the quantity Σe^2 terms for the two models can be the same if the coefficient of t^2 in the quadratic model is exactly 0—a very unlikely event.)

It is apparent that the difficulty with using R^2 is that it does not adjust for the different number of parameters in the different models. To correct for this problem, the *adjusted* R^2, usually denoted $\bar{R}^2$, is often used. The adjusted R^2 is defined to be:

$$\bar{R}^2 = 1.0 - \frac{\Sigma e^2/(n - k)}{\Sigma(Y - \bar{Y})^2/(n - 1)}, \tag{5.21}$$

where n is the number of observations on Y, and k is the number of parameters in the model ($k = 2$ in the linear and semilog models, and $k = 3$ in the quadratic model). The correction amounts to dividing both the error variation and the total variation by their respective degrees of freedom. The result is that $\bar{R}^2$ is smaller than R^2 in proportion to how many terms k have been used in fitting the model.

In Table 5.8 we present the R^2 and the $\bar{R}^2$ for the three time trend models fitted to our sales data. All of the figures are quite close to 1, indicating that all of the time trend models fit the data well. Based simply on the R^2, one might conclude that the choice between the quadratic trend line and the semilog trend was a toss-up. However, in terms of the adjusted R^2, it becomes apparent that the semilog trend line gives the best fit, since it does better than the quadratic model, and does this using fewer terms. The $\bar{R}^2$ is discussed somewhat further (in relation to statistical tests) in Chapter 6.

Table 5.8 R^2 and $\bar{R}^2$ for three sales revenue models

Model	R^2	$\bar{R}^2$
1. Linear	0.967	0.963
2. Quadratic	0.969	0.960
3. Semilog	0.969	0.965

Although the adjusted R^2 improves on the unadjusted R^2, one disadvantage concerning the $\bar{R}^2$ should be mentioned. In the linear and quadratic models, the left-hand side variable is Y. But in the semilog model, the dependent variable is $\log(Y)$. If Eq. (5.21) is used to judge the three types of models, there is a note of non-comparability involved. Because an $\bar{R}^2$ for a semilog model is higher than the $\bar{R}^2$ for linear and quadratic models, it does not follow that the semilog model is necessarily best. Tests to determine correct functional forms are quite complex and are beyond the present discussion. At this point we simply note that the $\bar{R}^2$ is a useful and inexpensive way to judge time trend models, although it does have certain imperfections.

When comparing time trend models, another method besides R^2 that is sometimes employed is the standard error of estimate. The standard error of estimate is defined by

$$s = \sqrt{\frac{\Sigma e^2}{n - k}}. \tag{5.22}$$

It has the advantage of adjusting for the number of terms in the model (k), and in this sense it is like the adjusted R^2. A disadvantage is that the error terms e are based on the left-hand side variable in the time trend model. When a linear or quadratic model is used, the errors describe the departure of the actual values from the trend line, but when a semilog model is used, the errors describe the departure of the log of the actual variables from the trend line. Thus, the standard error is not as useful as the adjusted R^2 for choosing among alternative models. Tables 5.2, 5.4, and 5.6 also contain the standard errors of the estimate for each of our three time trend models. These estimates are summarized in Table 5.9.

Table 5.9 Standard errors of the estimate for three sales revenue models

Model	Standard errors of the estimate
1. Linear	1.537
2. Quadratic	1.612
3. Semilog	0.011

Seasonal Each of the time series models discussed thus far was based on the implicit assumption that the data being used were either annual data (and thus lacking any seasonal pattern), or else that the seasonality had been removed. In this section we treat the case of quarterly or monthly data that contain a seasonal pattern. It will turn out to be possible to extend the trend line models to allow for both a time trend and a recurring seasonal pattern. The example will focus on monthly and quarterly data, but the methodology is completely general, and can be applied to weekly data, ten-day data, or data for any other time periods.

The trend models with seasonal patterns that we will discuss are based upon the trigonometric functions known as sine and cosine functions. Therefore, we begin with a review of some of the basic properties of these functions. Consider the angle θ that is pictured in Fig. 5.5. For the angle θ shown in the figure, the sine and cosine are defined as

$$\sin \theta \equiv Y/R$$
$$\cos \theta \equiv X/R \tag{5.23}$$

where R, X, and Y are the distances shown in the figure. Thus the sine and cosine of an angle measured in degrees is seen to be the ratio of certain distances.

From Fig. 5.5 it is apparent that the sine and cosine will change as the angle θ

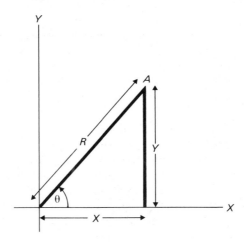

Fig. 5.5 The sine and cosine functions.

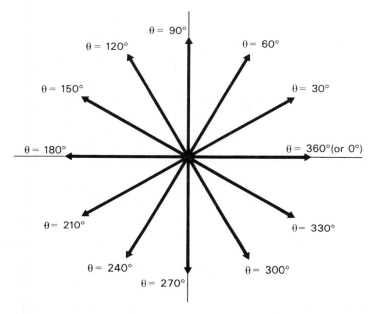

Fig. 5.6 Various angles θ moving through the circle.

changes. Figure 5.6 shows several different angles, and Table 5.10 shows the value of the sine and cosine function associated with various values of θ in the figure. Note that in Table 5.10 the sine and cosine functions make a complete revolution in moving from 0 to 360 degrees. The sine starts out at 0, $(\theta = 0°)$, rises to a peak at 1.0

Table 5.10 Values of sine and cosine functions for 0 to 360 degrees

Angle θ	Sine θ	Cosine θ
$0°$	0.000	1.000
30	0.500	0.866
60	0.866	0.500
90	1.000	0.000
120	0.866	−0.500
150	0.500	−0.866
180	0.000	−1.000
210	−0.500	−0.866
240	−0.866	−0.500
270	−1.000	0.000
300	−0.866	0.500
330	−0.500	0.866
360	0.000	1.000

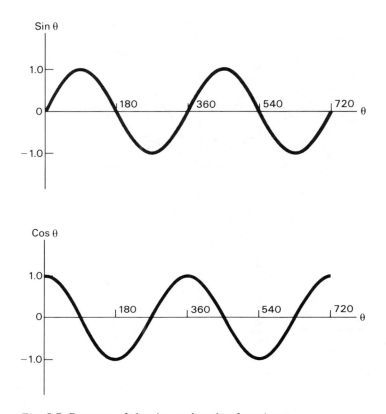

Fig. 5.7 Patterns of the sine and cosine functions.

$(\theta = 90°)$, then declines to -1.0 $(\theta = 270°)$, and finally returns to 0 $(\theta = 360°)$. The cosine function exhibits similar behavior, starting at 1.0 when $\theta = 0°$, falling to -1.0 when $\theta = 180°$, and then returning to 1.0 when $\theta = 360°$.

When the sine and cosine functions have passed through 360 degrees, they begin to repeat; that is, the sine and cosine of θ will be exactly equal to the sine and cosine of $(\theta + 360°)$. This repeating nature of the sine and cosine functions is what makes them so useful for the purposes of representing seasonal fluctuations in economic time series. To visualize the repeating nature of these functions, the sine and cosine functions are graphed in Fig. 5.7. The horizontal axis ranges from 0 to 720 degrees, so both the sine function and the cosine function make two complete cycles.

From Fig. 5.7 the possibility of employing sine and cosine functions to represent seasonal models should be obvious. We shall consider their applicability to monthly data first, then turn to quarterly and other types of data later.

Because the sine and cosine functions describe complete cycles in 360 degrees, a complete annual data cycle could also be viewed in terms of 360 degrees. Then when working with monthly data that comprises $\frac{1}{12}$ of the year, the appropriate angle θ that describes $\frac{1}{12}$ of 360 degrees is clearly 30 degrees. Consider then the time series model

$$\hat{Y}_i = b_1 + b_2 \sin(30°t) + b_3 \cos(30°t), \tag{5.24}$$

where Y is a time series of monthly data spanning two years. It is apparent then that t will range from 1 to 24 to describe the 24 months of the two-year period. As t takes on different values, the sine and cosine functions will describe a cyclical behavior. When $t = 1$, the sine and cosine of 30° will be used and this will represent the first month of data. When $t = 13$, the value of 30° times t will be 390° and, due to the repeating nature of the sine and cosine functions, the sines and cosines of 30° and 390° are identical. Thus, month one of year two will behave the same as month one of year one, and we have described a cyclical behavior that repeats itself every 12 months.

Equation (5.24) contains three coefficients: b_1, b_2, and b_3. The coefficient b_1 describes the level of the series, the base around which the series oscillates throughout the year. The coefficients b_2 and b_3 together describe the magnitude of the seasonal fluctuations and the starting point of the seasonal fluctuations. Figure 5.7 shows that by adding appropriate fractions of the sine and cosine functions, we can describe a stationary time series of any amplitude that starts at any point during the year.

The model above could be viewed as an extension of the simple moving average model. If the model had been simply

$$\hat{Y} = b_1, \tag{5.25}$$

then the task of estimating b_1 could be accomplished by taking a moving average. Addition of the sine and cosine terms generalizes this to the extent of modeling month-to-month fluctuations around this average.

Just as the moving average model had the drawback of not being able to capture time trends in a data series, the model with only three coefficients b_1, b_2, and b_3 also fails to capture any time trends that may be present in the data, in addition to the seasonality. A time trend can easily be added to the seasonal model by inserting time t as follows:

$$\hat{Y} = b_1 + b_2 t + b_3 \sin(30°t) + b_4 \cos(30°t). \tag{5.26}$$

It is clear that b_1 describes the level of the series, b_3 and b_4 describe the amplitude and start-up point, and b_2 describes an upward (or downward) drift of the whole process through time. The type of behavior described by this model is illustrated in Fig. 5.8.

Having described two types of seasonal models—stationary and with a time trend—it is appropriate to discuss how such models are actually fitted to a real data series. The answer is that the least-squares criteria employed earlier may again be used to estimate the b values that yield a minimum sum of squared errors for the model to be used. And when choosing among alternative seasonal models to fit to the data,

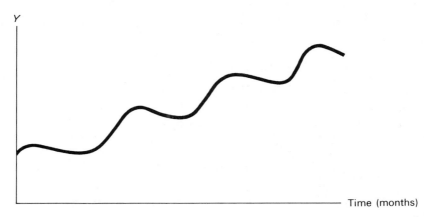

Fig. 5.8 The model $\hat{Y}_i = b_1 + b_2 t + b_3 \sin (30°t) + b_4 \cos (30°t)$.

the R^2 and $\bar{R}^2$ described earlier may again be useful to determine the seasonal model that provides the best representation of the data.

The seasonal modeling techniques based on the use of sine and cosine terms may be extended beyond the two simple models introduced above. Before exploring more complex seasonal forecasting models, we illustrate the estimate of one of these simple models.

In Table 5.11 monthly data on sales revenue for a particular year are displayed. As might be expected, there is a distinct seasonal pattern to sales revenue, with a peak in April. Inspection of the data in the table reveals that a simple trend line would not give a very good model of the data because a strong seasonal pattern is present. Accordingly, a trend line model that incorporates seasonal fluctuations is indicated, and we fit the model $Y = b_1 + b_2 t + b_3 \sin (30°t) + b_4 \cos (30°t)$, where t ranges from one to twelve months to describe the twelve months of data. The estimation of the parameters of Eq. (5.26) involves the use of the SIMPLAN ESTIMATE command for ordinary least squares, the results of which appear in Table 5.12.

Table 5.11 Sales revenue (figures in thousands)

January	79.4	July	99.3
February	76.2	August	101.8
March	118.1	September	89.1
April	140.9	October	76.6
May	130.0	November	72.8
June	120.6	December	60.2

The least-squares parameter estimates for Eq. (5.26) are given by Eq. (5.27)

$$\hat{Y} = 93.9 + 0.5t + 15.4\sin (30t) - 29.2\cos (30t). \tag{5.27}$$

In Table 5.12 we note that R^2 is equal to .84, and when adjusted for the four degrees of freedom lost in fitting the model, the adjusted R^2 becomes .78.

Table 5.12 Output of ESTIMATE command: a seasonal model with a trend.

```
ANALYSIS.

SIN30T=SIND(30*T)

ANALYSIS.

COS30T=COSD(30*T)

ANALYSIS.

ESTIMATE Y T SIN30T COS30T


LEAST SQUARES REGRESSION
```

ESTIMATED EQUATION IS: Y=0.49472*T+15.3739*SIN30T-29.1815*COS30T+93.8675			
INDEPENDENT VARIABLES	ESTIMATED COEFFICIENT	STANDARD ERROR	T- TEST
T	0.4947	1.6465	0.3005
SIN30T	15.3739	7.8679	1.9540
COS30T	-29.1815	5.1821	-5.6312
CONSTANT	93.8675	11.2524	8.3420

```
    NUMBER OF OBSERVATIONS USED =    12
    R-SQUARED=   0.8392                F-STATISTIC(  3,  8)=    13.9187
    ADJUSTED R-SQUARED=  0.7789        DURBIN-WATSON STATISTIC=    1.8581
    STANDARD ERROR=     12.0356        DEGREES OF FREEDOM FOR T-TEST=   8
    SUM OF SQUARED ERRORS=     1158.8542

ANALYSIS.
```

To get some better notion of how well the model fits the data, the data on sales are plotted in Fig. 5.9 along with the fitted model. The model rises to a peak in May (the observed data actually peak in April), then the model falls until the end of the year, when it predicts a slight upturn. If more data were used for the following years, the pattern of a peak in the summer and a low point in the winter would be found to repeat each year.

Having discussed the general way in which trend lines can be modified to reflect seasonal changes, it is now appropriate to consider a variety of models that can be constructed to capture seasonal patterns. These models all will involve some type of sine and cosine functions to capture the seasonality but, as will become apparent, the models can be applied to quarterly data as well as monthly, and to data that has other cycles besides annual cycles, or to data that represent a combination of superimposed cycles.

First, we consider several other models for monthly data with seasonal fluctuations. Beside the linear trend with sinusoidal fluctuations around the growth path, it is possible to have linear trend models with several other types of fluctuations around the long-run path. Often the observed cycle will not be purely annual, but will be composed of composite fluctuations—one that repeats annually and another that repeats every six months. To incorporate a cycle that repeats every six months, we simply add sine and cosine terms that involve $60°$ since this represents one-sixth

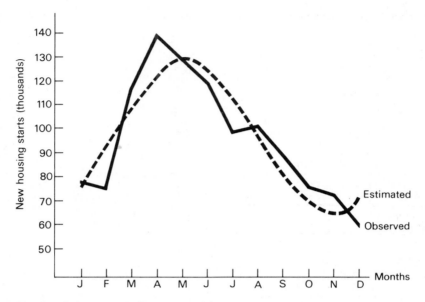

Fig. 5.9 Sales revenue (in thousands).

of the complete cycle. Thus a model for monthly data that contained both *annual* and *semiannual* cycles would be given by:

$$\hat{Y} = b_1 + b_2 t + b_3 \sin(30t) + b_4 \cos(30t) + b_5 \sin(60t) + b_6 \cos(60t). \quad (5.28)$$

This model is identical to Eq. (5.26) except for the addition of the terms involving 60°. Figure 5.10 displays a graph of a time series that follows the (exact) pattern described by the model above, for the coefficient (b) values shown in the figure.

A simple variation on the foregoing models involves models that allow for a trend in the fluctuations as well as a trend in the whole series. This is often desirable since the fluctuations in a series may not themselves be constant, but rather the fluctuations may themselves fluctuate. Typically, for a growing economic time series, the fluctuations will tend to widen through time. A model of this type that has annual fluctuations that become wider through time is described by the model:

$$\hat{Y} = b_1 + b_2 t + b_3 \sin(30t) + b_4 t \ \sin(30t) \quad (5.29)$$
$$+ b_5 \cos(30t) + b_6 t \cdot \cos(30t).$$

When this model is fitted to monthly data, it captures annual cycles because of the terms involving $b_3 \sin(30t)$ and $b_5 \cos(30t)$, but it allows these fluctuations to grow larger (or smaller) over time because of the terms involving $b_4 t \cdot \sin(30t)$ and $b_6 t \cdot (30t)$. A data series generated by such a model appears in Fig. 5.11.

Another variation on the same theme involves introducing six-month cycles into Eq. (5.29). The model then takes on the following form.

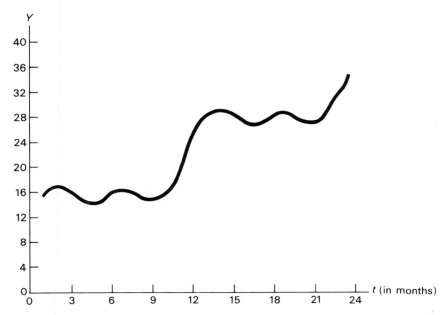

Fig. 5.10 A time series generated by the model
$Y = b_1 + b_2t + b_3 \sin(30t) + b_4 \cos(30t) + b_5 \sin(60t) + b_6 \cos(60t)$
$(b_1 = 10, b_2 = 1, b_3 = 4, b_4 = 1, b_5 = 2, b_6 = 5)$.

$$\hat{Y} = b_1 + b_2t + b_3\sin(30t) + b_4t \cdot \sin(30t) + b_5\cos(30t) \qquad (5.30)$$

$$+ b_6t \cdot \cos(30t) + b_7\sin(60t) + b_8\cos(60t).$$

This model has a regular yearly cycle (represented by the terms with b_3 and b_5), an upward drift through time (represented by the term b_2), yearly cycles that grow wider through time (denoted by the terms b_4 and b_6), and cycles that repeat every six months (denoted by the terms b_7 and b_8). Brown (1972, p. 183) found that this particular model worked well in describing monthly airline passenger traffic. A data series generated by such a model is graphed in Fig. 5.12.

The process of incorporating seasonal coefficients into time series models can easily be extended to meet particular modeling situations. The techniques are basically quite simple. For example, should an analyst have a time series that fluctuates annually about a constant mean, but the fluctuations seemed to widen through time, then the appropriate model would be Eq. (5.29) without the term involving b_2t. When faced with a monthly time series that exhibits very irregular fluctuations, the use of a model that incorporates sine and cosine terms of 30, 60, 90, and 120 degrees may be appropriate. The model would describe a time series with annual, half-yearly, four-month, and three-month cycles. Such a model can describe a very irregular and ill-behaved time series, but the large number of terms should be avoided unless simpler models have been tried and proved unsatisfactory.

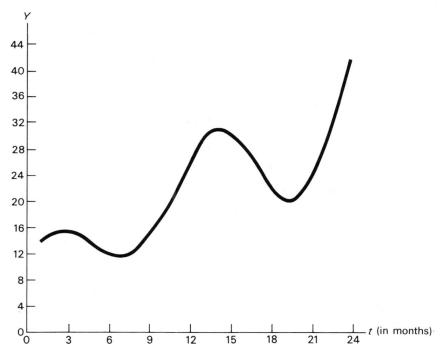

Fig. 5.11 A time series generated by the model
$\hat{Y}_i = b_1 + b_2 t + b_3 \sin(30t) + b_4 t \cdot \sin(30t) + b_5 \cos(30t) + b_6 \cdot \cos(30t)$
$(b_1 = 10, b_2 = 1, b_3 = 2, b_4 = .25, b_5 = 2, b_6 = .25)$.

When fitting and comparing different models as described above, the analyst may employ two criteria in selecting the appropriate model. First *a priori* considerations concerning the behavior of the time series may provide insights into the appropriate seasonal pattern and thus give guidance as to how many sine and cosine terms should be present. An analyst who has some feel for the data will generally know that they exhibit annual cycles or that they exhibit annual cycles with minor cycles at certain months. Such a feel for the data can be very valuable in fitting the time series model with an appropriate number of terms.

Second, statistical procedures are available for helping analysts select the best model for describing his or her time series. "Best" in this context means having the smallest sum of squared errors. Both the adjusted R^2 and the standard error of the estimate statistics can be employed to select among alternative models the one that provides the best fit to the data. The closer the $\bar{R}^2$ to 1.0, the better the model fits the data. The $\bar{R}^2$ for various models can be compared, and the one being closest to 1.0 may be selected. Alternatively, the standard errors of estimate can be compared, and the model providing the smallest standard error of estimate can be chosen.

The aforementioned models can easily be modified to accommodate data

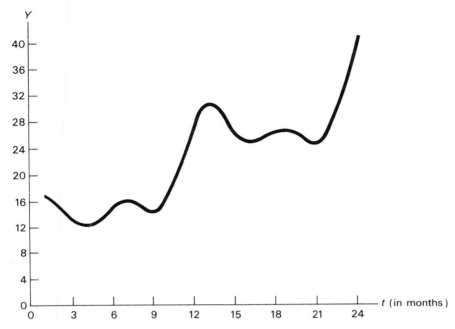

Fig. 5.12 A time series generated by the model
$$\hat{Y}_i = b_1 + b_2 t + b_3 \sin(30t) + b_4 t \cdot \sin(30t) + b_5 \cos(30t) + b_6 t \cdot \cos(30t)$$
$$\qquad + b_7 \sin(60t) + b_8 \cos(60t)$$
$$(b_1 = 10, b_2 = 1, b_3 = 2, b_4 = .1, b_5 = 2, b_6 = .1, b_7 = 2, b_8 = 2).$$

generated for time periods other than months. The technique is simply to choose fractions of 360° that are appropriate for the frequency of the data. For example, when dealing with quarterly data that have a repeating annual cycle that can be described by sine and cosine terms, we would use the model:

$$\hat{Y} = b_1 + b_2 t + b_3 \sin(90t) + b_4 \cos(90t). \qquad (5.31)$$

For quarterly data, we would have four observations per year. We would use the sines and cosines of 90° times t, where t denotes the quarter number beginning with the first quarter for which we have data. The appropriate choice is 90° because it is one quarter of 360°. If we want to use semimonthly (twice a month) data, we would employ sine and cosine terms involving 15° ($= 360°/24$). If we had data every two weeks such that there were 26 observations per year, we could use the model with $360°/26 = 13.85°$. And of course we could add higher frequency terms to any of these models to capture, say, six-month cycles if these were present.

In all of the time trend models discussed thus far, we have assumed that the coefficients of the model were estimated by the method of least squares; that is, if we fit a seasonal model to 36 monthly observations, our estimates of the b coefficients involve minimizing the sum of the 36 squared-error terms. A reasonable question to ask in time series analysis is whether all 36 monthly observations should get the same weight; that is, could it not be argued that the older observations deserve rather less weight since conditions now may be somewhat different from conditions many months ago, and more recent observations are more indicative of the future than are observations from the now distant past? The various models discussed so far can easily be modified to give coefficient estimates that minimize a weighted sum of squared errors where errors from the more distant past receive relatively less weight. Such models are called *exponential smoothing* models and *adaptive forecasting* models.

EXPONENTIAL SMOOTHING

To explore the simplest exponential smoothing model, let us return to the simple moving average. An alternative way of computing a moving average is given by

$$\hat{Y}_t = \hat{Y}_{t-1} + \frac{(Y_t - Y_{t-n})}{n},$$ (5.32)

where $\hat{Y}$ denotes the moving average and Y denotes an actual observation on the data. Following Brown (1972), let us assume that when we were ready to make our next forecast, we discovered that a computer error had somehow erased our data files, destroying all data prior to the present time period. In particular, Y_t still exists, but the value of Y_{t-n} has been unfortunately destroyed. In this situation, the moving average formula given by Eq. (5.32) would not be directly applicable since the old value to be removed from the average, Y_{t-n}, is not known.

In such a situation we could, however, estimate the value Y_{t-n} that we need to make the formula work. Our best estimate of the lost data point would be our most recent moving average value, $\hat{Y}_{t-1}$. If we were to use this value in Eq. (5.32) in place of Y_{t-n}, we would have the following formula:

$$\hat{Y}_t = \hat{Y}_{t-1} + \frac{(Y_t - \hat{Y}_{t-1})}{n}.$$ (5.33)

This formula can be rewritten in the following equivalent form:

$$\hat{Y}_t = \frac{1}{n}Y_t + \left(1 - \frac{1}{n}\right)\hat{Y}_{t-1}.$$ (5.34)

Simple exponential smoothing can now be summarized by the following variant of the foregoing equation:

$$\hat{Y}_t = \alpha Y_t + (1 - \alpha)\hat{Y}_{t-1},$$ (5.35)

where the value α is referred to as the smoothing constant, and it takes on a value between 0.0 and 1.0 that is selected by the user. The value of α is analogous but not identical to the term $\frac{1}{n}$. In the extreme case where $\alpha = 1$, it is obvious that the forecast $\hat{Y}_t$ is simply equal to the most recently observed value of the series, Y_t. For values of α between 0.0 and 1.0, the smoothed value $\hat{Y}_t$ consists of a weighted average of the smoothed value in the previous period and the present observation.

There are two important points concerning Eq. (5.35) that deserve note. First, the way in which more recent values of the data are handled differs from the moving average. The smoothed forecast value at any time is given by the previous smoothed values *plus* a fraction of the difference between the last smoothed value and the present period's realized value. To see this, note that Eq. (5.35) may be rewritten as

$$\hat{Y}_t = \hat{Y}_{t-1} + \alpha(Y_t - \hat{Y}_{t-1}). \tag{5.36}$$

When viewed in this form, it is apparent that exponential smoothing adjusts the previous forecast value $\hat{Y}_{t-1}$ by a fraction of the difference between this forecast and the value Y_t that was actually observed. When α is relatively small (.05 to .10) the smoothed values are revised moderately in response to the forecast errors, while larger values of α (.25 to .50) revise the smooth valued much more in response to a forecast error. Values greater than .25 are not often used since the smoothing process then tracks noise in the series to too great an extent.

A second point to note concerning exponential smoothing is that all values are not weighted equally as in the moving average Eq. (5.35). To see this point, note that Eq. (5.35) can be rewritten as

$$\hat{Y}_t = \alpha Y_t + (1 - \alpha)\hat{Y}_{t-1} \tag{5.37}$$

$$= \alpha Y_t + (1 - \alpha)(\alpha Y_{t-1} + (1 - \alpha)\hat{Y}_{t-2})$$

$$= \alpha Y_t + (\alpha - \alpha^2)Y_{t-1} + (1 - 2\alpha + \alpha^2)\hat{Y}_{t-2}$$

where in the second line we have substituted Eq. (5.35) lagged one time period. The point to note now about the smoothed value $\hat{Y}_t$ is how it depends on αY_t and $(\alpha - \alpha^2)Y_{t-1}$. For any value of α between zero and one, it is clear that the term Y_t receives more weight than does the older term Y_{t-1}. For example, if $\alpha = .3$ is employed, then the weights given to Y_t and Y_{t-1} are .3 and .21, respectively.

In general, exponential smoothing employs weights that decay with the age of the data series. The weights given to older observations decay *exponentially*, thus giving the process its name. Unlike the moving average, however, exponential smoothing does not only employ the last n values of a series in figuring the forecast. Rather, all past observations of Y are employed in calculating the smoothed value $\hat{Y}_t$, with the weights becoming steadily less as you go back through time. The weight given to the data point Y_{t-n} is given by the expression $\alpha(1 - \alpha)^n$. This expression is tabulated for various values of α and n in Table 5.13. In Fig. 5.13, we graph the weights given by exponential smoothing with $\alpha = .3$ and a moving average for six periods.

Two characteristics distinguish exponential smoothing from the moving average. First, exponential smoothing requires a smoothed value to get the process started, and second, exponential smoothing does not require that the complete data series be available for the computation of a forecast. Concerning the first point, it can be seen from Eq. (5.35) that the process requires an initial smoothed value (a value for $\hat{Y}_{t-1}$). How can such a value be obtained in practice?

There are at least three possibilities. The two simplest involve either using the actual value of Y_o to represent $\hat{Y}_o$, or else taking a moving average of several periods

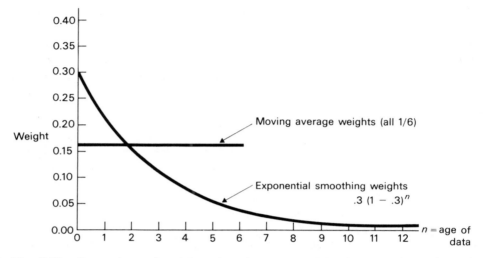

Fig. 5.13 Comparison of weights given by exponential smoothing ($\alpha = .3$) and moving average ($n = 6$).

and using this moving average in place of $\hat{Y}$. A third alternative suggested by Brown (1972) involves using the value that one expects the series to approach ultimately. Clearly, this value will not always be known, so a practical choice usually involves one of the two schemes previously mentioned. Fortunately, the exact choice is usually not particularly important if it is taken fairly far back in time and if the smoothing

Table 5.13 Weights for exponential smoothing for various values of α

Age of data n	Smoothing constant α				
	.10	.20	.30	.40	.50
0	.100	.200	.300	.400	.500
1	.090	.160	.210	.240	.250
2	.081	.128	.147	.144	.125
3	.073	.102	.103	.086	.063
4	.066	.082	.072	.052	.031
5	.059	.066	.050	.031	.016
6	.053	.052	.035	.019	.008
7	.048	.042	.025	.011	.004
8	.043	.034	.017	.007	.002
9	.039	.027	.012	.004	.001
10	.035	.021	.008	.002	.000
11	.031	.017	.006	.001	.000
12	.028	.014	.004	.000	.000

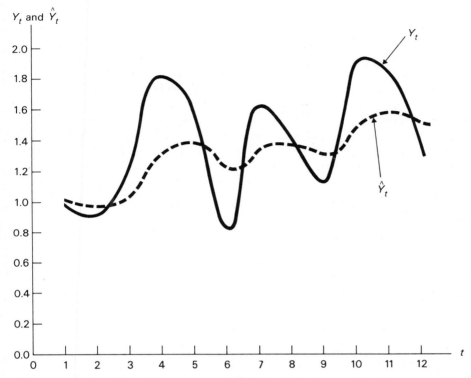

Fig. 5.14 Data series Y_t and the exponentially smoothed values $\hat{Y}_t$.

Table 5.14 Illustration of exponential smoothing ($\alpha = .25$)

t	Y_t	$\hat{Y}_t = .25 Y_t + .75 \hat{Y}_{t-1}$
1	1.00	1.37
2	.90	1.28
3	1.20	1.18
4	1.80	1.19
5	1.60	1.34
6	.80	1.40
7	1.6	1.25
8	1.4	1.34
9	1.1	1.36
10	1.9	1.29
11	1.8	1.44
12	1.3	1.53

Note: The value $\bar{Y}$ is used for the value $\hat{Y}_1$ to start the process off.

is carried on for a number of periods. This is because the weight given to a value in the past declines in importance with age, so whatever initial approximation is used for $\hat{Y}$, it will become less and less important through time.

Having discussed the basic method of exponential smoothing and having compared it with moving averages, we turn now to an example of this method. Table 5.14 contains a numerical example of a data series and the exponentially smoothed values of the series, using $\alpha = .25$. Note again that at this point we are talking about the exponential smoothing of a data series that is essentially stationary. The data in Table 5.14 are devoid of any significant time trend. The original values and the smoothed values are graphed in Fig. 5.14. Note that the smoothed values exhibit far fewer fluctuations than do the original data, as would be expected.

Table 5.15 Output of ADAPT command: Adaptive forecasting with constant model
ANALYSIS.

ADAPT Y 1-12 *CON *FAST

ADAPTIVE FORECASTING WITH:

```
*CON    CONSTANT PATTERN
*FAST       SMOOTHING CONSTANT .25
```

```
FINAL FITTED EQUATION IS:
    Y=1.47445
```

```
IN INITIAL FITTED EQUATION,  T=1 IN      1
IN FINAL FITTED EQUATION,    T=1 IN     13
```

	INITIAL EQUATION			FINAL EQUATION	
VARIABLE	ESTIMATED COEFFICIENT	STANDARD ERROR	T- TEST	ESTIMATED COEFFICIENT	STANDARD ERROR
CONSTANT	1.3667	0.11	12.63	1.4745	0.15

```
THE INITIAL EQUATION FITTED BY REGRESSION HAS:
    R-SQUARED=  0.0000          F-STATISTIC(  0, 11)=        ---
    ADJUSTED R-SQUARED=  0.0000   DURBIN-WATSON STATISTIC=    1.8168
    STANDARD ERROR=         0.3750  DEGREES OF FREEDOM FOR T-TEST= 11
```

```
THE FINAL EQUATION FITTED BY ADAPTIVE FORECASTING HAS:
    SUM OF SQUARED ERRORS=              1.8264
    STANDARD ERROR=          0.4075
```

TIME	SMOOTHED VALUE
1	1.3667
2	1.2750
3	1.1812
4	1.1859
5	1.3395
6	1.4046
7	1.2534
8	1.3401
9	1.3551
10	1.2913
11	1.4435
12	1.5326

ANALYSIS.

The smoothing was carried out by the SIMPLAN command ADAPT with the specification that the constant model (*CON) was to be used and $\alpha = .25$ (*FAST) was to be employed. The SIMPLAN output is shown in Table 5.15. Note that for an initial smoothed value ($\hat{Y}$), SIMPLAN uses the mean of Y, 1.3667. The standard error shown in the output (.11) is the standard deviation of the mean.

ADAPTIVE FORECASTING

When the method of moving averages is modified so that older observations receive less weight, the process is usually known as exponential smoothing. When the idea of less weight for older observations is applied to linear or quadratic time trend models or to sinusoidal models, the models usually go under the name of *adaptive forecasting* models. The reason is simply that when models contain a linear, quadratic, or sinusoidal function of time, future *forecasts* can easily be generated by plugging $t+1$, $t+2$, etc., into the model. And the forecasts are *adaptive* in the sense that some fraction of the forecast error is used in modifying model coefficients and future forecasts.

In this section we will discuss linear, quadratic, and sinusoidal models in which older observations are given less weight. The idea is entirely similar to the concept discussed under the heading of exponential smoothing. Some authors even use the term "exponential smoothing" for all of the models that we call exponential smoothing or adaptive forecasting models. However, as the models become more complex, the term adaptive forecasting is usually used, and we will follow this convention.

Since the mathematics of adaptive forecasting can become fairly tedious, we will not give the formulas for the adaptive forecasting models we discuss. The interested reader can refer to Brown (1972). Instead, we will focus on the implementation of these models.

The basic ideas behind all the adaptive forecasting models that we discuss can be

Table 5.16 Adaptive forecasting with linear model

Year	Y	$\hat{Y}$
1961	65.7	65.2
1962	66.7	66.7
1963	67.8	68.3
1964	69.3	69.7
1965	71.1	71.2
1966	72.9	72.7
1967	74.4	74.3
1968	75.9	75.8
1969	77.9	77.4
1970	78.6	78.9

Initial model estimated by least squares:
$\hat{Y} = 63.63 + 1.53t$ ($t = 1$ in 1961)
$\hat{Y} = 78.91 + 1.53t$ ($t = 1$ in 1971)

Table 5.17 Output from ADAPT command: adaptive forecasting with linear model

```
ANALYSIS.

ADAPT Y 1-13 *LIN

ADAPTIVE FORECASTING WITH:
```

```
*LIN   LINEAR PATTERN
*NORMAL  SMOOTHING CONSTANT .1
```

```
FINAL FITTED EQUATION IS:
   Y=78.9069+1.52793*T
```

```
IN INITIAL FITTED EQUATION,  T=1 IN     1
IN FINAL FITTED EQUATION,    T=1 IN    11
```

| VARIABLE | INITIAL EQUATION | | | | FINAL EQUATION | |
	ESTIMATED COEFFICIENT	STANDARD ERROR	T-TEST		ESTIMATED COEFFICIENT	STANDARD ERROR
CONSTANT	63.6267	0.25	254.45		78.9069	0.10
T	1.5279	0.04	37.91		1.5279	0.00

```
THE INITIAL EQUATION FITTED BY REGRESSION HAS:
   R-SQUARED=  0.9945           F-STATISTIC(  1,  8)=      1437.6294
   ADJUSTED R-SQUARED=  0.9938  DURBIN-WATSON STATISTIC=   1.4185
   STANDARD ERROR=        0.3660  DEGREES OF FREEDOM FOR T-TEST=  8
```

```
THE FINAL EQUATION FITTED BY ADAPTIVE FORECASTING HAS:
   SUM OF SQUARED ERRORS=         1.1834
   STANDARD ERROR=          0.3846
```

TIME	SMOOTHED VALUE
1	65.1545
2	66.7384
3	68.2637
4	69.7453
5	71.2276
6	72.7413
7	74.2841
8	75.8228
9	77.3579
10	78.9410

TIME	FORECASTED VALUE	APPROXIMATE STANDARD ERROR
11	80.4348	0.1413
12	81.9627	0.1465
13	83.4907	0.1514

```
ANALYSIS.
```

summarized as: (1) select a model that is believed to fit the data well (quadratic, linear, and sinusoidal, etc.); (2) get initial estimates of the model by applying the method of least squares; (3) revise the initial model coefficients by forecasting over the range of historical data and revising the model coefficients ("adapting") in accordance with the errors; and (4) use the revised model to produce forecasts into the future.

In the case of the constant model discussed above, we selected a constant model, and the initial estimate of the model was 1.3667. The model was revised on the available historical data to yield a final model estimate of 1.4745. This value would be our forecast for all future periods.

We will now illustrate the procedure with a linear adaptive forecasting model. The data and the historical adaptive forecasts are displayed in Table 5.16. The SIMPLAN output that produced these adaptive forecasts is shown in Table 5.17.

Several points can be seen from the output. First, since no particular smoothing constant was specified, the system supplied a "default" value of $\alpha = .10$, which is referred to as "normal" smoothing. Had the users wanted to request that more or less weight be given to older data, they could have included the options *SLOW or *FAST in their ADAPT command. SLOW smoothing corresponds to $\alpha = .05$, and this is appropriate if one believes that past data are reliable and should be given almost as much weight as more recent values. FAST smoothing corresponds to $\alpha = .25$, and this is employed if the users believe that past data are not likely to be very reliable and greater emphasis should be given to more recent values.

A second point to note from the output concerns the standard errors associated with the initial estimated equation and the final estimated equation. The standard error is defined by $s = \sqrt{\Sigma e^2 / (n-k)}$ where n = number of observations, k = number of right-hand side terms in the model, and e refers to the difference between estimated and actual values over the database period. The standard error is *smaller* for the least-squares estimates of the initial model, and *larger* for the final model produced by adaptive forecasting. This is not an indictment of the latter method, however, because adaptive forecasting has adjusted the model coefficients so as to minimize *weighted* forecast errors in which more recent time periods get more weight. What the larger standard error for the adaptive forecasting model says is that the model is giving considerable weight to minimizing errors in the recent past, but some larger forecast errors are occurring further back in the past because the process has acted to "forget" these older values.

Third, note that the forecasts cover (1) the historical period for which forecast

Table 5.18 Some adaptive forecasting models available in SIMPLAN

Model and SIMPLAN commands	Equation of model
Constant ADAPT Y *CON	$\hat{Y} = b_1$
Linear ADAPT Y *LIN	$\hat{Y} = b_1 + b_2 t$
Quadratic ADAPT Y *QUAD	$\hat{Y} = b_1 + b_2 t + b_3 t^2$
Constant with sinusoid ADAPT Y *S	$\hat{Y} = b_1 + b_2 \sin(30t)$ $+ b_3 \cos(30t)$
Linear trend with sinusoid ADAPT Y *LS	$\hat{Y} = b_1 + b_2 t + b_3 \sin(30t)$ $+ b_4 \cos(30t)$

and actual values may be compared, and (2) the future period, for which forecast and actual values cannot be compared until some time has elapsed.

The user who wants to generate exponential smoothing or adaptive forecasting models with SIMPLAN has a choice of a number of models that can be applied to forecast a time series. Complete details are available in SIMPLAN published by Addison-Wesley in 1978. As will be obvious to the reader, these adaptive forecasting models are all similar in nature to the sinusoidal time series models and linear and quadratic time trend models that were discussed in the previous section, so we will

Table 5.19 Output of ADAPT command: adaptive forecasting with linear time trend and superimposed sinusoid

```
ANALYSIS.

ADAPT Y 1-12 *LS

ADAPTIVE FORECASTING WITH:
```

```
*LS    LINEAR PATTERN WITH SUPERIMPOSED SINUSOID
*NORMAL  SMOOTHING CONSTANT .1
```

```
FINAL FITTED EQUATION IS:
  Y=99.7926+0.49453*T+15.3095*SIND(30*T)-29.1553*COSD(30*T)
```

```
IN INITIAL FITTED EQUATION,  T=1 IN    1
IN FINAL FITTED EQUATION,    T=1 IN   13
```

	INITIAL EQUATION			FINAL EQUATION	
VARIABLE	ESTIMATED COEFFICIENT	STANDARD ERROR	T-TEST	ESTIMATED COEFFICIENT	STANDARD ERROR
CONSTANT	93.8676	11.25	8.34	99.7926	2.28
T	0.4947	1.65	0.30	0.4945	0.03
SIND(30*T)	15.3738	7.87	1.95	15.3095	2.05
COSD(30*T)	-29.1814	5.18	-5.63	-29.1553	2.06

```
THE INITIAL EQUATION FITTED BY REGRESSION HAS:
  R-SQUARED=   0.8392        F-STATISTIC(  3,  8)=        13.9187
  ADJUSTED R-SQUARED=  0.7789  DURBIN-WATSON STATISTIC=   1.8581
  STANDARD ERROR=       12.0356  DEGREES OF FREEDOM FOR T-TEST=  8
```

```
THE FINAL EQUATION FITTED BY ADAPTIVE FORECASTING HAS:
  SUM OF SQUARED ERRORS=        1283.5898
  STANDARD ERROR=       12.6668
```

TIME	SMOOTHED VALUE
1	76.7772
2	93.8347
3	109.2286
4	123.3245
5	130.7899
6	127.3432
7	115.2906
8	97.6023
9	81.8166
10	70.6312
11	66.8376
12	71.7971

```
ANALYSIS.
```

merely summarize the types of models that will be employed. We will focus mainly on models for monthly data.

A summary of some of the most frequently used adaptive forecasting models is presented in Table 5.18. A glance at the table will make apparent the very close relationship to the models discussed previously. In addition to specifying the type of model to be used for a time series, the user must also indicate a smoothing constant (SLOW = .05, NORMAL = .10, FAST = .25) as discussed earlier. If none is specified, normal smoothing with $\alpha = .10$ is assumed.

Earlier in this chapter we discussed a sinusoidal model of sales revenue that was given in Table 5.12. The model was estimated by the method of least squares. The same model as estimated by adaptive forecasting is presented in Table 5.19. As is obvious from the table, the *initial model* estimated by least squares is the same as the least-squares model shown earlier. When the initial model is refined after making forecasts for all of the historical data, we have the final model, or the adaptive fore-casting model. It differs from the initial model in that the adaptive version weights the older errors less, and further the adaptive version has adjusted the time origin of the model so that the next time period into the future is time $t = 1$. This convention is adopted so that if an analyst has a variety of models that were estimated over *different* historical time periods (say, 1955–1975 in one case and 1960–1975 in another case), both models can use a vector t that has $t = 1$ in 1976 to generate future forecasts. This would not be possible if the model for 1955–1975 used 1955 for $t = 1$, and the model for 1960–1975 used 1960 for $t = 1$.

BOX–JENKINS

Box–Jenkins (1970) methods are among the most sophisticated time series methods currently available today. Moving averages, time trends, exponential smoothing, and adaptive forecasting can be mastered easily by analysts who have a basic knowledge of statistics. This is unfortunately not the case with Box–Jenkins methods. To employ Box–Jenkins methods with confidence, an analyst must be well versed in mathematical statistics. For this reason, we shall merely summarize some of the important aspects of Box–Jenkins models.

The basic idea of Box–Jenkins models is to represent a time series Y by a model of the following form:

$$\hat{Y}_t = a_1 Y_{t-1} + a_2 Y_{t-2} + b_1 e_{t-1} + b_2 e_{t-2}, \tag{5.38}$$

where the a's and b's are coefficients of the model, and the e's represent errors from previous forecasts. Equation (5.38) says that the present value of the time series Y_t depends linearly on past values of the time series (with weights a_1 and a_2) and also on past values of the error (with weights b_1 and b_2). Such a model is often referred to as an ARMA model because it involves an *autoregression* on past values of the Y's, and a *moving average* of past values of the errors. This moving average of error terms is slightly more general than the moving average discussed earlier in the sense that the b's in Eq. (5.38) do not necessarily add up to 1.0 and they are not all equal as they would be with an ordinary moving average. If the weights are not all equal but still sum to 1.0, we have what amounts to an exponential smoothing of the errors. If the weights are not all equal and do not sum to 1.0, we have something slightly more general than either a moving average or exponential smoothing, although the term "moving average" is still commonly applied to the weights given the error terms in Eq. (5.38).

In the equation above we have illustrated two autoregressive terms (Y_{t-1} and Y_{t-2}) and two moving average terms (e_{t-1} and e_{t-2}). In general, a Box–Jenkins model may contain any number of autoregressive or moving average terms, but for many practical applications it will be found that neither will exceed 2. The number of autoregressive terms is expressed as p, and the number of moving average terms is expressed as q. Thus the model of Eq. (5.38) would be described as a $p = 2, q = 2$ model. Often a time series can be modeled by a Box–Jenkins model in which either $p = 0$ or $q = 0$. In the former case, we simply have a moving average or exponential smoothing type of model, and in the latter case we have an autoregressive model.

Equation (5.38) gives a type of model that is appropriate for modeling a stationary time series. This general type of model is thus appropriate for estimating a series that fluctuates about a fixed mean. It provides a more complex description than does the moving average model or the simple exponential smoothing model, but it is limited to data that have no strong time trend. The model described by Eq. (5.38) can easily be modified to handle nonstationary time series. To understand how the Box–Jenkins model can be modified for data with a time trend, consider the data shown in Table 5.20.

In Table 5.20 are three time series generated by nonstochastic models. Three models are given: constant ($Y = 3$), linear ($Y = 3 + 2t$), and quadratic ($Y = 3 + 2t + t^2$), and the values of Y for $t = 1$ to $t = 10$ are tabulated. Along with the series Y is one or more columns of differences, or period-to-period changes in Y. The notation ΔY_t is used to denote the quantity $Y_t - Y_{t-1}$, and the values of ΔY_t are referred to as the first differences of the series. If we compute the differences of the differences, we have the differences in ΔY_t which are denoted by $\Delta^2 Y_t$ and are defined by $\Delta^2 Y_t =$

Table 5.20 Data generated from constant, linear, and quadratic models

time t	$Y = 3$	ΔY	$Y = 3+2t$	ΔY	$\Delta^2 Y$	$Y = 3+2t+t^2$	ΔY	$\Delta^2 Y$	$\Delta^3 Y$
1	3	-	5	-	-	6	-	-	-
2	3	0	7	2	-	11	5	-	-
3	3	0	9	2	0	18	7	2	-
4	3	0	11	2	0	27	9	2	0
5	3	0	13	2	0	38	11	2	0
6	3	0	15	2	0	51	13	2	0
7	3	0	17	2	0	66	15	2	0
8	3	0	19	2	0	83	17	2	0
9	3	0	21	2	0	102	19	2	0
10	3	0	23	2	0	123	21	2	0

$\Delta(Y_t - Y_{t-1}) = Y_t - 2Y_{t-1} + Y_{t-2}$. The term $\Delta^3 Y_t$ is similarly defined as $\Delta^3 Y_t = \Delta(Y_t - 2Y_{t-1} + Y_{t-2}) = Y_t - 3Y_{t-1} + 3Y_{t-2} - Y_{t-3}$. The terms $\Delta^2 Y_t$ and $\Delta^3 Y_t$ are known as the second and third difference of the series.

The important point to be observed from Table 5.20 is the behavior of the differences of the various models. In the case of the constant model $Y = 3$, it will be seen that the first differences are zero. In the case of the model $Y = 3 + 2t$, the first differences are nonzero, but the second differences are zero. For the model $Y = 3 + 2t + t^2$, the first and second differences are nonzero, but the third differences are zero. The general pattern of Table 5.20 is clearly thus: If the $(n + 1)$st difference of a series is zero, then the nth difference can be described by a constant model. Thus for the linear model, the $\Delta^2 Y$ terms all vanish, and the ΔY terms are all constant. And for the quadratic model the $\Delta^3 Y$ values are all zero, implying that the $\Delta^2 Y$ values are constant.

Since the Box–Jenkins model of Eq. (5.38) is appropriate for a stationary process, the generalization to a nonstationary time series is obvious from Table 5.20: given nonstationary data, compute differences of the data until the $(n + 1)$st differences all vanish. Then employ a Box–Jenkins model like Eq. (5.38) to predict the nth differences. For example, if the data seem to follow a linear trend, the second differences will be zero, and a Box–Jenkins model could be fitted to the first differences. Then forecasts of the differences (combined with knowledge of the most recent actual value) provide forecasts of the level of the series at some time in the future.

If the original data have been differenced once or twice before the model is fitted to the data, then the forecasts will give the first or second differences of the data series. These differences must be summed up to obtain an actual forecast. For example, if a model involved a first difference then we would have $\Delta Y_t = Y_t - Y_{t-1}$. If we desired a forecast of Y_t based on the differences, we could add ΔY_t to Y_{t-1}. But to find Y_{t-1}, we would add ΔY_{t-1} to Y_{t-2}. Since this summing process is referred to as integration in the case of continuous data, Box–Jenkins models involving differences are usually referred to as *autoregressive integrated moving average* models, or simply ARIMA models. While the ARIMA model is characterized by p autoregressive terms and q moving average terms, the ARIMA is characterized by p autoregressive terms, d differences, and q moving average terms. Thus, the model of Eq. (5.38) would be regarded as an ARIMA model of type (2,0,2).

To illustrate other simple Box–Jenkins models, Table 5.21 summarizes some ARIMA models that often occur in practical applications. Although Box–Jenkins models can have any number of autoregressive or moving average terms, in practice it is somewhat rare to have values of $p, d,$ or q that are in excess of 2.

When discussing the differencing of the data series above, it was assumed that the data were generated *exactly* by a constant, linear or quadratic process. In practice, the difference data will rarely be exactly as shown in Table 5.20. Simple statistical tests are employed to test whether the data series departs significantly from zero after differencing. If we cannot reject the hypothesis that the true value of all the differences. If the hypothesis is rejected, another differencing is performed. Usually values of d turn out to be 0, 1, or 2.

Table 5.21 Some Box–Jenkins models often met in practice

(0,1,0) model
This model is the familiar random walk model:

$$\Delta Y_t = e_t$$

$$\text{or} \quad Y_t = Y_{t-1} + e_t.$$

(0,1,1) model
This model involves 1 difference and 1 moving average term:

$$\Delta Y_t = b_1 e_{t-1}$$

$$\text{or} \quad Y_t = Y_{t-1} + b_1 e_{t-1}.$$

(1,1,1) model
This model involves 1 difference, 1 autoregressive term, and 1 moving average term:

$$\Delta Y_t = a_1 \Delta Y_{t-1} + b_1 e_{t-1}$$

$$\text{or} \quad Y_t = Y_{t-1} + a_1 \Delta Y_{t-1} + b_1 e_{t-1}.$$

(2,1,0) model
This model involves 1 difference and 2 autoregressive terms:

$$\Delta Y_t = a_1 \Delta Y_{t-1} + a_2 \Delta Y_{t-2}$$

$$\text{or} \quad Y_t = Y_{t-1} + a_1 \Delta Y_{t-1} + a_2 \Delta Y_{t-2}.$$

(0,1,2) model
This model involves 1 difference and 2 moving average terms:

$$\Delta Y_t = b_1 e_{t-1} + b_2 e_{t-2}$$

$$\text{or} \quad Y_t = Y_{t-1} + b_1 e_{t-1} + b_2 e_{t-2}.$$

Because Table 5.21 contains a number of different models, a natural question that arises is how does one select appropriate values of p and q once a d has been chosen as described above. The answer is that appropriate values of p and q may be inferred from the behavior of the autocorrelation coefficients for a time series. A table for a graph of these autocorrelation coefficients will provide immediate information on appropriate values of p and q, and attention can then shift to estimating actual values for the coefficients of the model.

The autocorrelation for sample data is defined by

$$r_k = \frac{\sum_{i=1}^{n-k} (Y_i - \bar{Y})(Y_{i+k} - \bar{Y})}{\sum_{i=1}^{n} (Y_i - \bar{Y})^2}, \quad \text{for} \quad k = 0, 1, 2, \ldots, \tag{5.39}$$

where $\bar{Y}$ is simply the mean of all n values of the time series. Thus r_0 is always one (the correlation of the series with itself), r_1 gives the correlation of the time series

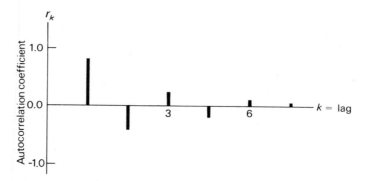

Fig. 5.15 Correlogram for the data of Table 5.22.

with the series lagged one period, r_2 is the correlation of the time series with the series lagged two periods, etc. A rule of thumb is that k need not be more than one-fourth of the sample size. Thus if the sample size is of $n = 100$, then at most $k = 25$ autocorrelation coefficients need be calculated.

Once the autocorrelation coefficients have been calculated, they are frequently plotted on a graph called a correlogram. Values of k (the lag length) are plotted along the horizontal axis and corresponding values of r_k are plotted on the vertical axis. In Table 5.22 we show values of the autocorrelation coefficients for a hypothetical time series, and in Fig. 5.15 we present the correlogram for the autocorrelation coefficients. The structure of the correlogram for a time series is often referred to as the autocorrelation function, or the ACF, of the time series.

Table 5.22 Values of the autocorrelation coefficient r_k for a time series

lag length k	value of r_k
0	1.00
1	.83
2	−.43
3	.25
4	−.18
5	.09
6	.05

In addition to finding the autocorrelation structure of the time series, it is usually also necessary to compute the partial autocorrelation coefficients for the time series. A partial autocorrelation coefficient between Y_t and Y_{t-1} is the correlation coefficient that results when holding constant for all other autocorrelations in the time series. Thus in calculating the partial autocorrelation coefficient between Y_t and Y_{t-1}, any relationship between Y_t and Y_{t-2} or Y_{t-1} and Y_{t-2} is held constant. The resulting partial autocorrelation coefficients are just like ordinary autocorrelation coefficients in the sense that they describe a relationship in terms of a value that ranges from -1.0 to $+1.0$. Like autocorrelation coefficients, the partial autocorrelation coefficients can be plotted in a correlogram similar to Fig. 5.15. The shape of the correlogram then reflects the partial autocorrelation function, or PACF, for the time series. As with the ACF, values of the partial autocorrelation coefficients are usually calculated for a maximum of $k = \frac{n}{4}$ periods.

Now the value of the ACF and the PACF can be readily related to the appropriate number of autoregressive and moving average terms in a Box–Jenkins model. There are three possibilities that can be readily isolated from inspection of the correlograms for the ACF and the PACF: (1) if the ACF gradually trails off to zero, but the PACF suddenly cuts off to zero, then a Box–Jenkins model involving only autoregressive terms is appropriate, and $(p,d,0)$ models are considered; (2) if the ACF suddenly cuts off to zero after several time periods, but the PACF gradually trails off to zero, then a Box–Jenkins model involving only moving average terms is appropriate, and $(0,d,q)$ models are considered; (3) if the ACF and the PACF both gradually trail off to zero and neither suddenly cuts off and falls to zero after a few time periods, then a Box–Jenkins model involving both autoregressive and moving average terms is appropriate, and (p,d,q) models are considered. Table 5.23 summarizes the alternatives.

Table 5.23 Behavior of the ACF and PACF and the choice of a Box–Jenkins model

		Behavior of the autocorrelation coefficients	
		Cut off	Trail off
Behavior of partial autocorrelation coefficients	Cut off	$p = 0$ and $q = 0$	$p > 0$ and $q = 0$
	Trail off	$p = 0$ and $q > 0$	$p > 0$ and $q > 0$

Table entries show appropriate type of Box–Jenkins model to model the behavior described by the ACF and PACF. Note that if both the ACF and the PACF cut off to zero very suddenly, Box–Jenkins models are inappropriate.

Once the autocorrelation coefficients and the partial autocorrelation coefficients have provided information on whether the model should include autoregressive terms, or moving average terms, or both, the user can proceed to estimate the appropriate coefficients (such as a_1, a_2, b_1, and b_2 of Eq. (5.38)) by appropriate means. Coefficient estimates are usually chosen according to the principle of least squares, but unlike all the previous models covered in this chapter, the equations that yield coefficient estimates for Box–Jenkins models are in general nonlinear simultaneous equations. Since some form of iteration is invariably necessary to solve nonlinear equations, the usual approach is simply to attempt a direct minimization of the sum of squared errors. The book by Box and Jenkins (1970) discusses fully the implementation of the computations.

As an example of a simple Box–Jenkins model, we present a model that describes the GNP implicit price deflator for the United States economy. The equation for the price deflator was developed by Naylor, Seaks, and Wichern (1972) in an attempt to compare Box–Jenkins model forecasting potential with the forecasting abilities of the Wharton Econometric Model. Based on the quarterly price deflator data from 1948 to 1964, examination of the data showed that one difference was necessary to make the data approximately stationary. The ACF and the PACF of the differenced data were then examined. Since the PACF cut off very quickly, and the ACF gradually trailed off to zero, a model involving only autoregressive terms was employed. The following model ($p = 1, d = 1, q = 0$) was finally estimated:

$$\Delta Y_t = .458 \Delta Y_{t-1} + .0025 \qquad (5.40)$$

or

$$Y_t = Y_{t-1} + .458(Y_{t-1} - Y_{t-2}) + .0025.$$

Since this particular equation involved only an autoregressive term and a constant, this particular model could have been estimated by a least-squares regression. But had the model contained moving average terms also, the model would have involved nonlinear estimation.

Since the Box–Jenkins methods provide the most complex methods now known for extrapolating a time series, it is impossible to give very complete coverage to the methods in any short space such as this. The foregoing discussion is of necessity rather incomplete, but it should suffice to give the reader some insight into the basic approach of Box–Jenkins model building, and how these models differ from the other types of model discussed in this chapter.

In summary, Box–Jenkins methods are a generalization of all of the other naive forecasting methods discussed in this chapter. Moving averages, time trends, exponential smoothing, and adaptive forecasting are each special cases of Box–Jenkins models. Although Box–Jenkins methods are alleged to be the most accurate time series methods presently available, they are also some of the most costly methods in terms of human expertise and computer time.

Gene Groff (1973) has recently cast some doubts on the forecasting performance of Box–Jenkins methods by comparing the forecasting accuracy of six adaptive forecasting methods with ten Box–Jenkins models. Applying these models to 63 different monthly sales series Groff concluded that

> the forecasting errors of the best of the Box–Jenkins models that were tested are either approximately equal to or greater than the errors of the corresponding exponentially smoothed models.

In other words, Groff's study raises a serious question as to whether or not the added cost and complexity of Box–Jenkins models are really worthwhile.

It is possible to link Box–Jenkins models to external variables including national economic indicators through the use of *transfer functions*. However, this method is somewhat cumbersome and difficult to use. More recently, a type of simultaneous equation, Box–Jenkins model has appeared.

LIMITATIONS OF TIME SERIES MODELS

Although time series forecasting models may be useful forecasting tools, they do have a number of limitations. First, since these methods are naive, mechanistic techniques, they provide little or no explanatory power; that is, they cannot be used to improve one's knowledge of the market. Second, forecasting models cannot be used to conduct "What if?" policy simulation experiments to simulate the effects of alternative marketing policies or assumptions about the national economy, competition, etc. Third, these techniques tend to be reliable for relatively short periods of time (usually less than 36 months). Fourth, in general, they produce accurate forecasts only for relatively stable, mature markets and they tend to miss turning points induced by changes in external factors which have an impact on the market.

However, in spite of these limitations, time series forecasting models can prove to be effective short-run forecasting tools and deserve serious consideration by corporate planners and model builders.

BIBLIOGRAPHY

Box, G. E. P., and G. M. Jenkins, 1970. *Time series analysis*. San Francisco: Holden-Day.

Brown, Robert G., 1972. *Smoothing, forecasting, and prediction*. Englewood Cliffs, N.J.: Prentice-Hall.

Chambers, John C., S. K. Mullich, and D. D. Smith, 1971. How to choose the right forecasting technique. *Harvard Business Review* (July-August): 45–74.

Groff, Gene K., 1973. Empirical comparison of models for short-range forecasting. *Management Science* 22 (September): 22–31.

Naylor, Thomas H., T. G. Seaks, and D. W. Wichern, 1972. Box–Jenkins methods: an alternative to econometric models. *International Statistical Review* 40 (2).

Nelson, C., 1973. *Applied time series analysis*. San Francisco: Holden-Day.

Pindyck, Robert S., and Daniel L. Rubinfield, 1976. *Econometric models and economic forecasts*. New York: McGraw-Hill.

6 Econometric Marketing Models: Methodology

TERRY G. SEAKS AND THOMAS H. NAYLOR

INTRODUCTION

Chapter 5 was concerned primarily with time series forecasting models in which a variable such as sales volume was expressed as a function of time only. No other indepedent variables were included as explanatory variables. As such, these models were naive, mechanistic, and devoid of explanatory power. Because the time series models included no management policy variables, no competitive variables, and no external economic indicators, it was not possible to conduct "What if?" simulation experiments.

This chapter discusses an alternative methodology for constructing marketing models (as well as many other kinds of models) that overcomes some of the limitations of time series forecasting models. Econometric marketing models provide the user with at least three important benefits not provided by the time series forecasting models described in the last chapter. First, with econometric models, it is possible to improve one's knowledge of the market for a particular product or an entire industry, since econometric models provide us with explanatory power. Second, econometric models enable us to evaluate the effects of alternative marketing policies on sales volume, sales revenue, and market share. Third, with econometric models we can also evaluate the effects on our market of alternative assumptions about the national economy as well as alternative policies which may be employed by our competition.

Unfortunately, econometric modeling is not without its disadvantages. First, econometric models tend to be more expensive than time series models in terms of the human effort required to develop them. Second, econometric models may require large amounts of data–data that may not be available in some industries. Third, successful econometric modeling is possible only if the analyst is well grounded in (1) econometric theory, (2) statistics, (3) microeconomic theory, and (4) modeling techniques. Fourth, the analyst must also become very familiar with the market of the product being modeled.

The approach which we take to econometric modeling involves four basic activities:

- Model specification
- Parameter estimation
- Validation
- Policy simulation

We begin by discussing the elements involved in specifying econometric models including the use of a market analysis questionnaire. Given an econometric model, we then turn to the problem of estimating the parameters of the model. A substantial portion of the chapter is devoted to the procedures and tests associated with the estimation of the parameters of econometric marketing models. In order to validate an econometric model and conduct policy simulation experiments with the model, it is necessary to solve the model. Thus the next three sections of the chapter treat model solutions, validation, and policy simulations.

Chapter 7 deals entirely with applications of econometric models including marketing models, industry models, and national econometric models. Our approach to this chapter is similar to our approach to Chapter 5, although it may well be the most complex chapter of the entire book. We rely almost exclusively on discussion, examples, and sample computer output. There will be relatively little mathematics, and very little in the way of proofs or derivations. Those interested in a technical and rigorous approach to the subject can pursue some of the references cited, but those who wish a readable, practical approach to econometrics as it is applied can read on without fear of cryptical matrix equations, moment generating functions, asymptotic distributions, and the like. We will provide citations and references for the important theorems and results we use, and a brief bibliography at the end of the chapter will serve as a guide for those interested in a more theoretical and rigorous approach.

MODEL SPECIFICATION

The first step in the development of an econometric marketing model calls for the specification of the mathematical equation or equations for the model: that is, we must define the output variables and come up with explicit mathematical relationships linking these variables to a set of explanatory variables on the right-hand side of the equation. For marketing policy models we are typically concerned with market share, sales, or revenue as output variables.

To illustrate how one goes about specifying a marketing model, consider the following generalized structure for a marketing model described by Eq. (6.1).

$$S = f(Z, C, X, S_{t-n}, \epsilon). \tag{6.1}$$

Suppose that we are dealing with a multiproduct firm; then we would need to specify at least one equation of the type given as Eq. (6.1) for every product produced by the firm. In Eq. (6.1) we used the symbol S to denote total sales volume for the given product. (S could also denote either market share or total revenue for that product.) On the right-hand side of the equation, the symbol f denotes a functional relationship. The explanatory variables on the right-hand side include Z, which is used to represent a variety of management policy variables. In the case of a marketing model, the relevant policy variables might include price, advertising, public relations, product quality, sales force, and distribution. Some of these variables might be expressed in dollar values; in other cases they may take the form of binary or dummy variables which simply indicate whether or not a particular policy is in effect. We utilize the symbol C in Eq. (6.1) to denote the influence of competitive variables on product sales. By competitive variables we mean those variables which are determined by the behavior of our competitors. These are variables over which our firm has little or no control. Although we may not be able to control the behavior of our competitors, we may be able to come up with reasonable hypotheses about how they behave. Among the competitive variables that we may want to include in a marketing model would be the price and advertising strategy of competing firms in our industry. Next, we use the symbol X to represent the effect of those variables that affect the sales of our firm but are not affected by the behavior of our firm. These would be national economic indicators for the countries in which our firm sells its product. Gross national product, total employment, unemployment and the consumer price index might all be examples of external economic indicators which affect the sales of our firm. It is also possible to include such variables as wars and natural disasters in the same category. While it is impossible to predict wars and natural disasters, it is not impossible to model the effects which these variables have on the sales of our products. In the case of national economic indicators, these must be read into the model from some outside source or generated by a national econometric model. To take the example of the United States, there are several service bureaus that sell national econometric forecasts for use in marketing models of the type described here.

Also included on the right-hand side of Eq. (6.1) is the variable S_{t-n}, which is a lagged output variable. In this case the subscript n can take on the values $1, 2, 3, \ldots$. The reason for including S_{t-n} is to allow for the possibility that sales in time period t depend in part on sales in $t-1, t-2, t-3, \ldots$. Although the inclusion of lagged output variables in a marketing policy model may cause us some difficulties with parameter estimation, lagged output variables nevertheless represent an important form of structural specification and should at least be mentioned.

Finally, the last variable to be included on the right-hand side of Eq. (6.1) is ϵ, which is used to denote a random error term. In a sense, ϵ represents a catchall variable that is included to account for that portion of the variation in S that has not been explained by the other four types of variables. We discuss the error term in detail later in this chapter.

In the case of a multiproduct firm in which there may be explicit interrelationships among the sales of the different products produced by the firm, we may want to take into consideration the substitutability or complementarity of different products in the firm's product line. In other words, if a firm happens to manufacture both trucks and truck tires, then it is reasonable to assume that the more trucks the firm sells, the more tires it will sell as well. Trucks and truck tires would be an example of complementary products. If we were explaining the sale of truck tires, then we probably would want to include truck sales as a right-hand side variable in our model. If, on the other hand, a firm produces radios in several different size and price ranges, then medium-priced radios may be a substitute for higher-priced radios, and this relationship must be taken into consideration in the firm's marketing policy model.

To further illustrate how one goes about constructing marketing models, consider the simple example given in Eq. (6.2).

$$S = \beta_0 + \beta_1 P + \beta_2 ADV + \beta_3 PR + \beta_4 P^c + \beta_5 ADV^c + \beta_6 GNP + \epsilon. \tag{6.2}$$

The coefficients $\beta_0, \beta_1, \ldots, \beta_6$ are parameters of the model which are to be estimated through the use of standard econometric techniques. Although Eq. (6.2) is a linear model, it contains many of the concepts required in building more complex, nonlinear marketing models. Equation (6.2) contains three marketing policy variables—price, advertising, and public relations. These variables are expressed, respectively, by the symbols P, ADV, and PR. Price will, of course, be measured in the appropriate monetary unit. Advertising may be measured either in monetary units or in some other form such as column inches for newspaper advertising, minutes or hours of television time, or number of billboards in place. Alternatively, advertising may also be expressed as a binary or dummy variable in such a way that ADV may take on a value of zero if a particular policy is not in effect, or it may take on a value of one if a policy has been implemented. The PR variable may be expressed in a similar form. Our example model also includes two competitive variables, P^c and ADV^c, which are used to denote the pricing and advertising policy of our competitor. If we have more than one competitor in this industry, it may be necessary to include competitive variables for each of the more important competitors in our industry. The next variable included in Eq. (6.2) is GNP, which is simply the notation for Gross National Product. GNP is included in order to illustrate the possible effect which the national economy may be exerting on the sales of our product. GNP is simply one of many possible national economic indicators that may be appropriate for our model. Unfortunately, there are no textbooks written to prescribe the best among the leading national economic indicators for particular products. Selecting the best indicators is a matter of experience and judgment. The final variable included in Eq. (6.2) is a normally distributed random variable ϵ which is assumed to have a constant variance and a zero expected value. We discuss it thoroughly later.

The model described in Eq. (6.2) above is admittedly simple, but it does include many of the important features of more complex marketing policy models. It should be emphasized that there is no point whatsoever in restricting ourselves to linear models for marketing policy. Indeed, it is quite likely that logarithmic, price–ratio, and higher-order-polynomial relationships will be encountered, giving rise to various forms of nonlinearity. The estimation methodology we present later will be applicable to linear models, logarithmic models, polynomial models, and a variety of relationships beyond the simple model in Eq. (6.2).

In the case of a multiproduct firm, we would find it necessary to produce an entire set of equations of the type exemplified by Eq. (6.2). If some products were either complements or substitutes, then we would have an interdependent system of simultaneous equations.

The approach taken above assumes that it is possible to model the firm's sales or market-share directly; that is, we have assumed that we can formulate an equation explaining the behavior of sales for each product produced by the firm. Unfortunately, in many instances this may not be possible. We may find it necessary to build a model of the entire industry and then to construct a separate model explaining our firm's share of the market. In this and the next chapter we present three examples of econometric industry models—textiles, tobacco, and coffee.

Generally speaking, we normally try the direct approach to marketing models, hoping to avoid the extra expense of modeling an entire industry. But in some cases this approach is an utter impossibility. Whether one can get by with the direct approach depends in part on the competitive structure of the industry. If the industry consists of a large number of firms and approaches the economist's ideal of a perfectly competitive industry or a monopolistically competitive industry, then the direct approach may be appropriate. However, if the industry is characterized by a relatively small number of firms and approaches what economists call an oligopoly, then one may be forced to model the entire industry.

The specification of marketing policy models is both an art and a science. On the other hand, it requires a considerable knowledge of the actual product markets of the firm. Marketing policy models should be based on sound judgment and sound economic theory. In other words, only those variables which make intuitive sense to the model builders and the market analysts should be included on the right-hand side of the model. One of the factors that differentiates marketing policy models from straight forecasting models is explanatory power. Marketing policy models are designed not only to perform policy simulation experiments to test the effects of alternative marketing policies on sales and revenue but are also useful devices for explaining the behavior of markets, thus enabling the firm's market analysts to obtain a more complete understanding of how the product markets function.

If we are going to build econometric models for more than a dozen products, then it pays to develop a market analysis questionnaire to be used to interview the respective product managers. The interviews should be conducted by the market analyst who will actually build the models. If the questionnaire is carefully designed, a good analyst can go directly from the answers to the questions to model specification.

There are at least two advantages to using a market analysis questionnaire. First, it puts the analyst in touch with the person who should know the most about the market for the product being modeled. Second, it reduces the number of return trips required by the analyst to obtain information from the project manager.

This approach was employed by Dresser Industries to specify the econometric models described in the paper by Charles H. Hatfield, Jr. and Bryant K. Kershaw in Chapter 11. At the end of this chapter we illustrate a market analysis questionnaire developed for Northwest Industries and successfully used by eight of their operating companies.

PARAMETER ESTIMATION

Once we have obtained a preliminary specification of our marketing policy model, we must then collect the approprate historical inputs as time series or cross-sectional data for estimating the parameters of the model. The decision to develop a marketing policy model is tantamount to a decision to commit the firm to the establishment and maintenance of a substantial marketing database. Indeed, the development of marketing policy models is virtually impossible unless the firm has an adequate marketing information system.

Generally speaking, we need a *minimum* of seven to ten observations to obtain the parameter estimates of relatively simple econometric equations. More complex models and equations involving more than, say, five or six right-hand variables may need substantially more historical observations for parameter estimation. Ideally, we would like to have in excess of 30 observations. Unfortunately, in the real world we frequently do not have the luxury of the number of observations that we would like to have. First, there is a problem as to whether or not the firm has been collecting historical data concerning its own pricing, advertising, public relations, sales force, product quality, and distribution policies. Frequently, a firm may find itself in a position in which it is simply impossible to construct a marketing model with the limited data available. However, if a firm is seriously considering building a marketing policy model within the next four to five years, then it may begin collecting the appropriate historical data now in order to be ready to produce workable marketing policy models four to five years in the future.

Another problem area concerning data is the fact that it may be extremely difficult to get information on pricing and advertising policies of competitors. Some industries have trade associations which produce reasonably good estimates of advertising budgets. In other industries, however, there may be virtually no data available on pricing, advertising, etc. for the different firms in the industry. The external variables generated by the national economy can be read in from national econometric models. In addition to providing national econometric forecasts, most of the firms which sell econometric models also provide their clients with historical data on the national economy. In many cases these data may be worth as much or more than the econometric models. By purchasing one's national economic data from one of the econometric service bureaus, one can be reasonably certain that the data are accurate and timely and based on the latest information available through published government sources. Collecting one's own national economic data can be an extremely frustrating process, for government economic series are constantly changing.

In many cases the historical data available for marketing models may be inadequate and the firm may have to supplement its existing supply of historical data through survey research. Through use of a carefully designed questionnaire, it may be possible to extract from the firm's customers or potential customers the information necessary to build a marketing policy model. Survey data are particularly useful in evaluating such abstract concepts as product quality and the effects of different forms of advertising on consumer behavior. Indeed, survey research may be the only way in which one can obtain reliable information of this type.

Once we have collected the necessary historical data and have specified the theoretical model which we intend to use, then we must *estimate* the values of the parameters of the model. We begin by assuming that the model takes the form of a linear equation, although this assumption is later relaxed in favor of several alternative forms of nonlinearity.

The simplest form of linear model relating an output variable Y to a right-hand side external variable X would be $Y = \beta_0 + \beta_1 X$. In such a model, Y is represented as an exact linear function of X, and β_0 and β_1 are called the parameters of the model. As X takes on different values, the model generates different values of Y by multiplying β_1 times X and adding β_0 to the result. If the value of β_1 is positive, then Y and X vary directly, and if the value of β_1 is negative, then Y and X vary inversely. The value of β_0 is interpreted as the value that Y takes on when X takes on the value zero. However, it will be seen that it is often difficult to assign much confidence to estimated values of β_0 since very often the data values from which the model is estimated will not approach the value of $X = 0$. Thus, in practice, it will be somewhat hazardous to put much weight on this estimate of β_0.

A graphical representation of the model $Y = \beta_0 + \beta_1 X$ is provided in Fig. 6.1. The graph depicts a direct relationship between X and Y, and the graph was generated by letting $\beta_0 = 3$ and $\beta_1 = .5$. In Chapter 5 the same type of model was encountered except that then Y was related to time instead of an explanatory external factor X. Also in Chapter 5 we were concerned only with mechanical methods for estimating the time trend model, so we were not concerned with a distinction between the true line and the estimated line, a distinction we now develop.

In developing a model that will be applicable to business and economic data, it is essential that the model incorporate some provision for randomness, inasmuch as economic relationships that we observe in the real world are never *exact* relationships such as the one pictured in Fig. 6.1. Rather than assuming that Y is an exact function of X,

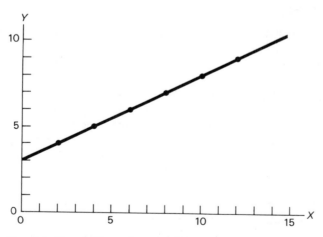

Fig. 6.1 Simple linear function $Y = 3 + .5X$.

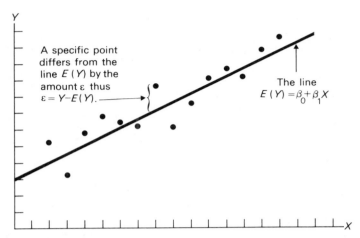

Fig. 6.2 The line $E(Y) = \beta_0 + \beta_1 X$ and data points generated by the model $Y = \beta_0 + \beta_1 X + \epsilon$ ($\beta_0 = 3, \beta_1 = .5$).

we can assume that Y is a function of X and a random error of ϵ. In this case the simplest linear model would be of the form:

$$Y = \beta_0 + \beta_1 X + \epsilon. \tag{6.3}$$

Data generated by a model of this form would not lie exactly along a straight line as in Fig. 6.1, but the data would lie *approximately* along a line. The deviations from the line $\beta_0 + \beta_1 X$ would of course depend on the size of the random error term ϵ.

Now the specific Y values do not coincide with the line, although the line shows where an average or typical Y value would fall. The line $\beta_0 + \beta_1 X$ shows the average of *expected* values of Y, and this is usually denoted by

$$E(Y) = \beta_0 + \beta_1 X. \tag{6.4}$$

And an actual value of Y will differ from its expected value by ϵ, so that $Y = E(Y) + \epsilon$ which is the same as writing $Y = \beta_0 + \beta_1 X + \epsilon$. Equation (6.3) is the theoretical *model* describing Y, while Eq. (6.4) represents the expected or average relationship between X and Y.

In Fig. 6.2 we show a set of 15 data points that are generated from the model $Y = 3 + .5X + \epsilon$ where ϵ is a random variable, the exact probability distribution of which will be discussed below. For the moment the important idea to note about the figure is that the points (the X and Y pairs) lie roughly along a line, but do not fall exactly on the line. The 15 points that are plotted in Fig. 6.2 are given in Table 6.1.

When we gather data on economic variables, we typically find ourselves in the position of having data like that shown in Table 6.1. Unfortunately, the exact parameters (intercept = 3, slope = .5) that underlie the relationship are unknown. The basic problem then is to estimate the parameters of the relationship between the two variables. Once we have done this, we will then have to analyze how good our estimates are likely to be, since there is always the chance that we have misguessed the true parameters by a large amount.

Ordinary Least Squares

The best known method for estimating the unknown parameters of economic models is the method of least squares. We have already seen its use in Chapter 5 for time trend models. In addition to being popular for its ease of use as seen earlier, the method possesses many good statistical properties which we discuss now.

The model that generated the data in Fig. 6.2 was of the form $Y = \beta_0 + \beta_1 X + \epsilon$ so that each particular Y value differed from the line $\beta_0 + \beta_1 X$ by the amount of the error term ϵ. If we were to select some values b_0 and b_1 to be our estimates of the parameters β_0 and β_1, then these values would define an estimated line $b_0 + b_1 X$. Using these estimated parameters (also called *estimated coefficients*), we could then compute an expected or predicted value of Y for each X. This computed value of Y is written as $\hat{Y}$ and thus we have

$$\hat{Y} = b_0 + b_1 X, \tag{6.5}$$

which is the estimated form of Eq. (6.4). It is analogous to Eq. (5.11) except for the switch of t and X.

It is important to understand the difference between the actual but usually unobserved line defined by $E(Y) = \beta_0 + \beta_1 X$ and the estimated line defined by $\hat{Y} = b_0 + b_1 X$. The difference is simply that the former is *the* line of average relationship that we seek to estimate, and the latter is *a* line that we use to estimate $E(Y)$. As we choose different values of b_0 and b_1, we have different estimating lines.

The method of least squares proceeds to estimate b_0 and b_1 such that the sum of

Table 6.1. Sample data plotted in Fig. 6.2.

x	y
1	3.05
2	5.65
3	2.70
4	6.05
5	7.15
6	6.15
7	5.90
8	8.65
9	4.95
10	7.10
11	8.80
12	9.60
13	8.60
14	10.60
15	11.55

the squared differences of the actual Y's from the estimated line is a minimum. That is, since any b_0 and b_1 will define a line $\hat{Y}$, we define the difference of actual Y values from the $\hat{Y}$ line by $e = Y - \hat{Y}$. The goal of least squares is to choose b_0 and b_1 so that the sum of the squared errors, Σe^2, is a minimum, where the summation extends over the sample size, n.

The calculation of the estimated coefficients b_0 and b_1 is a fairly easy and well-known process. If the sum of squared errors (which may be expressed for n observations on X and Y as $\Sigma(Y - b_0 - b_1X)^2$) is differentiated with respect to b_0 and b_1, two equations that describe b_0 and b_1 in terms of the observed values of Y and X result. The computer can easily solve these two equations to obtain b_0 and b_1. In Table 6.2, we show the estimated values of b_0 and b_1 that result from executing the SIMPLAN command ESTIMATE with the data for X and Y that were displayed in Table 6.2. (Readers who wish to explore the mathematics of the process in more detail will find that the book by Wonnacott and Wonnacott (1970) provides a very readable discussion of the mathematics involved. In equations (5.9) and (5.10) we gave the

Table 6.2 Output from ESTIMATE command: least-squares regression

```
ANALYSIS.

ESTIMATE Y X


LEAST SQUARES REGRESSION
```

ESTIMATED EQUATION IS: Y=0.49571*X+3.13429			
INDEPENDENT VARIABLES	ESTIMATED COEFFICIENT	STANDARD ERROR	T-TEST
X	0.4957	0.0794	6.2396
CONSTANT	3.1343	0.7223	4.3391

```
   NUMBER OF OBSERVATIONS USED =     15
  R-SQUARED=   0.7497          F-STATISTIC(  1, 13)=    38.9325
    ADJUSTED R-SQUARED=  0.7304    DURBIN-WATSON STATISTIC=   2.5801
    STANDARD ERROR=       1.3294   DEGREES OF FREEDOM FOR T-TEST= 13
  SUM OF SQUARED ERRORS=        22.9748

ANALYSIS.
```

equations for estimating the slope and intercept where t is the right-hand side variable. The corresponding equation when X is used should be obvious.)

The ESTIMATE command is followed first by a variable name that is to be the dependent (or left-hand side) variable, and thereafter the independent (or right-hand side) variable is specified. The coefficient value shown for X is the estimated b_1. The estimated value of b_0 is indicated next to the word "constant." Just as b_1 is the coefficient of the variable X, we may think of the intercept term b_0 as the estimated coefficient associated with a "constant" variable whose value is always one; that is, the estimated model $\hat{Y} = b_0 + b_1X$ could also be thought of as $\hat{Y} = b_0(1) + b_1X$.

The data that were used in the ESTIMATE command were produced by adding a random error term onto the exact model $E(Y) = 3 + .5X$. As is obvious from the computer output, the least-squares method managed to reproduce the original line fairly closely, but not exactly. The estimated line is $\hat{Y} = 3.13 + .496X$. Also the reader should note that the estimated line did not fit the data exactly, but errors were involved such that the sum of the squared errors was 22.9748 as shown on the printout.

Test Statistics

Having observed above that the least-squares line comes close to the true line, we now wish to investigate in some detail what we mean by "close." And in the process of discussing how close the least-squares line is to the true line, we will be able to devise means for testing whether an observed relationship between Y and X is likely to be a random occurrence, or whether the observed relationship is due to some systematic factors. Also the reason for distinguishing among the three separate Eqs. (6.3), (6.4), and (6.5) should become clear.

In the discussion above we began from a hypothesized true relationship line that was assumed to be of the form $E(Y) = \beta_0 + \beta_1 X$. Then for some values of X, the actual values of Y that we observed were generated by the process of adding a random error term ϵ to this equation, so that $Y = \beta_0 + \beta_1 X + \epsilon$. Obviously the values of Y will be influenced by the random error ϵ. The distribution of ϵ will thus clearly play a crucial role in influencing the values of b_0 and b_1, since they were computed from observed X and Y values and the latter values depend on ϵ.

In order to make statements about the way the least-squares estimators b_0 and b_1 behave, it is necessary to know something about the distribution of ϵ or else to be willing to make some assumptions about the behavior of ϵ. In practice one almost never has any reliable knowledge about the behavior of ϵ, so the practical solution is to make some reasonable assumptions. And, as will be seen later, the assumptions that are commonly made can frequently be tested to make sure that a model is not constructed on the basis of completely unrealistic assumptions about the error term.

In Fig. 6.3 we presented a scatter of points that resulted from adding random error terms ϵ to the line $E(Y) = 3 + .5X$. The particular values of the random error terms were obtained by generating values with these properties:

- $E(\epsilon) = 0$. On average the distribution of the error terms was zero. Since each Y value consisted of $E(Y) + \epsilon$, this implies that the values of Y center around the line given by $E(Y)$.
- $V(\epsilon) = \sigma^2$. All of the different error terms had the same variance, denoted by σ^2. In the example problem, a variance of 2.25 was used. This implies that the standard deviation of ϵ was the square root of 2.25, or 1.5.
- The error terms were independent of one another; that is, there was no correlation between the generated value of ϵ_1 and ϵ_2 nor between any other pair of error terms. Each realized value of this random error was independent of the other values.
- The error terms followed a normal distribution. The distribution of ϵ was the familiar bell-shaped curve known as the normal curve.
- The error terms were statistically independent of the values of X; that is, the values of ϵ were completely unrelated to the values of X.

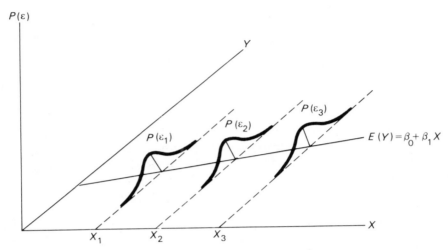

Fig. 6.3 Graphical display of the assumptions about ϵ.

Since these assumptions are very basic to the rest of the material in this chapter, we present a graphical display of these assumptions in Fig. 6.3. (The vertical axis represents the probability, $P(\epsilon)$, that the error term ϵ will take on a particular value.)

The assumption that $E(\epsilon) = 0$ is illustrated by the fact that the distribution of all the ϵ terms center on the line $E(Y) = \beta_0 + \beta_1 X$. The assumption that $V(\epsilon) = \sigma^2$ is illustrated by the fact that all the distribution curves have the same spread. The independence of different values of ϵ implies that wherever beneath the $P(\epsilon_1)$ curve the value of ϵ_1 actually falls (whether above or below the line $E(Y)$), there will be no relation between this value and other realized values such as ϵ_2 and ϵ_3. The normality assumption implies that each of the bell curves follows the normal distribution. The independence of ϵ and X implies that the realized values of ϵ will bear no relation to the level of X.

Although these are not the only assumptions that can be made (and later in this chapter we will deal with other assumptions that might be made), they are indeed quite simple. They are also very important assumptions for the following reason. Economists and statisticians have shown that if these assumptions hold regarding the true but usually unknown error ϵ, then application of the least-squares method to the observed values of Y and X yields estimators of β_0 and β_1 that have very desirable statistical properties. In particular, the least-squares estimators b_0 and b_1 of the true parameters β_0 and β_1 can be shown to be unbiased and minimum variance estimators. The fact that the estimators are unbiased guarantees that the values of b are distributed evenly around the corresponding parameter β, or that $E(b_0) = \beta_0$ and $E(b_1) = \beta_1$. The minimum variance property says simply that the spread of the distribution of b is minimum for the class of all unbiased estimators.

These properties can be easily illustrated. In Fig. 6.4 we show two estimators b_1 and b_1^* that could be used to estimate β_1. The estimator b_1 is unbiased, and this is illus-

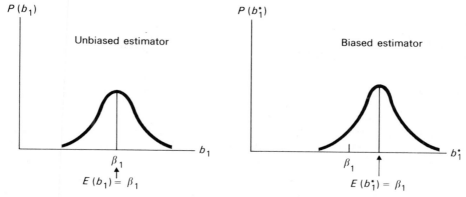

Fig. 6.4 Comparison of an unbiased estimator b_1 and a biased estimator b_1^*.

trated by the fact that its distribution centers on β_1. The estimator b_1^* is a biased estimator, and this is illustrated by the fact that the estimator does *not* have its distribution centered on β_1. Clearly, a lack of bias is a desirable property for an estimator to have, for it implies that coefficient estimates are on target on average.

Although the absence of bias is certainly one property that it is desirable for an estimator to have, it is not the only property that we would like in an estimator. Being "on target on average" may not be very good if the spread about the average is very wide. A good analogy might be that a set of forecasts for 12 consecutives quarters could be on target *on average*, yet no single forecast would be very close to the true value. In addition to the degree of bias, what is required is some indication that the *dispersion about the target be small*. And as mentioned above, it has been shown that the least squares estimators in fact yield the minimum dispersion or variance of all unbiased estimators.

In Figure 6.5 we compare two unbiased estimators of β_1 which we denote by b_1 and b_1^{**}. The least-squares estimator b_1 has smaller variance than the other unbiased

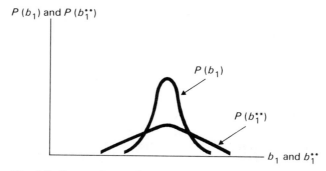

Fig. 6.5 Comparison of two unbiased estimators b_1 and b_1^{**} where b_1 is the more efficient.

estimator b_1^{**}. Its distribution clusters more tightly around the target. Since the distribution of b_1 has less extreme tails to its distribution, there is far less chance of coming up with a poor estimate when using b_1 instead of b_1^{**}. Statisticians often refer to the estimator with less variance or spread as being more *efficient*.

One of the important features of the least-squares estimators is that they are not only unbiased but they are also more efficient (have smaller variance) than any other unbiased estimators. Regardless of the data employed, if the assumptions mentioned above are met, then the application of the least-squares method will yield the most efficient unbiased estimators. (Strictly speaking, they are the most efficient unbiased estimators within the class of *linear* estimators; that is, estimators obtained by solving linear equations. This is a technical point that is of little import to our discussion.)

Although the foregoing discussion has usually referred to the slope coefficient estimator b_1, it should be noted that our results concerning bias and efficiency apply equally to both the slope and intercept estimators.

t-statistic   We are now in a position to consider the typical problem of an analyst who tries to measure the relationship between Y and X from observed data and determine if in fact there is any systematic relationship. If the assumptions given above are met, economists have shown that a relationship between Y and X can be tested statistically based on the use of a *t*-distribution. The test is based on the fact that $(b_0 - \beta_0)/s_{b_0}$ and $(b_1 - \beta_1)/s_{b_1}$ both follow the *t*-distribution, where s_{b_0} and s_{b_1} are the estimated standard errors of the least-squares coefficients. These standard errors are included in most standard computer program outputs for least squares. In the SIMPLAN output from the ESTIMATE command shown in Table 6.3, the standard errors are shown immediately to the right of the estimated coefficients.

Table 6.3 Output from the ESTIMATE command: testing the individual coefficients

```
ESTIMATE Y X

LEAST SQUARES REGRESSION
```

ESTIMATED EQUATION IS: Y=0.51393*X+3.32857			
INDEPENDENT VARIABLES	ESTIMATED COEFFICIENT	STANDARD ERROR	T- TEST
X	0.5139	0.0744	6.9037
CONSTANT	3.3286	0.6768	4.9178

```
   NUMBER OF OBSERVATIONS USED =    15
   R-SQUARED=   0.7857              F-STATISTIC(  1,  13)=   47.6614
   ADJUSTED R-SQUARED=  0.7692      DURBIN-WATSON STATISTIC=   2.5569
   STANDARD ERROR=       1.2457     DEGREES OF FREEDOM FOR T-TEST= 13
   SUM OF SQUARED ERRORS=       20.1717

ANALYSIS.
```

The procedure for carrying out the *t*-test is as follows. An analyst begins by formulating a null hypothesis. Since the case of no relationship between Y and X is captured by the case of $\beta_1 = 0$, this is very often the null hypothesis. A simple alternative hypothesis would be that $\beta_1 \neq 0$. Next the analyst must choose some probability level that will guide him or her in the selection of the null hypothesis or the alternative hypothesis; that is, based on the hypothesis that $\beta_1 = 0$, an analyst can compute a t-statistic, and from appropriate tables (discussed below) can determine how likely it is to have observed the least-squares results obtained if in fact the true state of nature was $\beta_1 = 0$. If this likelihood is too small, the hypothesis that $\beta_1 = 0$ can be discarded in favor of the alternative hypothesis that $\beta_1 \neq 0$. Since this is the same thing as concluding that there is some systematic relationship between Y and X, this procedure provides the analyst with a method for systematically testing for a relationship between variables.

We now illustrate this procedure for the sample data shown in Table 6.1. Note that in this case we are dealing with a problem where we know there is a relationship between Y and X because the values of Y were generated by adding a random error to a linear function of the values of X. However, our example provides a convenient illustration, since we are in the fortunate position of omniscience here: we constructed data for which we know there is a relationship, and we wish to apply the methodology *as if* we were ignorant of the relationship to see if we would in fact have discovered the relationship based on the methodology alone and not on the omniscience.

From the printout of the ESTIMATE command, we see that the least-squares estimate of b_1 is .4957 with a standard error estimated to be .0794. For the null hypothesis that $\beta_1 = 0$, we can compute the following t value:

$$t = \frac{.4957 - 0}{.0794} = 6.24 \tag{6.6}$$

Obviously, the t value for testing that a coefficient is equal to 0 is simply the ratio of the estimated coefficient to its estimated standard error. Since this computation is so easily performed and since this is a hypothesis that is so frequently of interest, this t value is often shown in the computer printout. In Table 6.3 the t values are printed next to the estimated coefficients and the estimated standard errors. Thus, to test whether a coefficient is statistically different from zero, an analyst need only consult the printout. As will be seen later, however, there are often circumstances in which the formula given above is useful. Such circumstances involve tests of hypotheses other than $\beta_1 = 0$.

To complete the test, an analyst need only select a desired probability or test level and compare the computed t value against the appropriate table value. This is most easily illustrated by the graph shown in Fig. 6.6. The graph shows values of the t distribution, a symmetric distribution that is centered on zero and has the property that the area under the curve is equal to one. As indicated on the graph, only five percent of the area under the curve lies outside of the limits indicated by $t = 2.160$ and $t = -2.160$. This area (shaded on the graph) is the area where a t value will fall only five percent of the time. The values ± 2.160 were determined by reference to Table B.1 of Appendix B. To find the appropriate value, one need only know the level of the test (five percent here) and the degrees of freedom. The degrees of freedom are shown to be 13 in the computer printout in Table 6.3. The degrees of freedom (or d.f.) can be found simply by subtracting from the sample size the number of coefficients estimated.

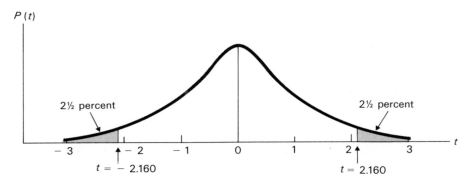

Fig. 6.6 Performing a t-test on $\beta_1 = 0$, a five percent test with 13 degrees of freedom (d.f.).

Since the present sample size is 15, and two coefficients are estimated (a slope and an intercept), d.f. $= 15 - 2 = 13$.

Since the computed t value of 6.24 falls outside of the region between ±2.160, we realize that there is less than a five percent chance of finding this computed t value if in fact the hypothesis $\beta_1 = 0$ were correct. Thus, we would reject the hypothesis that $\beta_1 = 0$ on the basis of the sample evidence, and instead accept the alternative hypothesis that $\beta_1 \neq 0$. In so doing, we are concluding that there is statistical evidence of a relationship between the observed values of Y and X.

How would the results have been interpreted if the computed t value had fallen between the values $t = -2.160$ and $t = 2.160$? Would this have been evidence that there was not a relationship between X and Y? The answer is no, this would not be a correct interpretation of the results. A t value within the interval ± 2.160 would mean that we could not reject $\beta_1 = 0$, but this is not at all the same thing as proving that β_1 *is* in fact zero. It would simply mean that for the data at hand this hypothesis could not be rejected. Saying something cannot be ruled out is not, however, the same thing as saying it is demonstrated to be true. We return to this point when we discuss a least-squares model with several variables on the right-hand side.

The test of the relationship between Y and X could also have been carried out by constructing a *confidence interval*. Since the computed b_1 value was .496, we could form a 95 percent confidence interval for the true value of β_1 by using .496 $\pm t \times$ .0794 where t denotes the correct t value (depending on d.f. and significance level) and the .0794 represents the estimated standard error of b_1 as shown in Table 6.3. The appropriate t value to use in constructing this confidence interval is exactly the same t value that was used in the hypothesis test, namely, 2.160. The correct 95 percent confidence interval for the true value of β_1 is thus seen to be .496 $\pm$ 2.160 $\times$ .0794 or .496 $\pm$ .172. The interval thus consists of all values between .324 and .668. Two features should be noted about this interval.

First, the interval does not contain the value 0, and this is no accident. Rejection of the hypothesis that $\beta_1 = 0$ is equivalent to saying that the corresponding confidence interval does not contain the value 0. A second point to note is that the confidence interval does in fact contain the correct value of β_1 (known to be .50 in this sample problem).

It is worth stressing that confidence intervals are rather unusual types of probabilistic statements. In fact, strictly speaking confidence intervals are not really *probabilistic* statements at all, in that probability is an *a priori* concept. Although we speak of a 95 percent confidence interval for the true value of β_1, this does *not* mean that there is a 95 percent chance that the true value of β_1 will fall within this interval. The reason is simply that β_1 is not random, but rather a fixed number. In our previous illustrative example we happened to know that it was .50, but in general the analyst will not know the value. The key point then is that once the confidence interval is constructed, it either does contain the true value of β_1 or it does not. The analyst who constructs a 95 percent confidence interval will either have bracketed the true value within his or her interval, or will have missed it on this particular problem. In other words, the procedure will bracket the true parameter 95 percent of the time if we compute numerous confidence intervals for different problems; that is, there is 95 percent confidence associated with the basic procedure, although for any specific problem the confidence interval is either correct in capturing the true parameter or it is incorrect and does not contain the true parameter.

Thus far we have assumed that we have no particular knowledge about the relationship of Y and X, and that we merely want to test the null hypothesis of $\beta_1 = 0$ against an alternative hypothesis that $\beta_1 \neq 0$. This is called a two-tail test because, as the graph in Fig. 6.6 illustrates, the rejection region includes areas in both the positive and negative extremes of the distribution. It will often be the case that we have enough *a priori* knowledge that we can frame a null hypothesis as $\beta_1 = 0$ and the alternative hypothesis as $\beta_1 > 0$; that is, we can effectively rule out a negative relationship based on theoretical considerations and test between the null hypothesis of no relationship and an alternative hypothesis of a positive relationship. It is intuitively reasonable that if one has this type of *a priori* knowledge about the possible sign of the relationship, then it ought to require less evidence from the sample to establish that a relationship exists. And this is indeed the case.

To construct a five percent test of the hypothesis that $\beta_1 = 0$ against the alternative that $\beta_1 > 0$, the appropriate procedure is to select a t value such that five percent of the area is left under the upper (positive) end of the curve. The situation is represented in Fig. 6.7 for the case of the sample problem we have been considering. For reasons that should be obvious after a glance at Fig. 6.7, this is known as a one-tail test. The appropriate t value to leave five percent of the area in the upper tail is found from the t tables (Table B.1) in Appendix B to be 1.771 when there are 13 d.f. as in this example. Comparison with Fig. 6.6 will show that in the case of a one-tail test, not quite so large a computed t value is required to reject the null hypothesis. The interpretation of this is simply that the *a priori* knowledge that a negative relationship can be ruled out, we then do not require as much evidence from our data to establish a positive relationship. Without previous knowledge about the direction of the relationship, the sample data must speak more loudly to reject the null hypothesis.

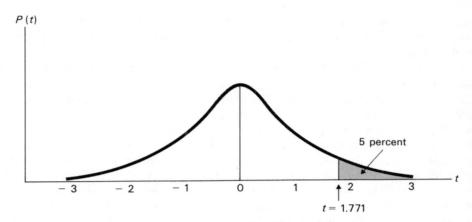

Fig. 6.7 Performing a t-test on $\beta'_1 = 0$, a five percent one-tail test with 13 d.f.

R-Square   A statistic that is often useful in interpreting a regression equation is the R-square (R^2) value that was discussed in Chapter 5. As mentioned there, the R^2 is a number between zero and one that measures the strength of the association between Y and X. If all of the Y values lie exactly on the estimated line $\hat{Y} = b_0 + b_1X$, then $R^2 = 1.0$, and if all of the Y values are completely randomly scattered around the estimated line, then $R^2 = 0$. Equation (5.20) provided an interpretation within the context of a time trend model, but the same interpretation discussed there can be applied here.

The R^2 value can also be interpreted in several other ways that are often useful. One interpretation is that R^2 is the square of the simple correlation coefficient between Y and X. The simple correlation coefficient is defined by the equation:

$$r = \frac{\Sigma(Y - \bar{Y})(X - \bar{X})}{\sqrt{\Sigma(Y - \bar{Y})^2\Sigma(X - \bar{X})^2}}, \tag{6.7}$$

and has a value that varies between -1 and $+1$. Negative values indicate an inverse relationship between X and Y, while positive values indicate a positive association. Values at the extremes of -1 and $+1$ occur only in the event of perfect inverse linear association and perfect positive linear association. In the event of no linear relationship between the X and Y values, the value of r is 0 as is the case with R^2.

In the regression example of Table 6.3, the R^2 was shown to be .7497. The square root of this value is .8658, which is the value that one obtains from Eq. (6.7). Simple correlations can be calculated with SIMPLAN by using the CORR command as illustrated in Table 6.4. The CORR command computes all possible simple correlation coefficients between the specified variable list (here simply X and Y), and displays them in a square table. Since the correlation of a variable with itself is one, there are always ones down the diagonal of the correlation matrix. Also, since Eq. (6.7) is symmetric with respect to X and Y, the correlation of X and Y is the same as the correlation of Y and X. For this reason the elements below the main diagonal in the correlation matrix will be identical to the corresponding elements above the main diagonal.

In the simple regression model with Y and X, there is a possible ambiguity as to the sign of r if it is computed by taking the square root of R^2. The solution is very simply that r will have the same sign as the slope coefficient b_1. The foregoing ESTI-MATE and CORR examples illustrate that this holds true.

R^2 is often interpreted as a percentage; that is, the value of R^2 for the example of .7497 could be regarded as 74.97 percent. The reason for this percentage interpretation is that Eq. (5.20) for R^2 can be reexpressed as:

$$R^2 = \frac{\Sigma(\hat{Y}-\bar{Y})^2}{\Sigma(Y-\bar{Y})^2} = \frac{\text{explained variation in } Y}{\text{total variation in } Y}, \tag{6.8}$$

where the explained variation is the variation or movement in Y that is *explained* by the right-hand side variable X. The movement is said to be explained in the sense that $\hat{Y}$ differs from $\bar{Y}$ because of the tendency of $\hat{Y}$ to rise or fall with different levels of X. This is illustrated graphically in Fig. 6.8.

Table 6.4. Output from CORR command: the simple correlation coefficient of X and Y

ANALYSIS.

CORR X Y

CORRELATION MATRIX BASED ON	15 OBSERVATIONS
X	Y
X 1.0000	0.8658
Y 0.8658	1.0000

ANALYSIS.

The matter of judging an R^2 is a matter about which there is some considerable debate, and there is limited agreement about the usefulness that can be attributed to the R^2 in all cases. As was stated above, an R^2 close to unity is in some sense "good" in that the right-hand side X variable explains a large proportion of the movement in Y. However, a problem arises in that this correlation can arise from a number of different sources, and a high R^2 may *not necessarily* mean a good model.

One would like to think that a high R^2 in some sense implies that X causes Y with some certainty, but in fact no such interpretation can be assigned to the R^2. There is no way that a statistical measure can establish or prove causation. What a statistical measure can do is show that a certain set of data is or is not consistent with a hypothesized causal relationship, but this does not consititute "proof." In fact, in a simple regression of Y on X, the resulting R^2 will be identical to the R^2 that results from running a regression of X on Y, so clearly the R^2 is of no use in determining if X caused Y or if Y caused X.

Another problem that arises in interpreting the R^2 is that equations estimated with time series data often will display a high value of R^2 (say, .80 or .90) because

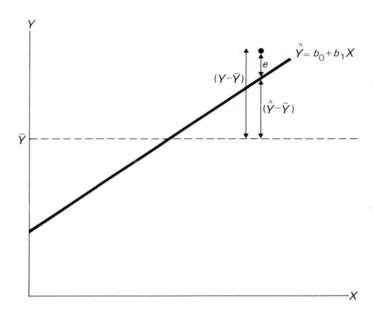

Fig. 6.8 Interpretation of R^2.

both X and Y share a common time trend that is strong. The time trend in many data series is, of course, the basis for the models of Chapter 5. Many general economic indicators that are only loosely related (for example, GNP, population, investment, money stock, etc.) may yet show a fairly high value of R^2 if one is regressed on another. This problem of spurious correlation due to time trends is sometimes summarized by pointing out that alcoholic beverage consumption through time correlates rather well with such things as church attendance and the number of ordained clergy! Clearly, no one would build a causal model along these lines, but uncritical use of the R^2 can sometimes lead one to almost the same type of erroneous result.

How is one to tell in practical situations whether a high R^2 is real or spurious? No hard and fast rules can be laid down, but two handy practical methods are often used. Neither rule can ever be a substitute for reason and good judgment on the part of the analyst. At best these rules can help an analyst uncover a suspected R^2 that is inflated by time trends. As a first check on the R^2, the model can often be reestimated in "first-difference" form; that is, instead of regressing Y on X, the analyst regresses the quarter-to-quarter or month-to-month change in Y on the corresponding change in X. Year-to-year, week-to-week, or other suitable periods may of course be used. The idea behind this is simply that if all the variables have in common is a time trend, then elimination of the trend by looking at changes should reduce the R^2 drastically and reveal the spurious relationship.

A second alternative accomplishes the same goal as trend removal, but accomplishes it in a somewhat different manner. If Y and X are both in "levels" (as opposed

Table 6.5 Data on sales volume and advertising

Period	S	ADV
1	1735.5	166.96
2	1782.4	177.12
3	1863.4	188.24
4	1971.1	204.64
5	2106.3	217.20
6	2206.9	227.52
7	2299.0	237.12

to first differences), then the trend common to both can be accounted for if Y is estimated not merely as a function of X, but rather as a function of both X and t, where t is a time trend variable; that is, a model of the form $Y = f(X, t)$ is estimated by least squares. Since this involves the concept of multiple regression which is not discussed until the next section of this chapter, we shall not pursue it here. The idea should become clear after reading the section on multiple regression.

To illustrate the use of the method of first differencing, we illustrate two simple regressions of sales volume (S) regressed on advertising expenditures (ADV). The data for the example appear in Table 6.5, and the SIMPLAN output for the model estimated in level and first difference form is shown in Table 6.6 and Table 6.7.

In Table 6.6 the SIMPLAN regression output shows that the regression of S on ADV yields an R^2 of .988, clearly a very high value. Also, the implementation of the t-test described earlier shows that the t value associated with the slope coefficient for ADV is very significant using any conventional test level (10 percent, 5 percent, or 1 percent). Despite the appearance of being a good model, most of the strong association is due to a time trend common to S and ADV. This is apparent from the results in

Table 6.6 Sales volume regressed on advertising expenditures

```
ANALYSIS.

ESTIMATE SALES ADV


LEAST SQUARES REGRESSION
```

ESTIMATED EQUATION IS: SALES=8.15927*ADV+341.175			
INDEPENDENT VARIABLES	ESTIMATED COEFFICIENT	STANDARD ERROR	T-- TEST
ADV	8.1593	0.4095	19.9265
CONSTANT	341.1743	83.5907	4.0815

```
NUMBER OF OBSERVATIONS USED =      7
R-SQUARED=   0.9876            F-STATISTIC(  1,  5)=    397.0818
ADJUSTED R-SQUARED=   0.9851   DURBIN-WATSON STATISTIC=   1.0338
STANDARD ERROR=       26.3957  DEGREES OF FREEDOM FOR T-TEST=  5
SUM OF SQUARED ERRORS=       3483.6672

ANALYSIS.
```

Table 6.7 Sales volume regressed on advertising expenditures in first difference form

```
ANALYSIS.

DSALES = SALES - SALES(-1)

ANALYSIS.

DADV = ADV - ADV(-1)

ANALYSIS.

ESTIMATE DSALES DADV


LEAST SQUARES REGRESSION
```

ESTIMATED EQUATION IS: DSALES=5.48721*DADV+29.753			
INDEPENDENT VARIABLES	ESTIMATED COEFFICIENT	STANDARD ERROR	T- TEST
DADV	5.4872	5.1359	1.0684
CONSTANT	29.7530	61.2109	0.4861

```
    NUMBER OF OBSERVATIONS USED =        6
         (        1 ADDITIONAL OBSERVATIONS DELETED FOR UNDEFINED DATA)
    R-SQUARED=    0.2220                F-STATISTIC(   1,    4)=      1.1415
    ADJUSTED R-SQUARED=     0.0275      DURBIN-WATSON STATISTIC=    1.1051
    STANDARD ERROR=         28.9856     DEGREES OF FREEDOM FOR T-TEST=   4
    SUM OF SQUARED ERRORS=          3360.6545

ANALYSIS.
```

Table 6.7 where the year-to-year changes in S are regressed on the corresponding changes in ADV. These results are not entirely surprising, since it is well known that advertising budgets are frequently expressed as a fraction of sales.

To compute the first differences of the data is a straightforward process. The command $DS = S - S(-1)$ causes the first differences of S to be computed and stored under the name DS. Then the same computation is implemented for ADV. The estimation is performed using DS and DADV instead of S and ADV. The results for the regression in first difference form are in sharp contrast to the results in level form. R^2 drops from 0.988 to 0.222. The $\bar{R}^2$ falls even more dramatically from 0.985 to 0.028. Clearly the original result was due mainly to the common time trend. Also it may be noted that the t-test on the slope coefficient for DADV is no longer significant at any conventional test level.

Although this example is rather simple, it serves to illustrate the dramatic changes that can occur when time series data are corrected for a trend. What might at first glance seem to be a very strong statistical relationship weakens considerably when first differences of the data are used.

If the foregoing example has served adequately to alert the reader that R^2 is a statistic that needs to be viewed with caution, it may then be safe to offer a few general guidelines that may be handy if not indiscriminately applied. In response to the question of what is a good R^2, we could venture these general guidelines. In the case of time series data where a trend is present, an R^2 should be at least 0.90 or 0.95 higher.

As should be obvious, this is *not* a sufficient condition for a good model, but it is roughly a necessary condition. Similarly, we might offer the rule of thumb that an R^2 of 0.50 is often regarded as good when working with the first differences of data and with certain cross-sectional data. While abuses of the R^2 as a measure of the quality of a model can easily occur, these heuristic rules may prove useful *if* they are used in conjunction with good judgment and the other statistical tests described in this chapter.

Multiple Regression

Up to this point we have been discussing how to estimate models with a single right-hand side variable. We now wish to broaden our investigation and look at the estimation of models with several right-hand side variables. Fortunately, almost all of the concepts presented thus far can be easily extended to the more general model with multiple right-hand side variables.

In multiple regression we hypothesize a model of the form $Y = \beta_0 + \beta_1 X_1 + \beta_2 X_2 + \epsilon$ which is assumed to have generated the observed values of Y in terms of several different right-hand side X's. The method can accommodate any number of X's, but it will often be convenient to deal with two X's. If the equation $Y = \beta_0 + \beta_1 X_1 + \beta_2 X_2 + \epsilon$ is the model that generates the observed Y values, it is analogous to the simple model for a single X and a single Y that was illustrated in Fig. 6.2. In that diagram we noted that the regression *line* was the average or expected value of Y, $E(Y)$, $= \beta_0 + \beta_1 X$, and the actual Y values came from adding a random error term ϵ to this line to give the observed scatter of points shown in Fig. 6.2. In the case of multiple regression, we have much the same situation, except that now the average or expected value of Y is no longer a line, but is rather a *plane*. This plane is given by the equation $E(Y) = \beta_0 + \beta_1 X_1 + \beta_2 X_2$ and the observed values of Y are assumed to differ from this plane by the additive error term ϵ.

One of the most important points about multiple regressions and one of the reasons for its popularity concerns the interpretation that is assigned to the values β_1 and β_2. These parameters obviously relate $E(Y)$ to X_1 and X_2. If we now ask the question, "What is the change in the average value of Y if X_1 changes *given that the effects of X_2 are held constant*?", the answer is the value of β_1. In the language of calculus, β_1 is the partial derivative of $E(Y)$ with respect to X_1. Similarly, β_2 shows the change that occurs in $E(Y)$ resulting from a small change in X_2, given that the effects of X_1 are held constant. This interpretation of the regression coefficients in multiple regression is one reason that the coefficients are sometimes referred to as *partial* regression coefficients.

It is important to stress that this concept of "holding constant" other variables is one of the crucial differences between multiple regression and the simple two-variable regression discussed earlier. If one wishes to measure the effect of X_1 on Y while holding constant for X_2, the proper way to proceed is *not* to regress Y on X_1 and simply ignore X_2. Rather, the correct procedure is to estimate the parameters of $Y = \beta_0 + \beta_1 X_1 + \beta_2 X_2 + \epsilon$ and then use the estimated value of β_1 to measure the effect of X_1 with X_2 held constant. To simply estimate Y as a function of X_1 will generally yield incorrect estimates of the partial effects of X_1, since the estimated value of β_1 will reflect not only the influence of X_1 but also some of the influence of X_2 which could not be apportioned to X_2 since that variable was omitted from the estimated equation.

In order to obtain estimators of the β's in the multiple regression model, the procedure is identical to that in the simple model with an X and a Y. The idea is to estimate the regression plane $E(Y) = \beta_0 + \beta_1 X_1 + \beta_2 X_2$ by $\hat{Y} = b_0 + b_1 X_1 + b_2 X_2$ where the b's are chosen so that the sum of squared errors Σe^2 (where $e = Y - b_0 - b_1 X_1 - b_2 X_2$ and there are as many e's as there are observations on the Y, X_1, and X_2 variables) is minimum. The exact calculations involved in obtaining the b's from the observed data are easily handled by the computer. The reader interested in more detailed information about these computations should see Kmenta (1971, pp. 350–351) or Wonnacott and Wonnacott (1970, pp. 244–246).

When we introduced the simple bivariate regression model, we did so by putting ourselves in the position of assuming we knew the values of β_0 and β_1, then generating Y values by adding random error terms ϵ to a set of X's. Then we argued that if certain basic assumptions held concerning the error term ϵ, the least-squares estimators b_0 and b_1 possessed desirable statistical properties. We then illustrated how the least-squares estimate did in fact come very close to reproducing the original values of β_0 and β_1 with which we started.

We could illustrate multiple regression in the same way, but instead we choose to start from the position of a given set of data for which we wish to estimate the β's. This will nearly always be the typical situation that the real world presents us with, since if the β's were known, we would never bother with estimating them in the first place. Just as the least-squares estimators have certain desirable properties in the case of simple regresssion, it can also be shown that they have the same properties in the case of multiple regression provided that the same five assumptions about the error term ϵ continue to hold. In brief, these assumptions are that: (1) the error terms have a mean of zero, (2) the error terms have the same variance, (3) different error terms are statistically independent, (4) the error terms are normally distributed, (5) the right-hand side variables are statistically independent of the error terms. Later in this chapter, we shall discuss some corrective procedures that can be applied if evidence indicates that these assumptions do not hold for a given set of data. We will also discuss how one can check the validity of these assumptions.

To illustrate the use of multiple regression, we present a simple model of the demand for automobiles. Conventional demand theory asserts that price and quantity will vary inversely if the effects of income (and possibly other prices) are held constant. In a classic study, Chow (1957, pp. 32, 65) gathered annual observations on price, quantity, and income to estimate a demand equation for automobiles in the United States. For price he used an average price of new cars, for quantity he utilized the stock of cars per capita (with old cars converted into an equivalent number of new cars units), and for income he employed a measure of permanent income. When Chow's demand equation was estimated with the SIMPLAN ESTIMATE command, the results which appear in Table 6.8 were obtained.

Abbreviating quantity, price, and income by their first letters, the estimated equation is $Q = -.0488P - .0255I - .725$. Thus, the quantity demanded is seen to be a positive

Table 6.8 A demand equation for automobiles

```
ANALYSIS.

ESTIMATE QUANTITY PRICE INCOME


LEAST SQUARES REGRESSION
```

ESTIMATED EQUATION IS: QUANTITY=-0.04886Z*PRICE+0.02549*INCOME-0.724657			
INDEPENDENT VARIABLES	ESTIMATED COEFFICIENT	STANDARD ERROR	T- TEST
PRICE	-0.0488	0.0042	-11.6159
INCOME	0.0255	0.0017	14.5901
CONSTANT	-0.7247	0.7148	-1.0137

```
NUMBER OF OBSERVATIONS USED =      28
R-SQUARED=    0.8952               F-STATISTIC(   2,  25)=      106.7306
ADJUSTED R-SQUARED=    0.8868      DURBIN-WATSON STATISTIC=    1.3087
STANDARD ERROR=         0.6176     DEGREES OF FREEDOM FOR T-TEST= 25
SUM OF SQUARED ERRORS=           9.5352

ANALYSIS.
```

function of income I and a negative function of price P, exactly as traditional demand theory would predict. Further, this equation permits us to derive different predictions of Q for various combinations of price and income that we might think would occur in the future.

When we discussed the simple regression model, the t-test was used to test the hypothesis that an individual slope coefficient was zero against the alternative hypothesis that the true value of the slope coefficient was not zero. The t values shown in the last column of Table 6.8 can be used in exactly the same way in this equation. Reference to Appendix B shows that for a one percent one-tail t-test with 25 degrees of freedom, the appropriate t value is 2.485. A one-tail test is logical since we would expect price to have either no effect, or a negative effect, and we would expect income to have either no effect or a positive effect.

Since the t value for income of 14.59 easily exceeds the table t value of 2.485, we would reject the hypothesis that income has no effect and accept that it is positively related to quantity. Similarly, since the t value of -11.62 for price is far below the t of -2.485 that leaves one percent in the lower tail, we would reject that price has no effect and accept that it is negatively related to quantity. Thus, even though we do not know the true values of the β's and must estimate them by least squares, our statistical estimates show us that if the correct theoretical specification is that quantity depends on price and income, then we can be very confident that the true values of the slope coefficients for price and income are not zero.

If we desired to construct a confidence interval for the true values of the slope coefficients, we could do so by utilizing the standard errors for the coefficients. Utilizing this information from Table 6.8, we would compute, say, a 95 percent confidence interval for the price coefficient as $-.0488 \pm t \times .0042$ where t is the appropriate value from Table B.1 of Appendix B. Since with a confidence interval we might err in either direction, we would want to use a t value that leaves 2.5 percent in each tail, or

5 percent overall, and this value for 25 degrees of freedom turns out to be 2.060. Thus, our confidence interval for the price coefficient would be $-.0488 \pm .0087$, or the interval $-.0575$ to $-.0401$. A similar interval for the true but unknown income coefficient can be computed to be $.0255 \pm .0035$ or $.0220$ to $.0290$.

F-statistic   The R^2 for the demand equation estimated by multiple regression can be interpreted in almost exactly the same way as the R^2 for the earlier equation estimated by simple regression. The value of .895 indicates that approximately 90 percent of the variation in the dependent variable is explained by the right-hand side variables.

In judging the R^2 for a multiple regression, we now face a slightly different situation. In regression it is possible to test statistically if the R^2 is different from zero. This amounts to a test of whether there is any explanatory power in the right-hand side variables in the model. In the case of the simple model discussed earlier, it can be shown that the test of $R^2 = 0$ vs. $R^2 > 0$ is identical to a two-tail test on the slope coefficient. Since we saw that a test on the slope coefficient could be carried out using the *t*-test, it follows that in the simple model a two-tail test on the slope coefficient is identical with a test on whether $R^2 = 0$. Asking whether there is any explanatory power in the model is identical with a test on whether the slope coefficient differs from zero by a two-tail test.

In the case of multiple regression where there are several right-hand side variables, clearly a test on $R^2 = 0$ cannot be equated with a *t*-test on a single coefficient for the simple reason that with several variables one would not know which coefficient to look at. Would R^2 be insignificant if all the *t*-tests were insignificant? Would R^2 be significant if all the *t*-tests were significant?

It turns out that neither of these propositions is correct, but there is yet a simple way to test $R^2 = 0$ against $R^2 > 0$ in the multiple regression model. Such a test does not look at any individual right-hand side variable, but rather looks at all the independent variables together and asks if they are *significant as a group*. To implement the test, one utilizes the F distribution and the calculated F value for a regression. In Table 6.8 the calculated *F*-statistic was found to be 106.73.

Unlike the *t*-test which may be either a one- or two-tail test, the F distribution always is a one-tail test (the positive tail). Large values of the computed *F*-statistic lead one to reject that $R^2 = 0$ in favor of $R^2 > 0$. Another difference between the t and the F is that the F distribution does not have a single number indicating degrees of freedom, but two values. These are shown in Table 6.8 where the F value is reported as $F(2,25)$, indicating 2 and 25 degrees of freedom. The first number is simply the number of *slope* coefficients in the model (one for price, one for income), and the second is the sample size N reduced by the total number of coefficients (counting slopes and the constant). Thus, for the sample size of 28 with two right-hand side variables plus a constant, the first value of d.f. is 2, and the second value of d.f. is 28 minus 3, or 25. In Table B.3 of Appendix B we observe that for a one-percent test for $F(2,25)$ the *F*-statistic is 5.57. Since the computed F value of 106.73 far exceeds the table value, we would clearly reject that $R^2 = 0$, and conclude that in fact the true value is nonzero. This is equivalent to concluding that the independent variables taken as a set are significant, although it does not guarantee that any individual variable is significant.

At this point it might be worthwhile to note a similarity between the t-statistic and the F-statistic. In multiple regression, the two statistics test different things, but in the case of simple regression the two statistics are in fact almost interchangeable. In the simple case, the two-tail, t-test will reveal a significant slope coefficient only if X plays some role in explaining Y, and if X does explain Y, then we would expect to find a significant R^2. In the simple model, one will find that a significant F-statistic associated with R^2 will coincide exactly with a significant two-tail t value on the slope coefficient. Thus, if one performs a t-test on the slope coefficient, it is unnecessary to test the R^2 since the results will be identical in the simple model. Hence, it would be unnecessary and useless to employ both the t-test and the F-test in the simple model, since there they test for the same thing. (The only way in which they can differ is if a one-tail, t-test is employed. Then the t and the F are not strictly related as described above.)

Adjusted R-square In Chapter 5 we defined the adjusted R^2 with reference to time trend models. Equation (5.21) provided the basic formula. In multiple regression we use the $\bar{R}^2$ as we did with time trend models to avoid an artificial inflation in R^2 as more right-hand side variables are added.

The reason that such an adjustment is desirable is easily seen by reference to Eq. (5.20). As successive independent variables are added to an equation, the least-squares method can always make the term Σe^2 smaller (except for the unlikely case that the additional variables have estimated coefficients that are all zero). Since the term $\Sigma(Y - \bar{Y})^2$ does not change as right-hand side variables are added, the formula for R^2 implies that R^2 can be made larger by adding *any* right-hand side variables to an equation. To avoid this automatic and possibly spurious increase in R^2, the formula is adjusted so that $\bar{R}^2$ is a statistic that may decrease, remain the same, or increase with the addition of right-hand side variables.

The adjusted R^2 shown in the printout has the property that it will only go up with the addition of a new variable if the t value associated with the new variable is more than 1.0 in absolute value. Thus, the adjusted R^2 requires that the additional variable have an estimated coefficient that is at least one standard error away from zero in order to show an increase in $\bar{R}^2$. While reliance on an increase in $\bar{R}^2$ is not quite the same thing as the requirement that a new variable have a statistically significant coefficient, the use of $\bar{R}^2$ instead of R^2 will at least partially protect the analyst from attaching unwarranted importance to added right-hand side variables.

Econometric Problems

The discussion of simple and multiple regression so far has been based on a number of assumptions that may not hold in all cases. In this section we will briefly outline some of the major econometric problems that analysts are likely to encounter in practice, and attempt to suggest procedures for circumventing some of these problems. Our objective is to acquaint readers with the types of problems encountered, the probable consequences, as well as possible solutions. References are given so that interested readers can pursue the various topics that may be of interest in their particular modeling problem.

Multicollinearity A problem that frequently arises with time series data and occasionally with cross-sectional data is the problem of multicollinearity. The problem is not that a particular assumption is incorrectly made, but rather that the data we are attempting to analyze came to us in such a way that we cannot answer all of the questions that we might wish to ask.

The essence of the problem is that when estimating a model of the form $Y = f(X_1, X_2)$ the right-hand side variables are rather highly correlated. If the X's are time series values, then they may be highly correlated simply because they all share a common strong time trend. If the X's are highly correlated and do not move independently of one another, then an attempt to estimate the model $Y = \beta_0 + \beta_1 X_1 + \beta_2 X_2 + \epsilon$ may make it difficult to determine precisely the influence of any single X. The association of Y with *both* X_1 and X_2 may be strong, and this may be reflected in a high value of R^2 and a high value of the F-statistic. However, it may yet be the case that neither X_1 nor X_2 has a significant t value! The reason for this perplexing situation is that a high degree of correlation between X_1 and X_2 will cause b_1 and b_2 to have large estimated standard errors. The large standard errors reflect the difficulty in allocating precisely the influence between the two variables, and when a t-test is computed according to $t = (b_i - \beta_i)/s_{b_i}$, the large values of s_{b_i} may cause small and insignificant t values. In this case, the small t values do not indicate a poor model with insignificant variables, because the F-statistic indicates that the right-hand side variables taken as a group explain a significant amount of the movement in Y. The problem is simply that one cannot decide whether the influence is due more to X_1 or X_2.

To repeat a point made earlier: a small t value does *not* prove that a variable is insignificant, rather, it simply implies that we cannot reject the hypothesis of insignificance. And in the case of multicollinearity, we cannot reject the null hypothesis because our data are not quite as rich in information content as we might like them to be.

The problem of multicollinearity can arise in other ways. If one has three right-hand side variables, X_1, X_2, and X_3, it may be the case that relating Y to X_1 and X_2 will yield significant t values for both variables, and the same result will arise if X_2 and X_3 are employed on the right-hand side. However, if X_1, X_2, and X_3 are all used on the right, it may happen that X_1 retains its significance while X_2 and X_3 both have very small t values. This will occur if X_2 and X_3 are highly correlated, and the precise effect due to the individual variables cannot be determined.

What do analysts do if they encounter the problem of multicollinearity? First, there is the question of what damage the problem does to the properties of the least-squares estimators. Fortunately, the answer is that the estimators retain their good qualities of unbiasedness (Fig. 6.4) despite multicollinearity. Although it is occasionally stated that multicollinearity may introduce bias into estimates, this is in fact not the case. Reference to the demonstration that the least-squares estimators are unbiased will show that this quality does not depend on the assumption that the independent variables are uncorrelated. (See, for example, Murphy 1973, p. 194.)

A second question concerns the seriousness of the problem. In the extreme case where two independent variables are exactly correlated (a simple correlation coefficient of $+1.0$ or -1.0), the least-squares method will break down. An attempt to estimate coefficients with such data will produce a message from the computer to the effect that an exact linear relationship between two (possibly more) variables prevents least-squares estimation. If one recalls the interpretation of the *partial* regression coefficients, it is easy to see why least-squares estimation breaks down in the case of perfect collinearity. Estimated regression coefficients show the estimated effects on Y of a change in one variable when all others are held constant. If two variables are exactly correlated, then it is impossible to speak of a small change in one variable with the rest of the variables held constant.

This extreme case of perfect collinearity fortunately does not arise too often in practice. (When it does, it is most often from an oversight, such as trying to estimate Y from X_1, X_2, and a weighted average of one-half the sum of X_1 and X_2, in which case the average is exactly correlated with the two variables from which it is constructed.)

Given the less extreme form of the problem (denoted by high F values, low t values), an analyst has few good alternatives. Since the problem originated with the particular sample of data used, gathering more data is one alternative. Other approaches that attempt to work with the given sample but apply more sophisticated methodology are described in most econometrics texts. The interested reader can consult Pindyck and Rubinfeld (1976, p. 68) and the references cited there.

Heteroscedasticity   One of the basic assumptions made about the behavior of the error term ϵ was that all values of ϵ shared the common variance σ^2. This was illustrated in Fig. 6.3 in which all of the bell-shaped curves had the same spread. If all of the distributions of the error terms do not have the same variance, the error term is said to be heteroscedastic, and the curves depicted in Fig. 6.3 would be of differing sizes. Some would show large variances, and some would show small variances.

If heteroscedasticity is present, the problem it poses is that the least-squares estimators are no longer efficient. They no longer have minimum variance (as depicted in Fig. 6.5). The estimators of the β's remain unbiased, but they no longer cluster most tightly around the target. The reason for this inefficiency can be visualized rather easily.

If the spread of some error terms is more than that of others, there is thus more noise and less information in the associated observation on Y and the X's. Since least-squares weights all errors equally in minimizing Σe^2, it is not taking advantage of the fact that some observations contain more information than others (by way of smaller error variances), and the associated least-squares estimators are not as efficient as some other estimators which utilize all of the information.

A further problem that is introduced by heteroscedasticity is that the t and F-statistics produced by least-squares estimators are no longer strictly valid. In all but severe cases they remain good approximations, but they are not exact. Thus, inferences based on these statistics may be incorrect.

Despite the damage done to the variances, t values, and F values, the least-squares estimators retain one good property in the face of heteroscedasticity: they remain unbiased; that is, the b's continue to be correct estimates of the β's on average. Thus, there is at least some comfort that the least-squares estimators do not lose all of their good properties if the assumption that $V(\epsilon) = \sigma^2$ is not valid.

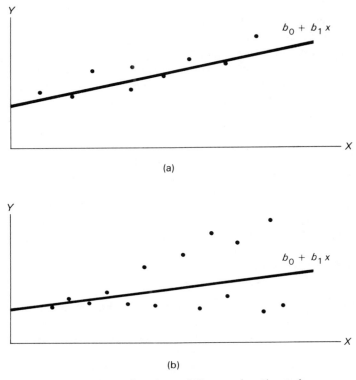

Fig. 6.9 Illustration of estimated line and estimated errors e with (a) no suggestion of heteroscedasticity and (b) strong suggestion of heteroscedasticity.

The detection of heteroscedasticity and the correction for it are both difficult in practice. One possible way to identify heteroscedasticity is to observe a plot of the estimated error and use this as an estimate of the spread of the distribution of the ϵ's. Figure 6.9 indicates what a heteroscedastic and nonheteroscedastic (homoscedastic) set of estimated errors e might look like. Unfortunately, the distribution of the e's depends on slightly more than the ϵ's, and one cannot always make reliable inferences from a plot of the e's. There are some statistical tests that can be applied to detect heteroscedasticity, but for a variety of reasons these are not always as useful as we might desire. A test due to Goldfeld and Quandt is perhaps the most useful of the tests available. It is based on dividing a regression sample up into subperiods for which the error variances are thought to be unequal, estimating the subperiods separately, and then comparing the estimated error variances with an F-test for the two subperiods to detect if there is a substantial difference. The test is described in detail in most standard econometrics texts. (See, for example, Murphy 1973, p. 304.)

Remedial methods of estimation are available if heteroscedasticity is established to be present, but the methods involved are too complicated to discuss in a survey chapter such as this. For the present purposes, it suffices to note that corrective procedures are available but even if such procedures are not employed in the face of heteroscedasticity, the least-squares estimators remain unbiased and the t and the F values remain approximately correct in most cases.

Autocorrelation Of the numerous econometric problems that an analyst may encounter, the problem of autocorrelation is among the most frequent. The problem of autocorrelation involves the violation of the assumption that the error terms ϵ are independently distributed. Instead of being uncorrelated, values in different time periods are correlated. (The problem can occur with cross-sectional data, but it is far more often a problem with time series data.) Hence, if the value of ϵ_t is correlated with the value of ϵ_{t-1}, the error terms are said to be autocorrelated. The problem with applying least squares to a set of data with autocorrelated errors is quite similar to the problems posed by heteroscedasticity in that the least-squares method will yield unbiased but not efficient estimates. Further, the t- and the F-tests will be incorrect.

Fortunately, there is a fairly straightforward test for the most common case of autocorrelation, and also a fairly good corrective procedure. The most common case of autocorrelation is so-called *first order autocorrelation*, which means that the relationship of ϵ_t and ϵ_{t-1} can be expressed as $\epsilon_t = \rho\epsilon_{t-1} + \mu_t$. The value of ρ is a number between -1 and $+1$ that is referred to as the autocorrelation coefficient, and μ_t is a random error term. Positive values of ρ lead to positive autocorrelation, while negative values lead to negative autocorrelation. The distribution of μ_t is assumed to be such that it has zero mean, constant variance, and no autocorrelation. Thus, the error terms ϵ_t are the fraction ρ of the previous error term, with a random error μ_t added on. There is thus both a deterministic and a random component to ϵ if first-order autocorrelation is present.

It should be apparent that if the value of ρ is zero, then the first-order autocorrelation scheme reduces to simply $\epsilon_t = $ a well-behaved error term, μ_t. This suggests that a test on $\rho = 0$ is a logical way to check for first-order autocorrelation, and this is the basic idea that lies behind the Durbin–Watson test for autocorrelation. If the null hypothesis of $\rho = 0$ is accepted, then there is no evidence of autocorrelation and we may have confidence that our least-squares estimators retain their desirable properties of both efficiency and unbiasedness, while rejection of the null hypothesis implies that least squares is unbiased but no longer efficient.

The Durbin–Watson value is produced by most computer programs, and for the multiple regression example in Table 6.8 the Durbin–Watson value was shown to be 1.31. This value can be compared against table values to test $\rho = 0$ against the alternative that $\rho \neq 0$, but there is one aspect of the test that is slightly more complicated than the usual t- or F-test. The Durbin–Watson (or D.W.) value does not have an accept–reject region like the t or F, but has instead three regions: accept–inconclusive–reject. The inconclusive region of the test arises from the fact that the D.W. value depends in part on the actual data values that analysts have employed in their regression. Although conceivably tables could be set up for different ranges of data, to do this would be immensely cumbersome. It is far easier to tabulate D.W. values with a range that will accept or reject for almost all conceivable data values, and another inconclusive range where the test depends on the actual values used to estimate the regression equation.

In Fig. 6.10 we show the construction of a D.W. test graphically. The diagram is analogous to Fig. 6.6 for a two-tail, t-test on a slope coefficient, except that we now have an inconclusive region as mentioned above. The inconclusive region is delimited by the values D_L and D_U, which signify "lower" and "upper," respectively. The terminology derives from checking for positive autocorrelation, which is indicated by D.W. values below 2.0, the approximate center of the distribution. If the computed value of D.W. is above D_U, we can accept that there is no evidence of autocorrelation. If the computed value of D.W. is below D_L, we reject the null hypothesis and conclude there is evidence of positive autocorrelation ($\rho > 0$). For values of D.W. between D_L and D_U, the test is inconclusive. Similarly, one can test for negative autocorrelation, and in this case values of D.W. in excess of $(4 - D_L)$ lead us to reject the null hypothesis in favor of the alternative hypothesis that there is negative autocorrelation. Values less than $(4 - D_U)$ let us accept the null hypothesis, and values between $(4 - D_U)$ and $(4 - D_L)$ lead to inconclusive results.

In Table B.4 of Appendix B the appropriate values of D_L and D_U to perform a five percent two-tail, t-test (leaving 2.5 percent in each tail) are seen to be 1.18 and 1.46 for a sample of size 30. Comparing the computed D.W. value of 1.31 from the sample regression in Table 6.8, it is seen that the test is inconclusive in this case. (To be slightly more precise, one could interpolate the table values for 25 and 30 observations in order to produce a value for 28, the actual sample size here. But this makes no difference in the outcome of the test.)

Suppose the test had indicated conclusively that there was evidence of positive autocorrelation? How could we proceed? One approach would be to accept the least-squares estimators, knowing they were still unbiased, but regarding the t and the F

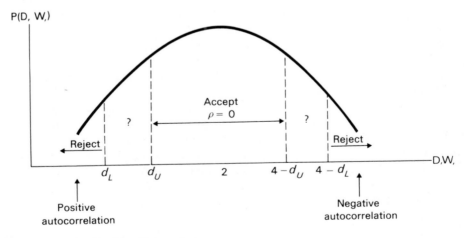

Fig. 6.10 The Durbin–Watson test.

values with some caution. Thus, one might interpret five percent significant levels as actually indicating 10 percent or 20 percent significance. Another approach would be to estimate the equation with a method that explicitly took account of the fact that the error terms in successive time periods were not independent.

Of the several methods available for estimating an equation with first-order auto-correlation, the most widely used method is probably the Cochrane–Orcutt procedure. To see how this method works, consider the true relationship $Y_t = \beta_0 + \beta_1 X_t + \epsilon_t$ where we have added subscripts t to denote time. If ϵ is first-order autocorrelated, then $\epsilon_t = \rho \epsilon_{t-1} + \mu_t$. Application of least squares to the autocorrelated equation would not be appropriate, in that the resulting estimators would be unbiased but not minimum variance. If we consider the model at time $t-1$ and multiply both sides of the equation by ρ, we would have $\rho Y_{t-1} = \rho \beta_0 + \rho \beta_1 X_{t-1} + \rho \epsilon_{t-1}$. If we now subtract this expression from the original model specification, the results are:

$$Y_t = \beta_0 + \beta_1 X_t + \epsilon_t$$

$$\underline{\rho Y_{t-1} = \rho \beta_0 + \rho \beta_1 X_{t-1} + \rho \epsilon_{t-1}}$$

$$Y_t - \rho Y_{t-1} = \beta_0(1-\rho) + \beta_1(X_t - \rho X_{t-1}) + \epsilon_t - \rho \epsilon_{t-1}. \qquad (6.9)$$

Although this last expression appears slightly messy at first glance, it possesses one very attractive property. The error term is seen to be of the form $\epsilon_t - \rho \epsilon_{t-1}$, and if the initial assumption was correct that $\epsilon_t = \rho \epsilon_{t-1} + \mu_t$, then it is apparent that the error term $\epsilon_t - \rho \epsilon_{t-1}$ is simply μ_t, a well-behaved nonautocorrelated error term. The importance of this is that ordinary least squares is then properly applied to the final equation above.

In practice, least squares cannot be immediately applied since ρ is not known in advance, but a simple solution is available. A least-squares regression of Y on X will produce residuals e_t from which one can estimate the autocorrelation coefficient ρ. Then with an estimated value denoted r, one can transform the Y and X values to obtain $Y_t - rY_{t-1}$ and $X_t - rX_{t-1}$ and a regression can be run with the transformed Y and X values. From these parameters and the original variables, one can obtain the residuals, obtain an improved r, transform the variables, and repeat the process. It can be demonstrated that this process will converge to values of b_0, b_1, and r that possess several desirable statistical properties, although not quite the properties of unbiasedness and minimum variance that were discussed earlier. One of the desirable properties of Cochrane–Orcutt estimators is consistency. We discuss this property later in conjunction with two-stage least squares.

In SIMPLAN Cochrane–Orcutt regression is requested by issuing the command REGR CORC ON prior to giving an ESTIMATE command. Then the estimated equation is revised by the method of Eq. (6.9). Space constraints do not permit further discussion here. The interested reader can see R. Britton Mayo's book, *Corporate Planning and Modeling with SIMPLAN*, Addison-Wesley, 1978.

Specification error   In the discussion so far we have assumed that it was known that the Y values were generated according to the model $Y = \beta_0 + \beta_1 X_1 + \beta_2 X_2 + \epsilon$, and the problem was to estimate the β's. It is very often the case, however, that one is not sure of exactly what are the correct right-hand side X's. We have seen already that the t-test on an individual coefficient can be used to judge significance, but the problem may be broader than simply choosing between two models that differ by a single variable. For example, there might be two possible specifications, say, $Y = f(X_1, X_2)$ and $Y = f(X_1, X_2, X_3, X_4)$, and it is desired to discriminate between the two models. If one incorrectly estimates the model $Y = f(X_1, X_2)$ when in fact the true model is $Y = f(X_1, X_2, X_3, X_4)$, then one has committed a specification error. The b_1 and b_2 coefficient estimates that are computed for the variables X_1 and X_2 will be biased by the fact that two causative variables $(X_3$ and $X_4)$ were incorrectly omitted from the regression; that is, b_1 and b_2 will not have as their expected values β_1 and β_2, and they will not correctly estimate the partial effect of X_1 and X_2.

The problem may be even broader than this in that there may be a set of perhaps a dozen potential right-hand side variables, and the analyst does not have a great deal of information on exactly which ones should be included in a model. What is to be done in this situation?

Space does not permit a discussion of the methodology that can be applied in such situations, but we can outline two general types of tests that are very powerful in such situations. Consider first the problem of distinguishing between two models such as $Y = f(X_1, X_2)$ and $Y = f(X_1, X_2, X_3, X_4)$. The problem can be attacked by estimating both models individually by least squares. The model with more right-hand side variables will then always have a smaller value for the sum of squared errors (ignoring the trivial case where the estimated coefficients for X_3 and X_4 are both exactly 0), and conversely the model with fewer right-hand side variables will have a larger value for the sum of squared errors. It is then possible to formulate an F-statistic based on the *excess* of sum of squared errors that results when several variables are left out of a model. Large values of the F-statistic imply that it was incorrect to omit these variables, while small values imply that the variables under consideration can be safely omitted. This general testing procedure can be applied to test a set of two, three, or any number of right-hand side variables that one wishes to consider jointly. Details of the test are set forth clearly in Murphy (1973, pp. 222–227) and other econometrics textbooks.

A more powerful and more general method for identifying an improperly specified model goes under the general heading of the Chow test. It too involves an F-statistic, but it operates in a slightly different fashion. The general idea behind the Chow test is to examine a model for stability over time. A correctly specified model will show only minor change in the estimated coefficient values if the model is estimated for two different time periods (say, 1970/I to 1974/IV and then 1975/I to 1978/IV), while a misspecified model is likely to exhibit very different coefficient values when estimated for the two different periods.

The test can be implemented in several different ways. One fairly simple method is based on requiring a model to show stability when its original data period is divided into two equal halves. Thus, if analysts constructed a model for 40 quarters, they might check to see if the model appeared to fit the first 20 quarters as well as the last 20 quarters. Another slightly more powerful application involves constructing a model from available data, and then after sufficient time has elapsed for the accumulation of further data, reestimating the model on the basis of the new data and seeing if the model exhibits stability. This is probably the strongest test that can be applied to an econometric model, and one that a good forecasting model should pass if it is to continue in use.

Although space does not permit a thorough discussion and illustration of the Chow test, we can note that it can be implemented with nothing more than the simple ESTIMATE commands that have been illustrated previously. A test statistic following the F distribution is formed by combining the values of the sum of squared errors from regressions for different periods. The test is discussed in detail in most econometrics texts. Murphy (1973, pp. 237–243), Johnston (1972, pp. 206–207), and Kelejian and Oates (1974, pp. 179–181) all provide discussions of the test.

Distributed lags   While for some models it is appropriate to consider that the current value of Y depends on the current value of one or more Xs, it is often the case that the current value of Y depends on the current *and* past values of one or more X's; that is, instead of a model such as $Y_t = f(X_t)$, we have a model of the form $Y_t = f(X_t, X_{t-1}, X_{t-2}, \dots)$. Since the influence of X is distributed over a number of lagged values, models of this type are known as distributed lag models.

One simple and often satisfactory method of dealing with such models is simply to apply least squares; that is, one could simply proceed to find the least squares estimate of the model $Y_t = \beta_0 + \beta_1 X_t + \beta_2 X_{t-1} + \beta_3 X_{t-2} + \epsilon$. To accomplish this in SIMPLAN, one could simply issue the command ESTIMATE Y X X(-1) X(-2), and the computer would provide least-squares estimates. If there were several different right-hand side variables that entered the model in contemporaneous and lagged form, one could estimate such a model with a command of ESTIMATE Y X X(-1) X(-2) Z Z(-1) Z(-2) where Y is modeled as a function of X and Z and lagged values of both variables.

Application of least squares to such distributed lag models yields estimates with the properties of unbiasedness and minimum variance if the standard assumptions are met. However, least-squares estimation may face a problem with multicollinearity. The use of independent variables such as X_t, X_{t-1}, and X_{t-2} may yield very large standard errors for individual coefficients, and thus very low t values. The highly correlated adjacent values of X make it difficult for the least-squares method to apportion the influence precisely. The problem will be worse if current and lagged values of several correlated variables are used on the right-hand side. Then not only will it be difficult to distinguish between the influence of X_t and X_{t-1}, but it will be difficult to distinguish among X_t, X_{t-1}, Z_t, and Z_{t-1}.

A variety of methods have been derived by economists to deal with distributed lag models. Typically, the methods of estimation attempt to reduce standard errors and obtain more precise coefficient estimates by utilizing some *a priori* information about the likely shape of the lag distribution. Such information is typically of two types. First, one may suspect that the influence of X decays over time, such that X_t exercises the greatest influence on Y_t, X_{t-1} exerts slightly less influence than does X_t,

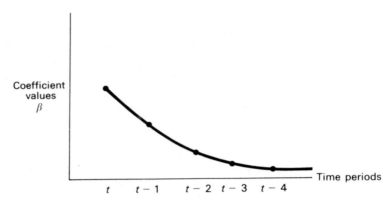

Fig. 6.11 How the coefficients of a Koyck model appear.

X_{t-2} exerts still less influence, etc. If this is the case, the values of the coefficients assigned to older values of X would be successively smaller. A plot of the coefficients for different time periods would appear as shown in Fig. 6.11.

A method known as the *Koyck* lag model estimates Y_t as a function of present and past values of X under the assumption that the influence of X decays geometrically. If analysts have knowledge that the influence of X will likely decay with time and if they are willing to assume that this decay is geometric, then the Koyck model can be used to drastically simplify the estimation of a model such as $f(X_t, X_{t-1}, X_{t-2}, \ldots,)$. In fact, it can be shown (Wonnacott and Wonnacott 1970, pp. 145–146) that the coefficients of such a model with geometric decay can be obtained by first performing a regression of the type ESTIMATE Y X Y(-1), and then suitably interpreting the estimated coefficients associated with X and $Y(-1)$. Thus, performing a regression of Y on X and the lagged value of Y is equivalent to running a regression of Y on all past values of X with the restriction that the influence of X decays geometrically with time. By accepting the notion of decaying weights, we have reduced the problem of estimating a large number of coefficients to merely two coefficients.

Another method of attempting to reduce the number of coefficients to be estimated in a distributed lag model is to require the coefficients to lie along a polynomial of a given degree. As long as the degree of the polynomial is less than the length of the distributed lag, then estimating the polynomial will greatly simplify the problem of estimation. This method is known as the *Almon* lag method.

The idea can be illustrated graphically in Fig. 6.12. There six coefficient values are to be estimated for the variables $X_t, X_{t-1}, \ldots, X_{t-5}$. If the distribution of the coefficients (shown by the dots) can be exactly or approximately represented by a second-degree polynomial (shown by the line), then estimation of three points to determine the polynomial will provide us with estimates of the six distributed lag coefficients. The number of coefficients to be estimated has been reduced from 6 to 3 (since 3 points determine a second-degree polynomial), and the result will be that the standard errors of the coefficients will be much smaller.

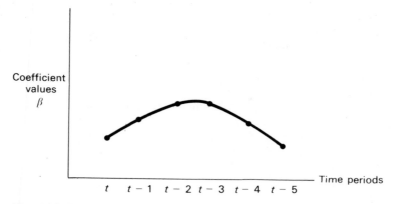

Fig. 6.12 How the coefficients of an Almon lag model appear.

An advantage of the Almon technique over the Koyck method is its ability to deal with lag structures that rise to a peak and then decay (Fig. 6.11), rather than decaying steadily from an initial value (Fig. 6.10). The Almon technique is flexible in the sense that a polynomial of low degree (say, degree 2, 3, or 4) can adapt itself to a variety of shapes, and the method thus differs from the Koyck technique which forces the idea of exponential decay upon the coefficients.

Almon lags are implemented in SIMPLAN by the DLAG command. Space does not permit a full discussion here, except to note that the output is very similar to that of an ESTIMATE command.

Nonlinear models At the outset of this chapter we began a discussion of estimating Y as a linear function of X, and with multiple regression we have broadened the discussion to estimating Y as a linear function of several X's. We now wish to point out that the methodology is not quite as restrictive as it might appear in confining itself to linear functions.

Suppose that one were interested in estimating a model of the form $Y = f(X)$ in which it was thought that the true relationship was quite probably a quadratic (similar to the quadratic models discussed in Chapter 5). Thus, Y is hypothesized to have been generated by a model of the form $Y = \beta_0 + \beta_2 X + \beta_2 X^2 + \epsilon$. If we define $X_1 = X$ and $X_2 = X^2$, it is clear that this quadratic model can be put into the form $Y = \beta_0 + \beta_1 X_1 + \beta_2 X_2 + \epsilon$, and thus all of our previous results for multiple regression apply completely. Thus, in order to estimate the coefficients of a quadratic model, one simply regresses Y on X and its squared value. This is exactly analogous to the quadratic time trend model of Eq. (5.13).

To carry out this process in SIMPLAN, one would need just two commands. Given data on, say, Y and X, the command XSQ = X * X could be used to generate the squared values. Then an ESTIMATE Y X XSQ would carry out the estimation of the quadratic relationship of Y to X. The $\bar{R}^2$ could be used to judge the goodness of fit, and the t-test could be applied to see if the coefficient of the squared term appeared to be significant. In this way one could see if a hunch about a quadratic relationship was supported by the data.

The same idea can be extended a step further by incorporating linear and squared terms for two different variables in a model. Thus, least squares can be used to estimate the relationship $Y = f(X_1, X_1^2, X_2, X_2^2)$ where X_1 and X_2 are two different independent variables that are thought to influence Y. Application of the t test to the terms involving X_1^2 and X_2^2 will reveal whether these terms are significant or whether the simpler model $Y = f(X_1, X_2)$ can be used.

Another possible functional form that can be estimated and tested with regression is a form that allows for the possibility of *interaction* between X_1 and X_2. It is often the case that the influence of X_1 on Y is related to the level of X_2 and the influence of X_2 on Y is related to the level of X_1. A model that captures quadratic effects and also allows for the possibility of interactions is a model of the form $Y = f(X_1, X_1^2, X_2, X_2^2, X_1 X_2)$. Thus, there are five right-hand side variables, with the fifth being the product of X_1 and X_2. A test of the significance of this term amounts to a test of the proposition that X_1 and X_2 interact with one another to influence Y. Such a model could be estimated by issuing the commands X1SQ = X1*X1, X2SQ = X2*X2, (the quadratic terms), X1X2 = X1*X2 (the interaction term), and then finally ESTIMATE Y X1 X1SQ X2 X2SQ X1X2 (to carry out the estimation).

Aside from using powers and products of terms in a model, frequently we may want to employ *logarithmic transformations* of either or both of the left-hand side and right-hand side variables. For example, often we estimate $Y* = \beta_0 + \beta_2 X* + \epsilon$, where $Y* = \log(Y)$ and $X* = \log(X)$. Such a model is useful when it is thought that a *percentage* change in X is associated with a *percentage* change in Y, rather than that a change in the *level* of X is associated with a change in the *level* of Y. We omit the algebra involved in the demonstration, and simply state that if the model involving the logarithms of both variables is used, then b_1 tells us the percent change in Y that results from a one percent change in X. (See Kmenta 1971, p. 458, for the algebra.) An estimated value of β_1 in excess of unity implies that a one percent change in X causes more than a one percent change in Y, while an estimated coefficient less than unity implies the converse. The t-test can be employed to test the hypothesis that $\beta_1 = 1$, against a two-sided alternative that $\beta_1 \neq 1$ by utilizing the formula $t = (b_1 - \beta_1)/s_{b_1}$. Here the value of 1.0 would be substituted for β_1, and the values of b_1 and s_{b_1} would be obtained from the computer printout. Then one could proceed exactly as was illustrated with Fig. 6.6.

The estimation of this so-called double log model is easily implemented in SIMPLAN. The statements YLOG = LOG(Y) and XLOG = LOG(X) would cause the computer to generate the necessary logarithmic values of the data and then the command ESTIMATE YLOG XLOG would carry out the estimation and return the coefficient estimates for the model $\log(Y) = \beta_0 + \beta_1 \log(X) + \epsilon$.

Simultaneous Equations

In the discussion so far we have dealt with different types of models of the general form $Y = f(X_1, X_2)$ where there was a clear idea that the variables on the right influ-

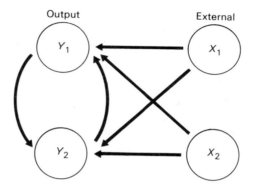

Fig. 6.13 Causal diagram for $Y_1 = f(Y_2, X_2)$ and $Y_2 = f(Y_1, X_1)$.

enced the variable on the left. We have not, however, dealt with the problem of two-way causation that was briefly introduced in Chapter 2. The problem of *simultaneous equations* occurs when we have models of the form:

$$Y_1 = f(Y_2, X_2)$$
$$Y_2 = f(Y_1, X_1). \tag{6.10}$$

That is, in one equation Y_1 is a dependent variable, but in another equation Y_1 functions as an independent variable. The variable Y_2 functions in exactly the same way.

The variables Y_1 and Y_2 are output variables and can be solved simultaneously for their respective values. (This is a simple generalization of the idea that a model of the form $Y = f(X_1, X_2)$ can be used to forecast values of Y.) Output variables are simply identified by the facts that (1) they always appear on the left-hand side of at least one equation and (2) they may appear on the right-hand side of one or more equations. External variables may also appear in simultaneous equation models, and they are simply identified by the fact that they appear only on the right-hand side of equations. Above X_1 and X_2 were illustrative of external variables.

Figure 6.13 illustrates via a simple causal diagram the type of system interaction that is captured by the two equation model $Y_1 = f(Y_2, X_2)$ and $Y_2 = f(Y_1, X_1)$. One important point to note from this diagram is that even though X_2 appears only on the right-hand side of the equation for Y_1, it affects both Y_1 and Y_2. The same argument applies to X_1. The reason that X_2 affects Y_1 and Y_2 is simply that Y_1 and Y_2 are simultaneously determined, and even though X_2 appears to influence only Y_1, because Y_1 acts upon Y_2, so too does X_2 ultimately. This is the reason for the intersecting arrows going from X_1 to Y_2 and from X_2 to Y_1 in Fig. 6.13.

The identification problem   In the foregoing discussion of two simultaneous equations, the reader may have wondered why we included X_1 and X_2 at all. Wouldn't it have been simpler to talk of the two simultaneous equations $Y_1 = f(Y_2)$ and $Y_2 = f(Y_1)$? It would indeed have been simpler in the sense of having fewer variables, but it would

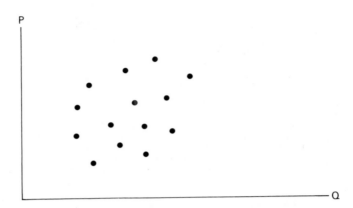

Fig. 6.14 A collection of values for prices (P) and quantity (Q): an identification problem.

run into a great difficulty known as the *identification problem*. Briefly, the identification problem occurs in a model where "everything depends on everything else." In such a model it is impossible to identify or isolate separate causal equations. The problem is basically a difficult mathematical problem, but it can be given a graphical treatment for a simple case.

To make our model realistic, consider the case where Y_1 and Y_2 represent price P and quantity Q in an economic model. Economic theory asserts that P and Q are simultaneously determined at the intersection of the supply curve and the demand curve, the two equations of our model. Thus, two intersecting equations can in theory be used to solve for values of the two output variables of the model.

Consider now the problem of analysts who gather data on P and Q and find their data give them the scatter of points shown in Fig. 6.14. From this collection of points, how can one proceed to estimate the demand equation and supply equation; that is, how can one estimate $Y_1 = f(Y_2)$ and $Y_2 = f(Y_1)$? If we perform a least-squares regression such as ESTIMATE Y1 Y2 and ESTIMATE Y2 Y1, how do we know which is the demand equation and which is the supply equation, or is either the correct equation? We have a problem of being able to *logically* identify or spot the two equations, and this problem precedes and makes impossible any meaningful estimation of the two equations. This problem was briefly alluded to in Chapter 2 in the discussion of a demand equation. The situation in which "everything depends on everything else" leaves us stuck.

Consider, however, a slight modification of the problem. Although demand theory asserts that the quantity demanded depends on price, that is not usually the only determinant of quantity. As was seen in the example in Table 6.8, a demand equation typically includes income on the right-hand side; that is, the demand equation is of the form $Y_1 = f(Y_2, X_2)$ in which quantity demanded Y_1 depends on price Y_2 and income X_2. We denote income by the variable X_2 to indicate that income is external and does not itself appear on the left-hand side of any equation. This is logical, for while income

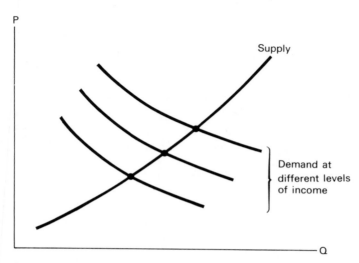

Fig. 6.15 A supply and demand curve: identifying the supply
curve.

may influence quantity demanded, it is not reasonable that the quantity demanded
would influence income.

If we then consider the two equations $Y_1 = f(Y_2, X_2)$ (the demand curve) and
$Y_2 = f(Y_1)$ (the supply curve), we could envision a situation such as that depicted in
Fig. 6.15. There we illustrate the supply curve along with several different demand
curves, the different demand curves resulting from different levels of income X_2. It
will be noted that the intersection of the different demand curves with the single supply
curves causes the supply curve to be traced out or identified by the intersection of the
two curves.

If the state of nature is such that $Y_1 = f(Y_2, X_2)$ and $Y_2 = f(Y_1)$ and we observe
the three dotted points in Fig. 6.15, our knowledge about the variables in the model
(the presence of income in the demand equation) lets us be sure that the three points
in fact lie along a supply curve. What has happened is that the presence of the external
variable income X_2 in the demand equation has enabled us to identify the supply
equation. How is this? The key lies not so much in the presence of X_2 in the demand
equation as it does in its *absence* from the supply equation. The fact that X_2 did not
occur in the supply equation means that the supply curve will not move in response to
changes in X_2, while the demand curve will shift. And this shifting of the demand curve
while supply holds still causes the demand curve to "cut" the supply curve at different
points and thus identify the supply curve for us.

The fact that the absence of an external variable from the supply equation enabled
us to identify it is an example of a proposition known as the order condition for identification. The name "order" derives from the size or order of a certain matrix expression,
but the basic idea of the order condition is easily grasped. To be able to identify and

estimate an equation in a system of simultaneous equations, it is necessary that there be an *absent* external variable for each right-hand side output variable. Thus, the supply equation which is of the form $Y_2 = f(Y_1)$ has one right-hand side output variable. The system of which it is part has one external variable (X_2 = income) which is absent from this equation. Thus we can identify and estimate this equation.

One can also apply this rule to the demand equation $Y_1 = f(Y_2, X_2)$. Here there is one right-hand side output variable (Y_2 = price), but the only external variable associated with the system is *not* absent (X_2 = income appears on the right). Thus the demand equation is not identified and cannot be estimated if the system from which it comes is correctly described by the two equations $Y_1 = f(Y_2, X_2)$ and $Y_2 = f(Y_1)$.

Suppose instead of these two equations that the supply and demand equations were $Y_1 = f(Y_2, X_2)$ and $Y_2 = f(Y_1, X_1)$ where now X_1 is some factor that influences the supply equation but does not directly influence the demand function. The variable X_1 might represent some cost factor or perhaps the availability of a raw material. In this case, both the supply and demand equations are now identified and can be estimated, since there is one absent external variable from each equation and there is one right-hand side output variable in each equation.

In the case of the demand equation for automobiles presented earlier, the equation was identified in that the supply of automobiles was reasonably thought to be dependent on a number of external factors that were absent from the demand equation and thus permitted it to be identified.

Checking for the identification of an equation can sometimes be a bothersome task in that one must enumerate all of the external variables in a system, and then check that one (or more) are excluded for each right-hand side output variable. Fortunately, the type of estimation procedure that is appropriate for estimating equations embedded in a simultaneous system of equations provides a kind of automatic check on the order condition for identification. We will discuss this further below when we discuss the appropriate means of estimating equations in a simultaneous system.

Two-stage least squares   The method of ordinary least squares that results from an ESTIMATE command has good statistical properties in many circumstances, but unfortunately the method of least squares turns out to be particularly inappropriate for estimating an equation that is part of a simultaneous system of equations. The reason for this can be explained as follows. Recall from the first discussion of least squares that one of the five basic assumptions made about the behavior of the true regression line $Y = \beta_0 + \beta_1 X + \epsilon$ was the right-hand side variable X and the error term ϵ were independent of one another. If one estimates a single equation out of a system of equations, this assumption of independence of the right-hand side variables and the error term *cannot possibly hold*. To see why this is so, consider the equation to be estimated as $Y_1 = f(Y_2, X_2) + \epsilon_1$ and $Y_2 = f(Y_1, X_1) + \epsilon_2$.

Consider now the first equation, and note that the model will generate values of Y_1 and Y_2 given values of X_1, X_2, ϵ_1, and ϵ_2. We see ϵ_1 and X_2 along with Y_2 enter the right part of the first equation to determine Y_1. In the second equation we see that Y_1 is one of the factors influencing Y_2. And herein lies the problem. Since ϵ_1 is related to

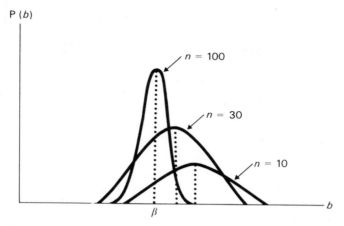

Fig. 6.16 Illustration of the distribution of a consistent estimator.

Y_1 in the first equation, and Y_1 is related to Y_2 in the second equation, it must also be true that Y_2 and ϵ_1 have some relationship to one another in the first equation. Thus, the assumption that the right-hand side variables are independent of the error terms cannot possibly hold in a system of simultaneous equations. The very fact of simultaneity causes the output variables (right-hand side Y's) to be correlated to some degree with the error terms in the equations.

If least squares is applied to estimate such an equation, it can be shown that the resulting estimators are biased. They will always be centered on the wrong target, and the direction of the bias will generally not be known. Clearly, application of least-squares estimation to a system of simultaneous equations poses some serious problems.

To get around the problem of bias, economists generally apply a method known as *two-stage least squares*, often abbreviated TSLS or 2SLS. As the name implies, the method involves the application of least squares in two separate steps. The resulting estimators turn out to have good statistical properties (better than the application of least squares), although the TSLS estimators do not have the property of being minimum variance unbiased estimators.

The most important statistical property possessed by the TSLS estimator is the property of *consistency*. The idea of consistency is easily illustrated with the aid of Fig. 6.16. The basic concept of a consistent estimator is one whose distribution—though possibly biased—clusters ever more tightly on the correct parameter as the sample size increases. In Fig. 6.16, we show the distribution of a consistent estimator b of a parameter β. In the diagram it is important to notice that there are different distributions of b associated with different sample sizes n, and that the center of the distribution of b for small samples is not necessarily β. However, as sample size grows larger, two things happen: the distribution of b tends more and more to center on β and the distribution of b has less and less spread. Were we dealing with an inconsistent estimator (such as least squares applied to a simultaneous equation model), there would not be a tendency for the distribution to shift more and more onto the correct target. An inconsistent estimator would begin off target and remain off target regardless of the sample size used.

Consistency is a somewhat weaker condition than minimum variance unbiasedness. With a consistent estimator we can say only that the bias disappears as the same size grows large, while for an unbiased estimator there is no bias for any size sample.

The idea of the two-stage, least-squares method and how it obtains consistent estimators can be described in simple terms, although the computations are usually rather involved. Consider again the simple model $Y_1 = f(Y_2, X_2) + \epsilon_1$ and $Y_2 = f(Y_1, X_1) + \epsilon_2$. If the model is linear in the parameters to be estimated the model equations then take the form $Y_1 = \alpha Y_2 + \beta X_2 + \epsilon_1$ and $Y_2 = \alpha' Y_1 + \beta' X_1 + \epsilon_2$ where we use α for the coefficient of the output variables and β for the coefficient of the external variables and the second equation is distinguished from the first by the primes which follow the coefficients (α' and β'). We omit the constant term for simplicity, but as will be seen below these can be produced by the computer easily.

Least squares is not applicable to the two equations because in the first Y_2 is correlated with ϵ_1, while in the second equation Y_1 is correlated with ϵ_2. The idea behind two-stage least squares is to devise a way around this correlation in the first stage, and then proceed to the estimation of the equation in the second stage. This is accomplished for the first equation as follows. In stage one we take the right-hand side variable Y_2 and regress it on all of the external variables in the model, X_1 and X_2. The estimated values of Y_2 from this regression can be denoted $\hat{Y}_2$. In stage two we now estimate the equation by regressing Y_1 on $\hat{Y}_2$ and X_2. These are almost the original right-hand side variables of the model, except that Y_2 is replaced by $\hat{Y}_2$. The results of this regression are that we obtain values a and b which are consistent estimators of the model parameters α and β.

The reason for the use of $\hat{Y}_2$ instead of Y_2 in stage two is that $\hat{Y}_2$ is not correlated with the equation error term ϵ_1. The reason is simply that $\hat{Y}_2$ was constructed as an exact linear function of X_1 and X_2, two external variables that were independent of the error term. Thus, a linear function of X_1 and X_2 will also be independent of the error term, and application of a second stage of least squares to estimate the equation will be appropriate.

The second equation can be estimated in a similar way. The right-hand side variable Y_1 can be regressed on the external factors in the model X_1 and X_2 yielding values $\hat{Y}_1$. Then, in a second-stage regression we can regress Y_2 on $\hat{Y}_1$ and X_1 to obtain values a' and b' that are consistent estimators of the population parameters α' and β'.

Although we have described TSLS in the context of a two-step process, the process can be carried out in one simple operation with the aid of an appropriate computer program such as SIMPLAN. While the (inappropriate) least-squares estimators could be computed for the two equations by the commands ESTIMATE Y1 Y2 X2 and ESTIMATE Y2 Y1 X1, the TSLS command is slightly more complex. In addition to specifying the equation to be estimated, one must also supply the list of all the external variables so that the computer can use these in the first stage of the estimation. This first stage is then carried out by the computer, but typically only the second stage with the estimated coefficients is printed for the user to see.

The TSLS command to estimate the first equation of our model would be TSLS Y1 Y2 X2 *EXOG X1 X2. Everything up to the asterisk reads like an ordinary regression command, except that we have specified TSLS instead of ESTIMATE. The phrase "*EXOG" is a keyword that indicates a list of external (exogenous) variables for the entire model follows, and after this word the variables X_1 and X_2 are listed. With the information on the external variables following *EXOG, the computer then can identify right-hand side output variables (such as Y_2 in the first equation) by their absence from the list following *EXOG. The computer can then perform the necessary first-stage regression, obtain the necessary hatted values, and proceed to obtain the desired estimates in the second stage of the estimation process. In a similar fashion, the second equation could be estimated by the command TSLS Y2 Y1 X1 *EXOG X1 X2. Chapter 7 contains several examples of the SIMPLAN TSLS command.

We mentioned above that the computer can check that the order condition for identification is met if we employ TSLS. The computer can check that an equation is identified based on the information in a TSLS command. Since all the exogenous or external variables are listed after the keyword *EXOG, the computer can figure out which variables following the TSLS are output variables. Then for each output variable, there must be an absent external variable that is listed after *EXOG but not after TSLS. The computer can thus check the order condition for identification and spare the analyst the burden.

To complete our discussion of TSLS, we need only to mention the test statistics associated with the TSLS coefficient estimates. The TSLS method produces test statistics that are analogous to those for an ordinary regression: t values, F values, D.W. values, and an R^2. By and large, these have *approximately* the same interpretation, but these statistics do not behave in exactly the same way for two-stage least squares as they do for ordinary least squares.

The t and the F values are basically similar, except that these values from a TSLS command must now be regarded as approximately t-distributed and approximately F-distributed, rather than following these distributions exactly. Thus, one can perform t-tests as was illustrated in Figs. 6.6 or 6.7 and F-tests, except that now the tests must be regarded as approximately correct and not exactly correct. To be cautious in such situations, one suggested approach is to regard a test of a given level as really being a test at the next lower level. Thus, one might interpret a five percent test as really implying ten percent significance, and a one percent test might imply five percent significance.

The D.W. value can be similarly regarded as an approximation. The D.W. statistic was originally derived for the case of ordinary least-squares regression, and thus is not strictly applicable to a TSLS regression, but it still may give a rough idea of the problem of autocorrelated errors. One rule of thumb for checking for positive autocorrelation is that D.W. values between 1.5 and 2.0 imply no autocorrelation, values between 1.0 and 1.5 are inconclusive, while values of the D.W. below 1.0 probably indicate the presence of autocorrelated errors. There is a version of TSLS that carries out a

Cochrane–Orcutt type of correction, but space does not permit its discussion here. The reader interested in this problem can see Kelejian and Oates (1974, pp. 261–264).

The R^2 is the one statistic that is perhaps most different in the case of an ordinary regression and a two-stage regression. In an ordinary regression the value of the R^2 is always between 0 and 1, and the R^2 can be interpreted as a ratio of explained variation in the dependent variable. In the case of TSLS, the R^2 is not necessarily on the interval 0 to 1, and it is sometimes perplexing to see an R^2 of, say, $-.3$ result from a TSLS regression. This does not indicate a computer program error, and it may not even indicate a poor model. It simply indicates that a statistic which is useful for an ordinary regression equation is not always useful for a TSLS regression equation. The real test of a TSLS equation is how well the equation interacts with the rest of the equations of the model of which it is a part, and this is a question of the simulation performance of the entire model. We discuss this question below and in the following chapter.

Other simultaneous equation estimators We have discussed TSLS because it is the simplest and most widely used method for dealing with the problem of estimating a system of simultaneous equations. It is not, however, the only means available. Economists have developed at least half a dozen other methods that yield consistent estimates, and under some conditions these other methods can yield estimates that are superior to the TSLS estimates. However, the other methods are often quite involved and expensive in terms of both computing time and the time of the analyst. The analyst's time is often taxed heavily by other methods because the complexity of the estimation methods requires very detailed and lengthy specification of the model in order for the other methods to be applied. A check with most of the standard econometrics texts will acquaint the reader with some of the more sophisticated methods. They are rather rarely employed in the construction of actual models. Ordinary least squares and two-stage least squares are the workhorses that practicing econometricians apply in 95 percent of their work.

SOLUTION OF ECONOMETRIC MODELS

As noted above, the R^2 is not a very useful statistic for a TSLS equation. The real question is not how well does one equation fit, but how well does the entire set of equations fit. To investigate this question, we must solve the entire model simultaneously. We discuss solving simultaneous equation models below.

Before we do so, however, we illustrate a slightly simpler type of multiple equation model, the recursive model. We have made reference to recursive models in Chapter 2. While simultaneous equation models typically require TSLS estimation, recursive models can be estimated with ordinary least squares.

Recursive Models

Recursive models consist of equations which, if placed in the proper order, are such that the left-hand dependent variable in each equation can be isolated and solved in terms of given external variables and policy variables, lagged output variables whose values were generated in previous time periods, and current output variables which have already been solved in previous equations. Recursive models are easily solved by algebraic substitution once they have been put in a causally ordered sequence. Sometimes it may be difficult to determine the causal ordering of a set of recursive equations and it may be easier to treat the model as a simultaneous equation model.

To illustrate the nature of recursive models we shall examine two example models –a market model and an econometric model of the textile industry.

A market model   The basic supply–demand model known as the *cobweb model* is a typical recursive model. The variables of the model are defined as follows:

P_t = price in period t

QD_t = quantity demanded in period t

QS_t = quantity supplied in period t

The model consists of two behavioral equations:

$$QD_t = A - BP_t \tag{6.11}$$

$$QS_t = C + DP_{t-1}. \tag{6.12}$$

The market is assumed to be cleared each period by the identity.

$$QS_t = QD_t. \tag{6.13}$$

Substituting Eqs. (6.11) and (6.12) into Eq. (6.13) we get

$$P_t = \frac{1}{B}(A - C - DP_{t-1}). \tag{6.14}$$

By changing the order of the equations, the model can be solved recursively with the following SIMPLAN program:

```
10 QS = C + D * P(-1)
20 QD = QS
30  P = (A - C - D * P(-1))/B
```

For given values of the parameters A, B, C, and D, the market model will generate the time paths (solutions) for price, quantity demanded, and quantity supplied. The coefficients A, B, C, D, could be estimated by least squares.

A model of the textile industry   The following recursive model of the United States textile industry was developed by several Duke University economists. The variables and equations are defined below. The coefficients were estimated by least squares. We omit values of R^2, t-tests, etc., to save space.

Output Variables

D_A = Apparel retail sales in millions of dollars

O_A = Index of production of apparel products

D_T = Shipments of textile mill products, in billions of dollars

O_T = Index of production of textile mill products

N_{PT} = Production and related workers on the payrolls in textile manufacturing in thousands

$E_{\bar{w}/m}$ = Average weekly gross earnings per production worker in textiles, in dollars

P_T = Index of prices of textile products and apparel

II_T = Net profit after taxes in textile mill products quarterly in millions of dollars

I_T = Investment in new plant and equipment quarterly in billions of dollars

External Variables

DPI = Disposable personal income in billions of dollars

CPI = Consumer price index

A_D = Magazine advertising for apparel and accessories in millions of dollars

INV_A = Inventories of apparel retail stores in millions of dollars

IP_{DG} = Index of production of durable goods

INV/UO = Ratio of inventories to unfilled orders for textile mill products

P_W = Index of wool prices

Status Variables

M = Monthly dummy variables, numbered 1 for January, 2 for February, . . . , and 12 for December.

T = Trend dummy variable numbered 1 through 144.

AD_A = Moving average of D_A

AO_A = Moving average of O_A

AD_T = Moving average of D_T

Identities

$$AD_A(t) = \frac{1}{3} \sum_{r=1}^{3} D_A(t-r) \tag{6.15}$$

$$AO_T(t) = \frac{1}{6} \sum_{r=7}^{12} O_A(t-r) \tag{6.16}$$

$$AD_T(t) = \frac{1}{12} \sum_{r=1}^{12} D_T(t-r) \tag{6.17}$$

Behavioral Equations

Apparel demand:

$$D_A(t) = -552.71 + 300.81\left[\frac{DPI(t-1)}{CPI(t-1)}\right] + 96.94[A_D(t-1)]$$
$$+ 55.19[A_D(t-2)] + 94.38[A_D(t-3)] + 34.83[M] \qquad (6.18)$$

Apparel output:

$$O_A(t) = -4.38 + .01824[AD_A(t)] - 30.70[INV_A(t-1)] \qquad (6.19)$$

Demand for textile mill products:

$$D_T(t) = .3029 + .0014[AO_A(t)] + .00064[IP_{DG}(t-1)] + .0083[M] \qquad (6.20)$$

Output of textile mill products

$$O_T(t) = 58.99 + 41.20[D_T(t)] - 14.45\left[\frac{INV}{UO}(t-1)\right] \qquad (6.21)$$
$$- .515[M] + .082[T]$$

Employment of production workers:

$$N_{PT}(t) = 1684.29 + .4745[O_T(t)] + .9623[O_T(t-1)] \qquad (6.22)$$
$$+ .6041[O_T(t-2)] + .7305[O_T(t-3)]$$
$$- 411.72\left[\frac{DPI(t-1)}{CPI(t-1)}\right]$$

Earnings

$$E_{\bar{w}/m}(t) = .3153 + .427[N_{PT}(t)] + .2421[T] \qquad (6.23)$$

Prices:

$$P_T(t) = 169.07 - 8.41\left[\frac{INV}{UO}(t-1)\right] + .5722[E_{\bar{w}/m}(t)] \qquad (6.24)$$
$$+ .7986[P_T(t-1)]$$
$$+ .0342[P_w(t-1)] - .0682[T]$$

Profit:

$$\Pi_T(t) = -463.43 + 1.80[P_T(t)] - 1.39[P_T(t-1)] + 41.28[D_{\hat{r}}(t)] \qquad (6.25)$$
$$- 58.65\left[\frac{INV}{UO}(t-1)\right] + 1.78[E_{\bar{w}/m}(t)]$$

Investment:

$$I_T(t) = -.869 + .2524[AD_T(t)] + .000075[T] \qquad (6.26)$$

The solutions to the textile model appear in Figs. 6.17 through 6.25. Both the actual observed values of each output variable and the simulated values are plotted.

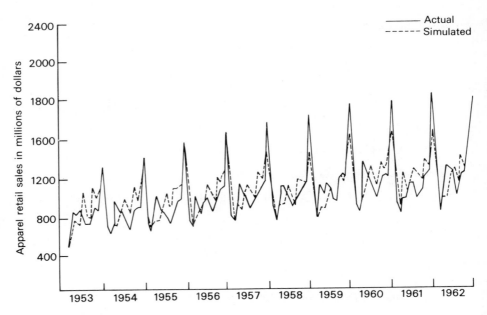

Fig. 6.17 Apparel demand.

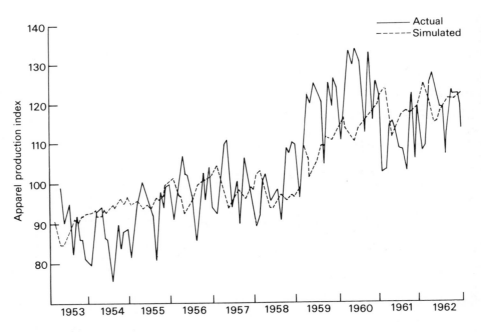

Fig. 6.18 Apparel output.

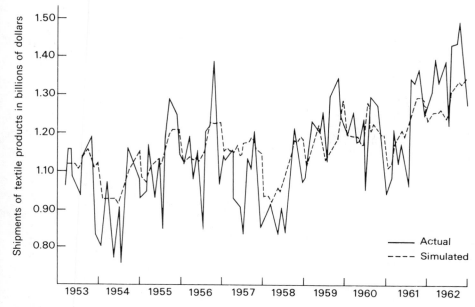

Fig. 6.19 Demand for textile mill products.

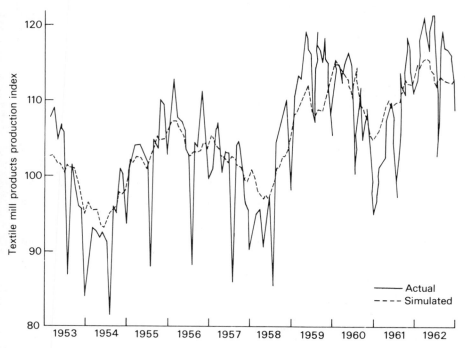

Fig. 6.20 Output of textile mill products.

Fig. 6.21 Employment of production workers.

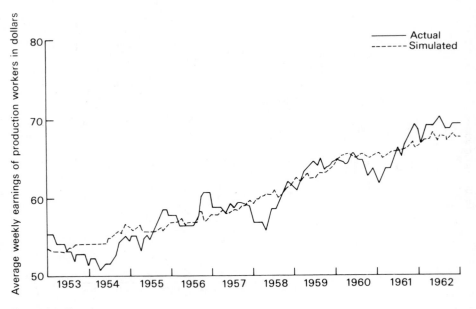

Fig. 6.22 Earnings.

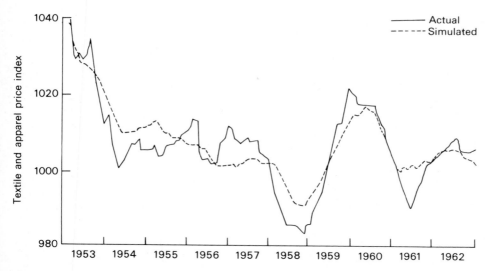

Fig. 6.23 Prices.

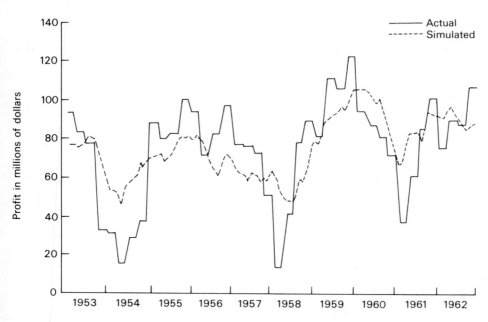

Fig. 6.24 Profit.

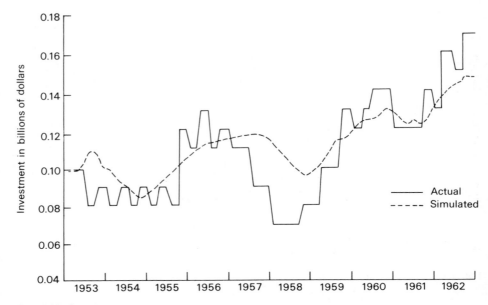

Fig. 6.25 Investments.

Simultaneous Equation Models

The fundamental problem with a simultaneous equation model is that of solving the model for the output variables. We discuss here the Gauss–Seidel method, a fairly simple method that works very well in practice. Further, the method can be applied to linear models, as well as nonlinear models that contain logs, squared terms, etc.

Consider the system of equations:

$$Y_1 = f(Y_2, X_2) \tag{6.27}$$

$$Y_2 = f(Y_1, X_1).$$

It is assumed that we have values of X_1 and X_2 for all periods, and the goal is to obtain solution values of Y_1 and Y_2 for the corresponding time periods.

We begin by making some initial guesses as to the values of Y_1 and Y_2. These values may come from an informed guess or recently observed values of the variables. Denote these values as Y_1^0 and Y_2^0. Substituting these values on the right-hand side of the model, we obtain:

$$Y_1^1 = f(Y_2^0, X_2) \tag{6.28}$$

$$Y_2^1 = f(Y_1^0, X_1).$$

The superscript one denotes the values after one iteration. If we repeat the process using the values Y_1^1 and Y_2^1 on the right-hand side, we obtain:

$$Y_1^2 = f(Y_2^1, X_2) \tag{6.29}$$
$$Y_2^2 = f(Y_1^1, X_1).$$

The superscript two denotes results after two iterations. After n iterations, the equations will be of the form

$$Y_1^n = f(Y_2^{n-1}, X_2) \tag{6.30}$$
$$Y_2^n = f(Y_1^{n-1}, X_1).$$

Iteration continues until the values Y_1 and Y_2 show no further change from iteration to iteration, or we can use the criterion of no further relative change. This can be formalized as saying the system is solved when the following inequalities are satisfied:

$$\left| \frac{Y_1^n - Y_1^{n-1}}{Y_1^{n-1}} \right| < .001 \tag{6.31}$$

$$\left| \frac{Y_2^n - Y_2^{n-1}}{Y_2^{n-1}} \right| < .001$$

The speed of convergence can often be increased if the iteration in Eq. (6.30) is modified slightly. In Eq. (6.30) it is apparent that once the first equation is evaluated, we have a new value of Y_1^n and we can utilize this value in the second equation in place of Y_1^{n-1}. With this change the Gauss–Seidel iteration becomes:

$$Y_1^n = f(Y_2^{n-1}, X_2) \tag{6.32}$$
$$Y_2^n = f(Y_1^n, X_1).$$

Two factors influence convergence in this algorithm. The first is the procedure of normalization; that is, the choice of the variable in each equation to be written on the left-hand side with unit coefficient and expressed as a function of all other variables. In almost all equations this normalization procedure can be carried out in a variety of ways. Some normalizations lead to convergence and some to divergence.

The other factor affecting convergence is the ordering of the equations in the case where we substitute in a given iteration a value computed earlier in the same iteration. This is not of any consequence if there are only two equations, but is important if there are several. As with normalization, some orderings lead to convergence while others cause divergence. No simple rule is available for the optimal ordering, and some experimentation may be necessary to find an ordering that will give a convergent solution. This is a consequence of the particular iterative procedure used here and not of the exact solution of the model itself. In particular, even if a fully simultaneous solution of the model always converges, an attempt to solve by iteration with an erroneous ordering will lead to divergence.

The Gauss–Seidel method has among its advantages the fact that it usually converges quickly (10–20 iterations in many cases) and that it can handle linear and nonlinear models. Conceptually linear equations can be solved directly by elimination of variables, but the use of the Gauss–Seidel method makes it possible to treat simultaneous equation models as a general class without regard to whether the equations are linear or nonlinear. Among its disadvantages are that some rearrangement of the equations may be necessary to make the method converge in the linear case, and the method may possibly fail to converge at all in the case of nonlinear equations. In practice the latter occurrence is rare, but it is a possibility with any method for solving nonlinear equations.

The SOLVE command of SIMPLAN utilizes the Gauss–Seidel method to solve linear and nonlinear simultaneous equation models. We illustrate it in Chapter 7.

VALIDATION

The validation of econometric models includes three basic steps–rationalism, empiricism, and prediction. We shall briefly summarize each of these steps.

By *rationalism*, we mean that econometric models must be based on sound economic and market theory. The raison d'être for the questionnaire approach described at the beginning of this chapter was to provide a sound rationale on which to base econometric marketing models.

With regard to *empiricism*, we examine such test statistics as R^2, t-statistics, F-statistic, and Durbin–Watson statistic. Ideally, we would like to have econometric estimations characterized by high R^2s (close to 1.00), statistically significant coefficients (t-statistics greater than 2.00), high F-statistics, Durbin–Watson statistics which are not statistically significant, and signs which make intuitive sense. Rarely are all of these criteria satisfied by a single estimating equation. We tend to worry if the sign of a particular equation is contrary to our intuitive understanding of the system. For example, a positively sloped demand function makes us nervous. On the other hand, we may be willing to include the variable in the model if it has the right sign, even though it is barely statistically significant.

There are at least two reasons for subjecting the assumptions of our model to empirical tests. First, we may save ourselves a lot of programming time and computer running time by performing some simple empirical tests at this stage rather than waiting until we have conducted extensive computer simulation runs to determine that a particular variable was incorrectly included or excluded from the model. By detecting specification errors at an early stage we may save a great deal of work and a considerable amount of computer time. A second reason for our interest in the verification of assumptions is that while we are ultimately interested in the model's forecasting performance, we are also interested in the explanatory power of the model. To be specific, if the model begins to forecast badly, we may want to try to ascertain why it is tracking the behavior of the actual system poorly. A model based on assumptions which are nonsensical may be extremely difficult to understand. When this is the case, the job of correcting or modifying a model which is performing badly may be a demanding task. In many instances we may be primarily concerned with forecasting ability but have a genuine interest in trying to understand the behavior of the system as well. For a marketing manager, a model which predicts well but is difficult or impossible to understand may be of very limited value as an operational tool.

In the final analysis, *prediction* is probably the most powerful test of the validity of a computer simulation model; that is, if we are consistently able to forecast the behavior of sales, revenue, or market share with a high degree of accuracy through the use of a simulation model, then our confidence in the validity of the model increases. But to say that we are primarily concerned with the predictive capabilities of a simulation model still raises a number of serious methodological questions.

Suppose, for example, that the model has been estimated over a database for the period 1956–1970 but that marketing policy simulations are to be conducted over the period 1971–1980. As an initial step in validating our model, we would certainly want to simulate the behavior of the system over the database 1956–1970. This type of validation experiment is known as *ex-post* validation. Unless the model is able to predict the past behavior of the system over the database, we will have only limited confidence in its ability to predict the future. Ideally, we would like to validate the model over the database using a different set of data from that used to actually estimate the model. Unfortunately, in actual practice this is likely to be extremely difficult if not impossible. Ultimately we would like to validate the model on the basis of its prediction of the future 1971–1980. Even so, there is no assurance that because the model has performed well on an ex-post basis it can also perform well on an *ex-ante* basis in the future. In a sense, once we have validated the model on an ex-post basis it becomes an act of faith as to whether or not the model will do well in future applications. It is safe to say that if we have a complete understanding of the inner workings of the model and have carefully verified all the assumptions of the model that we are likely to have greater confidence in the ex-ante forecasting performance of the model than if we did not fully understand the assumptions underlying the model.

The two most common goodness of fit tests for validating the forecasting performance of econometric models are mean percent absolute errors and Theil's inequality coefficients. The SIMPLAN VALIDATE command automatically generates both of these statistics for comparing a predicted series P_i with an actual observed series A_i.

Mean percent absolute error   The mean percent error statistic is calculated by the expression

$$\frac{1}{n} \sum \left| \frac{P_i - A_i}{A_i} \right| \tag{6.33}$$

where P_i denotes the predicted value generated by the econometric model and A_i denotes the corresponding actual observed value of the variable.

Theil's inequality coefficient   Theil's inequality coefficient U provides another index which measures the degree to which an econometric model provides retrospective predictions P_i of observed historical data A_i:

$$U = \frac{\sqrt{\frac{1}{n} \sum (P_i - A_i)^2}}{\sqrt{\frac{1}{n} \sum P_i^2} + \sqrt{\frac{1}{n} \sum A_i^2}} \tag{6.34}$$

U varies between 0 and 1. If $U = 0$, we have perfect predictions. If $U = 1$, we have very bad predictions. It is somewhat analogous to a correlation coefficient except that close fits are denoted by values close to 0. The correlation coefficient is of no use in validation since it would yield the same value for the series $P = 1, 2, 3, A = 10, 20, 30$ and $P = 1, 2, 3, A = 1, 2, 3$. The first values of P and A would represent horrible forecasts, and the latter values would represent perfect forecasts. For both series $r = 1.0$, but only for the latter series does $U = 0$ indicating the two series are identical.

POLICY SIMULATION

Once we have come up with a model which has passed the aforementioned validity tests, we must then turn our attention to the question of marketing policy simulation experiments with the model. It should be noted that the procedures of specification, estimation, and validation described above are likely to be repeated many times before we develop a marketing model for which marketing managers are willing to accept the results as a reasonable representation of the actual system. In other words, we are only ready to consider marketing policy simulation experiments if marketing management is willing to place their confidence in the results of the policy simulation experiments run on the corporate marketing model. Typically, we will have to alter the specifications of our model, reestimate the parameters, change the computer program, and replicate the validity checks many times before we come up with a model which will be satisfactory to the management.

Following is a list of five different types of variables that may be used for conducting "What if?" simulation experiments with econometric marketing models:

1. *Marketing Policy Variables*

   a. Price
   b. Advertising expenditures
   c. Advertising strategies
   d. Public relations
   e. Product quality
   f. Size and quality of sales force
   g. Distribution system

2. *Competitive variables*

   a. Price
   b. Advertising
   c. Other

3. *Industry variables*

   a. Volume
   b. Price
   c. Inventories

4. *External economic variables*

   a. National economy
   b. Regional economy
   c. International economy

5. *Other external variables*

   a. Government regulations
   b. Strikes
   c. Wars
   d. Natural disasters
   e. Weather

Management must fully understand that the forecasting accuracy of econometric models depends entirely on the accuracy of the assumptions we make about the competitive variables, industry variables, external economic variables, and other external variables. Management must be strongly encouraged to participate in the process of specifying the policy assumptions and external assumptions which drive the model. In this fashion, management will then also share in the risk associated with the model's forecasting performance.

There are two important aspects of marketing policy simulations conducted with an econometric model. They include experimental design and data analysis.

Experimental design   Since a computer simulation experiment is indeed an experiment, it follows that we should give careful attention to the problem of experimental design. The problem of experimental design is also, in part, a political problem. Suppose that we are considering an experiment with a marketing policy model which contains ten price policies, five advertising policies, six research and development policies, and four distribution policies. In order to conduct an experiment which considers all of the logical possibilities described in the preceding sentence, we will need to conduct twelve hundred experiments, the number of logical possibilities being the product of all policy alternatives for each policy under consideration. We must try $10 \times 5 \times 6 \times 4$ or 1200 logical possibilities if we want to consider all of them. This type of experiment is called a *full-factorial design* in the literature on experimental design. In essence, we are confronted with the problem of too many managerial policy variables. If the model happens to contain, say, 150 to 200 equations, then we might consume an enormous amount of computer time examining all the logical possibilities in this experiment. Furthermore, this is actually a relatively small number of policy combinations. In actual marketing applications the number of policy alternatives might be much larger than the number mentioned as an example.

By this time it should be apparent to the reader that the first part of the problem of experimental design is in impressing upon the users or marketing managers that we can consider only those policies which they believe to be absolutely essential. We do not want to run policy simulation experiments to evaluate policies which are clearly nonfeasible or nonacceptable for political reasons. It is essential at this stage that we try to convince management to reduce its policy set to those policies which are politically feasible and which would be implemented if they proved to yield acceptable results from the marketing policy simulaton experiments.

However, we may be able to influence management only so far. We still may end up with a totally unmanageable number of policy configurations after the screening exercises above have been implemented. At this point we may need to call in a statistician to help us. There exist a number of techniques known in the literature as experimental designs which enable one to reduce the size of a full-factorial experiment. However, in cutting down the number of design points we actually run in the experiment, we must give up some information. The book edited by Thomas H. Naylor entitled *The Design of Computer Simulation Experiments* (Duke University Press, 1969) describes a number of experimental designs which can be used to solve the problem of too many marketing policy variables.

In summary, the problem of experimental design is both a political and a statistical problem. As is the case with the practical applications of simulation methodology to marketing policy, the problem of experimental design requires a considerable amount of experience and good judgment as well as a knowledge of scientific techniques and processes.

Data analysis   Finally, once we have actually conducted policy simulation experiments with the marketing policy model, the question arises as to how we interpret the results. Again, as was the case with all the previous steps, the analysis of the data generated by the simulation experiments depends to a great extent on our experimental objectives. We must ask if our objective began as one of optimization or if we were simply attempting to explore the effects of a number of different marketing policies on the behavior of sales. Were we primarily interested in parameter estimation, hypothesis testing, the construction of confidence intervals, or the ranking of output variables? Depending on the answers to these questions, there is a variety of statistical techniques available for analyzing data generated by computer simulation experiments.

The importance which we attach to these aspects of our methodology depends a great deal on the problems we are attempting to solve through the use of marketing policy models as well as our experimental objectives. Frequently, analysts have directed all too little attention to the question of data analysis with simulation experiments. While in some cases this may be totally justified, one should be aware of the possible risks in passing over questions of data analysis. Indeed, it may virtually impossible to interpret the results of a simulation experiment unless we give at least some thought to the question of data analysis. Naylor's book referenced in the preceding section describes a multiplicity of techniques for the analysis of data generated by computer simulation models.

MARKET ANALYSIS QUESTIONNAIRE

1. Product name _____

2. Date _____

3. Name of product manager or analyst _____

_____

4. Number of firms in the market _____

5. Market share _____%

6. The five largest firms in the market:

Firm name   Market share

   a. _____   _____

   b. _____   _____

   c. _____   _____

   d. _____   _____

   e. _____   _____

7. Description of product

_____

_____

_____

8. The major markets in which the product is sold

   a. _____   _____%

   b. _____   _____%

   c. _____   _____%

   d. _____   _____%

   e. _____   _____%

9. The major countries in which the product is sold

   a. _____   _____%

   b. _____   _____%

   c. _____   _____%

   d. _____   _____%

   e. _____   _____%

10. Six important leading indicators

Indicator   *Lag*

a. _____   _____

b. _____   _____

c. _____   _____

d. _____   _____

e. _____   _____

f. _____   _____

11. Which of the following best describes the market?

a. Perfect competition _____

b. Monopoly_____

c. Monopolistic competition _____

d. Oligopoly_____

12. What is the basis for competition?

a. Price _____

b. Advertising_____

c. Quality _____

d. R&D _____

e. Service_____

f. Promotion _____

13. How does the quantity demanded respond to price changes?

_____

_____

_____

_____

14. Are there a number of major customers? If so, please list them.

a. _____

b. _____

c. _____

d. _____

e. _____

15. Is the demand for the product highly seasonal?

_____

_____

_____

16. Has this product been modeled using econometric or time series methods?

_____

17. List any special promotional programs and their dates.

a. _____   _____

b. _____   _____

c. _____   _____

d. _____   _____

e. _____   _____

f. _____   _____

g. _____   _____

18. Describe the channels of distribution for the product.

_____

_____

_____

_____

19. Are there any apparent nonlinear relationships in the model?

_____

20. What about the quality of the data? How far back do the time series go?

_____

_____

21. Are there any close substitutes for the product?

a. _____

b. _____

c. _____

d. _____

22. Are there any other products whose sales are closely related to the sales of this product (complementary goods)?

    a. _____

    b. _____

    c. _____

23. Can you think of any other unique features of the market for this product?

    a. _____

    b. _____

    c. _____

    d. _____

    e. _____

24. Are there any other variables which help explain the sales volume of this product?

    a. _____

    b. _____

    c. _____

    d. _____

25. Do you feel it is necessary to develop a model of the entire market for the product? What characteristics of the market should be modeled?

    _____

    _____

    _____

26. What are the most important determinants of market share?

    a. _____

    b. _____

    c. _____

    d. _____

    e. _____

BIBLIOGRAPHY

Chow, Gregory, 1957. *The demand for automobiles in the United States*, Amsterdam: North Holland.

Johnston, J., 1972. *Econometric methods*. New York: McGraw-Hill.

Kelejian, Harry H., and Wallace E. Oates, 1974. *Introduction to econometrics: principles and applications*. New York: Harper & Row.

Kmenta, Jan, 1971. *Elements of econometrics*. New York: Macmillan.

Murphy, James L., 1973. *Introductory econometrics*. Homewood, Ill.: Richard D. Irwin.

Pindyck, Robert S., and Daniel L. Rubinfeld, 1976. *Econometric models and economic forecasts*. New York: McGraw-Hill.

Wonnacott, Ronald J., and Thomas H. Wonnacott, 1970. *Econometrics*. New York: Wiley.

7 Econometric Marketing Models: Applications

THOMAS H. NAYLOR AND TERRY G. SEAKS

Chapter 6 developed the methodology for building econometric models. This chapter describes the application of this methodology for a number of specific examples.

In the section entitled Corporate Marketing Models we describe two specific econometric models—the *New York Times* model and the Dresser Industries model. In both models the direct approach for market modeling has been employed; that is, demand equations have been estimated directly for each of the various products and services offered by the two companies. No attempt was made to model the respective industries, but rather the individual firm's demand curves were estimated for each product without regard for the entire market or industry.

Sometimes the direct approach proves to be impossible, and it becomes necessary to construct models of entire industries or markets and then develop separate equations linking the company's market share or sales volume to the industry's performance. The next two models presented in this chapter fall into this category. They include a pharmaceutical industry model and a battery industry model. In both cases, market share models were constructed and linked to the industry models.

The pharmaceutical and battery industry models were basically single-equation industry models. The next two models are much more complex in scope. They are multiequation models of the tobacco industry and the world coffee market, respectively.

Next we turn to national econometric models and include an illustrative example of a simple macroeconometric model. A section is also included that proposes a set of criteria for evaluating econometric service bureaus. Finally, several other applications of econometric models, unrelated to marketing, are also summarized.

CORPORATE MARKETING MODELS

The *New York Times* Model

Chapter 11 contains a write up describing the *New York Times* Corporate Planning

Model. It is an excellent example of an integrated planning model in which the financial model is linked to a production model and both are driven by an econometric marketing model. In this section we shall outline the econometric marketing model in some detail. It consists of 12 equations which explain circulation and 38 equations which explain advertising linage. The variables and equations are described below:

Circulation variables:

CIRCD	Daily circulation
CIRCS	Sunday circulation
SC4	National daily
SC9	National Sunday
SC11	City daily home delivery
SC12	Suburban daily home delivery
SC14	City Sunday home delivery
SC15	Suburban Sunday home delivery
SC16	City daily newsstand
SC17	Suburban daily newsstand
SC18	City Sunday newsstand
SC19	Suburban Sunday newsstand

Advertising linage variables

AMUSE	Total amusements
AMUSESUN%	Sunday amusements as a percentage of total amusements
EMP	Total help wanted classified
SL2101	Department store daily
SL2102	Amusements daily
SL2103	Real estate display daily
SL2103A	Classified apartments daily
SL2103B	Classified real estate daily
SL2107	Retail other daily
SL2202	General daily
SL2202A	Other general daily
SL2399	Automotive daily
SL2400	Financial daily
SL2501	Help wanted classified daily
SL2503	Other classified daily
SL2503A	Other classified except real estate daily

SL2600	Help wanted display daily
SL3102	Amusements Sunday
SL3103	Real estate display Sunday
SL3103A	Classified apartments Sunday
SL3103B	Classified real estate Sunday
SL3501	Help wanted classified Sunday
SL3600	Help wanted display Sunday
SL4101	Department store Sunday
SL4107	Retail other Sunday
SL4202	General Sunday
SL4202A	Other general Sunday
SL4399	Automotive Sunday
SL4400	Financial Sunday
SL4503	Other classified Sunday
SL4503A	Other classified except real estate Sunday
SL5999	Sunday magazine
SL6999	Book review
SL7999	Special sections
SUN%	Sunday help wanted display as percentage of total display
SUN%3501	Sunday help wanted classified as a percentage of total classified
TOTAPT	Total classified apartments
TOTDISP	Total help wanted display

External variables

CDAUTO	Personal consumer expenditures auto
CDMV&P	Personal consumption expenditures motor vehicles and parts
CNDUM	Dummy for loss of NYC newspapers
CN72	Real personal consumption expenditures nondurables
CPI	Consumer price index
CS72	Real personal consumer expenditures other services
EEA	Employment nonagricultural establishments
EHH	Total employment household survey
GNP	Gross National Product

GNPK72	Real potential GNP
HHNETWORTH	Household net worth
HUSTS	Housing starts
ICR	Residential construction expenditures
INVNF72	Inventories–constant dollars
JFRB	FRB production index
JFRBM	FRB production index manufacturing
JS&P	Standard & Poor's combined index or stock prices
LC	Civilian labor force
MONEY	Money Supply
NEST22&	Noninstitutional population 22 and over
N16&	Noninstitutional population 16 and over
PGNP	GNP deflator
P3	Suburban and city daily price
P4	National daily price
P8	Suburban and city Sunday price
P9	National Sunday price
RMMBCAAANS	Moody's AAA Corporate bond rate
RU	Unemployment rate
SF72	Real final sales
STRIKE2	Strike dummy variable
STRIKE2A	Strike dummy variable
STRIKE 3	Strike dummy variable
TIME	Trend variable
UCAPFRBM	FRB index of capacity utilization
VACR	Vacancy rate
YD72	Real disposable income
ZA	Corporate profits after taxes

Circulation equations

Sunday circulation
$$CIRCS = SC9 + SC14 + SC15 + SC18 + SC19$$

Daily circulation
$$CIRCD = SC17 + SC16 + SC12 + SC11 + SC4$$

National daily

$$SC4 = -142.16 + .22144*SC9 + .0057300*(SL2022 + SL2501 + SL2503)$$
$$+ .34473*SC4(-1) + 1.6413 * EHH + .84302 * P9 - 4.0371 * P4$$
$$+ 17.978 * STRIKE2 + 12.532 * STRIKE2A - 19.878 * STRIKE3$$

National Sunday

$$SC9 = 395.42 + 526.78 * (CPI - CPI(-1)) + .60837 * SC4 - 1.8062 * EHH$$
$$- 1.1354 * P9 + 2.4923 * P4 + .33235 * SC9(-1)$$

City daily home delivery

$$SC11 = -94.053 - .80112 * P3HD - .023381* SC16 + .49019 * SC14$$
$$+ 1.9608 * EHH - .99487 * CNDUM - 5.9084 * STRIKE2 - 12.503$$
$$* STRIKE3$$

Suburban daily home delivery

$$SC12 = -32.244 + 2.1913 * EHH + 1.4658 * TIME - 4.4427 * P3HD$$
$$- .53389 * SC17 - 13.158 * CNDUM - 24.453 * STRIKE3 - 29.462$$
$$* STRIKE2A - 10.226 * STRIKE2$$

City Sunday home delivery

$$SC14 = -1.3539 + .30103 * (SC11 + SC16) - 2.0433 * RU + 1.8727 * P3HD$$
$$- .62865 * P8HD + 3.8678 * CNDUM - 29.899 * STRIKE3 - 31.330$$
$$* STRIKE2 - 11.321 * STRIKE2A$$

Suburban Sunday home delivery

$$SC15 = 64.476 - 1.4540 * RU + .41481* SC17 + .41932 * SC12 + .65213$$
$$* TIME - 1.0543 * P8HD - 52.889 * STRIKE3 - 36.570$$
$$* STRIKE2A - 50.731 * STRIKE2$$

City daily newsstand

$$SC16 = 283.27 + .031376 * (SC18 + SC19) - .19847 * (SC11 + SC12)$$
$$- 6.4878 * P3 + 1.1469 * P8 + .018695 * (SL2107 + SL2501)$$
$$- 10.697 * CNDUM + 30.447 * STRIKE2 - .029908 * STRIKE3$$

Suburban daily newsstand

$$SC17 = 59.955 + .081756 * (SC19 + SC15) - .15321 * SC12 + .44807$$
$$* SC17(-1) - .79927 * P3 + .0082488 * (SL2501 + SL2107)$$
$$- 7.6248 * CNDUM + 31.882 * STRIKE2 + 19.989 * STRIKE3$$

City Sunday newsstand

$$SC18 = 112.66 + 271.01 * (CPI - CPI(-1)) + .42557 *SC18(-1) + .35497$$
$$* (SC11 + SC16) + 4.4971 *P3 - 1.8154 * P8 - .47245 * RU$$
$$+ 40.325 *STRIKE2 + 33.891 * STRIKE3$$

Suburban Sunday newsstand

$$SC19 = 90.428 - 466.24 * (CPI - CPI(-1)) + .45843 * SC17 - 1.1078 * P8$$
$$+ 2.0552 * TIME - 6.3173 * CNDUM + 36.263 * STRIKE2 + 41.348$$
$$* STRIKE3 + 32.387 * STRIKE2A$$

Advertising linage equations

Total amusements
$$AMUSE = -1094.41 + 1.7663 * (5.0000 * CIRCD + CIRCS)/ 6.0000 + 3.0298$$
$$* (CS072 + CS072 (-1) + CS072 (-2) + CS072 (-3)$$
$$+ CS072 (-4)/5.0000 - 217.26 * STRIKE 2 - 457.48$$
$$* STRIKE2A$$

Sunday amusements as a percentage of total amusements
$$AMUSESUN\% = .15393 + .0075474 * CIRCS/CIRCD + .25569$$
$$* AMUSESUN\% (-1) + .27865 * AMUSESUN\% (-2)$$
$$+ 2.481 * STRIKE2A$$

Total help wanted classified[1]
$$EMP = EXP (10.010 - 1.5761 * LOG (CIRCS/CIRCD) * 6.3240$$
$$* LOG (GNP72/GNP72 (-1)) - .93403 * LOG ((RU + RU (-1)$$
$$+ RU (-2) + RU (-3)) / 4.0000) - .33148 * STRIKE2 - 11.247$$
$$* STRIKE2A - .071687 * SLOW - .13253 * EMPDUM)$$

Department store daily
$$SL2101 = EXP (-.092991 + .16772 * LOG (SL4101) + .65982$$
$$* LOG (CIRCD) - .30405 * LOG ((RU + RU (-1) + RU (-2)$$
$$+ RU (-3) + RU (-4) + RU (-5) + RU (-6))/ 7.0000) + .051172$$
$$* XTIME - .0002/ 970 * XTIME ** 2.0000 - .31390 * STRIKE2$$
$$- 9.3630 * STRIKE2A - .19057 * STRIKE3)$$

Amusements daily
$$SL2102 = (1.0000 - AMUSESUN\%) * AMUSE + ADDSL2102$$

Real estate display daily
$$SL2103 = 30.681 + .20147 * SL2103 (-1) + .26794 * SL2103 (-2) + 7.4149$$
$$* HUSTS - 23.494 * STRIKE3 - 83.243 * STRIKE2A + 27.424$$
$$* SLOW$$

Classified apartments
$$SL2103A = .632 * TOPAPT + ADDSL2103A$$

Classified real estate daily
$$SL2103B = -1114.5 + 1.3643 * SL3103B + 28.442 * TIME - .17020 * TIME$$
$$** 2$$

Retail other daily
$$SL2107 = EXP (-.88690 - .64886 * LOG (CIRCS/CIRCD) + .78388$$
$$* LOG (GNP72) + .028473 * TIME - .00018934 * TIME ** 2.0000$$
$$+ .29578 * LOG (SL4107) - .28662 * STRIKE2 - .068273$$
$$* STRIKE3 - 8.0614 * STRIKE2A)$$

General daily
$$SL2202 = SL2202A + SL2102 + SL2103$$

Other general daily
$$SL2202A = 699.87 + .15357 * SL4202A + 1.9610 * CIRCD - 7.1671$$
$$* CS072 + 25.228 * (EEA - EEA (-4)) - 407.39 * STRIKE2$$
$$- 1266.9 * STRIKE2A - 143.17 * STRIKE3 - 89.755 * SLOW$$

Automotive daily
$$SL2399 = 416.03 + .08971 * CIRCD - 417.80$$
$$* (CDMV\&P/ NEST22\&) / PGNP - 24.652 * RU - 158.92$$
$$* (HHNETWORTH - HHNETWORTH (-4))/HHNETWORTH(-4))$$
$$+ .27780 * SL2399 (-1) - 60.022 * STRIKE2 - 101.30$$
$$* STRIKE3 - 263.05 * STRIKE2A$$

Financial daily
$$SL2400 = 31.338 + .0016017 * SL4400 * (CIRCD + CIRCD (-1)$$
$$+ CIRCD (-2) + CIRCD (-3)) / 4.0000 + 917.19 * MONEY (-1)$$
$$- MONEY (-3)) / MONEY (-3) -1.5328 * (GNPK72 - GNP72)$$
$$+ 88.970 * RMMBCAAANS - 68.632 * STRIKE2 - 99.541$$
$$* STRIKE3 - 346.16 * STRIKE2A$$

Help wanted classified daily
$$SL2501 = (1 - SUN\%3501) * EMP + ADDSL2501$$

Other classified daily
$$SL2503 = SL2503A + SL2103A + SL2103B$$

Other classified except real estate daily
$$SL2503A = -74.086 + .85439 * CIRCD - 7.1613 * RU + 106.54$$
$$* ERRORDUM + 2.0895 * (.25000 * CDMV\&P72 + .30000$$
$$* CDMV\&P72 (-1) + .20000 * CDMV\&P72 (-2) + .15000$$
$$* CDMV\&P72 (-3) + .10000 * CDMV\&P72 (-4)) - 139.69$$
$$* STRIKE2 - 569.15 * STRIKE2A - 46.828 * STRIKE3$$

Help wanted display daily
$$SL2600 = 36.680 + .50340 * SL2600 (-1) -1.9315 * RU + .4767 * ZA$$
$$- 4.8008 * RMMBCAAANS - 10.112 * STRIKE2 + .47671$$
$$* STRIKE2A + 7.1146 * SLOW + 20.933 * NASSA$$

Amusements Sunday
$$SL3102 = AMUSESUN\% * AMUSE + ADDSL3102$$

Real estate display Sunday
$$SL3103 = 152.53 + 2.5988 * APTDUM + .10970 * SL3103 (-1) + .19166$$
$$* SL3103 (-2) - 36.388 * STRIKE2 - 267.94 * STRIKE2A$$
$$- 41.421 * STRIKE3$$

Classified apartments Sunday
$$SL3103A = .368 * TOTAPT + ADDSL3103A$$

Classified real estate Sunday

$$SL3103B = 293.705 - 79.59 * STRIKE2 - 50.0140 * STRIKE3 - 402.69$$
$$* STRIKE2A - 53.703 * SLOW - 25.578 * VACR + 4.8844$$
$$* ((ICR + ICR(-1) + ICR(-2) + ICR(-3) + ICR(-4))/5)$$
$$+ .94323 * TIME$$

Help wanted classified Sunday

$$SL3501 = SUN\%3501 * EMP + ADDSL3501$$

Help wanted display Sunday

$$SL3600 = 329.81 + .47967 * SL3600(-1) - 30.892 * RU + 4.3013 * ZA$$
$$- 23.188 * RMMBCAAANS - 126.46 * STRIKE2 - 296.74$$
$$* STRIKE2A + 84.997 * NASSA$$

Department store Sunday

$$SL4101 = RES4101 + 2236.2 - .11765 * XTIME ** 2.0000$$

Retail other Sunday

$$SL4107 = EXP(4.6778 - .20134 * LOG(CIRCS/CIRCD) - .0087670$$
$$* LOG(RU) - .0023954 * TIME + .37363 * LOG(SL2107)$$
$$- .14530 * STRIKE2 - 7.2375 * STRIKE2A - .12025 * STRIKE3)$$

General Sunday

$$SL4202 = SL4202A + SL3102 + SL3103$$

Other general Sunday

$$SL4202A = 468.46 + .26778 * SL2202A + 2.1910 * CS072 + 25.155$$
$$* (EEA - EEA(-4)) - 102.05 * STRIKE2 - 695.99$$
$$* STRIKE2A - 66.233 * STRIKE3 + 98.068 * SLOW$$

Automotive Sunday

$$SL4399 = -367.29 - .62065 * JS\&P + .26134 * CIRCS + .56958 * TIME$$
$$+ 438.49 * (CDMV\&P / NEST22\&) / PGNP - 62.622 * STRIKE2$$
$$- 60.427 * STRIKE3 - 93.336 * STRIKE2A$$

Financial Sunday

$$SL4400 = 154.05 - 24.037 * HUSTS + .00014986 * SL2400 * (CIRCS$$
$$+ CIRCS(-1) + CIRCS(-2) + CIRCS(-3)) / 4.0000 - 18.583$$
$$* RMMBCAAANS + 21.777 * STRIKE2 - 22.959 * STRIKE3$$
$$- 42.130 * STRIKE2A$$

Other classified Sunday

$$SL4503 = SL4503A + SL3103A + SL3103B$$

Other classified except real estate Sunday

$$SL4503A = -435.03 + .38957 * SL2503A + .36070 * CIRCS + 14.419 * RU$$
$$+ 3.5157 * CDAUTO + 5.2823 * CDAUTO(-3) - 165.33$$
$$* STRIKE2 - 278.12 * STRIKE2A$$

Sunday magazine
$$SL5999 = EXP (7.7758 - .63788 * LOG ((RU + RU (-1) + RU (-2)$$
$$+ RU (-3)) / 4.00000 - 11.222) * STRIKE2A - .12729$$
$$* STRIKE2 - .34779 * STRIKE3)$$

Book review
$$SL6999 = 410.92 + 1.6349 * TIME - 32.612 * P6999 - 17.120 * RU$$
$$- 39.492 * STRIKE2 - 36.418 * STRIKE3 - 319.96 * STRIKE2A$$
$$+ 22.374 * SLOW$$

Special sections
$$SL7999 = -369.51 + 8.9244 * EEA + .24963 * SL7999 (-1) - 165.70$$
$$* STRIKE2A$$

Sunday help wanted display as percentage of total display
$$SUN\% = .25829 + .42423 * SUN\%(-1) + .29656 * SUN\%(-2)$$

Sunday help wanted classified as a percentage of total classified
$$SUN\%3501 = .098196 + .0030864 * TIME - .012624 * STRIKE2 - .031217$$
$$* STRIKE2A + .12084 * (CIRCS/CIRCD$$
$$+ CIRCS (-1) / CIRCD (-1) + CIRCS (-2) / CIRCD (-2)$$
$$+ CIRCS (-3) / CIRCD (-3)$$
$$+ CIRCS (-4) / CIRCD (-4)) / 5.0000$$

Total classified apartments
$$TOTAPT = 164.72 + 39.099 * APTDUM + 151.98 * VACR - 159.90$$
$$* STRIKE2 - 1175.4 * STRIKE2A - 80.063 * SLOW$$

Total help wanted display
$$TOTDISP = 835.911 + 8.7957 * (.35000 * ZA + .30000 * ZA (-1) + .15000$$
$$* ZA (-2) + .10000 * ZA (-3) + .10000 * ZA (-4)) - 59.589$$
$$* (.38000 * RU + .27000 * RU (-1) + .19000 * RU (-2)$$
$$+ .11000 * RU (-3) + .50000 * RU (-4)) - 56.102$$
$$* RMMBCAAANS - 101.33 * STRIKE2 - 389.10 * STRIKE2A$$
$$- 50.667 * SLOW + 181.06 * NASSA$$

The Dresser Industries Model

Chapter 11 contains a detailed description of a planning model for one of the operating companies of Dresser Industries. The econometric marketing model which drives the model contains 45 equations (15 products sold in three markets). Each of the 45 demand functions is of the following form:

$$Q_i = f(P_i, M_1, \ldots, M_k, E_1, \ldots, E_n, Q_1, \ldots, Q_j, \ldots, Q_m) \tag{7.1}$$

where

Q_i = Quantity demanded of the ith product–market items

P_i = Relative price of the ith product–market to fabricated metal prices

M = Management decision variable

E = Economic indicator of market activity

Q_j = Quantity demanded of complementary products sold by Dresser in the same market where $j \neq i$

Sample equations for specific product–market combinations are included in the more extensive write up of the model in Chapter 11.

INDUSTRY MODELS

A Pharmaceutical Industry Model

The pharmaceutical industry in the United States is unique in terms of the richness of the marketing data available within the industry. Although the most advanced econometric modeling in the industry has been done by the Swiss pharmaceutical company, CIBA-GEIGY, several American drug companies are now beginning to experiment with econometric marketing models.

Several versions of the following econometric model specification have been successfully implemented by American drug firms:

$$S_i = f(M_i, PE_i, QPE_i, DE_i, QDE_i, P_i), \tag{7.2}$$

where

S_i = Sales volume for product i

M_i = Market sales volume for the therapeutic market class of product i

PE_i = Promotional expenditures for product i

QPE_i = Quality of promotional effort for product i

DE_i = Detailing effort (sales calls on physicians) for product i

QDE_i = Quality of detailing message for product i

P_i = Relative price of product i

The market sales volume for the therapeutic market class of each product M_i is expressed as a separate regression equation for each product. Initial specifications of the market equations expressed M_i as a function of time only. Empirical testing of the model suggested that a number of the drug markets were indeed influenced by the national economy. The M_i equations were then respecified including national economic indicators as external variables. Products from the following therapeutic class markets have been modeled:

1 Anti-infectives

2 Analgesics and anti-inflammatory

3 Psychopharmaceuticals

4 Cough and cold preparations

5 Cardiovasculars

6 Nutritional sufficiency

7 Oral contraceptives

8 Diabetic therapy

9 Anticholinergics and antispasmodics

10 Antiobesity

A Battery Industry Model

A leading manufacturer of batteries has specified and estimated the following equation to explain industry sales for batteries:

$$S = f(MV, PC, INV, TEMP, Q_2, Q_3, Q_4), \tag{7.3}$$

where

S	=	Sales volume
MV	=	Population of motor vehicles two years old and older
PC	=	Personal consumption
INV	=	Change in business inventories
TEMP	=	Temperature variations from norm to first and fourth quarters
Q_2	=	Second quarter dummy variable
Q_3	=	Third quarter dummy variable
Q_4	=	Fourth quarter dummy variable

A Tobacco Industry Model[2]

In this section we shall summarize an econometric model of the American tobacco industry for the period 1949 through 1966. The model contains 19 equations and is divided into three major blocks: (1) leaf production, (2) leaf price, and (3) cigarettes. The variables of the model are defined below. Further explanation of the variables is provided in the discussion of the models individual equations

Output variables

AFR	Free market acreage (acres)
AVAL	Acre value (dollars)
AFRMAL	Free market acreage less allotment (acres)
UND	Underage (acres)
A	Actual acreage (acres)
Q	Leaf production (1000 lbs)

QNET	Leaf production less leaf pledged (1000 lbs)
SQNET	Ratio of net leaf supply to domestic disappearance (usage)
SQ	Ratio of leaf supply less exports only to domestic disappearance (usage)
PACT	Leaf price (cents)
PFR	Free market leaf price (cents)
SPMFP	Support price minus free market price (cents)
T	Leaf pledged by growers at support price (1000 lbs)
CCON	Cigarette consumption (billions cigs.)
CPRO	Cigarette production (billions cigs.)
LFPCIG	Leaf per cigarette (lbs/1000 cigs.)
CDIS	Disappearance (usage) into cigarette production (1000 lbs)
DDISP	Domestic leaf disappearance (usage) (1000 lbs)
STK	Stock of leaf at end of crop year (1000 lbs)

External variables

OTHDIS	Disappearance into other products (1000 lbs)
PCAPY	Disposable income per capita (dollars)
RDISY	Real disposable income (billions dollars)
RPCIG	Real price of cigarettes retail (cents/pack)
TIME	Time
TXFWD	Tax free withdrawals and exports (billions cigs.)
WPX	Wholesale price index
X	Exports of leaf (1000 lbs)
YPA	Yield per acre (lbs)

Policy variables

AL	Allotment of acres (acres)
LBDMY	Dummy variable for first-year poundage program
SBDMY	Dummary variable for Soil Bank
SP	Support price (cents)

The model consists of 19 equations which represent the tobacco industry over the period 1949–1966. Since the model is recursive, the seven behavioral equations were estimated by ordinary least squares. The remaining 12 equations are identities. It is convenient to consider the model in three blocks. Block 1 of six equations explains total leaf production and the effect of the government restriction on output. Block 2, Eqs. (7.10) through (7.16), describes the determination of leaf price and the effect of the government support price. Block 3, Eqs. (7.17) through (7.22), is concerned with the cigarette manufacturing portion of the industry.

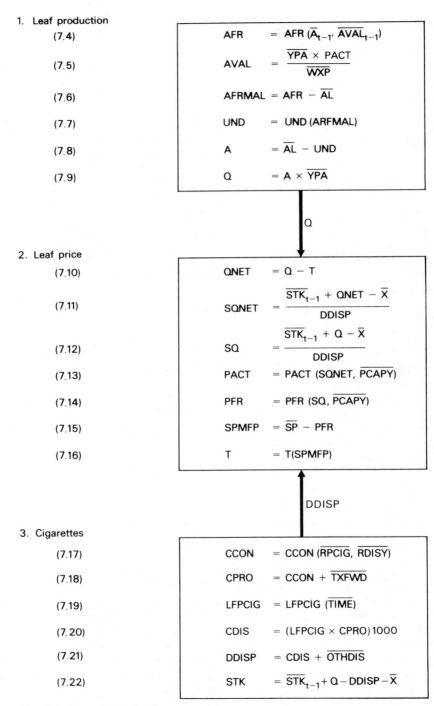

Fig. 7.1 Flowchart of tobacco model.

To illustrate the order in which the blocks must be solved and to provide an initial overview of the model, we have included a flowchart (Fig. 7.1). As indicated in the chart, Blocks 1 and 3 must be solved first for the values of Q and DDISP, and then Block 2 may be solved for the remaining variables. Bars are placed over predetermined variables.

1. Leaf Production The justification for treating leaf production separately from price determination is that the tobacco leaf market is of the cobweb type; that is, price and production are not determined simultaneously. Rather, production depends upon *lagged* price and can be determined first. Since price depends upon current production, it can logically be determined after production has been fixed. In more concrete terms, tobacco growers decide on leaf production in the spring based upon the price received for the crop in the preceding fall. The tobacco is then harvested in July and August and taken to market. Since the growers normally have no storage capability, the leaf production is thrown upon the market in perfectly inelastic supply (modified somewhat by the control program).

We have found it useful to treat the average amount of leaf produced per acre, YPA, as external to the model; that is, YPA depends largely upon weather, technical change and, since 1965, YPA has been subject to governmental limitation. If price is multiplied by YPA, we obtain the variable acre-value, AVAL. Consequently, we view the grower as possessing a supply function of acreage, A, which responds to the lagged price of acres or $AVAL_{t-1}$. Under free market conditions we would like to estimate the acreage equation $A = f(AVAL_{t-1})$. For example, the line OB in Fig. 7.2 could represent such an equation.

There would be no problem in estimating OB if we had reason to believe that all observable points actually lie on OB. Unfortunately, we have reason to believe otherwise. If the government should have set the allotment for acreage at OC acres when $AVAL_{t-1}$ was OD, then the point observed in that year would have been point T. Clearly, point T does not lie on the acreage supply equation.

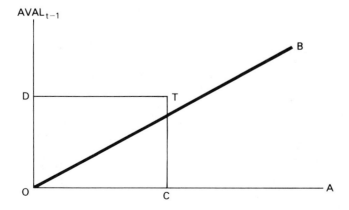

Fig. 7.2 Free market acreage.

Rather than attempting to estimate A, we estimate the difference between A and acreage allotment AL. This difference or underage, UND, is the number of acres not planted even though permitted by the allotment. The hypothesis is that UND will be lower the greater is the economic incentive to growers.

We have estimated hypothetical free market acreage, AFR, and have used the excess of AFR over AL as a measure of the growers' incentive to reduce UND. The AFR equation was estimated by using 1910–1930 data. Thus, since the government control program did not go into effect until after 1933, the 1910–1930 data points should all lie on the line OB in Fig. 7.2. Of course, in using the equation we must make the rather strong assumption that the structure of supply has not changed over this long period of time. The excellent statistical results for these equations offer some support for this assumption.

Based upon the hypothesis that A depends upon the *expected* AVAL, we can develop A as a function of A_{t-1} and $AVAL_{t-1}$. Equation 7.4 is the acreage equation estimated with 1910–1930 data. Since it will be used in the model to generate acreages for the 1949–1966 period which would have occurred had the free market structure of 1910–1930 prevailed, we will label it the free market acreage equation. The only other behavioral equation in the first six is Eq. (7.7), the underage equation. As hypothesized, the coefficient of AFRMAL is negative and is statistically significant.

One further point should be made about the UND equation. Two dummy variables were used to account for unusual events affecting UND. One dummy variable represents the effect of the Soil Bank program which was in effect in 1956, 1957, and 1958. Since the program was announced too late in 1956 to affect growers' decisions, the dummy variable SBDMY represents 1957 and 1958 only. The second dummy variable, LBDMY, represents the effect of a change in allotment after planting was over in 1965. The original allotment was set at 515,425 acres in December 1964. However, in May 1965, the allotment was increased to 607,335 acres as a result of the passage of a new governmental control program (the new program permits control of poundage as well as acreage).

Free market acreage[3]

$$\log AFR = -1.2098 + 0.8566 \log \overline{A}_{t-1} + 0.4825 \log \overline{AVAL}_{t-1} \qquad (7.4)$$
$$(0.6066)\ (0.0683) \qquad\qquad (0.1242)$$

$$\overline{R}^2 = 0.9150$$

$$DW = 2.3247 \qquad\qquad (1910\text{--}1930)$$

$$SE = 0.1302$$

Acre value

$$AVAL = \frac{\overline{YPA} \times PACT}{\overline{WPX}} \qquad (7.5)$$

Free market acreage less allotment

$$AFRMAL = AFR - \overline{AL} \qquad (7.6)$$

Underage

$$UND = 26.9640 - 0.0160 \text{ AFRMAL} + 46.3971 \text{ SBDMY} + 33.6419 \text{ LBDMY}$$
$$(6.6716) \ (0.0085) \qquad\quad (5.2275) \qquad\qquad (7.5373)$$

$\bar{R}^2 = 0.8296$ (7.7)

$DW = 1.5642$ (1949–1966)

$SE = 6.8986$

Actual acreage

$$A = \overline{AL} - UND \tag{7.8}$$

Leaf production

$$Q = A \times \overline{YPA} \tag{7.9}$$

2. Leaf Price   In Eqs. (7.10) through (7.11) we attempt to integrate the government support price for leaf into the determination of price. The essence of this part of the model is that the amount of leaf pledged by growers at the support price, T, and the market price of leaf, PACT, are mutually dependent. That is, PACT depends upon T and T depends upon PACT.

The statement that T depends upon PACT requires further explanation. We hypothesize that T depends upon the difference between SP and the hypothetical free market price, PFR. Thus, PFR is analogous to AFR since it represents what the price would have been if the government control program had not been in effect. Since we used the parameter estimates from the PACT equation to generate the artificial PFR series (to be described below), it is in this special sense that we view T and PACT as simultaneously determined. While we would have preferred a simultaneous estimation of the T and PACT equations, this was not possible because of the non-existence of actual data on PFR.

We now turn to Eq. (7.13), the PACT equation, in order to explain the derivation of the free-market price, PFR. First, however, we need to explain the explanatory variables used.

A number of studies of the tobacco industry have all found that an important variable in explaining price is a variable resembling our SQNET. This variable is the ratio of the total supply of leaf available to total usage of leaf, or disappearance. As such, SQNET represents an inventory stock to sales ratio concept. Cigarette manufacturers have often stated that they seek to maintain a ratio of total supply of leaf to current usage of about 2.5 to 1. A main reason for such large inventories is the two- to three- year aging requirement of tobacco leaf. The numerator of the variable SQNET is equal to the sum of the stock of tobacco on hand at the beginning of the market period and leaf production minus exports and minus tobacco pledged under the support program, T. The numerator is then divided by the current domestic usage of tobacco leaf, DDISP. The expectation that the coefficient of this variable in the PACT equation should be negative is confirmed by the statistical results.

The second variable, PCAPY, is an income variable which accounts for shifts in demand over the period. It has a positive coefficient as expected. Perhaps the most serious omission is a variable to account for the quality of leaf.

The derivation of PFR from Eq. (7.13) is accomplished by setting T equal to zero; that is, if the government is not intervening in the market, total pledges of leaf will be zero. Hence, Eq. (7.14) is simply Eq. (7.13) with T set equal to zero. PFR is always less than PACT, as expected.

Equation (7.16) is the T equation. The goodness of fit of this equation, as measured by the coefficients of determination, is poorer than for any of the other equations. However, the regression coefficient is of the expected sign and is statistically significant. We should also mention that in *estimating* the equation a value of PFR was used which differs slightly from the PFR given in Eq. (7.14). The "adjusted" PFR used was determined by first calculating a predicted *difference* between PACT and PFR for each year by subtracting Eq. (7.14) from Eq. (7.13). Then the predicted difference was subtracted from the observed market price to obtain "adjusted" PFR.

Leaf production less leaf pledged

$$QNET = Q - T \tag{7.10}$$

Ratio of net leaf supply to domestic disappearance

$$SQNET = \frac{\overline{STK}_{t-1} + QNET - \overline{X}}{DDISP} \tag{7.11}$$

Ratio of leaf supply less exports to disappearance

$$SQ = \frac{\overline{STK}_{t-1} + Q - \overline{X}}{DDISP} \tag{7.12}$$

Actual leaf price

$$\log PACT = -0.2833 \log SQNET + 0.5858 \log \overline{PCAPY} \tag{7.13}$$
$$(0.1108) \qquad\qquad (0.0189)$$
$$\overline{R}^2 = 0.7873$$
$$DW = 1.6657$$

Free market leaf price

$$\log PFR = -0.2833 \log SQ + 0.5858 \log \overline{PCAPY} \tag{7.14}$$

Support price less free market price

$$SPMFP = \overline{SP} - PFR \tag{7.15}$$

Leaf pledged under support program

$$\log T = 5.4038 + 0.1472 \, SPMFP \tag{7.16}$$
$$(0.1609) \ (0.0352)$$
$$\overline{R}^2 = 0.4922$$
$$DW = 1.2729$$

3. Cigarettes Equation (7.17) is the demand function for cigarettes. In view of the oligopolistic pricing behavior of the cigarette manufacturers, it seems reasonable to treat the price of cigarettes as an external variable.

The demand function displays properties similar to those which have been obtained by a number of other investigators. For example, the price elasticity of demand for cigarettes is $-.43$ and the income elasticity is .77. Other analyses have shown that the price elasticity of demand for cigarettes is between $-.3$ and -9.4, and the income elasticity of demand about .5. A dummy variable used to represent the 1964 Surgeon General's report on the link between cancer and smoking proved to be insignificant.

The other estimated equation in this block is the technical relation between leaf disappearance and cigarette production. Thus Eq. (7.19) is a regression of tobacco leaf per cigarette, LFPCIG, on time. It reveals that LFPCIG is declining exponentially at about three percent per year. The ratio of flue-cured leaf price to Burley price was also tried as an independent variable, but it proved to be statistically insignificant.

Domestic cigarette consumption

$$\log \text{CCON} = -0.4250 \log \overline{\text{RPCIG}} + 0.7721 \log \overline{\text{RDISY}} \tag{7.17}$$
$$(0.1349) \qquad\qquad (0.0765)$$

$$\bar{R}^2 = 0.9094$$

$$\text{DW} = 0.5900$$

Cigarette production

$$\text{CPRO} = 20 \times \text{CCON} + \overline{\text{TXFWD}} \tag{7.18}$$

Leaf per 1000 cigarettes

$$\log \text{LFPCIG} = 0.6161 - 0.0289 \overline{\text{TIME}} \tag{7.19}$$
$$(0.0156)\ (0.0017)$$

$$\bar{R}^2 = 0.9531$$

$$\text{DW} = 1.3836$$

Disappearance into cigarette production

$$\text{CDIS} = (\text{LFPCIG} \times \text{CPRO})/1000 \tag{7.20}$$

Domestic leaf disappearance

$$\text{DDISP} = \text{CDIS} + \overline{\text{OTHDIS}} \tag{7.21}$$

Leaf stock

$$\text{STK} = \overline{\text{STK}}_{t-1} + Q - \text{DDISP} - \bar{X} \tag{7.22}$$

Validation In order to gain some additional insight concerning the validity of our model, we treated it as a closed-loop simulation model; that is, for given starting values of the lagged output variables and given values of the external variables and the policy variables, we solved the model each period for the current values of the 19 output variables. The values of the output variables generated in one period were fed back into the model in future periods in the form of lagged output variables. The error terms in the behavioral equations were suppressed. In this manner we generated the time paths for the 19 output variables over the period 1949 through 1966.

Figures 7.3 through 7.8 contain graphs of six of the variables whose time paths were simulated. For the purpose of comparisons, the actual time paths of these six variables are also plotted. On the basis of these graphical comparisons of the simulated output of the model and the actual time paths of the corresponding variables, we conclude that our model does a reasonably good job of simulating the behavior of the tobacco industry between 1949 and 1966.

A Coffee Market Model[4]

With the interest exhibited in the price of coffee in 1977, it seems appropriate to include an econometric model of the world coffee market in this section.

On the demand side, the world coffee market is divided into three sections: (1) United States, (2) Western Europe and Canada, and (3) the rest of the world. On the supply side, there are three major categories of coffee: (1) Brazils, (2) mild arabicas (typically from Colombia), and (3) robustas (typically from Africa).

The model explicity incorporates the International Coffee Agreement into its structure. The policy variables included in the model are export quotas set by the International Coffee Agreement.

Output variables

BMIN = Brazilian minimum export price (United States cents/pound)

EXB = Total exports of Brazils

EXM = Total exports of milds

EXR = Total exports of robustas

INV1 = Actual inventory in the United States at the end of the quarter

INV1* = Planned inventory in the Unites States at the beginning of the quarter $(\text{INV1}_t = \text{INV1}_{t-1})$

M1B/POP1 = Per capita imports of Brazils to the United States

M1M/POP1 = Per capita imports of milds to the United States

M1R/POP1 = Per capita imports of robustas to the United States

M2B/POP2 = Per capita imports of Brazils to Canada plus a group of European countries (Belgium, Luxembourg, the Netherlands, Germany, France, Italy, the United Kingdom, Norway, Sweden, Denmark, Austria, and Portugal)

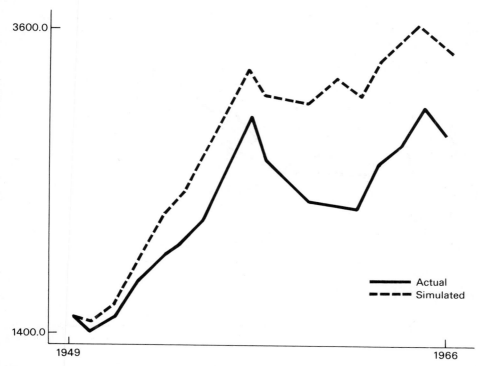

Fig. 7.3 Flue-cured underage (1000 acres).

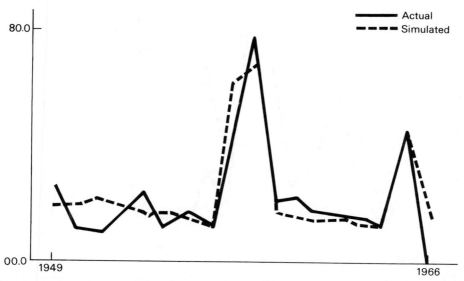

Fig. 7.4 Stocks of flue-cured tobacco leaf (1000 lbs).

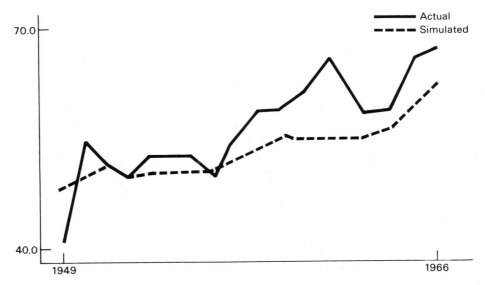

Fig. 7.5 Actual price of flue-cured tobacco leaf (cents).

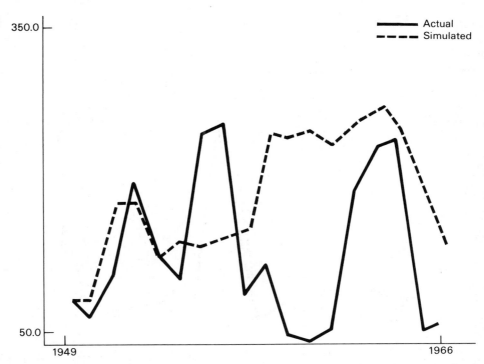

Fig. 7.6 Volume of flue-cured tobacco leaf pledged by growers at support price (1000 lbs).

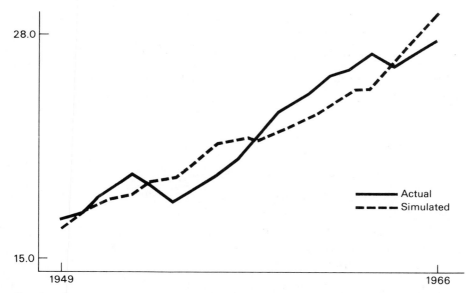

Fig. 7.7 Domestic cigarette consumption (United States) (billions of cigarettes).

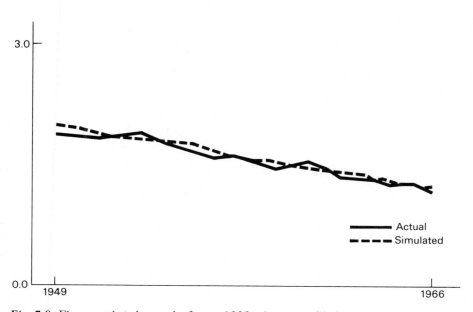

Fig. 7.8 Flue-cured tobacco leaf per 1000 cigarettes (lbs/1000 cigarettes, ratio estimate).

M2M/POP2 = Per capita imports of milds to Canada plus the same group of European countries

PB   = World market price of Brazils (United States cents/pound)

PM   = World market price of milds (United States cents/pound)

PR   = World market price of robustas (United States cents/pound)

External variables

CPI1 = United States consumer price index for food

CPI2 = Consumer price index for all consumer products for Canada plus the group of European countries

M3B   = Imports of Brazils to the rest of the world (total Brazilian exports minus imports to the United States and the group of European countries plus Canada)

M3M   = Imports of milds to the rest of the world

M3R   = Imports of robustas to the rest of the world

POP1 = Total United States population

POP2 = Total population of Canada plus the group of European countries

QB   = Exportable production of Brazils (annual)

QM   = Exportable production of milds (annual)

QR   = Exportable production of robustas (annual)

Q1   = Dummy variable set equal to 1 in quarter 1 of calendar year and 0 otherwise

Q2   = Dummy variable set equal to 1 in quarter 2 of calendar year and 0 otherwise

Q3   = Dummy variable set equal to 1 in quarter 3 of calendar year and 0 otherwise

T   = Time trend

W   = Dummy variable: 1 denotes severe frost or drought, 0 otherwise

Y1   = United States per capita income deflated by consumer price index (seasonally adjusted)

Y2   = OECD index of industrial production for the group of European countries plus Canada (weighted by each country's share of total green coffee imports in 1962)

Policy variables

EXQB = Export quota for Brazils set by International Coffee Agreement (I.C.A.)

EXQM = Export quota for milds set by I.C.A.

EXQR = Export quota for robustas set by I.C.A.

The Model The econometric model described in the following paragraphs is based on the decision rule that Brazil simply attempts to maintain the price established in the preceding period. Figure 7.9 contains a generalized flowchart of the logic of the overall model. We now turn to a detailed description of the equations of the model.

In Block 1 we compute the minimum Brazilian exports price BMIN.[5]

$$BMIN = \underset{(17.49)}{0.81744}\, PB_{t-1} - \underset{(-1.84)}{0.000134}\, STOCK* - \underset{(-2.70)}{7.3796}\, W_{t-4} + \underset{(2.43)}{5.8188} \quad (7.23)$$

$$\begin{array}{cc} \bar{R}^2 & \text{D.W.} \\ 0.92 & 2.7 \end{array}$$

The minimum price (BMIN) is largely determined by Brazilian price in the preceding quarter. The additional terms adjust for an undervaluation or overvaluation in the lagged world market price (PB_{t-1}). The STOCK variable represents Brazil's expected end-of-the-year addition to stocks if minimum price remains unchanged. Brazil will usually permit fairly substantial fluctuations in stocks in order to stabilize prices. However, the negative coefficient associated with the STOCK variable implies that, at times, the size of stocks causes Brazil to adjust minimum price. Thus, if expected stocks are unreasonably large, Brazil will lower minimum price in order to increase exports. Conversely, if expected stocks are very low, Brazil will consider increasing prices. Such a price increase will both ration remaining supplies of fresh coffee and increase profits.

The second extra variable in the BMIN equation is a frost dummy variable lagged four quarters. After a severe frost, buyers will build up inventories as a hedge against a future short supply. This inventory buildup will increase prices. The minus sign of the dummy variable coefficient indicates a return to normality after such an inventory buildup.

Once the minimum export price is set, if there is no International Coffee Agreement, the world market price of Brazils is determined in block 3. It is just the minimum price plus a proportional markup for transportation and handling. (The world market price does have a tendency to rise above the minimum price floor in the flurry of buying following a frost scare.)

The world market price of Brazils is given by.

$$PB1 = \underset{(68.79)}{1.0713}\, BMIN + \underset{(6.26)}{17.9216}\, W_{t-2} \quad (7.24)$$

$$\begin{array}{cc} \bar{R}^2 & \text{D.W.} \\ 0.93 & 1.75 \end{array}$$

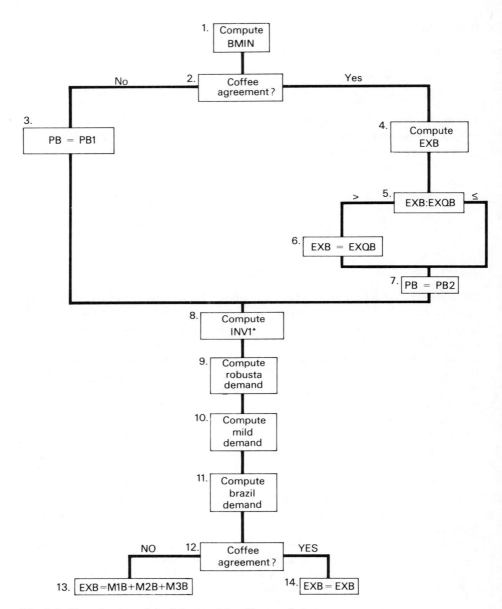

Fig. 7.9 Flowchart model of the world coffee market.

This formulation of the Brazilian price equation is designed for periods in which no International Coffee Agreement is operative. It is not suitable for periods in which quota constraints actually limit Brazilian exports. In such periods we would expect exports to influence world market price.

Let us reexamine the causal chain linking Brazilian government policies with world market price. Brazilian exports enter into this chain in the following manner. The Brazilian government sets the minimum price. The level of the minimum price limits the flow of exports, since exports at prices below the minimum are prohibited. Finally, the supply of exports largely determines world market price.

In the original formulation of the Brazilian sector we omitted exports from the causal chain. This formulation was designed for periods with no effective export ceiling. In such periods the export supply function is horizontal at the minimum price level. Thus, minimum price determines world market price; and exports equal world demand at this price.

However, in periods of international cooperation, the quota ceiling effectively limits exports; the export supply function becomes vertical at the point where exports equal export quotas. In this case, when Brazilian exports equal the export quota, the world market price is that price at which world demand equals world supply; that is, the price at which the demand for Brazil equals the export quota of Brazils. In other words, in periods of international cooperation the world market price of Brazils varies with the supply of Brazilian exports. The Brazilian minimum price is still an important instrument. However, it is now set high enough that exports are less than or equal to the export quota. Thus, the formulation of the Brazilian section in periods of international cooperation will be as follows. We will not change the minimum price equation, but we will introduce two alternative explicit expressions for Brazilian exports. We will use either:

$$EXB = EXQB \qquad (7.25)$$

or

$$EXB = 0.02526 \text{ QB} - 31.894 \text{ BMIN} + 1083.86 \text{ W}_{t-2} \qquad (7.26)$$
$$(1.76) \qquad (-2.79) \qquad (1.91)$$

$$- 826.81 \text{ Q1} - 918.4 \text{ Q2} + 5217.5$$
$$(7.29) \qquad (-3.12) \qquad (7.29)$$

$$\begin{array}{cc} \bar{R}^2 & \text{D.W.} \\ 0.53 & 2.48 \end{array}$$

whichever is smaller. (See Blocks 4 through 6 in Fig. 7.9.)

Export Eq. (7.26) reflects the importance of the minimum export price (BMIN) as a policy instrument designed to regulate the flow of Brazilian exports (EXB). Since exports are not permitted at prices below the minimum, high minimum prices will hold down exports and vice versa. The negative coefficient associated with minimum price in Eq. (7.26) implies the desired inverse relationship between minimum price and Brazilian exports.

Given Brazilian exports, we can estimate the price of Brazils in Block 7 from the following equation:

$$PB2 = -0.0080 \text{ EXB} + 13.26 \text{ } W_{t-2} + 79.775 \qquad (7.27)$$
$$(-4.55) \qquad (2.27) \qquad (11.07)$$

$$\begin{array}{cc} \bar{R}^2 & \text{D.W.} \\ 0.28 & 0.63 \end{array}$$

The coefficient associated with Brazilian exports (EXB) is negative. Thus, when Brazil permits substantial exports, the price of Brazils (PB) must fall to ensure that all these exports are sold. On the other hand, when exports are low—either because of Brazilian government controls or International Coffee Organization quotas—PB rises in order to ration limited supplies among potential buyers.

In our empirical analysis we discovered that changes in aggregate inventories were extremely important in explaining changes in United States demand for each of the three types of coffee. Therefore, United States inventories were included as an output variable.

Actual inventory data relates to the levels of stocks at the end of each period. It is inventory *plans* that influence imports within each period. Since no data on inventory plans exist, we assumed that inventory plans were formulated at the beginning of the period, and that these plans were always realized. The last assumption guarantees that actual inventories at the end of the period always equal planned inventories at the beginning of the period. On the basis of these assumptions, we include a planned inventories equation as one of the first links in the causal chain of the block recursive model. The planned inventories equation was fitted using actual end-of-period inventories. The empirical function takes the following form:

$$INV1* = 52.90 \text{ } (PB_{t-1} - PB_{t-2}) + 48.23 \text{ POP1}_t \qquad (7.28)$$
$$(2.22) \qquad (5.48)$$

$$+ 0.40 \text{ } (INV1_{t-1} - INV1_{t-2}) + 652.44 \text{ } W_{t-4} - 5726.08$$
$$(2.56) \qquad (2.21) \qquad (-3.58)$$

$$\begin{array}{cc} \bar{R}^2 & \text{D.W.} \\ 0.56 & 1.84 \end{array}$$

Since no inventory breakdown by type of coffee was available, we assumed the price of Brazils to be characteristic of the general price situation. We assumed further that United States dealers base their expectations of current price changes on past price changes. Here the positive price-change coefficient suggests that dealers have elastic price expectations; and thus, an increase in price triggers inventory buildups as a hedge against still greater price increases expected in the future.

The positive and highly significant coefficient associated with population is easily explained. Under normal conditions, dealers seek to maintain inventories proportional to expected sales. Since total sales tend to rise with population growth, we would expect inventories to vary directly with population.

Finally, the positive coefficient associated with W_{t-4} indicates a tendency to increase inventories four quarters after a frost occurs. Since frost normally occurs at the beginning of the Brazilian coffee year in July or August, a four quarter lag implies an inventory buildup when the damaged crop first comes to market. A preference for new-crop coffee among dealers and a knowledge that new-crop coffee will be in short supply during the coming year explains the significance of the four-period lag.

Theoretically, one might assume that the demand for Brazils is a function of the prices of all three types of coffee, while the demand for milds and robustas varies inversely with their respective prices and directly with the price of Brazils. In actually fitting the demand equations, it was impossible to obtain significant estimates for all the substitution effects which we postulated. However, in order to avoid the possibility of rejecting a true hypothesis about these substitution effects, we followed our theoretical demand equations and retained all price coefficients including those not significantly different from zero.

In the following pages we will present three different empirical models of the mild and robusta demand sectors. The models differ from one another chiefly with respect to the amount of simultaneity hypothesized among the price, demand, and export–supply equations for each of the two varieties. The models also possess a number of common features. These include the general form of the mild and robusta demand equations and the specific coefficient estimates for the two Brazilian demand equations. In estimating United States and European demand for each of the three coffee varieties, we begin by postulating the following basic demand equation:

$$M_i/POP = f(PB, PR, PM, T, CPI, INV1_{t-1}, Q_1, Q_2, Q_3) \qquad (7.29)$$

In this equation we hypothesize that per capita imports of variety i vary directly with the prices of substitutes including other varieties of coffee and all foods. We also consider the possibilities that imports vary with income, or that the intercept of the demand equation varies with time or with the particular quarter of the coffee year. In addition, we hypothesize that United States imports vary directly with additions to inventories.

For each variety some of these coefficients were not significantly different from zero. In fitting each demand equation we retained all coffee price variables including those with nonsignificant coefficients. However, we discarded all other variables the coefficients of which were not significantly different from zero.

For the robusta and mild demand sectors of our model we have developed three alternative models.

In Model 1, as in the other two models, we determine the price of Brazils recursively at the beginning of the period. We then fit mild and robusta total export equations and regional demand equations. Equating total demand for each of the two varieties with total supply, we can determine the robusta and mild equilibrium prices for the period. Given the prices of all three types of coffee, we can estimate the demand for Brazils from equations which are recursive to the model.

Model 1 follows closely our theoretical model in which Brazil sets the price and then acts as the residual supplier. One serious drawback is that, although the Brazilian price appears as an explanatory variable in the mild and robusta equations, the Brazilian price coefficient is not significant in the mild demand equations and is only weakly significant in the robusta equations. Therefore, in Model 1 Brazilian price has only a minor influence on mild and robusta demand and prices. *A priori* information, on the other hand, would lead us to suspect that the price of Brazils substantially influences the other two prices. Indeed, one major difficulty in determining the influence of Brazilian price on mild and robusta demand is derived from the high degree of multicollinearity among the three price variables.

Model 1: the robusta sector

$$EXR = 11.9473\ PR + 0.1852\ QR \tag{7.30}$$
$$(2.22) \qquad (13.38)$$

$$\begin{array}{cc} \bar{R}^2 & \text{D.W.} \\ 0.66 & 2.76 \end{array}$$

$$M1R/POP1 = -0.1054\ PR + 0.0845\ PB + 0.2728\ CPI1 \tag{7.31}$$
$$(-2.09) \qquad (1.97) \qquad (3.14)$$

$$+ 0.004597\ Y1 + 0.001415\ (INV1_t - INV1_{t-1})$$
$$(2.04) \qquad\qquad (4.54)$$

$$- 0.5341\ Q2 - 1.1880\ Q3 - 32.5612$$
$$(-1.61) \qquad (-3.66) \qquad (-5.24)$$

$$\begin{array}{cc} \bar{R}^2 & \text{D.W.} \\ 0.75 & 1.15 \end{array}$$

$$M2R/POP2 = -0.01891\ PR + 0.01463\ PB + 0.01626\ Y2 \tag{7.32}$$
$$(-1.28) \qquad (1.41) \qquad (3.95)$$

$$+ 0.01306\ CPI2 + 0.3485\ Q1 + 0.4633\ Q2$$
$$(1.90) \qquad\qquad (2.69) \qquad (3.64)$$

$$\begin{array}{cc} \bar{R}^2 & \text{D.W.} \\ 0.81 & 1.76 \end{array}$$

$$EXR \equiv M1R + M2R + M3R \tag{7.33}$$

Model 1: the mild sector

$$EXM = 0.2187\ QM + 900.7278\ Q1 \tag{7.34}$$
$$(44.35) \qquad (5.30)$$

$$\begin{array}{cc} \bar{R}^2 & \text{D.W.} \\ 0.58 & 2.36 \end{array}$$

$$M1M/POP1 = -0.2799\ PM + 0.1782\ PB - 0.2640\ T \tag{7.35}$$
$$(-2.24) \qquad (1.50) \qquad (-5.14)$$

$$+ 0.002008(\text{INV1}_t - \text{INV1}_{t-1}) + 0.01348 \text{ Y1}$$
$$(3.72) \qquad\qquad\qquad\qquad (8.36)$$

$$+ 1.2707 \text{ Q1} - 1.3892 \text{ Q2} - 1.3341 \text{ Q3}$$
$$(1.97) \qquad (-2.25) \qquad (-2.05)$$

$$\begin{array}{cc} \bar{R}^2 & \text{D.W.} \\ 0.49 & 1.90 \end{array}$$

$$\text{M2M/POP2} = -0.04820 \text{ PM} + 0.03409 \text{ PB} + 0.01467 \text{ Y2} \qquad (7.36)$$
$$(-2.45) \qquad (1.54) \qquad (3.01)$$

$$+ 0.02365 \text{ CPI2} + 0.2292 \text{ Q2}$$
$$(2.92) \qquad\quad (1.88)$$

$$\begin{array}{cc} \bar{R}^2 & \text{D.W.} \\ 0.88 & 2.14 \end{array}$$

$$\text{EXM} \equiv \text{M1M} + \text{M2M} + \text{M3M} \qquad (7.37)$$

Model 2 differs from Model 1 in two ways: (1) it contains explicit price functions for milds and robustas and (2) it does not contain explicit supply functions for those varieties. Both the price of milds and the price of robustas are largely determined by the level of the Brazilian price; consequently, Model 2 avoids the major shortcoming of Model 1. However, in Model 2 the exportable production of robustas and milds enters only as a ceiling to exports whereas during the period studied mild and robusta exports have been highly correlated with production. This correlation is consistent with our theoretical model in which we hypothesized that current production strongly influences mild and robusta export supplies. (In Model 1 the relation between production and exports is explicit.)

Model 2: the robusta sector

$$\text{PR} = -0.001829 \text{ EXR} + 0.5663 \text{ PB} \qquad (7.38)$$
$$(2.21) \qquad\qquad (12.40$$

$$\begin{array}{cc} \bar{R}^2 & \text{D.W.} \\ 0.53 & 0.73 \end{array}$$

$$\text{M1R/POP1} = -0.1088 \text{ PR} + 0.08705 \text{ PB} + 0.2760 \text{ CPI1} \qquad (7.39)$$
$$(2.14) \qquad (2.01) \qquad (3.15)$$

$$+ 0.004554 \text{ Y1} + 0.001422 \, (\text{INV1}_t - \text{INV1}_{t-1})$$
$$(2.00) \qquad\qquad (4.53)$$

$$- 0.5378 \text{ Q2} - 1.1880 \text{ Q3} - 32.8173$$
$$(-1.61) \qquad (-3.63) \qquad (-5.23)$$

$$\begin{array}{cc} \bar{R}^2 & \text{D.W.} \\ 0.75 & 1.15 \end{array}$$

$$\text{M2R/POP2} = -0.01914 \text{ PR} + 0.01478 \text{ PB} + 0.01624 \text{ Y2} \qquad (7.40)$$
$$(-1.30) \qquad (1.42) \qquad (3.94)$$

$$+ 0.01310 \text{ CPI2} + 0.3484 \text{ Q1} + 0.4632 \text{ Q2}$$
$$(1.90) \qquad (2.69) \qquad (3.64)$$

$\bar{R}^2$	D.W.
0.81	1.76

$$\text{EXR} \equiv \text{M1R} + \text{M2R} + \text{M3R} \qquad (7.41)$$

Model 2: the mild sector

$$\text{PM} = -0.003314 \text{ QM} + 1.03378 \text{ PB} + 18.3125 \qquad (7.42)$$
$$(-2.73) \qquad (14.37) \qquad (2.71)$$

$\bar{R}^2$	D.W.
0.88	0.96

$$\text{M1M/POP1} = -0.2291 \text{ PM} + 0.1319 \text{ PB} - 0.2480 \text{ T} \qquad (7.43)$$
$$(-1.83) \qquad (1.11) \qquad (-4.88)$$

$$+ 0.001918 \, (\text{INV1}_t - \text{INV1}_{t-1}) + 0.01303 \text{ Y1}$$
$$(3.64) \qquad (8.19)$$

$$+ 1.2447 \text{ Q1} - 1.4126 \text{ Q2} - 1.4460 \text{ Q3}$$
$$(1.99) \qquad (-2.35) \qquad (2.27)$$

$\bar{R}^2$	D.W.
0.52	1.88

$$\text{M2M/POP2} = -0.0430 \text{ PM} + 0.02846 \text{ PB} + 0.01533 \text{ Y2} \qquad (7.44)$$
$$(-2.17) \qquad (1.28) \qquad (3.17)$$

$$+ 0.02261 \text{ CPI2} + 0.2295 \text{ Q2}$$
$$(2.81) \qquad (1.90)$$

$\bar{R}^2$	D.W.
0.88	2.16

$$\text{EXM} \equiv \text{M1M} + \text{M2M} + \text{M3M} \qquad (7.45)$$

Model 3 is unique in treating third-region imports of milds and robustas as residuals. This formulation implies that mild and robusta suppliers simply dump their extra coffee on third-country markets. There is some evidence that at least Colombia may do this. However, large quantities of coffee can be dumped in this way only at prices much below the world market price. And our model makes no provision for a third-region price different from the world market price.

The model has the distinct advantage of accurately reflecting the nature of the data used. Since no comprehensive quarterly information on third-region imports is available, the data relating to third-region imports are simple residuals. Therefore, they include a very large error component, which is ignored in the other models. Furthermore, Model 3 has a desirable simplicity in being almost completely recursive. Finally, the inclusion of explicit functions to explain both prices and exports has the advantage of recognizing both the importance of the price of Brazils in determining the prices of milds and robustas and the tendency for exports of these two coffee types to be closely tied to their respective exportable productions. Thus, Model 3 is also consistent with our theoretical models.

Model 3: the robusta sector

$$PR = 0.001581 \ EXR + 0.5790 \ PB \qquad\qquad (7.46)$$
$$(1.96) \qquad\qquad (12.98)$$

$$\begin{array}{cc} \bar{R}^2 & \text{D.W.} \\ 0.54 & 0.52 \end{array}$$

$$EXR = 11.6284 \ PR + 0.1860 \ QR \qquad\qquad (7.47)$$
$$(2.08) \qquad\quad (12.97)$$

$$\begin{array}{cc} \bar{R}^2 & \text{D.W.} \\ 0.66 & 2.76 \end{array}$$

$$M1R/POP1 = -0.02429 \ PR + 0.02259 \ PB + 0.1958 \ CPI1 \qquad\qquad (7.48)$$
$$(0.87) \qquad\quad (0.83) \qquad\qquad (2.78)$$

$$+ \ 0.005631 \ Y1 + 0.001246 \ (INV1_t - INV1_{t-1})$$
$$(2.85) \qquad\qquad (4.62)$$

$$- \ 0.4461 \ Q2 - 1.1881 \ Q3 - 26.3869$$
$$(1.51) \qquad\quad (4.07) \qquad\quad (5.40)$$

$$\begin{array}{cc} \bar{R}^2 & \text{D.W.} \\ 0.80 & 1.16 \end{array}$$

$$M2R/POP2 = 0.01092 \ PB - 0.01303 \ PR + 0.01692 \ Y2 \qquad\qquad (7.49)$$
$$(1.36) \qquad\quad (-1.25) \qquad\quad (4.30)$$

$$+ \ 0.01204 \ CPI2 + 0.3499 \ Q1 + 0.4657 \ Q2$$
$$(1.82) \qquad\qquad (2.71) \qquad\quad (3.68)$$

$$\begin{array}{cc} \bar{R}^2 & \text{D.W.} \\ 0.82 & 1.73 \end{array}$$

$$M3R \equiv EXR - M1R - M2R \qquad\qquad (7.50)$$

Model 3: the mild sector

$$EXM = 0.2187 \ QM + 900.7278 \ Q1 \qquad\qquad (7.51)$$
$$(44.35) \qquad\quad (5.30)$$

$$\begin{array}{cc} \bar{R}^2 & \text{D.W.} \\ 0.58 & 2.36 \end{array}$$

$$PM = -0.002196 \ EXM + 1.0647 \ PB + 12.6732 \qquad (7.52)$$
$$ (-2.54) \qquad\quad (15.94) \qquad (2.44)$$

$$\begin{array}{cc} \bar{R}^2 & D.W. \\ 0.89 & 0.73 \end{array}$$

$$M1M/POP1 = -0.1525 \ PM + 0.06227 \ PB - 0.2241 \ T \qquad (7.53)$$
$$ (-2.23) \qquad (0.88) \qquad\quad (-5.85)$$

$$+ \ 0.001782 \ (INV1_t - INV1_{t-1}) + 0.01234 \ Y1$$
$$(3.68) \qquad\qquad\qquad\qquad (9.73)$$

$$+ \ 1.2057 \ Q1 - 1.4480 \ Q2 - 1.6143 \ Q3$$
$$(1.97) \qquad\quad (-2.46) \qquad (-2.77)$$

$$\begin{array}{cc} \bar{R}^2 & D.W. \\ 0.54 & 1.91 \end{array}$$

$$M2M/POP2 = -0.03127 \ PM + 0.01574 \ PB + 0.01682 \ Y2 \qquad (7.54)$$
$$ (2.18) \qquad\quad (0.95) \qquad\quad (3.75)$$

$$+ \ 0.0203 \ CPI2 + 0.2301 \ Q2$$
$$(2.70) \qquad\quad (1.92)$$

$$\begin{array}{cc} \bar{R}^2 & D.W. \\ 0.88 & 2.19 \end{array}$$

$$M3M \equiv EXM - M1M - M2M \qquad (7.55)$$

Finally, the Brazilian demand equations are given below.

Brazilian demand equations

$$M1B/POP1 = -0.2279 \ PB + 0.1898 \ PM + 0.02654 \ PR \qquad (7.56)$$
$$ (-2.56) \qquad (2.94) \qquad\quad (0.57)$$

$$+ \ 0.006338 \ Y1 + 0.004469 \ (INV1_t - INV1_{t-1})$$
$$(-3.59) \qquad\quad (9.83)$$

$$+ \ 1.3528 \ Q1 - 1.3397 \ Q3 + 24.3761$$
$$(2.74) \qquad\quad (-2.72) \qquad (6.35)$$

$$\begin{array}{cc} \bar{R}^2 & D.W. \\ 0.82 & 1.73 \end{array}$$

$$M2B/POP2 = -0.07849 \ PB + 0.02145 \ PR + 0.02964 \ PM \qquad (7.57)$$
$$ (-2.78) \qquad\quad (1.33) \qquad\quad (1.44)$$

$$- \ 0.09118 \ T + 0.04939 \ Y2 - 0.5894 \ Q2$$
$$(-4.63) \qquad (9.24) \qquad\quad (-3.53)$$

$$\begin{array}{cc} \bar{R}^2 & D.W. \\ 0.66 & 1.16 \end{array}$$

NATIONAL ECONOMETRIC MODELS

Since many econometric marketing models are driven by national economic indicators such as Gross National Product, consumption, investment, employment, etc., we must consider the question of how we obtain historical data and forecasts for national economic indicators. In the United States there are now a number of different service bureaus which offer national economic databases and econometric forecasts for macroeconomic series. Figure 7.10 contains a flowchart describing one well-known national econometric model, the UCLA Econometric Model. Before discussing these econometric forecasting services, we shall briefly describe an example of a national econometric model. It is a six-equation model of the economy of the United States. Then we shall outline a set of criteria for choosing an econometric service bureau.

An Example Model [6]

Problem formulation Suppose that we are interested in testing the effects of one or more governmental fiscal policies on the behavior of the economy of the United States. To be more specific, suppose that we are interested in the effects that (1) the governmental wage bill, (2) governmental demand, and (3) business taxes have on (1) consumption, (2) wages, (3) profits, (4) investment, (5) capital stock, and (6) national income.

Model formulation Given the objective mentioned above, it follows that we should formulate an econometric model that relates the six output variables defined above to the three policy variables. Needless to say, a realistic model explaining the behavior of these six output variables would probably be quite complex. Clearly, these six output variables are going to be influenced by variables other than the three policy variables listed above. For this reason, a valid model of the economy of the United States probably requires as many as 100 equations. In these models our six output variables would be explained in terms of a multiplicity of other output, policy, and external variables. However, for expository purposes we shall consider a somewhat less complex six-equation econometric model of the United States economy. This model has two principal attributes. First, it is a relatively simple model. Second, it possesses many of the characteristics of more complex econometric models. The model's small size makes it possible to illustrate estimation and simulation without consuming too many pages.

The model consists of the following policy variables, output variables, and function relationships.

Policy variables

$W2_t$ = governmental wage bill

G_t = governmental demand

T_t = business taxes

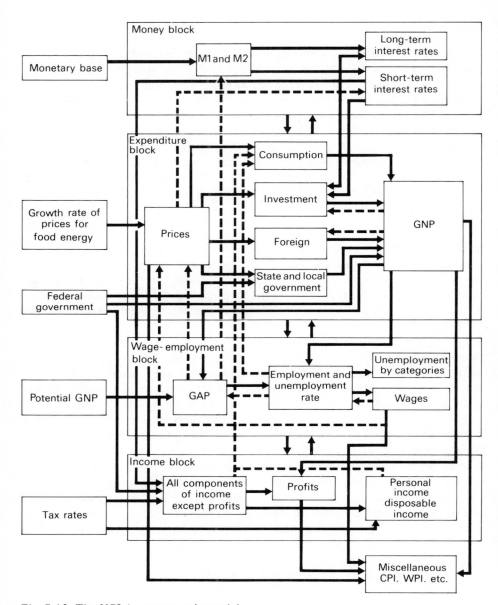

Fig. 7.10 The UCLA econometric model.

Output variables

C_t = consumption

$W1_t$ = private wage bill

P_t = nonwage income (profits)

I_t = net investment

K_t = capital stock at end of period t

X_t = national income

Behavioral equations

Consumption function

$$C_t = a_1 + a_2 (W1_t + W2_t) + a_3 P_t + a_4 P_{t-1} \qquad (7.58)$$

Investment function

$$I_t = b_1 + b_2 P_t + b_3 P_{t-1} + b_4 K_{t-1} \qquad (7.59)$$

Demand for labor function

$$W1_t = c_2 + c_2 X_t + c_3 X_{t-1} + c_4 t \qquad (7.60)$$

Identities

National income equation

$$X_t = C_t + I_t + G_t \qquad (7.61)$$

Profit equation

$$P_t = Y_t - W1_t - W2_t \qquad (7.62)$$

Capital stock equation

$$K_t = K_{t-1} + I_t \qquad (7.63)$$

Parameter estimation   Since the model simultaneously explains the six output variables, the behavioral equations should be estimated by two-stage least squares (TSLS). For this purpose the external variables are all those variables in the model that are not output variables, namely P_{t-1}, K_{t-1}, X_{t-1}, G, W2, T, and, t, the time trend. The estimation of the three behavioral equations using SIMPLAN is illustrated in Tables 7.1 through 7.3. Note that as equations are estimated, they are *stored* in the computer as part of a model named "Klein." The key parts of Table 7.1 are enclosed in boxes.

After the behavioral equations are estimated and stored, the identities need to be added to complete the model. In Table 7.4 we show the SIMPLAN output involved in this. As a listing of the model shows, the three estimated equations have line numbers 10, 20, and 30. Line 10 is changed so that the variable W1W2 used in estimation is expanded into its parts W1 + W2, and then the three identities are added to lines 40, 50, and 60. A complete list of the SIMPLAN model is shown at the end of Table 7.4.

Table 7.1 Estimation of the consumption function of the Klein model

ANALYSIS.

```
TSLS C P P(-1) W1W2 *EXOG P(-1) K(-1) X(-1) TIME T G W2

TWO STAGE LEAST SQUARES

ESTIMATED EQUATION IS:
   C=0.0173*P+0.21623*P(-1)+0.81018*W1W2+16.5547
```

INDEPENDENT VARIABLES	ESTIMATED COEFFICIENT	STANDARD ERROR	T- TEST
P	0.0173	0.1312	0.1319
P(-1)	0.2162	0.1192	1.8137
W1W2	0.8102	0.0447	18.1106
CONSTANT	16.5547	1.4680	11.2772

```
EXOGENOUS VARIABLES USED IN FIRST STAGE ARE:
      P(-1)
      K(-1)
      X(-1)
      TIME
      T
      G
      W2
      CONSTANT
```

```
   NUMBER OF OBSERVATIONS USED =      21
   R-SQUARED=  0.9767              F-STATISTIC(  3, 17)=    237.6552
   ADJUSTED R-SQUARED=  0.9726     DURBIN-WATSON STATISTIC=  1.4851
   STANDARD ERROR=       1.1357    DEGREES OF FREEDOM FOR T-TEST= 17
   SUM OF SQUARED ERRORS=     21.9253
```

ANALYSIS.

```
STORE KLEIN 10
```

KLEIN   WILL BE CREATED AS A NEW MODEL BEGINNING AT LINE   10
ANALYSIS.

Validation We are now ready to simulate the model. We will provide the model with actual values of the external variables and ask it to perform an expost simulation of the output variables. The SIMPLAN results are shown in Table 7.5. There the first "model" command specifies a convergence criterion as discussed in Eq. (6.32), which indicates a limit of 30 iterations, and indicates that a simultaneous model (as opposed to recursive model) is to be dealt with. The "solve" command requests the Gauss–Seidel method. Upon achieving convergence, the results are printed. Values for the output variables are the simulated values, while values for the external variables are the real historical values. We have boxed the values of X. These constitute the simulated values of real GNP for the years shown.

With the solution of the model available, we can now check any or all of the output variables to see how well the simulated values compare with the actual values. If a copy of the original data on X was kept in file 2, then once model solutions are obtained for X the command "VALIDATE X(2) X" will compare the actual values and the simulated values. Results are shown in Table 7.6. There the mean absolute error in X is seen to be about 5.3, or about 9.5 percent. Theil's inequality

Table 7.2 Estimation of the investment function of the Klein model

```
ANALYSIS.

┌────────────────────────────────────────────────────────────────┐
│ TSLS I P P(-1) K(-1) *EXOG P(-1) K(-1) X(-1) TIME T G W2         │
├──────────────────────────────────────────────────────┘         │
│ TWO STAGE LEAST SQUARES                                │         │
├──────────────────────────────────────────────────────┘         │
│ ESTIMATED EQUATION IS:                                          │
│   I=0.15022*P+0.61594*P(-1)-0.157787*K(-1)+20.2782              │
├──────────────────────────────────────────────────────────────┤ │
```

INDEPENDENT VARIABLES	ESTIMATED COEFFICIENT	STANDARD ERROR	T- TEST
P	0.1502	0.1925	0.7802
P(-1)	0.6159	0.1809	3.4044
K(-1)	-0.1578	0.0402	-3.9297
CONSTANT	20.2782	8.3832	2.4189

```
EXOGENOUS VARIABLES USED IN FIRST STAGE ARE:
    P(-1)
    K(-1)
    X(-1)
    TIME
    T
    G
    W2
    CONSTANT

   NUMBER OF OBSERVATIONS USED =    21
   R-SQUARED=  0.8849             F-STATISTIC( 3, 17)=      43.5589
   ADJUSTED R-SQUARED=  0.8646    DURBIN-WATSON STATISTIC=   2.0853
   STANDARD ERROR=      1.3071    DEGREES OF FREEDOM FOR T-TEST= 17
   SUM OF SQUARED ERRORS=      29.0469

ANALYSIS.

┌─────────────────┐
│ STORE KLEIN 20  │
└─────────────────┘

KLEIN  WILL BE UPDATED BEGINNING AT LINE    20
ANALYSIS.
```

coefficient is close to zero (.05) indicating little inequality between the two series. In a similar fashion it would be easy to validate other variables in the model.

Once the model has been estimated and validated, it would be a simple process to conduct policy simulations. Entering different values of G, T, and W2 and then solving the model would be a straightforward process. Simulating the model into the future would also be a simple process, requiring only the values to be assumed by the external variables.

Although the Klein model is short and simple, the foregoing example should give the analyst a feel for how such models are implemented in practice.

Criteria for Evaluating Econometric Service Bureaus

In the early 1970s a number of organizations began offering macroeconomic databases and econometric forecasting services in the United States. These services are provided by a wide range of different types of organizations including independent private corporations, divisions of large conglomerates, university-owned research institutes, nonprofit economic research organizations, and various governmental agencies. Given the diversity in the scope of econometric services offered by these

Table 7.3 Estimation of the demand for labor function of the Klein model

```
ANALYSIS.
```

```
TSLS W1 X X(-1) TIME *EXOG P(-1) K(-1) X(-1) TIME T G W2

TWO STAGE LEAST SQUARES

ESTIMATED EQUATION IS:
    W1=0.43886*X+0.14667*X(-1)+0.1304*TIME+1.50031
```

INDEPENDENT VARIABLES	ESTIMATED COEFFICIENT	STANDARD ERROR	T-TEST
X	0.4389	0.0396	11.0815
X(-1)	0.1467	0.0432	3.3981
TIME	0.1304	0.0324	4.0260
CONSTANT	1.5003	1.2757	1.1761

```
EXOGENOUS VARIABLES USED IN FIRST STAGE ARE:
    P(-1)
    K(-1)
    X(-1)
    TIME
    T
    G
    W2
    CONSTANT
```

```
    NUMBER OF OBSERVATIONS USED =      21
    R-SQUARED=  0.9874                     F-STATISTIC(  3, 17)=   444.5649
    ADJUSTED R-SQUARED=  0.9852            DURBIN-WATSON STATISTIC=   1.9634
    STANDARD ERROR=       0.7672          DEGREES OF FREEDOM FOR T-TEST= 17
    SUM OF SQUARED ERRORS=  10.0050
```

```
ANALYSIS.

STORE KLEIN 30

KLEIN   WILL BE UPDATED BEGINNING AT LINE    30
ANALYSIS.
```

organizations, it seems appropriate that we outline a set of criteria that might be used in selecting a particular service bureau.

In the following paragraphs we shall describe twelve criteria for evaluating econometric modeling services:

- Databases
- Forecasting accuracy
- Relevance of forecasts
- Number of equations
- Short-term model
- Long-term model
- Industry forecasts
- Industry models
- Fee schedule
- Software
- Consulting
- Availability

Databases Perhaps the single most important service offered by econometric service bureaus is historical macroeconomic data which are accurate, consistent, up to date, and easily accessible through time-sharing computer terminals. Indeed, it can be argued that the prices charged by many service bureaus are justified primarily by the databases which they provide. Trying to keep track of changes in economic data generated by various government agencies is not a job which many companies are willing to undertake on their own.

Table 7.4 Adding the identities to the Klein model

```
ANALYSIS.

EDIT KLEIN

EDIT.
LIST



KLEIN
```
```
   10  C=0.0173*P+0.21623*P(-1)+0.81018*W1W2+16.5547
   20  I=0.15022*P+0.61594*P(-1)-0.157787*K(-1)+20.2782
   30  W1=0.43886*X+0.14667*X(-1)+0.1304*TIME+1.50031
```
```
EDIT.
```
```
CHANGE 10 /W1W2/(W1+W2)/

   10  C=0.0173*P+0.21623*P(-1)+0.81018*(W1+W2)+16.5547
```
```
EDIT.
```
```
40  X=C+I+G
```
```
EDIT.
```
```
50  P=X-W1-T
```
```
EDIT.
```
```
60  K=K(-1)+I
```
```
EDIT.
SAVE

SAVED.
EDIT.
LIST



KLEIN
```
```
   10  C=0.0173*P+0.21623*P(-1)+0.81018*(W1+W2)+16.5547
   20  I=0.15022*P+0.61594*P(-1)-0.157787*K(-1)+20.2782
   30  W1=0.43886*X+0.14667*X(-1)+0.1304*TIME+1.50031
   40  X=C+I+G
   50  P=X-W1-T
   60  K=K(-1)+I
```
```
EDIT.
END

ANALYSIS.
```

For those who are just beginning to work with econometric models, the NBER (National Bureau of Economic Research) database may prove to be an attractive alternative. It contains over 3000 economic time series, is available on numerous computer service bureaus, can be installed on the user's in-house computer, and is moderately priced. Alternatively, one service bureau has over 35,000 series available including state and regional databases as well as macroeconomic data for Canada, Japan, and most countries of Western Europe.

Forecasting accuracy We have repeatedly emphasized throughout this book that econometric models should not be justified solely on the basis of forecasting accuracy. National econometric models are not exceptions to this rule. If one is primarily interested in using a national econometric model for forecasting the future, one

Table 7.5 Simulating the Klein model

ANALYSIS.

MODEL CONVERGENCE .0001 ITERATIONS 30 SIMULTANEOUS ON

ANALYSIS.

SOLVE KLEIN

RESULTS OF KLEIN -- DEFAULT FILE IS FILE   1

TIME	C(1)	G(1)	I(1)	K(1)
1	39.8	2.4	2.7	182.8
2	45.1	3.9	1.3	184.1
3	47.2	3.2	2.4	186.5
4	50.5	2.8	4.9	191.5
5	53.3	3.5	5.6	197.0
6	55.1	3.3	5.9	202.9
7	54.0	3.3	3.6	206.5
8	51.0	4.0	0.2	206.7
9	48.9	4.2	−1.1	205.6
10	50.0	4.1	0.2	205.8
11	52.5	5.2	1.0	206.8
12	53.3	5.9	−0.2	206.6
13	53.1	4.9	−0.7	205.9
14	51.6	3.7	−1.7	204.2
15	52.5	4.0	−0.8	203.4
16	53.7	4.4	−0.5	202.9
17	54.9	2.9	−0.6	202.3
18	54.0	4.3	−1.3	201.0
19	57.3	5.3	0.1	201.2
20	61.1	6.6	1.8	202.9
21	64.0	7.4	2.4	205.3
22	69.8	13.8	3.1	208.4

TIME	P(1)	T(1)	TIME(1)	W1(1)
1	12.7	3.4	−11.0	28.8
2	13.8	7.7	−10.0	28.9
3	18.0	3.9	−9.0	30.9
4	19.8	4.7	−8.0	33.8
5	22.0	3.8	−7.0	36.5
6	20.7	5.5	−6.0	38.1
7	16.8	7.0	−5.0	37.0
8	14.4	6.7	−4.0	34.2
9	15.8	4.2	−3.0	32.0
10	17.6	4.0	−2.0	32.7
11	15.9	7.7	−1.0	35.1
12	15.5	7.5	0.0	36.0
13	13.6	8.3	1.0	35.4
14	14.5	5.4	2.0	33.7
15	14.7	6.8	3.0	34.2
16	14.9	7.2	4.0	35.5
17	13.2	8.3	5.0	35.7
18	14.6	6.7	6.0	35.7
19	17.0	7.4	7.0	38.3
20	18.3	8.9	8.0	42.2
21	18.9	9.6	9.0	45.2
22	23.4	11.6	10.0	51.6

Table 7.5 (continued)

TIME	W2(1)	X(1)
1	2.2	44.9
2	2.7	50.3
3	2.9	52.8
4	2.9	58.2
5	3.1	62.3
6	3.2	64.3
7	3.3	60.8
8	3.6	55.3
9	3.7	52.0
10	4.0	54.3
11	4.2	58.7
12	4.8	59.0
13	5.3	57.3
14	5.6	53.6
15	6.0	55.7
16	6.1	57.5
17	7.4	57.3
18	6.7	57.1
19	7.7	62.7
20	7.8	69.4
21	8.0	73.8
22	8.5	86.6

ANALYSIS.

should proceed with extreme caution. National econometric models forecast well during periods of relatively stable economic behavior such as the period 1960 through 1968. They perform very badly during periods of uncertainty of the type experienced between late 1973 and early 1976. It is always interesting to watch econometric service bureau representatives squirm when confronted with the question, "How well did your model forecast the 1974–1975 recession?"

The fact that the forecasting track records of these models leaves something to be desired does not render them useless. They may still prove to be extremely powerful tools for answering "What if?" questions about the national economy.

Since 1973, Stephen K. McNees of the Federal Reserve Bank of Boston has published an annual report comparing the forecasting performance of the major econometric forecasting models in the United States. His reports appear in the *New England Economic Review*. Although these reports are not easily read by lay people, they do nonetheless contain valuable information concerning the forecasting performance of the leading national econometric models.

Relevance of forecasts For many companies, the number of macroeconomic variables required to do successful econometric modeling may be relatively small. Some marketing models necessitate highly disaggregated industry data. The selection of an appropriate economic database involves matching the user's particular database requirements with the databases which are currently available.

Number of equations The number of equations contained in national econometric models varies from fewer than 100 equations to nearly 1500 equations. The real issue is not how many equations are in the model, but rather whether or not the right series are included in the model in order to meet the user's particular needs.

In general, large econometric models are difficult to manage, hard to understand

Table 7.6 Checking the actual and simulated values of the GNP

```
ANALYSIS.

VALIDATE X(2) X
```

MODEL VALIDATION		
MEAN ABSOLUTE ERROR = 5.3448		
MEAN PERCENTAGE ERROR = 9.4674		
THEIL'S INEQUALITY COEFFICIENT U = 0.0541		
APPROXIMATE STANDARD ERROR OF U = 0.0540		

TIME	X(2) ACTUAL	X SIMULATED	DIFFERENCE
2	45.6000	50.3476	-4.7476
3	50.1000	52.8497	-2.7497
4	57.2000	58.2290	-1.0291
5	57.1000	62.3318	-5.2318
6	61.0000	64.3123	-3.3123
7	64.0000	60.8106	3.1894
8	64.4000	55.2750	9.1250
9	64.5000	52.0187	12.4813
10	67.0000	54.2927	12.7073
11	61.2000	58.7028	2.4972
12	53.4000	58.9759	-5.5759
13	44.3000	57.2776	-12.9776
14	45.1000	53.5879	-8.4879
15	49.7000	55.7304	-6.0304
16	54.4000	57.5505	-3.1505
17	62.7000	57.2815	5.4185
18	65.0000	57.0589	7.9411
19	60.9000	62.7097	-1.8097
20	69.5000	69.4340	0.0660
21	75.7000	73.7540	1.9460
22	88.4000	86.6344	1.7656

```
ANALYSIS.
```

when something is wrong, and expensive to run. An obvious question is whether the increased power achieved with a 1000-equation model is worth the increased computer charges and loss of user orientation caused by the increased complexity of the model. In general, larger models are not necessarily more useful or more accurate models.

Short-term model Several of the econometric forecasting services offer two different types of national econometric forecasting models—short-term models and long-term models. Short-term forecasting models are usually quarterly models the time horizon of which typically extends out for three years. The forecasting accuracy of the short-term models tends to be more accurate than the forecasting accuracy of the long-term models.

Again, it is a matter of finding a short-term forecasting model tailored to meet the needs of a particular econometric modeling application.

Long-term model For long-term, strategic planning, a different type of national econometric model is required; namely, a long-term econometric model. Long-term models are typically annual models capable of producing forecasts for periods of ten to fifteen years into the future.

For certain industries such as electric utilities, long-term forecasts are absolutely essential, given the long lead times required to develop additional generating capacity. Long-term econometric forecasting is, at best, very tenuous business. Corporate planners should use long-term econometric models merely as a guide to the future and not as tools for forecasting the future.

Industry forecasts As part of their econometric services, some bureaus offer their clients forecasts by industry down to the two-digit SIC code level. In some cases these forecasts are produced by an input–output model driven by the bureau's macro-econometric model. In other cases, individual econometric equations are specified for a limited number of variables for each industry. In general, the forecasting track record of these industry forecasts has not been impressive. This is not surprising, since it is unlikely that a given bureau could possess expertise on all categories of industry.

Industry models On the other hand, some bureaus have special expertise on a limited number of industries and have applied this expertise to develop highly sophisticated industry models for such industries as steel, agriculture, petrochemical, and energy. Some of these models represent the state of the art of econometric modeling and may prove to be quite useful to companies in the appropriate industries.

Fee schedule Numerous pricing options are available for econometric services ranging from "full service" packages in which the user has no choice in the options included in the package to flexible pricing options in which the user may select among various alternatives including databases, models, consulting support, etc.

Software Several of the econometric services are offered on computer service bureaus and provide their own econometric software. In selecting econometric software, the reader may wish to refer to the checklist provided in Chapter 2 entitled "Elements of a Planning and Modeling System."

Consulting   Since in-house econometricians are still few and far between even among the largest companies in the United States, the availability of consulting support for econometric modeling may prove to be important. However, if econometric models are built by outside consultants, they may lack the support needed to gain acceptance by the management. Outside consultants should be used to train in-house analysts on the development of econometric models and to guide the project to completion.

Availability   Several of the econometric service bureaus make their services available on outside time-sharing bureaus as well as on the client's in-house computer. Obviously, this type of flexibility is highly desirable because it provides the user with the option of beginning an econometric project on a service bureau and then switches the project to his or her in-house computer if the time-sharing charges become excessive.

Unfortunately, some econometric databases and models are available only on time-sharing bureaus. The user then becomes a captive client of the bureau.

OTHER ECONOMETRIC MODELS

Contrary to what may have been implied thus far in this chapter, econometric modeling has many other applications as a planning tool and is by no means restricted to marketing applications. Econometrics can be useful as an analytical tool in a wide variety of situations involving behavioral equations including supply forecasting, price projections, production cost models, interest rate projections, personnel planning, and demographic projections.

Supply Models

With the likelihood of continuing energy problems as well as dwindling supplies of numerous natural resources, supply models may become increasingly important. The ability to forecast supplies of production factor inputs may prove to be critical to the survival of some industries. Econometric models offer one alternative way of improving our ability to forecast the availability of inputs into the production process.

Pricing Models

Given that inflation seems to have become a fact of life, the necessity to be able to forecast factor input prices today has become much more important than it was in the 1960s. Again, econometric models may be used to improve our knowledge of the price structure of the production inputs which are required by a given company. As usual, one must be careful not to expect too much from price forecasting models and one must know the limitations of such models.

Production Cost Models

The Dresser Industries Model described in Chapter 11 contains an interesting application of econometrics to production cost models. Shortages of energy and other natural resources will create increased pressure on management scientists to develop viable production cost models. Chapter 8 contains an alternative methodology for developing production cost models based on activity analysis.

Banking Models

A plethora of econometric applications can be found in banks and bank holding companies ranging from forecasting interest rates, demand deposits, and time deposits to models for explaining loan demand. Although the number of banks using econometric modeling is still relatively small, the number seems to be increasing.

Personnel Planning Models

Personnel planning and forecasting can also be facilitated through the use of econometric modeling techniques. CIBA–GEIGY has successfully applied econometric models to personnel planning problems.

Demographic Models

Sales of many consumer products are highly correlated with population growth. Demographic trends may be particularly important in international marketing planning. Below is a simple demographic model for Taiwan.

$$B = -2.27EX + 3.63CMR + 1.09D_{-2} \tag{7.64}$$

$$D = .001NNP - .117LIT_{-2} + 547.2 \, PPS \tag{7.65}$$

$$POP = POP_{-1} \, (1 + B/1000 - D/1000) \tag{7.66}$$

where

$$
\begin{aligned}
B &= \text{birthrate per 1000} \\
D &= \text{death rate per 1000} \\
POP &= \text{population in thousands} \\
EX &= \text{expenditures on family planning per 1000 population} \\
CMR &= \text{crude marriage rate per 1000} \\
NNP &= \text{real per capita net national product} \\
LIT &= \text{literacy rate} \\
PPS &= \text{percentage of population over age 60}
\end{aligned}
$$

NOTES

1. EXP indicates that the expression within the parentheses represents the power to which the natural logarithm base e is to be raised.
2. This model is based on a paper by J. M. Vernon, N. W. Rives, and Thomas H. Naylor entitled, An econometric model of the tobacco industry. *Review of Economics and Statistics* 49 (May, 1969): 149–157.

3. The numbers within the parentheses below the coefficients denote the standard errors of the individual coefficients.

4. This section is based on the unpublished Ph.D. dissertation of Mary Lee Epps at Duke University entitled, *A computer model of the world coffee economy*, April 30, 1970. The version of the model which appears in this book was previously published in an article by Mary Lee Epps, Thomas H. Naylor, and Maocyr Fioravante entitled, A quarterly econometric model of the world coffee market, which appeared in *Revista Brasileira de Economia*, 1972.

5. The numbers within the parentheses below the coefficients are *t*-statistics.

6. This model is based on a model by Lawrence R. Klein as discussed in *Principles of Econometrics* by Henri Theil, New York: Wiley, 1971.

8   Production Planning Models

INTRODUCTION

Although the use of production planning models in industry goes back well over 20 years, relatively few companies have developed production planning models which are integrated into overall business planning models. Dresser Industries, the *New York Times,* and CIBA–GEIGY are exceptions to this rule. (These models are all described in Chapter 11.) Most of the production planning models which have been developed by management scientists are stand-alone models, not linked to financial or marketing models.

Virtually every major oil refinery in the world employs some type of mathematical programming model to generate refinery schedules. Mathematical programming models, inventory control models, queueing models, and job-shop scheduling models are widely used as short-term, operational planning tools. Thus far, they have seldom been used as strategic planning tools to evaluate the effects of long-run production plans and strategies. Yet why have so few firms developed integrated production planning models tied to financial and marketing models? There appear to be several reasons for the delayed interest in production planning models.

In the 1960s the top priorities among most business firms in the western hemisphere were expansion, growth, and increased market share. There were no energy problems; shortages of factor inputs were rare; and prices of factors of production were relatively stable. The binding constraint on corporations was a demand constraint rather than a supply constraint. But the 1970s produced an entirely different corporate environment characterized by energy problems, shortages of a variety of factor inputs including oil, gas, and coal, and dramatic increases in factor input prices. In many industries, market demand constraints were replaced by supply constraints. As supply constraints become more important, there is every reason to expect more companies to begin giving higher priority to integrated production planning models.

Since production models originated as operational planning tools, there has always been a timing interface problem in linking models intended to facilitate weekly or monthly scheduling with annual or five-year planning models of a more aggregate nature.

Finally, production planning models have tended to be much more complex than financial models or even marketing models. Top management is likely to find it much easier to relate to financial planning models than to sophisticated mixed integer programming models, goal programming models, or dynamic programming models.

This chapter examines two alternative approaches to production models for strategic planning purposes—marginal analysis and activity analysis. In each case we shall outline the assumptions underlying the model, describe the model, summarize the practical implementation of the model, and indicate some of its limitations.

A MARGINAL ANALYSIS MODEL

Assumptions

The assumptions underlying the marginal analysis production model of the firm are outlined below (Mauer and Naylor 1964; Naylor and Vernon 1968):

- The firm may sell its products as a monopolist or as a perfect competitor.
- The firm may purchase factor inputs as a monopolist or as a perfect competitor.
- The objective of the firm is to maximize profit subject to the technical constraints imposed by its production function.
- The firm possesses a production process that is capable of transforming a maximum of m variable factors of production into p products. (There are no limitations on the availability of the factors.)
- A continuous production function exists (with nonvanishing first-order and second-order partial derivatives) that relates the set of independent factor variables to the set of independent product variables.
- The production function is such that the quantity of output produced for a given product represents the maximum amount of that product that can be produced from specified factor input quantities along with specified product quantities for the remaining $p - 1$ products.
- The exact nature of the firm's production function has been predetermined by a set of technical decisions by the firm's engineers and technicians.
- The production function is characterized by a decreasing marginal product for all factor–product combinations, a decreasing rate of technical substitution between any two factors, and an increasing rate of product transformation between any two products.
- All of the firm's factors and products are perfectly divisible.
- The parameters which determine the firm's total revenue function, production function, and total cost equation will not change over the time period which is being considered.
- The parameters which determine the firm's total revenue function, production function, and total cost equation are not permitted to be random variables.

The Model

The product–factor transformation process of the firm is given by

$$Q(Z_1, \ldots, Z_k, \ldots, Z_p, X_1, \ldots, X_i, \ldots, X_m) = 0 \tag{8.1}$$

where

$$Z_k \geqslant 0 \text{ are products } (k = 1, \ldots, p), \tag{8.2}$$

and

$$X_i \geqslant 0 \text{ are factors } (i = 1, \ldots, m). \tag{8.3}$$

Equation (8.1) may be conveniently rewritten as

$$Q(Z_k, X_i) = 0 \ (k = 1, \ldots, p \text{ and } i = 1, \ldots, m) \tag{8.4}$$

where Z_k and X_i are defined by Eqs. (8.2) and (8.3). For any given set of factors, X_1, $\ldots, X_m$, there may be several technically feasible sets of products, $Z_1, \ldots, Z_p$. Assign arbitrary values to $p-1$ of these products and determine the largest value of the remaining product which is consistent with Eq. (8.4). This will assume a single-valued production function. If all but one of the factors of the products are assigned, then the remaining product is fully determined. It is further assumed that the production function is defined over the domain of nonnegative factors and products and that within the domain of definition it has continuous partial derivatives of first and second order.

Let R denote the firm's total revenue function and let C denote the firm's total cost function.

$$R = R(Z_1, \ldots, Z_k, \ldots, Z_p). \tag{8.5}$$

$$C = C(X_1, \ldots, X_i, \ldots, X_m). \tag{8.6}$$

The firm's profit function is defined as

$$\pi = R - C. \tag{8.7}$$

The objective of the firm is to maximize total profit, Eq. (8.7), subject to the technical constraints imposed by its production function, Eq. (8.4).

Optimal Decision Rules

The optimality conditions for the marginal analysis model of the firm may be derived in a straightforward manner by use of the Lagrangian multiplier method. In the case of the competitive firm, these optimality conditions take the form of the following economic decision rules:

Rule 1. The price ratio of any two products must equal the marginal rate of product transformation between the two products.

Rule 2. The price ratio of any two factors must equal the marginal rate of technical substitution between the two factors.

Rule 3. The price ratio of any factor–product combination must be equal to the marginal product for the particular factor–product combination.

The Dresser Industries Model

It will probably come as no surprise to the reader when we suggest that the marginal analysis model has not been used extensively as a strategic planning tool. The assumptions underlying the production function are seldom realized in actual production situations. In the following section some of the limitations of the marginal analysis model as a production planning tool are spelled out in detail.

However, Chapter 11 contains an interesting example of the practical application of a marginal analysis production model which has been used by Dresser Industries. The Dresser production model is an integrated planning model for one of the operating divisions of Dresser Industries. It is linked to the division's financial and marketing models.

The particular division of Dresser Industries which has been modeled produced 15 different products. The production function for each product is given by

$$Q_i = Q_i(VLO_i, DM_i, MF_i, AG_i, INV_i, TECH_i) \tag{8.8}$$

where

Q_i = output quantity of the ith product

VLO_i = direct labor required for Q_i for the ith product

DM_i = direct material required for the ith product

MF_i = manufacturing cost required for Q_i for the ith product

AG_i = administrative and general cost required for Q_i for the ith product

$TECH_i$ = technological change in production processes of the ith product

The production function, Eq. (8.8), is used to derive the appropriate cost functions for the Dresser model as well.

The Dresser Industries marketing model consists of 45 econometric equations. Once a demand forecast has been produced for each of the fifteen products, the production model generates the costs associated with satisfying demand. The front-end of the Dresser model is a revenue-expenditure model which is driven by the marketing model and the production model, respectively.

THE ACTIVITY ANALYSIS MODEL

Assumptions

The activity analysis or linear programming model of the firm is based on the following assumptions (Naylor 1966; Naylor and Vernon 1968):

·   The firm has p activities available, where an activity is defined as a particular way of combining a maximum of m variable factors for the production of a unit of output. A unit of output is analogous to a unit of product, but the firm may produce more than one product. Since a given product may be produced by several different activities each using different factor input ratios, the number of activities may exceed the number of products.

· The prices of the firm's variable factors and products are fixed and known. (Perfect competition is assumed.)

· The objective of the firm is to maximize profit subject to the constraints imposed by the nature of its activities and the amounts of fixed factors which are available.

· Each activity is characterized by a set of ratios of the quantities of the factors to the levels of each of the outputs. These ratios are constant and independent of the extent to which each activity is used. (The firm's production functions are homogeneous of degree one; that is, constant returns to scale are assumed.)

· The firm is constrained in its selection of activity levels by its fixed endowments of certain resources (fixed factors) required to support the p activities. (The firm's fixed factors are perfectly divisible in use but there is an upper limit on the total quantity of each fixed factor available.)

· Two or more activities can be used simultaneously, subject to the limitations of the fixed factors available to the firm and, if this is done, the quantities of the outputs and inputs will be the arithmetic sums of the quantities which would result if the activities were used separately.

· The exact nature of the firm's activities has been predetermined by a set of technical decisions by the firm's engineers and technicians.

· All of the firm's factors and products are perfectly divisible. (This assumption may, of course, be relaxed if one desires to formulate an integer linear programming model.)

· Neither the factor prices, product prices, nor the coefficients which determine the firm's activities (input–output coefficients) will change over the time period which is being considered.

· Neither the factor prices, product prices, nor the coefficients which determine the firm's activities are permitted to be random variables.

Production Function Comparison

Since most of the differences between marginal analysis and activity analysis (linear programming) models concern the production function, it seems appropriate to explore this concept in some detail.

Under the assumptions of conventional marginal analysis, the firm's production function is said to be a function of the quantities of fixed and variable factors which are used in the firm's production process. For any given factor quantities, the dependent variable represented by the function is usually defined as the maximum quantity of the particular product that can be produced, in a given state of technology, from the specified factor quantities.

The marginal analysis production function implies that a physical maximization of output for given levels of input has already been achieved. In essence this implies that the profit maximization problem of the firm is a two-stage problem. The first stage consists of deriving a prescription for achieving the *physical* maximization presupposed in the definition of the production function; that is, stage one is equivalent to determining the technology for the firm. The second stage is merely the problem of maximizing total profit subject to the conditions imposed by the production function.

It should be pointed out that the first of the firm's two decision problems can be solved independently of the second, but the second problem must be solved either simultaneously with the first problem or after the solution to the first problem has been obtained.

The distinction between the types of problems for which conventional marginal analysis and linear programming are best suited may be clarified by further examining the nature of the two different types of productive decisions made by the firm. The firm is assumed to have certain fixed factors at its disposal and access to variable factors through the open market.

The first decision is usually considered to be a technical decision; that is, the firm must decide on the technology to be applied in the production of the set of product possibilities available to it. This involves determining the maximum quantity of output for each product variable attainable from specified factor quantities along with other specified product quantities.

Once technology is determined or has been fixed by the previous decision, the second decision is concerned with which products should be produced, and in what quantities, so as to maximize total profit. It should be remembered that at this point a decision to produce a particular set of products at a particular level of output automatically determines the level of factor usage for the firm because the production function prescribes the exact proportions for each level of output for all possible product combinations.

The marginal analysis model of the firm is concerned only with the second type of decision problem of the firm because it assumes that the firm's technological problem has already been solved. Robert Dorfman (1951, p. 10) has summarized some of the difficulties involved in attempting to solve the second of the firm's two decision problems by marginal analysis.

. . . Machinery, and especially the more advanced types, is likely to be inflexible with regard to the factors which must be combined with it and with regard to the rate and character of its output. Thus, when it has been determined to use a certain number of units of a specific machine, several of the other variables in the production function have been determined at the same time. It will not then be possible to move freely from point to point on the production surface except in an indirect manner.

The type of decision which faces a firm using industrial processes is therefore essentially different from the decision contemplated by marginal analysis. The firm may decide the extent to which to use each of the types of equipment it owns at any time. In that case any variation in the use of equipment implies simultaneous variation in the use of factors complementary to that equipment. The firm may choose among a number (generally finite) of ways of applying its equipment. Or it may select among a number of types of equipment offered for its purchase. All of these differ in two respects from the kind of decisions treated by marginal analysis. First, they affect the quantities of a group of distinct inputs and outputs simultaneously. Second, the range of choice does not lie along a continuous scale, but involves selection among discrete alternatives. The effects of such decisions are therefore not adequately expressed by the theoretical operation of partial differentiation with respect to the quantities of separate inputs and outputs.

In other words, the difficulty in solving the firm's second decision problem (profit maximization subject to the constraints imposed by the production function) stems from the fact that the solution of the firm's technological problem may yield a production function which does not possess such properties as continuity, concavity, and nonzero first- and second-order partial derivatives. Marginal analysis may not be at all appropriate for solving the second type of decision problem in industrial environments similar to those outlined by Dorfman. Linear programming was devised specifically to circumvent the difficulties described by Dorfman in solving the firm's second-stage decision problem.

Furthermore, linear programming can handle both decision problems simultaneously; that is, linear programming determines both the quantities of the products to be produced *and* the optimal technological arrangement of productive activities.

In the final analysis the principal difference between the assumptions underlying marginal analysis models for the firm and linear programming models of the firm lies in the difference between the definitions of an "activity." These salient differences have been summarized by Dorfman (1951, p. 15) as follows:

> ... the [activity] of linear programming is a more specifically defined concept than the production function of marginal analysis. Indeed, a production function is a family of [activities] which use the same factors and turn out the same products. If we compare any two points on a production surface, if the internal ratios of the inputs and outputs at the two points are the same, they will represent different levels of the same [activity]. Otherwise they will represent different [activities]. The production function thus is a tool for exhibiting and comparing different but related [activities]. What it fails to present adequately is the consequence of using several [activities] in parallel, and such combinations of [activities] are characteristic of modern industry.

We turn now to the explicit formulation of the linear programming model. This will be followed by a comparison of the optimality conditions of the marginal analysis model and the linear programming model.

The Model

Consider a firm that has p independent activities available, where an activity is defined as a particular way of combining a maximum of m variable factors with a maximum of n fixed factors for the production of a unit of output. We then let

Z_k = the level of the kth activity, $(k = 1, \ldots, p)$

X_{ik} = the total quantity of the ith variable factor required by the kth activity, $(i = 1, \ldots, m; k = 1, \ldots, p)$

Y_{jk} = the total quantity of the jth fixed factor required by the kth activity, $(j = 1, \ldots, n; k = 1, \ldots, p)$

Y_j = the quantity of the jth fixed factor which is currently available to the firm, $(j = 1, \ldots, n)$

a_{ik} = the quantity of the ith variable factor required by one unit of the kth activity, $(i = 1, \ldots, m; k = 1, \ldots, p)$

b_{jk} = the quantity of the jth fixed factor required by one unit of the kth activity, $(j = 1, \ldots, n; k = 1, \ldots, p)$

P_k = the competitive price per unit of the kth activity, $(k = 1, \ldots, p)$

C_i = the competitive price per unit of the ith variable factor, $(i = 1, \ldots, m)$

K_{jk} = the cost of converting one unit of the jth fixed factor for use in the kth activity, $(j = 1, \ldots, n; k = 1, \ldots, p)$

The firm's profit function may then be stated as follows:

$$\Pi = \sum_{k=1}^{p} P_k Z_k - \sum_{i=1}^{m} \sum_{k=1}^{p} C_i X_{ik} - \sum_{j=1}^{n} \sum_{k=1}^{p} K_{jk} Y_{jk}. \tag{8.9}$$

By definition, in linear programming, each activity is characterized by certain ratios of the quantities of the factors to each other and to the levels of each of the outputs. These ratios are defined to be constant and independent of the extent to which each activity is used. Hence, it becomes necessary to impose the following definitional constraints on our problem.

$$X_{ik} = a_{ik} Z_k \quad (i = 1, \ldots, m; k = 1, \ldots, p) \tag{8.10}$$

$$Y_{jk} = b_{jk} Z_k \quad (j = 1, \ldots, n; k = 1, \ldots, p). \tag{8.11}$$

The firm is constrained in its selection of activity levels by its fixed endowments of certain resources required to support the p activities.

$$\sum_{k=1}^{p} Y_{jk} \leqslant Y_j \quad (j = 1, \ldots, n). \tag{8.12}$$

Summarily, the mathematical problem of the firm is one of determining those values of Z_k, X_{ik}, and Y_{jk} which will maximize

$$\Pi = \sum_{k=1}^{p} P_k Z_k - \sum_{i=1}^{m} \sum_{k=1}^{p} C_i X_{ik} - \sum_{j=1}^{n} \sum_{k=1}^{p} K_{jk} Y_{jk}, \tag{8.13}$$

subject to:

$$X_{ik} = a_{ik} Z_k \quad (i = 1, \ldots, m; k = 1, \ldots, p) \tag{8.14}$$

$$Y_{jk} = b_{jk} Z_k \quad (j = 1, \ldots, n; k = 1, \ldots, p) \tag{8.15}$$

$$\sum_{k=1}^{p} Y_{jk} \leqslant Y_j \quad (j = 1, \ldots, n) \tag{8.16}$$

Although this constrained optimization problem can be solved by the simplex method, our principal concern here is not with the technique by which one would solve the problem, but rather how to interpret the solution.

Optimal Decision Rules (Naylor and Vernon 1968)

For the purpose of comparison with the marginal analysis model of the firm, the optimality conditions for our linear programming model of the firm may be summarized in the form of the following decision rules.

Rule 1. The unit price of each activity must be less than or equal to the sum of the imputed costs of the fixed and variable factors used to produce one unit of that activity. (The term *imputed cost* is used to mean a valuation based on alternative factor uses internal to the firm.)

Rule 2. For each variable factor–activity combination the unit price of the given variable factor must be greater than or equal to the marginal value imputed to the variable factor with regard to the given activity.

Rule 3. The cost of covering one unit of a given fixed factor for use in a given activity must be greater than or equal to the net marginal value imputed to the given fixed factor used in the given activity, that is, the marginal value imputed to a unit of the fixed factor used in the given activity minus the marginal value imputed to one unit of the fixed factor.

Rule 4. The firm's total profit after paying the costs of its scarce resources (fixed factors) must be equal to zero.

Rule 5. The total value imputed to the scarce resources available to the firm must be equal to the imputed value of the scarce resources used by the firm in manufacturing operations.

A Petroleum Refining Industry Model

Adams and Griffin (1972) have developed an economic-linear programming model of the U.S. petroleum refining industry. The structure of the model is outlined in simplified form in Fig. 8.1. The Wharton Long-term Industry Model, on the left-hand side, determines the economic environment in which the refinery model operates. Given the stocks of petroleum consuming equipment, economic activity generates product demands. A simple inventory adjustment to normal levels is also assumed. Imports and exports of products are treated as exogenous variables.

Given product demands, inventory adjustments, and net imports, the requirements for the petroleum products are determined, and they become output constraints in the linear programming model. Other inputs include the capacities of various types of refining equipment available and crude oil prices, both of which are exogenous variables. Crude oil supplies are adjusted to satisfy refining needs. Constraints in the model include product quality specifications, process capacities, and product output requirements. The objective is to minimize the cost of producing the given outputs. The linear programming solution determines the volume of crude oil inputs required, the capacity utilization measures, total operating costs, and the outputs of by-products such as residual fuel oil. Product prices are computed on the basis of a markup over crude cost, utilization of capacity, inventory levels, and a general inflation measure. By sub-

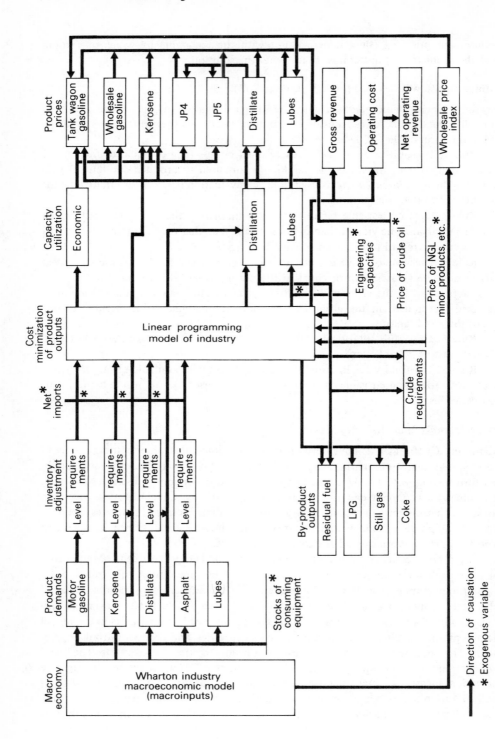

Fig. 8.1 A simplified structure of the petroleum industry model.

tracting operating costs as calculated by the model from a measure of gross revenue, an estimate of net operating revenue is obtained.

It would appear to be only a matter of time before this methodology will be adopted by most oil refineries and chemical processing plants.

Activity Analysis without an Objective Function

Given the difficulty in reducing corporate planning problems to the optimization of a single objective such as profit maximization or cost minimization, a number of companies have developed production planning models based on a variant of activity analysis in which no attempt is made to optimize with respect to production.

Given a demand forecast X, where X is a vector of different products, the resources required to satisfy demand are given by the expression

$$R = AX, \tag{8.17}$$

where A is an input-output matrix with elements a_{ij} denoting the quantity of input i required to produce one unit of product j. If we have the prices of the input resources (labor, materials, capital, etc.) denoted by the vector P, then the operating cost C can be calculated by

$$C = P' \cdot R. \tag{8.18}$$

By adjusting for inventories, cost of goods sold CGS can be obtained from

$$CGS = f(C). \tag{8.19}$$

The result of this approach is an experimental method for long-run strategic planning in which the planner can evaluate the effects of alternative production plans, resource constraints, and resource prices.

Some may argue that this approach which is sometimes called a material-parts explosion is in reality not a model, but merely cost accounting. Indeed, this is the case. Whatever one chooses to call this method, it does represent a practical way to evolve into the use of production planning models. For process-oriented industries this approach is likely to be easy to implement. On the other hand, it would be particularly difficult to apply to a job shop.

Example Models

One of the CIBA–GEIGY (Rosenkranz 1978) business planning models has an interesting linear programming model embedded within its production component. Given demand forecasts for 35 product groups which have been generated by econometric marketing models, the linear programming model minimizes the production and distribution costs for sales from 65 countries produced in ten different plant locations. Both the marketing model and the production–distribution model are in turn linked to a front-end financial model for the particular division of CIBA–GEIGY. This model is described in more detail in Chapter 11.

The activity analysis approach without an objective function has been successfully employed by Inland Steel, Potlatch, Monsanto, and the *New York Times*. The Inland

Steel model (Boulden 1975) divides the production of steel into four basic processes or activities: (1) conversion of ores to molten iron, (2) conversion of molten iron to steel ingots, (3) processing of ingots, and (4) finishing the steel to various end products. This model drives a financial model for the steel division of the company which generates pro forma cash flow statements, balance sheets, and income statements. A similar model has been developed by Potlatch, a major forest products company. The *New York Times* model is described in Chapter 11.

BIBLIOGRAPHY

Adams, F. Gerard, and James M. Griffin, 1972. An econometric-linear programming model of the U.S. petroleum industry. *Journal of the American Statistical Association* **67** (September): 542–551.

Boulden, James B., 1975. *Computer-assisted planning systems*. New York: McGraw-Hill.

Dantzig, George B., 1963. *Linear programming and extensions*. Princeton, N.J.: Princeton University Press.

Dorfman, Robert, 1951. *Application of linear programming to the theory of the firm*. Berkeley, Calif.: University of California Press.

————, 1953. Mathematical, or "linear," programming. *American Economic Review* (December).

————, Paul A. Samuelson, and Robert Solow, 1958. *Linear programming and economic analysis*. New York: McGraw-Hill.

Mauer, William A., and Thomas H. Naylor, 1964. Monopolistic-monopsonistic competition: the multi-product, multi-factor firm. *Southern Economic Journal* (July): 38–43.

Naylor, Thomas H., 1965. A Kuhn–Tucker model of the multi-product, multi-factor firm. *Southern Economic Journal* (April).

————, 1966. The theory of the firm: a comparison of marginal analysis and linear programming. *Southern Economic Journal* (January).

————, and John L. Vernon, 1968. *Microeconomics and decision models of the firm*. New York: Harcourt, Brace.

————, and John L. Vernon, 1971. *Introduction to linear programming*. Belmont, Calif.: Wadsworth.

Rosenkranz, Friedrich, 1978. *An introduction to corporate modeling*. Durham, N.C.: Duke University Press.

9

A Corporate Planning Model

THOMAS H. NAYLOR AND
W. CORBETT ROUSE

INTRODUCTION

TV Limited is the American subsidiary of the multinational Swiss electronic firm known as Zeta Electronics, Ltd. TV Limited (TVL) is a manufacturer of television sets. In early 1976, TVL had just received its year-end financial reports for 1975. The Director of Corporate Planning at TVL was interested in developing a corporate planning model to facilitate the formulation of the next five-year plan for the company. At present the company has a manual strategic planning system, but it has proved to be somewhat rigid and inflexible. Specifically, the Director of Corporate Planning was interested in acquiring the capability to answer "What if?" questions to evaluate alternative marketing and financial policies in light of possible scenarios which might evolve for the economy of the United States. TVL is heavily dependent on the U.S economy, since over 80 percent of its market is in the United States.

GOALS AND OBJECTIVES

The Director of Corporate Planning at TVL envisaged a fully integrated business planning model for TVL based on certain guidelines provided by the Vice-President of Corporate Planning for the parent company, Zeta Electronics, Ltd.

The model was to consist of a front-end financial model driven by a marketing model and a production model as illustrated in Fig. 9.1. Based on historical data since 1966, the financial model was to produce annual financial reports for the period 1976 through 1980. The financial reports would include an income statement (Table 9.21), a balance sheet (Table 9.22), and a set of financial ratios (Table 9.23). In addition, the model was expected to generate a five-year market forecast (Table 9.19) and a five-year production forecast (Table 9.20).

After a careful review of the planning requirements for TVL, the Director of Corporate Planning determined that it was important for management to monitor a

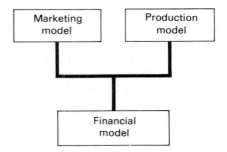

Fig. 9.1 Flowchart for the TVL corporate planning model.

total of 32 different output variables. These variables would become the major indicators by which management would judge the performance of the company. It followed that these variables would also serve as the output of the TVL Corporate Planning Model.

After consultation with the President, Vice-President of Finance, Treasurer, Vice-President of Marketing, and Vice-President of Manufacturing, the Director of Corporate Planning decided that it would be desirable to attempt to link the TVL Model to the economy of the United States. It was felt that both long- and short-term interest rates were important external financial variables that should be treated as input into the model as well as several other measures of overall economic activity. After repeated experimentation, national income was selected as a good leading indicator for television sales in the U.S. These external variables were included in the model.

Since the primary objective of the model was to evaluate the impact of alternative management strategies on the performance of the company, a great deal of attention was given to the selection of the policy variables to be included in the model. Nine policy variables were integrated into the model. The policy variables included three marketing policy variables—advertising expenses, the price of color TV sets, and the price of black-and-white (b&w) TV sets.

On the financial side, management could control the number of shares of stock outstanding, the price to be charged if additional shares were to be sold, and whether or not dividends were declared. Management could also establish a minimum cash balance such that if cash dropped below this minimum, the cash gap could be made up by drawing on the company's short-term line of credit. TVL could also elect whether or not to acquire additional long-term debt or retire some of its existing debt.

In planning for the next five years, management wanted to be able to consider different financial and marketing strategies and to be able to anticipate their likely impact on TVL's market performance and financial condition. Among the kinds of "What if?" questions of interest to management were the following. What will be the impact on total revenue if we raise prices and hold advertising expenditures constant? If we double our advertising budget, how much cash will we need? Should we sell additional stock to finance our expansion and growth or should we acquire additional long-term debt? Is our cash management policy effective? What if interest rates go up? What if the U.S. economy goes into recession again?

Following is a list of the 32 output variables, three external variables, and nine management policy variables which appear in the TVL Model. We define each variable and specify the units associated with it.

Output Variables

Variable	Name (units)
AP	Accounts payable ($1000)
AR	Accounts receivable ($1000)
BW	B & w TV sales (1000)
CA	Current assets ($1000)
CASH	Cash ($1000)
CGS	Cost of goods sold ($1000)
CL	Current liabilities ($1000)
COLOR	Color TV sales (1000)
CR	Current ratio (ratio)
CS	Common stock ($1000)
DIV	Dividends ($1000)
EPS	Earnings per share ($/share)
ES	Earned surplus ($1000)
INTEREST	Interest ($1000)
INV	Inventory ($1000)
LTD	Long-term debt ($1000)
MA	Miscellaneous accruals ($1000)
NET	Net profit ($1000)
NPLANT	Net plant and equipment ($1000)
NPTSR	Net profit to sales ratio (ratio)
NSHARES	Number of shares (1000)
OA	Other assets ($1000)
OE	Operating expenses ($1000)
PBT	Profit before taxes ($1000)
RTAX	Reserve for federal income taxes ($1000)
RTE	Retained earnings ($1000)
SALES	Sales revenue ($1000)
STD	Short-term debt ($1000)
TA	Total assets ($1000)

TAX	Federal income taxes ($1000)
TE	Total expenses ($1000)
TL	Total liabilities ($1000)

Input Variables

External

Variable	*Name* (*units*)
LTR	Long-term interest rate
STR	Short-term interest rate
Y	National income ($billion)

Policy

Variable	*Name* (*units*)
ADV	Advertising expenses ($1000)
DPS	Dividends per share ($1)
MIN	Minimum cash balance ($1000)
NDEBT	New long-term debt ($1000)
NOMINAL	Nominal value per share ($1)
NSHARES	Number of shares (1000)
PBW	Price of b&w TV sets ($1)
PC	Price of color TV sets ($1)
REPAY	Repayment of long-term debt ($1000)

HISTORICAL DATA

Three types of historical data were available to TVL for the development of its corporate planning model—marketing, production, and financial data.

Table 9.1 contains marketing data over the 1966–1975 period. The data include price and volume data by product as well as advertising expenditures and national income for the United States.

Unfortunately, TVL's manufacturing cost accounting data were somewhat limited. Production volume (assumed to be equal to sales volume) by product, cost of goods sold, and inventory data appear in Table 9.2.

Relatively complete financial data were available including annual income statement data (Table 9.3), balance sheet data (Table 9.4), and selected financial ratios (Table 9.5).

External Assumptions

The TVL Model was based on a set of assumptions about the external environment of the firm. These assumptions were assumed to be beyond the control of TVL's management but of vital importance to the future of the company.

Table 9.1 TVL historical marketing data (1966–1975)

Year	Color TV sales Volume (1000)	Price ($1)	B&W TV sales Volume (1000)	Price ($1)	Advertising Expenses ($1000)	National Income ($billion)
1966	17.1	260	12.3	138	1,600	414.5
1967	19.9	264	15.3	138	1,760	427.3
1968	20.4	270	15.2	146	1,792	457.7
1969	21.7	270	15.4	150	1,840	481.9
1970	24.4	276	18.5	150	2,000	518.1
1971	27.9	280	20.0	160	2,160	564.3
1972	30.4	280	21.3	160	2,240	620.6
1973	31.5	280	21.8	160	2,272	653.6
1974	33.6	283	23.0	164	2,368	701.3
1975	34.2	285	23.7	164	2,400	723.5

Table 9.2 TVL historical production data (1966–1975)

Year	Color TV volume (1000)	B&W TV volume (1000)	Total volume (1000)	Cost of goods sold ($1000)	Inventory ($1000)
1966	17.1	12.3	29.4	3010.3	1167.2
1967	19.9	15.3	35.2	3829.8	1546.7
1968	20.4	15.2	35.6	3709.1	1545.4
1969	21.7	15.4	37.1	4084.5	1470.4
1970	24.4	18.5	42.9	5040.0	2092.1
1971	27.9	20.0	47.9	5616.1	2202.4
1972	30.4	21.3	51.7	6556.0	2026.4
1973	31.5	21.8	53.3	6277.1	2584.7
1974	33.6	23.0	56.6	6640.0	2656.2
1975	34.2	23.7	57.9	6953.2	2863.1

In forecasting sales volume for color and b&w TV sets, national income in the United States was found to be a good leading indicator. For this reason national income data were tabulated in Table 9.6.

The production model employed by TVL was relatively primitive and reflected the dearth of accurate cost accounting data available to build such a model and the fact that management was more concerned with marketing and financial problems than with production problems. Both cost of goods sold and work-in-process inventory were assumed to be driven entirely by sales. No data were available on specific factor input costs. The external production assumptions are spelled out in Table 9.7.

Finally, the financial module of the TVL Model was based on a set of rather detailed assumptions explaining the relationship between TVL's financial structure and its external environment. These assumptions appear in Table 9.8 and include assump-

Table 9.3 TVL historical income statement data (1966–1975)

	1966	1967	1968	1969	1970	1971	1972	1973	1974	1975
Sales revenue	6143.4	7365.0	7727.2	8169.0	9509.4	11012.0	11920.0	12308.0	13280.8	13633.8
Expenses										
Cost of goods sold	3010.3	3829.8	3709.1	4084.5	5040.0	5616.1	6556.0	6277.1	6640.0	6953.2
Advertising expenses	1600.0	1760.0	1792.0	1840.0	2000.0	2160.0	2240.0	2272.0	2368.0	2400.0
Operating expenses	233.4	287.2	293.6	326.8	399.4	451.5	512.6	516.6	531.2	545.4
Interest	354.4	343.9	720.4	636.3	563.6	1022.4	704.2	1273.1	1616.7	1553.8
Total expenses	5198.2	6220.9	6515.1	6887.6	8003.0	9250.0	10012.8	10338.8	11155.9	11452.4
Profit before taxes	945.2	1144.1	1212.1	1281.4	1506.4	1762.0	1907.2	1969.2	2124.9	2181.4
Federal income taxes	453.7	554.9	593.9	627.9	745.8	881.0	953.6	984.6	1062.4	1090.7
Net profit	491.5	589.2	618.2	653.5	760.6	881.0	953.6	984.6	1062.5	1090.7
Dividends	360.2	362.3	363.4	367.8	371.6	372.5	370.6	369.5	370.1	375.6
Retained earnings	131.3	226.9	254.8	285.7	389.0	508.5	583.0	615.1	692.4	715.1

Table 9.4 TVL historical balance sheet data (1966–1975)

	1966	1967	1968	1969	1970	1971	1972	1973	1974	1975
Assets										
Cash	800.2	421.3	1354.4	2344.4	2071.2	3111.3	2078.1	2554.4	4215.0	5168.1
Accounts receivable	491.5	626.0	734.1	939.4	950.9	991.1	1192.0	1232.3	1300.1	1363.4
Inventory	1167.2	1546.7	1545.4	1470.4	2092.1	2202.4	2026.4	2584.7	2656.2	2863.1
Current assets	2458.9	2594.0	3633.9	4754.2	5114.2	6304.8	5296.5	6371.4	8171.3	9394.6
Net plant and equipment	5212.9	5715.3	7316.8	7747.6	7906.6	9867.8	9126.7	11244.1	13436.0	14635.2
Other assets	102.3	140.9	181.5	220.7	259.2	300.8	341.0	384.4	424.3	464.9
Total assets	7774.1	8450.2	11132.2	12722.5	13280.0	16473.4	14764.2	17999.9	22031.6	24494.7
Liabilities										
Accounts payable	150.5	210.6	222.5	265.5	352.8	365.0	393.4	345.2	398.4	417.2
Short-term debt	1107.8	975	1610.0	2272.5	2261.3	2840.0	1956.1	2652.3	3674.3	4316.1
Reserve for federal taxes	450.0	560.0	600.0	625.0	740.0	890.0	1000.0	1010.0	1025.0	1050.0
Miscellaneous accruals	22.5	28.1	34.6	43.6	53.2	64.9	81.1	101.4	127.7	159.7
Debt repayment	90.6	92.5	92.0	94.9	95.6	100.1	100.4	110.6	115.3	118.0
Current liabilities	1821.4	1866.2	2559.1	3301.5	3502.9	4260.0	3531.0	4219.5	5340.7	6061.0
Long-term debt	2417.0	2417.0	4179.2	4772.3	4342.7	6390.0	4401.3	6365.5	8660.9	9711.3
Common stock	2000.0	2500.0	2500.0	2500.0	3000.0	3000.0	3500.0	3500.0	3500.0	3500.0
Earned surplus	1535.7	1667.0	1893.9	2148.7	2434.4	2823.4	3331.9	3914.9	4530.0	5222.4
Total liabilities	7774.1	8450.2	11132.2	12722.5	13280.0	16473.4	14764.2	17999.9	22031.6	24494.7

Table 9.5 TVL historical financial ratio data (1966–1975)

	1966	1967	1968	1969	1970	1971	1972	1973	1974	1975
Earnings per share	4.92	4.71	4.95	5.23	5.07	5.87	5.45	5.63	6.07	6.23
Current ratio	1.35	1.39	1.42	1.44	1.46	1.48	1.50	1.51	1.53	1.55
Net profit to sales ratio	0.08	0.08	0.08	0.08	0.08	0.08	0.08	0.08	0.08	0.08

tions about interest rates, expenses, tax rates, depreciation, accounts receivable, and accounts payable. In each case, the external financial assumptions were made over the period between 1976 and 1980.

Table 9.6 External marketing assumptions

Year	National Income (Y) ($billion)
1976	750.20
1977	775.40
1978	788.90
1979	800.00
1980	822.50

Table 9.7 External production assumptions

1. *Cost of goods sold* (CGS) equals 60% of sales (SALES).
2. *Work-in-process inventory* (INV) equals 20% of sales (SALES).

Table 9.8 External financial assumptions

1. *Long-term interest rate* (LTR) equals 10%
2. *Short-term interest rate* (STR) equals 12%
3. *Operating expenses* (OE) equal 10% of sales (SALES)
4. *Federal income tax rate* equals 50%
5. *Accounts receivable* (AR) equal 10% of sales (SALES)
6. *Depreciation* for plant and equipment is assumed to be 5% per year
7. *Other assets* (OA) increase by $40,000 each year
8. *Accounts payable* (AP) equal 6% of cost of goods sold (CGS)
9. *Miscellaneous accruals* (MA) increase by 25% per year

POLICY ASSUMPTIONS

In addition to a set of external assumptions, the TVL Model was also based on a set of managerial policy assumptions for the coming five-year period. Marketing policies included price and advertising (Table 9.9). The policy assumptions underlying the production model were relatively simplistic (Table 9.10). However, it should be pointed out that with adequate technical and cost accounting data, an in-depth activity analysis production model could have been specified. Such a model would have linked production volume to resource requirements (raw materials, labor, capital, etc.). Given a sales forecast, an activity analysis model would generate a resource demand forecast and the cost of the resource needed to satisfy demand. Companies like Inland Steel, Potlatch, and Monsanto utilize a production modeling technique of this type.

Consistent with the emphasis placed on financial analysis by TVL's management, Table 9.11 contains a set of seven financial policy assumptions on which the model is based.

Table 9.9 Marketing policy assumptions

Year	Color TV price ($1)	B&W TV price ($1)	Advertising expenses ($1000)
1976	300	180	3000
1977	310	190	3000
1978	320	200	3000
1979	330	210	3000
1980	340	220	3000

Table 9.10 Production policy assumptions

1. *Two products*–color TV sets (COLOR) and black and white TV sets (BW).
2. *Production output approximately equals sales volume* for both color TV sets (COLOR) and (BW) sets.
3. *No adjustments* made in sales (SALES), output, or cost of goods sold (CGS) to reflect changes in work-in-process inventory (INV).

Table 9.11 Financial policy assumptions

1. *Dividends per share* (DPS) equal $2.15.
2. *If cash* (CASH) *is less than the required minimum cash balance* (MIN), additional short-term debt (STD) equal to 1.33 times the cash deficit is generated; otherwise, STD equals STD of last period.
3. *No new long-term debt* (NDEBT) is contemplated.
4. *Nominal value per share* (NOMINAL) based on average value of previous shares sold equals $20 per share.
5. *Number of common shares outstanding* (NSHARES) equals 225,000.
6. *Annual repayment of long-term debt* (REPAY) equals $100,000.
7. *No additional plant and equipment* (NPLANT).

MODEL SPECIFICATION

Marketing Model

Specification To explain the behavior of color and b&w TV sales volume, the following two-equation econometric model was formulated.

$$COLOR = a + bPC + cBW + dADV + eY \tag{9.1}$$

$$BW = f + gPBW + hCOLOR + iADV + jY \tag{9.2}$$

In reality, many different behavioral equations were specified. Equations (9.1) and (9.2) represent the result of screening out numerous unacceptable equation specifications. Equation (9.1) states that color TV sales volume (COLOR) is related to the price of color sets (PC); the number of b&w sets sold (BW), since they are substitutes for color sets; total advertising expenditures (ADV) and national income (Y). On the other hand, in Eq. (9.1), we observe that b&w TV sales volume (BW) is assumed to be linked to the price of b&w sets (PBW), the number of color sets sold (COLOR), advertising expenditures (ADV), and national income (Y). Many other national macroeconomic indicators were considered, but national income proved to yield the best statistical fit.

In summary, Eqs. (9.1) and (9.2) represent a hypothesis about the sales behavior of the two kinds of TV sets manufactured by TVL. But in Table 9.1 we have ten years of historical data on each of the variables included in Eqs. (9.1) and (9.2). Armed with this data, it is possible to estimate the coefficients $a, b, c, \ldots, f, g, h, \ldots$, of the two models, subject these parameter estimates to a series of statistical tests, and evaluate the dynamic properties of the model. Once an acceptable model has been specified and estimated, then it can be used to generate forecasts for each type of TV set.

Estimation Table 9.12 contains the printout of the estimation of the parameters of the COLOR equation using ordinary least squares to estimate each equation separately. The estimated equation is given by

$$COLOR = 11.271 - .133PC - .228BW + .024ADV + .013Y. \qquad (9.3)$$

The first thing we note in Eq. (9.3) is the signs of the coefficients. The signs of PC and PBW are both negative as would be expected. The negative signs respectively imply that the law of demand is at work in the color TV market and that color TV sets and b&w sets are substitutes. In Table 9.12, we also examine the R^2s and the t-statistics. The exceptionally high R^2s indicate that the right-hand variables have explained most of the variance in COLOR. The t-statistics indicate that all of the right-hand side variables are statistically significant at the .05 level.

Table 9.12 Estimation of color TV equation

Least-squares regression
estimated equation is

$COLOR = -0.1334*PC - 0.2283*BW + 0.0237*ADV + 0.0132*Y + 11.2709$

Independent variables	Estimated coefficient	Standard error	t-test
PC	− 0.1334	0.0200	− 6.6704
BW	− 0.2283	0.1122	− 2.0336
ADV	0.0237	0.0022	10.7829
Y	0.0132	0.0017	7.7233
CONSTANT	11.2709	3.9949	2.8213

Number of observations used = 10
$R^2 = 0.9999$
Adjusted $R^2 = 0.999$
Standard error = 0.0966
F-statistic (4, 5) = 9302.4648
Durbin–Watson Statistic = 1.6503
Degrees of freedom for t-test = 5

Table 9.13 displays the results of estimating Eq. (9.2). The estimated equation is

$$BW = -7.360 - .121PBW - .499COLOR + .027ADV + .005Y. \qquad (9.4)$$

The interpretation of Eq. (9.4) is similar to that of Eq. (9.3). Both equations were estimated through the use of a special purpose planning and modeling system known as SIMPLAN. Since Eqs. (9.1) and (9.2) represent a system of simultaneous equations, the user may want to consider reestimating the equations using a technique like two-stage least squares, which takes the simultaneity into consideration.

Table 9.13 Estimation of b&w TV equation

Least-squares regression
Estimated equation is:

$$BW = -0.210*PBW - 0.4989*COLOR + 0.0267*ADV + 0.0054*Y - 7.3610$$

Independent variables	Estimated coefficient	Standard error	t-test
PBW	-0.1210	0.0094	-12.8993
COLOR	-0.4989	0.1068	-4.6693
ADV	0.0267	0.0017	15.4040
Y	0.0054	0.0022	2.4010
CONSTANT	-7.3610	1.4601	-5.0416

Number of observations used = 10
$R^2 = .9998$
Adjusted $R^2 = 0.9997$
Standard error = 0.0684
F-statistic (4, 5) = 7337.0156
Durbin–Watson statistic = 1.8930
Degrees of freedom for t-test = 5

Although Eqs. (9.3) and (9.4) both produced excellent statistical fits, the reader should be aware that these equations are the results of numerous other specifications and estimations that were rejected either because the models did not make sense or because of unacceptable R^2s or t-statistics.

Validation The model set forth in Eqs. (9.1) and (9.2) does appear to be based on rational economic theories. According to economic theory we would expect the signs of coefficients b and g to be negative. The law of demand provides the rationale for this assertion. Since COLOR and BW are substitute products, we would assume that coefficients c and h would also be negative. Economic theory would also lead us to assume that increased advertising expenditures and increased income would increase the quantity demanded of a given product. Therefore, we would anticipate that coefficients d, e, i, and j would all be positive.

As we have previously indicated, Eqs. (9.3) and (9.4) have good R^2s and good t-statistics and the signs of the coefficient are consistent with our *a priori* understanding of the TV market. In other words, we can have confidence in the model's explanatory power.

Finally, the most severe test of the validity of our model is its ability to accurately forecast the behavior of the system it was designed to emulate. This implies that the model must be solved simultaneously for COLOR and BW over time based on given values for PC, PBW, ADV, and Y. We can then compare the simulated values of the two output variables COLOR and BW with their actual observed historical values.

Through the use of the VALIDATE command in SIMPLAN, actual and simulated values of COLOR and BW are tabulated in Table 9.14 and the mean percent absolute errors are computed as well. As we can see from the mean percent errors, the model tracks the actual values of COLOR and BW very well. The SOLVE command of SIMPLAN makes use of the Gauss–Seidel method to solve the equations dynamically over time. The method can also be used with larger numbers of equations and with nonlinear equations.

Table 9.14 Validation of marketing model

| Year | Color TV sales volume | | | B&W TV sales volume | | |
	Actual	Simulated	Difference	Actual	Simulated	Difference
1966	17,100	17,555.5	55.5	12,300	12,335.0	35.0
1967	19,900	19,903.6	3.6	15,300	15,303.9	3.9
1968	20,400	20,295.7	− 104.3	15,200	15,159.0	− 41.0
1969	21,700	21,700.4	0.4	15,400	15,386.3	− 13.7
1970	24,400	24,463.5	63.5	18,500	18,474.1	− 25.9
1971	27,900	27,974.3	74.3	20,000	20,033.3	33.3
1972	30,400	30,323.1	− 76.9	21,300	21,301.0	1.0
1973	31,500	31,404.0	− 96.0	21,800	21,794.0	− 6.0
1974	33,600	33,627.6	27.6	23,000	23,021.0	21.0
1975	34,200	34,261.4	61.4	23,700	23,678.8	− 21.2

Mean absolute error = 56.4   Mean absolute error = 20.2
Mean percentage error = 0.2203   Mean percentage error = 0.1188

The fact that the model tracks well historically is no guarantee that the model will forecast accurately between 1976 and 1980. Unless there is additional information to the contrary, then this is probably the best we can do. We shall now proceed to use Eqs. (9.3) and (9.4) in the integrated TVL Corporate Planning Model.

Production Model

There are only two production equations in the TVL Model. Equation 40 in the income statement model (Table 9.15) states that cost of goods sold (CGS) will on the average be equal to approximately 60 percent of sales revenues (SALES). Equation 200 in the Balance Sheet Model (Table 9.16) assumes that the value of the company's work-in-process inventory (INV) will be approximately 20 percent of the sales revenue (SALES).

Table 9.15 TVL Income statement model

```
 10  COLOR = 11.270 − .133*PC − .228*BW + .024*ADV + .013*Y
 20  BW = − 7.360 − .121*PBW − .499*COLOR + .027*ADV + .005*Y
 30  SALES = PC*COLOR + PBW*BW
 40  CGS = .60*SALES
 50  OE = .10*SALES
 60  INTEREST = STR*STD + LTR*LTD
 70  TE = CGS + ADV + OE + INTEREST
 80  PBT = SALES − TE
 90  TAX = .5*PBT
100  NET = PBT − TAX
110  DIV = DPS*NSHARES
120  RTE = NET − DIV
```

Table 9.16 TVL Balance sheet model

```
130  CASH = TL − AR − INV − NPLANT − OA
140  IF CASH < MIN
150  STD = STD + 1.33*(MIN−CASH)
160  ELSE
170  STD = STD(− 1)
180  END
190  AR = .10*SALES
200  INV = .20*SALES
210  CA = CASH + AR + INV
220  NPLANT = .95*NPLANT(− 1)
230  OA = OA(− 1) + 40
240  TA = CA + NPLANT + OA
250  AP = .06*CGS
260  RTAX = TAX
270  MA = 1.25*MA(− 1)
280  CL = AP + STD + RTAX + MA + REPAY
290  LTD = LTD(− 1) + NDEBT − REPAY
300  CS = NOMINAL*NSHARES
310  ES = ES(− 1) + RTE
320  TL = CL + LTD + CS + ES
```

Financial Model

The financial model consists of three separate models: (1) income statement model, (2) balance sheet model, and (3) financial ratio model. To specify a financial model, an analyst must sit with someone within the company who is very familiar with the company's financial structure and examine each line item of the three financial reports to be generated by the model. The assumptions on which each of the three models were based were previously summarized in Tables 9.8 and 9.11.

Income Statement   Table 9.15 contains the SIMPLAN equations for the income statement model. The model contains 12 equations—one equation for each line item in the income statement (Table 9.21).

Statements 10 and 20 in Table 9.15 correspond respectively to Eqs. (9.3) and (9.4) of the marketing model. The asterisks (*) denote multiplication. Otherwise, the two statements are identical to the two previously estimated econometric equations for COLOR and BW sales volume. Total sales revenue (SALES) is the sum of the revenue from color TV sets and b&w TV sets.

The cost of goods sold equation, statement 40, was previously specified in conjunction with the production model. Advertising expense (ADV) is a policy variable. Its values are given in Table 9.9 for the period 1976–1980.

Short-term interest is the product of the short-term interest rate (STR) and short-term debt (STD). Long-term interest is the product of the long-term interest rate (LTR) and long-term debt (LTD). Total interest (INTEREST) is calculated in statement 60 and is the sum of short-term interest and long-term interest.

Total expenses (TE) and profit before taxes (PBT) are accounting identities and are defined by SIMPLAN statements 70 and 80, respectively. Federal income taxes (TAX) are computed in statement 90 assuming a tax rate of 50 percent. Net profit (NET) is defined by statement 100. Total dividends paid (DIV) is the product of dividends per share (DPS) and the number of shares outstanding (NSHARES). Finally, retained earnings (RTE) are calculated in statement 120.

Balance sheet   The equations for the balance sheet model are specified in Table 9.16. The output report generated by the model appears in Table 9.22.

The balance sheet is balanced with the cash account. In statement 130 cash (CASH) is defined as the sum of liabilities and equity (TL) less all assets other than cash. If cash (CASH) is less than the required minimum cash balance (MIN), additional short-term debt equal to 1.33 times the cash deficit (MIN-CASH) is generated by statement 150.

In statements 190 and 200 accounts receivable (AR) and work-in-process inventory value (INV) are expressed as 10 percent and 20 percent of sales revenue (SALES), respectively. Current assets (CA) are defined as the sum of cash (CASH), accounts receivable (AR), and inventory (INV) in statement 210.

Depreciation is subtracted from net plant and equipment (NPLANT) in statement 220 at the rate of five percent per year. Other assets (OA) are incremented by $40,000 in statement 230 and total assets (TA) are defined by statement 240.

Turning to the liabilities side of the balance sheet, accounts payable (AP) are computed in statement 250 as a fixed percentage (six percent) of cost of goods sold (CGS). Short-term debt (STD) was previously calculated in statement 170. The reserve for federal income taxes (RTAX) is equal to federal taxes for the year (TAX).

Miscellaneous accruals (MA) in statement 270 are assumed to increase by 25 percent each year. Retirement of long-term debt (REPAY) is a policy variable. Current liabilities (CL) are summed in statement 280. Long-term debt (LTD) is defined as last year's long-term debt plus any new debt (NDEBT) less payments of the debt (REPAY).

If we assume the nominal value per share of stock is the average price paid to the company for all outstanding shares, then the total paid in value of the common stock (CS) is the product of the nominal value per share (NOMINAL) and the number of outstanding shares (NSHARES). This relationship appears in statement 300.

Finally, earned surplus (ES) is updated in statement 310 and total liabilities (TL) are computed in statement 320.

Financial ratios   Three financial ratios are calculated in the simple model which appears in Table 9.17. These ratios include earnings per share (EPS), the current ratio (CR) and the ratio of net profit to sales revenue (NPTSR). Statements 330, 340, and 350 contain the definitions of each of these three respective ratios. The output generated by this model is displayed in Table 9.23.

Table 9.17 TVL financial ratio model

330 EPS = NET/NSHARES
340 CR = CA/CL
350 NPTSR = NET/SALES

Corporate planning model   In Table 9.18 the integrated corporate planning model is listed. It includes all of the equations from the income statement, balance sheet, and financial ratio models. Statements 10, 20, and 30 constitute the marketing models and statements 40 and 200 represent the production relationships. In a manner similar to Fig. 9.1 we have a front-end corporate financial model which is being driven by an econometric marketing model and a relatively simple production model.

POLICY SIMULATION EXPERIMENTS

Scenario 1

Given the external assumptions of Tables 9.6, 9.7, and 9.8 and the policy assumptions of Tables 9.9, and 9.11, we now employ the corporate model listed in Table 9.18 to produce a five-year plan for TVL. The plan will produce a total of five output reports over the period 1976 through 1980. The reports include a market forecast (Table 9.19), a production forecast (Table 9.20), a projected income statement (Table 9.21), a projected balance sheet (Table 9.22), and a projected financial ratio statement (Table 9.23).

From a financial standpoint, this scenario assumes no change in the financial relationships of the past. Advertising expenses will be held fixed at $3 million per year, and the prices of color and b&w TV sets will be increased each year. TVL subscribes to an econometric forecasting service which has provided it with five-year projections of national income, short-term interest rates, and long-term interest rates.

The simulated results of Scenario 1 appear in Tables 9.19 through 9.23. Since the TVL Model is a simultaneous equation model, it must be solved using the Gauss–Seidel method of SIMPLAN. This calculation is executed for all five years by the single SIMPLAN command SOLVE, after setting model options for simultaneous solution and time range.

Table 9.18 TVL corporate planning model

```
 10  BW = —0.1210*PBW—0.4989*COLOR+0.0267*ADV+0.0054*Y—7.3610
 20  COLOR = —0.1334*PC—0.2283*BW+0.0237*ADV+0.0132*Y+11.2709
 30  SALES = PC*COLOR + PBW*BW
 40  CGS = .60*SALES
 50  OE = .10*SALES
 60  INTEREST = STR*STD + LTR*LTD
 70  TE = CGS + ADV + OE + INTEREST
 80  PBT = SALES = TE
 90  TAX = .5*PBT
100  NET = PBT — TAX
110  DIV = DPS*NSHARES
120  RTE = NET — DIV
130  CASH = TL — AR — INV — NPLANT — OA
140  IF CASH < MIN
150  STD = STD + 1.33*(MIN — CASH)
160  ELSE
170  STD = STD(— 1)
180  END
190  AR = .10*SALES
200  INV = .20*SALES
210  CA = CASH + AR + INV
220  NPLANT = .95*NPLANT(— 1)
230  OA = OA(— 1) + 40
240  TA = CA + NPLANT + OA
250  AP = .06*CGS
260  RTAX = TAX
270  MA = 1.25*MA(— 1)
280  CL = AP + STD + RTAX + MA + REPAY
290  LTD = LTD(— 1) + NDEBT — REPAY
300  CS = NOMINAL*NSHARES
310  ES = ES(— 1) + RTE
320  TL = CL + LTD + CS + ES
330  EPS = NET / NSHARES
340  CR = CA / CL
350  NPTSR = NET / SALES
```

Table 9.19 TVL market forecast (1976–1980)

Year	Net profit ($1000)	Total revenue ($1000)	Color TV Sales Volume (1000)	Price ($1)	B&W TV Sales Volume (1000)	Price ($1)	Advertising expenses ($1000)	National income ($billion)
1976	658.2	19318.0	44.80	300.00	32.66	180.00	3000.00	750.20
1977	721.2	19704.8	43.94	310.00	32.02	190.00	3000.00	775.40
1978	772.6	20014.2	42.93	320.00	31.38	200.00	3000.00	788.90
1979	817.6	20280.7	41.89	330.00	30.75	210.00	3000.00	800.00
1980	864.9	20562.6	41.00	340.00	30.11	220.00	3000.00	822.50

Table 9.20 TVL production forecast (1976–1980)

Year	Net profit ($1000)	Color TV volume (1000)	B&W TV volume (1000)	Total volume (1000)	Cost of goods sold ($1000)	Inventory ($1000)
1976	658.2	44.80	32.66	77.46	11590.8	3863.6
1977	721.2	43.94	32.02	75.96	11822.9	3941.0
1978	772.6	42.93	31.38	74.31	12008.5	4002.8
1979	817.6	41.89	30.75	72.64	12168.4	4056.1
1980	864.9	41.00	30.11	71.11	12337.6	4112.5

Table 9.21 TVL projected income statement: Scenario 1 (1976–1980) ($000)

	1976	1977	1978	1979	1980
Sales revenue	19318.0	19704.8	20014.2	20280.7	20562.6
Expenses					
Cost of goods sold	11590.8	11822.9	12008.5	12168.4	12337.6
Advertising expenses	3000.0	3000.0	3000.0	3000.0	3000.0
Operating expenses	1931.8	1970.5	2001.4	2028.1	2056.2
Interest	1479.0	1469.0	1459.1	1449.0	1439.0
Total Expenses	18001.6	18262.4	18469.0	18645.5	18832.8
Profit before taxes	1316.4	1442.4	1545.2	1635.2	1729.8
Tax	658.2	721.2	772.6	817.6	864.9
Net profit	658.2	721.2	772.6	817.6	864.9
Dividends	483.7	483.7	483.7	483.7	483.7
Retained earnings	174.5	237.5	288.9	333.9	381.2

Scenario 2

The second scenario generated by the TVL Model assumes that the price of a color set will be $285 and the price of a b&w set will be $164 for the five-year period beginning in 1976. Advertising expenditures will rise according to the schedule in Table 9.24. Otherwise, there are no changes in the original financial, marketing, and production assumptions which were spelled out in Tables 9.6 through 9.11. For Scenario 2, we only display the income statement and the balance sheet projections in Tables 9.25 and 9.26, respectively.

Other Scenarios

There are literally countless other scenarios which could be run with the TVL model ranging from experiments with alternative forms of external financing to different assumptions about interest rates and the national economy. Scenarios could also be generated for alternative cash management policies, depreciation policies, and federal tax policies. For each scenario, we can produce any combination of the output reports

Table 9.22 TVL projected balance sheet: Scenario 1 (1976–1980) ($000)

	1976	1977	1978	1979	1980
Assets					
Cash	5273.7	6077.1	6918.5	7792.3	8699.9
Accounts receivable	1931.8	1970.5	2001.4	2028.1	2056.3
Inventory	3863.6	3941.0	4002.8	4056.1	4112.5
Current assets	11069.1	11988.6	12922.7	13876.5	14868.7
Net plant and equipment	13903.4	13208.3	12547.8	11920.5	11324.5
Other assets	504.9	544.9	584.9	624.9	664.9
Total assets	25477.4	25741.8	26055.5	26421.9	26858.1
Liabilities					
Accounts payable	695.4	709.4	720.5	730.1	740.3
Short-term debt	4316.1	4316.1	4316.1	4316.1	4316.1
Reserve for tax	658.2	721.2	772.6	817.6	864.9
Miscellaneous accruals	199.6	249.5	311.9	389.9	487.4
Repayment	100.0	100.0	100.0	100.0	100.0
Current liabilities	5969.3	6096.2	6221.1	6353.7	6508.7
Long-term debt	9611.3	9511.3	9411.3	9311.3	9211.3
Common stock	4500.0	4500.0	4500.0	4500.0	4500.0
Earned surplus	5396.8	5634.3	5923.1	6256.9	6638.1
Total liabilities	25477.4	25741.8	26055.5	26421.9	26858.1

Table 9.23 TVL projected financial forecast: Scenario 1 (1976–1980)

	1976	1977	1978	1979	1980
Earnings per share	2.93	3.21	3.43	3.63	3.84
Current ratio	1.85	1.97	2.08	2.18	2.28
Net profit to sales ratio	0.03	0.04	0.04	0.04	0.04

Table 9.24 TVL revised marketing policy assumptions: Scenario 2

Year	Color TV price ($1)	B&W TV price ($1)	Advertising expenses ($1000)
1976	285	164	3200
1977	285	164	3350
1978	285	164	3550
1979	285	164	3700
1980	285	164	4000

Table 9.25 TVL projected income statement forecast: Scenario 2 (1976–1980) ($000)

	1976	1977	1978	1979	1980
Sales revenue	20481.9	21835.5	23567.6	24870.2	27476.6
Expenses					
Cost of goods sold	12289.0	13101.3	14140.6	14922.1	16486.0
Advertising expenses	3200.0	3550.0	3550.0	3700.0	4000.0
Operating expenses	2048.2	2183.5	2356.8	2487.0	2747.7
Interest	1479.1	1469.1	1459.0	1449.1	1439.0
Total expenses	19016.3	20103.9	21506.4	22558.2	24672.7
Profit before taxes	1465.4	1731.6	2061.2	2312.0	2803.9
Federal income taxes	732.7	865.8	1030.6	1156.0	1401.9
Net profit	732.7	865.8	1030.6	1156.0	1402.0
Dividends	483.7	483.7	483.7	483.7	483.7
Retained earnings	249.0	382.1	546.9	672.3	918.2

Table 9.26 TVL projected balance sheet forecast: Scenario 2 (1976–1980) ($000)

	1976	1977	1978	1979	1980
Assets					
Cash	5115.6	5878.4	6715.6	7734.8	8764.4
Accounts receivable	2048.2	2183.5	2356.8	2487.0	2747.7
Inventory	4096.3	4367.1	4713.5	4974.0	5495.3
Current assets	11260.1	12429.0	13785.9	15195.8	17007.4
Net plant and equipment	13903.4	13208.3	12547.8	11920.5	11324.4
Other assets	504.9	544.9	584.9	624.9	664.9
Total assets	25668.4	26182.2	26918.6	27741.2	28996.7
Liabilities					
Accounts payable	737.3	786.1	848.4	895.3	989.2
Short-term debt	4316.1	4316.1	4316.1	4316.1	4316.1
Reserve for tax	732.7	865.8	1030.6	1156.0	1401.0
Miscellaneous accruals	199.6	249.5	311.9	389.9	487.4
Repayment	100.0	100.0	100.0	100.0	100.0
Current liabilities	6085.7	6317.5	6607.0	6857.4	7294.7
Long-term debt	9611.3	9511.3	9411.3	9311.3	9211.3
Common stock	4500.0	4500.0	4500.0	4500.0	4500.0
Earned surplus	5471.4	5835.4	6400.3	7072.5	7990.7
Total liabilities	25688.4	26182.2	26918.6	27741.2	28996.7

which were produced by Scenario 1, or easily specify only certain variables to be printed after the model has been solved.

EXTENSIONS OF THE MODEL

It is, no doubt, obvious to the reader that the model chosen to illustrate the methodology of corporate modeling in this chapter is a very simple model. In the interest of making the model easy to explain and interpret, numerous simplifying assumptions had to be made. We shall conclude this chapter by proposing a number of possible extensions to the TVL Model.

Marketing

First, the marketing model could easily be extended to include more than two products. Second, it may be possible to find other policy variables such as research and development expenditures which are statistically significant in some equations. Third, for some products it may be necessary to consider the relationship to TVL's competitors. Fourth, other national economic indicators may be important in some equations. Fifth, the final model should be reestimated using two-stage least squares.

Production

Our production model is in need of substantial improvement. First, product output should be linked to the actual resources required to produce a unit of output. Given a sales forecast for a particular product, we should be able to say how much it will cost to produce sufficient output to satisfy demand. Obviously, we will need good cost accounting data as well as a detailed description of the input–output relationships for each product; that is, for each product j we need to know how much of input i is required to produce a unit of j, and we need to know this information for all inputs and outputs. Second, we need to introduce inventories more explicitly into the model.

Financial

There are several directions we could go with the financial model. First, it could be converted into a much more detailed and more sophisticated cash management model. Second, the tax component could be considerably expanded. Third, inflation and changes in foreign currency exchange rates may also be introduced. Fourth, the model could be modified for short-term profit planning rather than five-year, strategic planning. Fifth, several of the assumed value models including accounts receivable and accounts payable could be replaced by econometric relationships. Sixth, the debt structure of most large companies is more complex than that of TVL. A more realistic model would take this factor into consideration.

Corporate

Since TVL is a subsidiary of Zeta Electronics in Switzerland, the management of Zeta may want to have similar models constructed for each of its subsidiaries. These separate business planning models could then be consolidated into an integrated corporate planning model for Zeta Electronics. In other words, each business would develop its own planning model and use it to develop its own five-year plans. However, the Vice-President of Corporate Planning for Zeta Electronics could maintain a duplicate database and model for each business and perform his own "What if?" experiments with the separate business models or with the consolidated corporate model.

10

The Politics of Corporate Model Building[1]

INTRODUCTION

Even with the increased usage of corporate planning models in recent years, the percentage of corporations which have experience with corporate models remains relatively small. Why aren't more corporations using these models today? Why are the corporate model users restricted to the larger corporations? Are the primary constraints impeding the use of these models technical problems, computer hardware problems, or political problems?

It is our strong conviction that the mathematical and computer tools for constructing effective corporate planning models have existed for over 20 years. That there are no more corporate models in use is in no sense a reflection of technical limitations of these tools. Rather the most severe limitation on the expanded use of the models is almost entirely a human problem.

At the heart of the problem is the fact that people—management scientists and operations research specialists—who have attempted to construct these models in the past frequently did not possess the necessary political and human relations skills required to produce effective corporate planning models. In the 1960s management science and operations research were, in many cases, oversold to corporate management. Promises were made for which the model builders could not deliver results. Due dates and schedules were not met. Managerial expectations, inflated by over-zealous model builders, were not fulfilled. Frustration, anger, and complete disillusionment on the part of management followed in the wake of these events. It was, therefore, not surprising to find many corporate executives backing off from management science in the late 1960s or at least viewing computers and model builders with a jaundiced eye.

But perhaps it is not really surprising to find that model builders are not effective politicians, for there is little or nothing in their formal academic training which prepares them to cope with the many practical, political problems which one typically encounters in implementing corporate models in the real world. Most academic courses in management science taught at universities these days provide minimal guidance in dealing with what we shall call the "politics of planning and modeling." All too often academic operations research courses are little more than courses in applied mathematics. Too little attention is given to the human side of model building. Yet countless management scientists have learned the hard way that sophisticated mathematics and computer techniques are neither necessary nor sufficient to provide top management with an effective decision-making tool. Indeed, there is increasing evidence that the politics of model building may be the single most important factor in determining the success or failure of a particular corporate modeling project.

In the following pages we shall outline some of the political problems involved in developing and implementing corporate models. We shall attempt to provide some practical, political guidelines for corporate model builders and model users. We shall examine some of the political conditions which have existed both with successful corporate models and with failures.

CORPORATE MODELING GOALS

Fundamental to an understanding of the politics of corporate model building is an understanding of the goals of those who build and use corporate models. Frequently the goals articulated by corporate model builders in the daytime, while they are on the job, bear little resemblance to their real goals–goals which one frequently learns about in the evening after a few drinks.

It is interesting to note the number of corporate model builders who have discovered that participating in a corporate modeling project offers one a unique opportunity to glean an understanding of the inner workings of a corporation—an understanding which can be employed to the political advantage of the model builder if the model proves to be a success. In other words, a clever model builder can use the corporate model as a political tool to enhance his or her own career in corporate management. To the extent that this point is recognized by the model builder's colleagues, the possibility that the model will be perceived as a threat is indeed a reality. Whether motivated by petty jealousy or fear of losing one's job, an envious colleague who does not expect to share in the spoils may be fully capable of sabotaging a technically sound corporate modeling project.

In some cases, a corporate model is not only perceived as a threat, but is, in fact, a threat. Consider the case of a Dallas manufacturing firm. The Dallas firm is decentralized around 12 product groups headed by vice-presidents who had previously enjoyed a high degree of autonomy. A desire to improve the effectiveness of the profit plans of the divisions motivated the president of the firm to commission the development of a corporate simulation model. There was little doubt that the president of the Dallas firm was sending a message to the division vice-presidents to the effect that "somebody in Dallas cares." In these circumstances the company president was clearly using the model as a political strategy.

Many different goals and objectives motivate corporate executives to undertake the development and use of corporate models. In addition to the obvious objective of having a tool to evaluate alternative managerial policies, some chief executives have discovered that a corporate model is a very effective tool for making presentations to the board of directors, stockholders' meetings, or lending officers of banks and other financial institutions. In some cases, the company president and vice-president of finance have been known to use the corporate model to support their positions concerning a proposed investment, new venture, etc.

More recently we have seen some corporate executives view corporate models with a type of naive optimism. Having transcended the period of skepticism and distrust of mathematics and computers, there are increasing numbers of corporate executives who perceive corporate models as some type of panacea. This type of corporate officer is potentially quite dangerous. If model builders are not aware of the unrealistic expectations of such an executive, they may be incurring a substantial risk. The day of reckoning arrives when the model does not produce the results expected by the naive user—results which were totally beyond the reach of the model in the first place.

In summary, the goals of model users and model builders may be quite diverse, and sometimes they may even be in conflict. Both model users and model builders would be well advised to be on the lookout for hidden agenda which may be more important than stated agenda. To protect themselves, model users (managers) should make certain they understand their own goals as well as the stated and implied goals of the model builders. On the other hand, model builders must necessarily try to ascertain *all* of the user's goals whether they be openly stated or otherwise.

POLITICAL CONFLICTS

In the preceding paragraphs, we acknowledged the possibility of conflicting goals among those who use corporate models and those who build them. In this section, we shall classify other political conflicts which typically arise in conjunction with corporate modeling activities. We have chosen to classify these situations as (1) corporate planning politics, (2) functional area politics, (3) organizational politics, and (4) geographic politics.

Corporate Planning Politics

In those companies which have a vice-president (or director) of corporate planning, the corporate planning department was probably created by and for the benefit of the president of the company. In most cases, the corporate planning department is a relatively new department—probably less than ten years old. For purposes of discussion, let us assume that the corporate planning department has the primary responsibility for developing a corporate planning model.

The first person who is likely to feel threatened by the project is the chief financial officer (vice-president of finance, treasurer, controller, etc.). Prior to the advent of the corporate planning department, the president probably relied on the vice-president of finance for financial planning and financial forecasting. For this very reason, the vice-president of finance is likely to feel that the vice-president of corporate planning is infringing on his or her territory. A threatened financial officer is not likely to be very cooperative in providing the planning department with the much needed historical data required to develop a corporate financial model. Yet the success of the model is heavily dependent on the availability of financial data. Conflicts between the vice-president of planning and the chief financial officer are not unusual in large corporations. The only person who can alleviate problems of this type is the president. If the president is truly committed to corporate planning and corporate modeling, he or she will find it quite easy to sit with the vice-presidents of finance and planning to resolve the conflict. On the other hand, if the president is not committed to corporate modeling, an aggressive vice-president of finance can quickly undermine the credibility of the model.

It is interesting to compare the political position of corporate planning to the political position of state government planning in the United States. State planning directors are among the most frustrated and powerless officials in state government. Again the reasons are political and have their origins in the way in which state planning has evolved in the United States. The reason we have state planning divisions is not because we have enlightened state governors who sought the establishment of state planning. Rather, the reason is that in the 1960s the federal government decreed that to be eligible for certain federal grants states had to have state planning divisions— and not only that, the federal government agreed to pay most of the bills. The fact that the impetus for state planning came from outside the states and not from the governors goes a long way in explaining the difference in political clout between corporate planners and state planners. Corporate planners serve at the pleasure of the company president, and that is a good thing.

Although the corporate planning function is still a relatively new activity in many corporations, the fact that the vice-president of planning typically reports directly to the president means that primary responsibility for the corporate planning model should reside in his or her hands. Only with adequate political support from the president is it possible to create an environment conducive to effective corporate modeling.

Functional Area Politics

We have already alluded to the potential political rivalry which may exist between corporate planning and corporate finance and the implications which this rivalry may have on corporate modeling. Unfortunately, this is only one of many possible sources of political conflict which may affect the success of corporate modeling.

Another type of functional rivalry frequently encountered is the conflict between the management science (or operations research) department and the data-processing department. Although primary responsibility for the corporate model should be delegated to the corporate planning department, the actual model building is likely to be done by the company's management science group. If there were ever two groups who should cooperate, they would be management scientists and data-processing people. Several types of problems frequently emerge between these groups. First, the in-house computer may be saturated with routine accounting and data-processing applications thus providing the management scientists with minimal amounts of computer time and abysmal turn-around time. In part, this problem depends on where data processing fits into the corporate organization chart. If data processing reports to accounting or finance, therein may lie the crux of the problem. Model building will always be given a lower priority than will accounting applications.

A second problem situation arises when there is excess capacity on the in-house computer, but the management scientists prefer the convenience of an outside time-sharing vendor. The director of data processing wants to centralize all computing on the in-house computer. The management scientists, in turn, view this as an infringement on their automony. Tempers flare, time-sharing bills soar, and the in-house computer which contains the corporate database is underutilized.

An extreme case involving both of these problems occurred several years ago in one of the divisions of Motorola. The situation was so bad that the director of operations research and the director of data processing literally did not speak to each other. All model building was done on outside time-sharing computers, yet the corporate database was on the company's in-house computer—a tragic waste of talents and resources. On the other hand, the North Carolina National Bank seems to have come up with one possible solution to this problem. The Bank's data-processing management vigorously promotes the use of the in-house computer. Users are permitted to experiment with outside time-sharing applications, but data-processing management and the management science department work with users to bring the applications in-house.

To the extent that a corporate model involves finance, marketing, and production submodels, the potential for political conflict with the respective functional areas of the company exists. The vice-president of finance may feel that his or her department should have primary responsibility for the financial model. The head of market research may have his or her own ideas about sales forecasting and marketing policy models. Obviously what one hopes to achieve is the strong support of each of the functional areas without engaging in political infighting over the possession, development, or use of the model. The cooperation of the major functional areas of the company is crucial to the success of the model.

Organizational Politics

A host of political conflicts are possible in decentralized firms that develop planning models for each division and each of these models is linked into an overall corporate model. Among the sticky questions that arise are the following: Should the division models be developed, controlled, and up-dated by the divisions or the corporate planning department? Should each division model have a unique model structure or should a common structure be used for each division? Who can access each division's database? Who can access the corporate database? What accuracy requirements should be imposed on the divisions for profit plans generated by the division models? Who is responsible for the accuracy of division profit plans and projections produced by the division models? These are not easy questions to answer, but we shall set forth a few guidelines which may prove to be helpful.

First, the corporate planning department should be responsible for specifying the model structure for the divisions. Second, wherever possible a common model structure for each of the divisions is a desirable feature. Third, division models should not be developed independently of the corporate planning department. This classic mistake was made by a division of Motorola. One of the divisions built a stand-alone financial model without consulting the people who were building the Motorola corporate financial model. As might be expected, a strained relationship developed between the corporate model builders and the division model builders leading to a loss of credibility for the division model. Fourth, the division model should be responsible for maintaining the database for the division model. Fifth, division management should be encouraged to use the division model for division level planning. Sixth, corporate management should have access to the division models but not vice versa. Seventh, although the corporate staff should have the prime responsibility for developing division models, every effort should be made to enlist the knowledge and experience of the division staff in model development.

Finally, we predict that in the near future the subject of more than one Ph.D. dissertation will be the impact of corporate planning models on organizational structure. This is a fascinating and timely question about which we have insufficient historical data to generalize.

Geographic Politics

The major oil companies in the United States are among the leading users of management science techniques such as mathematical programming. Many of these firms also have corporate financial models which are used in their New York and Chicago corporate headquarters. Surprisingly, in spite of over 20 years of experience with the use of linear programming to schedule oil refineries, there appears to be minimal communication between these corporate model builders and the refinery model builders in places such as Houston and Dallas. A combination of geography and oil company politics seems to have led to an inefficient use of models by the industry which has the longest track record in the use of corporate models. The result of this phenomenon is that none of the United States oil companies has truly integrated corporate planning models. In most cases, the models are stand-alone financial models that are not linked to drilling and refinery operations at all. Given today's computer and telecommunication technology, this situation is astonishing. It does not exactly instill confidence in the industry's long-range planning ability.

HOW TO SELL A CORPORATE MODEL

As a group, management scientists and operations researchers are not known for their sales abilities or political astuteness. Indeed, the political ineptness of model builders has played a major role in impeding the state of the art of corporate modeling. The heavy emphasis on mathematics and statistics in their formal education does little or nothing to improve the ability of model builders to communicate with the management and other model users. Their inability to draw management into the model-building process has led to numerous corporate modeling failures. If management scientists spent 20 percent less time solving differential equations and inverting matrices during their academic careers and 20 percent more time learning how to define problems and interact with management, corporate modeling would take a great forward leap.

Admittedly, selling something as abstract as a computer model is much more difficult than selling a refrigerator or an automobile. The fact that it is virtually impossible to quantify the benefits to be derived from developing a corporate model (before it is actually built) makes the task of selling a corporate model even more difficult. More timely, more accurate, and more complete information for forecasting and planning are the major benefits of corporate planning models. Although it is relatively easy to establish the cost of a corporate model, the projected benefits can be estimated only through small pilot modeling projects and reference to comparable firms which have had experience with corporate models.

Probably the most effective strategy for convincing a skeptical manager of the benefits of a corporate model is to construct a simple corporate financial model for projecting the firm's profit and loss statement, balance sheet, and cash flow. With the new planning and modeling systems, such a model can be constructed in a matter of hours. The prospective user can experiment with the model by selecting alternative financial policies and having the model produce alternative financial scenarios.

A modular, stepwise approach is recommended with visible results presented to management as soon as possible. Start with a simple financial model and gradually add embellishments to the model. Keep the model as simple as possible in the early stages. Lead management by the hand until confidence is established in the model. Avoid the use of technical jargon. Learn to speak management's language.

As a first step in presenting corporate models to uninitiated managers, the analyst should attempt to assist management in defining their own problems, goals, and objectives. Corporate models should be related to specific problems articulated by management. The quickest way to enlist a negative response is to present corporate models in the abstract rather than in relationship to real problems perceived by management.

Sometimes the proper choice of words is extremely important. We recall the case of the president of a bicycle tire manufacturer who stated quite emphatically that his company had no problems and therefore did not need a corporate model. When reminded of the energy crisis, tight money, decreasing productivity, and the other problems confronting firms at that time, he steadfastly denied the need for a model. Sitting at the president's side was the vice-president of finance who indicated that he never knew from one month to the next what his cash requirements would be. Yet the president refused to acknowledge the presence of any problems. As it turned out, the president seemed to be hung up on the use of the word "problem." We later discovered that if we had used terms like "goals" and "objectives" rather than the word "problem" that we might have elicited a more positive response. The company president simply did not want to admit to an outsider in the presence of his colleagues that he had any problems.

Interestingly enough, some managers have discovered that it is the model builders and not the model users who assume the greatest share of the risk associated with the use of corporate models. If the model yields inaccurate or ineffectual results, the blame can easily be placed on the management scientists. But if the model yields useful, accurate projections, management can take full credit for the success of the model. In summary, clever managers can easily put themselves in a "no lose" position concerning corporate modeling.

RESPONSIBILITY FOR THE MODEL

The director of corporate planning is the obvious person to assume the responsibility for coordinating the development, maintenance, and use of the corporate model. Orchestrating the development of a corporate model involves coordinating the efforts of the management scientists who actually build the model based on assumptions and data collected from financial, marketing, and production analysts.

Managing a corporate model is not unlike managing any other research and development project and the director of corporate planning or whoever directs the project need not have expertise or previous experience with modeling. The important thing is for the project leader to know how to ask the right questions about the development of the corporate model. The following checklist contains a sample of the type of questions which must be raised repeatedly by the director of corporate planning. What are the goals and objectives of the project? What kind of output will be produced? How much will it cost to produce and maintain the model? When can we expect some visible results from the model? What can be said about the validity of the results generated by the model? What are the assumptions underlying the model? Is the model oriented toward managerial users or not? If project directors keep hammering away with these questions, it makes little or no difference whether they understand the mathematical and computational details of the model.

It goes without saying that the team leader plays an all-important role in facilitating communications between the model builders and the model users (management). The team leader provides the interface between the technicians, the users, and the functional specialists who really understand the inner workings of the business.

Finally, the director (or vice-president) of corporate planning is also the protector of the model. It is this individual's responsibility to sell the results of the model to management and to defend it in the event of attack from the president, board of directors, stockholders, or other parties with an interest in the firm. The larger the model, the more protection is required. On more than one occasion corporate models have fallen into disrepute as a result of the loss of their political protector.

DEVELOPMENT OF THE MODEL

As previously suggested, the coordination of model development should reside in the hands of the director of corporate planning. With the availability of planning and modeling software systems, relatively simple, deterministic financial models can be built by financial analysts with little or no previous modeling experience. However, more complex financial models involving risk analysis and systems of simultaneous equations require analysts with more sophisticated analytical skills. Although software packages such as SIMPLAN facilitate the development of forecasting, econometric, and production models, management science skills are required to specify, estimate, and validate models of this type.

Whether a corporation should have a separate management science department is an open question. If such a department exists, then the human resources of the department should be utilized. If there is no management science department, it is still essential that the corporate modeling team have management science skills available to it.

Another important aspect of corporate modeling is the involvement of staff personnel from the relevant functional areas of the company—finance, marketing, and production. If the financial model is to have credibility, there must be substantial involvement of accountants and financial analysts who are familiar with the firm's financial structure. Furthermore, the vice-presidents of finance or other financial officers should be involved in the problem definition stage. Financial management should also be given the option to review continuously the assumptions underlying the model as well as sample output reports. Over the long run, it is desirable to train several people from each functional area to participate on the modeling team. One of the obvious benefits of this strategy is that communications remain open between corporate planning and finance, marketing, and production.

USE OF THE MODEL

If a corporate model is to be little more than an academic exercise, it is extremely important that the users include some combination of the following people: president, vice-president of finance, treasurer, controller, vice-president of sales or marketing, vice-president of production, or vice-presidents of one or more product divisions. Indeed, if some subset of the management is not committed to the development and use of the model, the entire effort should probably be abandoned or at least delayed until such time that there is adequate political support at the top.

In companies such as AVCO, Pillsbury, Memorex, Northwest Industries, and Santa Fe Industries the presidents of the companies have used the model. At AVCO, a corporate financial model has been used at meetings of the board of directors. Prior to AVCO board meetings, financial scenarios are prepared with the model by the vice-president of finance and the vice-president of corporate planning. These scenarios are presented to the board.

For several years, Terrance Hanold, Chairman of the Executive Committee and former President of Pillsbury, has had his own computer terminal linked to a corporate planning model. He described the situation at Pillsbury in an article in *Managerial Planning* (September–October, 1973).

All levels of Pillsbury management are able to address themselves more consistently and in a more professional manner to the conduct of the business which they are charged with prosecuting. All levels of Pillsbury management have access to current data, identical in content, describing the present state of things, as well as to an immense body of historical data.

Since through the use of planning models, he now sees his own activity in the perspective of all related operations, we require a manager to be both specifically responsible within his own area and widely contributive to the areas that his actions affect.

All levels of Pillsbury management have an increasing stock of electronic and mathematical tools, many in a time-shared remote access mode, for the assembly, classification, transmission, analysis, evaluation, and projection of banked data—both to solve present problems and to forecast future conditions.

Perhaps the most dramatic corporate modeling success story ever recorded is the case of the Memorex Target Company (TARCO) Model. In the summer of 1973 there was a flurry of rumors to the effect that one or more companies might be contemplating acquiring Memorex—a company which was incurring substantial financial losses and was falling behind on the repayment schedule on the $130 million it owed the Bank of America. By October of 1973, it was apparent that there were no takers for Memorex and that it would have to work out its financial problems with the bank alone. It was at this point in time that the president became seriously interested in the TARCO Model.

The TARCO Model was designed to calculate a coordinated plan of production volume, lease/sales mix, financial statements, and lease fundamentals that meet the user's objectives for up to 40 periods. The user may select any two of the following items as objectives to be met in each period:

- operating profit
- manufacturing output
- equipment sales
- NRI (net installed revenue increment)
- cash in flow from operations
- new leases

After specifying the planned objectives and entering approximately 30 revenue, cost, expense, and cash flow items, a sequence of mutually consistent outputs is calculated and printed. Output options include profit and loss statements, cash flow statements, expense budgets, and return on investment analyses.

The Memorex president discovered he could do some very interesting things with the TARCO Model. He could simulate the effect on Memorex's financial structure of a decision on the part of the Bank of America to call the $130 million loan. This scenario was, of course, tantamount to the death of Memorex. He could also run financial scenarios reflecting an extension of the loan, refinancing the loan, and increasing the line of credit offered by the bank. Each time the vice-president from the bank came to negotiate, the TARCO Model was used by the president of Memorex to present the firm's case. On December 31, 1973, the bank renegotiated the repayment schedule on the loan and extended Memorex's line of credit. In 1975, Memorex began operating on a profitable basis again.

The interesting thing about the Memorex Model was its simplicity. It consisted of 18 definitional equations (accounting identities) and 20 unknowns. Memorex had a well-defined problem—survival. The model had the political support of the president. All of this adds up to an environment in which success comes as no surprise to anyone.

We believe this example illustrates the fact that major accomplishments are possible even with a very simple corporate financial model, provided the problem is narrowly defined and the model is supported by top management.

More recently, the president of Northwest Industries began using his own computer terminal, an executive database, and corporate planning models to evaluate the performance of the ten operating companies of Northwest.

We believe that within five years, this degree of participation of corporate management in the use of computer planning models will have become commonplace among larger corporations (corporations with sales in excess of $50 million). But with current trends in computer hardware, corporate modeling software, and telecommunications equipment, the use of corporate planning by top management of very small firms (with sales less than $1 million) may become almost routine. The cost of building and using corporate financial models on remote conversational terminals linked to central computers owned by time-sharing utilities has become so economical that even small firms can now afford to use corporate models. Indeed, it can be argued that such problems as cash management, financial forecasting, and profit planning are even more important to smaller firms than to larger firms. Literally every firm has cash management problems. They either have too much cash or too little cash. Conversational financial models are particularly useful as cash management tools.

SOME THINGS A CORPORATE MODEL CANNOT DO

One of the more ambitious corporate modeling projects to date is the Texas Manufacturing Company (TMC) Model. (The name has been changed to protect the innocent.) During the early stages of development of the model after the objectives of the project had been thoroughly aired, the director of corporate planning raised an amazing question about the model. He wanted to know if the TMC Model would have the capability to forecast the market share of each of TMC's competitors in each market in which TMC participated. To give you some indication as to the magnitude of the question posed by the director of corporate planning, TMC sells hundreds of different products in at least 30 major markets each of which has anywhere from five to 50 competitors in it. The corporate planning director was quickly informed that even if TMC utilized the services of the Central Intelligence Agency to collect data on each of its competitors, there was no way that the TMC Model could forecast the market share of each of TMC's competitors. He was further informed that forecasting TMC's market share by product group was in itself a monumental task and that the modeling staff would consider itself fortunate if it could achieve this goal.

This anecdote illustrates an important point. Not only is it desirable to communicate to management the expected benefits to be derived from using a corporate model but it is equally important to inform management as to the limitations of the model. In other words, for the mutual protection of both the model builders and the model users, we recommend the preparation of two lists at the outset of the project: (1) a list of what the model *can* be expected to achieve and (2) a list of things the model *cannot* possibly do. Following the aforementioned episode, the director of planning at TMC was provided with the two lists outlined below:

TMC Model Can:

- Take variables (actions) over which management has direct control (price, sales force, etc.) and project those over which management has only indirect control (sales, market share, etc.).
- Test the effects of different market strategies without having to experience them.
- Provide a systematic approach for forecasting in which the influence of each action can be isolated for review and action.
- Project industry sales and price and TMC sales by product category. From these, relative price, market share, etc. will be computed.
- Improve the accuracy of all forecasts.
- Explain "why" for the forecasts.
- Evaluate financial impacts of decisions.

TMC Model Cannot:

- Evaluate individual competitor reaction on market share.
- Forecast specific market volume.
- Forecast sales by region.
- Predict events which occur discontinuously such as wars, strikes, etc.
- Explain any aspect of production.

It is also important for management to understand that although it is impossible to predict or model such phenomena as wars, strikes, floods, earthquakes, and political events, it may indeed be possible to model the effects of such events on the behavior of the company.

Although we cannot predict whether or not there will be another "Watergate Affair" or whether the Arabs will cut off the supply of crude oil again, we can simulate the likely consequences of such events on the financial performance of the firm.

THE ROLE OF OUTSIDE CONSULTANTS

Relatively few of the successful corporate simulation models have been built by outside consultants. Upon reflection, this fact is really not so surprising. The very nature of a corporate planning model implies substantial interaction between the model builders and management. If the model is built by outsiders, this type of continuous interaction is very difficult to achieve. The primary responsibility for developing the model should reside inside the company. If the firm does not have the appropriate modeling skills in-house, then it should either delay the project or hire some individuals with management science skills.

In 1972 when Dresser Industries decided to move ahead on the development of a corporate planning model, there was not one person inside the company who had any previous modeling experience. The outside consultant's recommendation to management was that Dresser employ a full-time person with management science and econometric skills to direct the project and gradually build up a technical staff. The consultant's role in the project consisted of helping Dresser locate the right person to direct the modeling project and to come in for a day or so every three or four months to review the progress of the project.

Basically, what we are advocating is a do-it-yourself approach to corporate modeling. Models built in-house by insiders have much more credibility than models built by outside consultants and then handed over to management on a silver platter.

Not only should corporate planning models not be built by consultants but "canned" corporate models should also be avoided. The state of the art of corporate modeling has not yet developed to the point where one can develop a canned computer model that is sufficiently general to be adapted to any type of firm. Although some aggressive software sales people try to lead you to believe that effective canned corporate models do exist, in reality, there is no such product on the market and, furthermore, such a software product is not likely to exist any time soon.

MODEL CREDIBILITY

In Chapter 6, we suggested a three-step procedure for validating computer-based planning models—rationalism, empiricism, and forecasting. While these three steps may be necessary steps in validating a corporate simulation model, the ultimate test of the validity is whether or not top management uses the model on a continuous basis to make policy decisions. A valid model is one that is used for corporate planning. An invalid model is a model that is not used by management. In other words, validation has a lot to do with believability and credibility.

To achieve credibility for a corporate simulation model, one must build the user (management) into the entire model building process. Not only must management be involved in problem definition, but management must be consulted concerning data availability, specification of the model, and output reports, to mention only a few aspects of the entire process. Models presented to management as a fait accompli without substantial managerial input are likely to end up on the shelf and not be taken seriously. To ensure model credibility requires considerable effort on the part of the model builder and maybe even a little luck. Model credibility is really the essence of the politics of model building.

IMPLEMENTATION

Just as we have previously advocated a modular, stepwise approach to the development of corporate planning models, a similar strategy seems appropriate for implementing the model. As each step or module is completed, it should be pressed into service for testing, evaluation, and eventually productive use. We should try to avoid the experience of the large electric utility which spent 20 work-years developing an integrated planning model and then hired an outside consultant to tell management what to do with the model.

Our philosophy of corporate modeling calls for getting some form of the model, even if it is simple, up and running as soon as possible. The sooner you have something to show, the greater the chances of obtaining management acceptance and support. This is the real advantage of starting the corporate modeling process with a relatively simple corporate financial model. Within two weeks it is possible to provide financial management with useful results from a simple corporate financial model.

WHY SOME MODELS FAIL

It goes without saying that not all corporate modeling stories have been success stories. Indeed, there have been some monumental failures. Some are well known. Others are not so well known. It is our view that one may learn more about how to build effective, useful corporate planning models through the careful examination of the failures rather than just considering the successful models. In this section, we shall outline 12 reasons why some corporate planning models have failed.

1. The Ill-Defined Problem

Perhaps the single most important step in the corporate modeling process is problem definition. Once the problem has been clearly defined, much of what follows represents a series of technical details. But formalizing problem definition for corporate management can prove to be an elusive process. It is that aspect of corporate modeling that most resembles an art rather than a science. Many a corporate modeling project has gone astray because of vagueness in setting the goals and objectives of the project. If six months to a year after the project is underway the model builders discover that they have misunderstood management's goals and objectives, the entire project may be in deep trouble. Valuable corporate resources may have been spent trying to solve the wrong problem.

We were once approached by the director of corporate planning of a West Coast manufacturer of computer peripheral equipment who wanted us to build a corporate financial model for his company. After spending a day with the planning director, we discovered that he had a very specific optimization model in mind. We further observed that the planning director was unwilling to discuss the possible relevance of any other modeling approach. Upon probing more deeply, we determined that not only did the director of corporate planning not understand the methodology he was insisting that we use but neither could he articulate the project objectives. At least the objectives he expressed were in no sense compatible with the modeling techniques being proposed.

A corporate modeling team leader who neither understands the problem to be solved nor the modeling techniques to be employed is on a one-way trip to disaster.

Alternatively stated, an analyst with a methodology in search of a problem is equally dangerous.

2. Unfulfilled Expectations

Related to the pitfalls of ill-defined problems is the problem of unrealistic expectations on the part of management. As previously mentioned, some corporate executives have adopted the very risky posture of viewing corporate models as some type of panacea. Although it is desirable to have management's confidence in corporate modeling, their overconfidence can be a dangerous thing. There comes a day of reckoning when management expects to see results. If their expectations are unrealistic, but the model builders are unaware of the extent of the problem, then there is a good chance that the expectations will be unfulfilled. Unfulfilled managerial expectations can lead to misunderstandings and termination of the project.

3. Inadequate Documentation

Inadequate user documentation and technical documentation can easily lead to the demise of a corporate model. First, a certain amount of documentation is required just to acquaint management with the use of the model. This type of documentation should be nontechnical in nature and written in the style and language of management. Second, user documentation is particularly important for maintaining continuity in the use of the model. If the original users are transferred to a new position or for some other reason cease being users, then inadequate documentation may become a serious obstacle preventing others from using the model. Third, technical documentation is equally important for model builders, computer programmers, and computer operators. Corporate models require continuous modification, maintenance, and updating—all of which are impossible without good documentation.

Unfortunately, model builders and programmers frequently do not like to document their work. In some cases, they are not very good writers either. There is no ideal solution to the problem of model documentation, but some combination of users, model builders, and programmers must resolve this problem if the model is to survive.

4. Excessive Use of Technical Jargon

The burden of the responsibility for communications rests in the hands of the model builders and not in the hands of management. It is not incumbent on management to familiarize themselves with the technical jargon of econometrics, statistics, and computer science. The model builders must not only understand management's problems, but they must learn to speak the language of management as well. The politics of corporate modeling involves a continuous selling and reselling of concepts which may seem strange and unrealistic to management. One of the quickest ways to turn management off to modeling is to present corporate modeling in a highly abstract, technical manner. The use of computerese and technical jargon is cited as having contributed to the failure of more than one computer model.

5. Failure to Produce Useful Results

Obviously, if a corporate planning model does not produce the types of results for which it was intended or if nonmodeling techniques yield more useful results than the model, no amount of political savvy will be sufficient to bail out the project. There are at least two ways in which this situation can arise. First, the model may prove to be ineffective as a planning tool because of some misunderstanding concerning problem definition and project objectives; that is, maybe the model was designed to be an effective tool for solving a particular problem, but that problem turns out not to be the "right problem." Second, sometimes model builders encounter serious practical problems in developing a model which does precisely what it was intended to do. With financial models this seldom happens, but with econometric marketing models there is no guarantee that one will be able to come up with an acceptable model. Insufficient data, theoretical problems, and statistical problems can all lead to serious problems in the development of econometric models. With econometric models, science and technology can take you only so far. In the final analysis, experience, judgment, and even a little luck are required to produce operational, policy analytic, econometric models.

However, insufficient data need not necessarily prove to be an insurmountable obstacle. Indeed, in some cases, historical data may even be misleading. For example, historical data on the petroleum industry in the 1960s and early 1970s is of limited value in projecting the future of the industry or firms in the industry. Of more importance for future planning for the oil industry is imagination and a knowledge of the politics of the Middle East. Once a corporate financial model has been developed, the number of potential applications of the model which require little or no data is almost limitless. A clever corporate planner can go a long way toward producing useful results with limited empirical data.

6. Failure to Meet Deadlines

One should never forget that managing a corporate planning model is like managing a large research and development project. One of the problems encountered with the Boeing Model was that it took three to four times longer to develop than was promised. The fact that the model of a major oil company required 23 work-years to complete strongly implies that there was a serious slippage in the schedule for the model. Unmet deadlines and schedules are the joint responsibility of the modeling team leader and the model builders. Schedules should be set, and if deadlines are consistently unmet, corrective management action must be taken. Specific target outputs should be established for delivery on specific dates. Management should expect to receive definite results according to a preannounced schedule.

In preparing a model-building schedule, one should anticipate problems and delays and make allowance for these in the schedule. For example, econometric models frequently require repeated specification, estimation, and validation. To obtain one good equation may require as many as 25 alternative specifications of the model.

7. Insufficient Data

A proverbial problem in building corporate models is insufficient data. The decision to develop a corporate model is tantamount to a commitment to develop a comprehensive database or management information system. Data problems are less acute for financial modeling than for marketing and production modeling. If there is any one type of data which a firm is likely to have available in machine-readable form, it is accounting and financial data. (The IRS provides certain incentives toward this end.) However, marketing and production data are another story. Time series data on pricing, advertising, marketing, and the behavior of competitors are particularly difficult to obtain. Obtaining production data may require time-and-motion studies as well as engineering analyses.

8. Unfavorable Cost-Benefit Ratio

There is no denying the fact that a full-scale corporate model can become an expensive undertaking. Management scientists, computer programmers, data collection, computer time, national economic forecasts, computer software, and consulting services are among the items contributing to the total cost of a corporate model. Although one electric utility holding company spent nearly two million dollars to build a financial model, corporate financial models can be built these days for less than $5000.

Again, as mentioned before, precise cost-benefit calculations are hampered by the fact that it is not possible to quantify the benefits of corporate models—the benefits of more accurate, more timely information for the control of the firm.

But the same type of cost control practices used in the effective management of research and development projects are relevant to corporate planning models.

Many companies have begun with a one-year pilot project with a strict budget. The results are reviewed at the end of the first year to determine whether or not the project will be continued. Dresser Industries successfully employed this strategy. During the first year of development of their model, management set very specific targets to be achieved within a predetermined budget. At the end of the first year, the results were weighed against the project costs and a decision was made to continue the project a second year.

9. Inadequate Human Engineering

Several years ago the Wells Fargo Bank developed a corporate simulation model for security analysts in the bank. The primary objective was to generate more accurate, systematic, and consistent estimates of income statements and balance sheets for companies which are of investment interest to the bank. Nine months after the model was finished not one of the 100 analysts who had been introduced to the model was using it. Among the reasons given for the lack of interest in the model was inadequate "human engineering."

> The model was not "human engineered" by someone familiar with the thought processes of a noncomputer-oriented user. We did not investigate the psychological aspects of the user being confronted by a dialogue with a computer.

Both corporate simulation models and corporate simulation languages must be user-oriented; that is, they must be designed in such a manner that the user feels comfortable with their use.

10. Inaccurate Results

In spite of recent improvements in computer modeling technology, forecasting accuracy remains one of the most elusive goals of corporate modeling. If the only objective of the project is forecasting accuracy, then the project should probably not be undertaken in the first place. Although corporate models can lead to improved forecasting accuracy, there are other uses of corporate models which are more important such as policy analysis, scenario generation, and "What if?" simulations.

If all that one is interested in is forecasting accuracy, then one may not need to go to the trouble to build an econometric model. Naive forecasting techniques such as time trends and exponential smoothing may suffice. Alternatively, judgmental forecasts may be more accurate than are forecasts produced by corporate models. One of the problems with the Wells Fargo Bank model was that judgmental forecasts of security analysts turned out to be more accurate than are the forecasts produced by the model. This is always an awkward position in which to find oneself.

We are reminded of the early forecasting objectives set for the Dresser Industries Model. It was stated emphatically that management would not tolerate forecasting errors greater than five percent. Needless to say, with hundreds of different products involved, this target was later revised upwards.

No matter how you slice it, forecasting is a tough business.

11. Dependence on One Person

During the development stages of a corporate model, it is almost unavoidable for the project to be highly dependent on the team leader. Furthermore, it can be argued that this is even a good thing, particularly if the team leader is a good sales person and an entrepreneur. But there comes a point in time when this type of dependence may become a liability; that is, if the success of the model continues to depend upon the support or involvement of one person, then a potentially unstable situation exists. If the prime mover of the model leaves the company or changes jobs, the model may be left high and dry. This was the situation several years ago at Corning Glass. The project director retired and another key employee left the company. The model was left without adequate technical or political support and was permitted to die. Poor documentation makes a corporate model particularly vulnerable to the key employee problem. Dependence on a single person was a contributing factor which led to the demise of the model of a large oil company in the 1960s.

12. Inadequate Political Support

The evidence is overwhelming that the most highly successful corporate planning models have not necessarily been the most complex or the most sophisticated. The more successful corporate models (Northwest Industries, *New York Times*, Monsanto, Eli Lilly, and Ross Laboratories) have been models that have enjoyed the strongest political support from top management. Indeed, some of the most successful and most useful models have been among the simplest models to date. It is better to have a relatively simple model that management can understand than a more sophisticated model that management does not understand and does not utilize.

Ultimately, what the politics of model building is really all about is obtaining and maintaining the political support of top management for the continued development and use of the corporate model.

SOME UNSUCCESSFUL CORPORATE MODELS

Case 1

Between 1965 and 1968, a major oil company developed what was probably the first large-scale corporate planning model ever built. The stated objective of the model was "to provide management with a fast, reliable method for forecasting the financial performance of the company based on any set of anticipated conditions." Certainly this was an ambitious objective. Twenty-three work-years were required to develop the model including 13 work-years to "familiarize management with the operation of the model." The total elapsed time for development was 3.5 calendar years.

The model required 1500 inputs per year to produce 5200 output items and 142 pages of computer printout per year. Output reports included an income statement, a capital investment schedule, a sources-and-uses of funds statement, a rate of return analysis, and a financial summary statement. The model consisted of over 2000 equations. By any reasonable criteria, this was a large financial planning model. Yet the model has not been used since 1969. Why was the model shelved?

The official reason given for taking the model out of service was that the company merged with another oil company in 1969, and the accounting systems of the firms were mutually incompatible. The model was programmed in FORTRAN and FORTRAN is not noted for its flexibility. With the merger, databases had to be reorganized, equations had to be respecified, and reports had to be changed, each of which is difficult to do in a scientific programming language like FORTRAN. In 1965 when the programming was begun on the original model, FORTRAN was really the only option available. None of the special purpose planning and modeling software systems was available in 1968. In other words, inadequate computer software played a major role in the demise of the model.

Among the unanswered questions are: (1) Why was the model so big? (2) Why did it take 23 work-years and 3.5 calendar years to implement? (3) Why did it produce so much output?

For the model to have required 2000 equations easily makes it one of the world's largest financial planning models. It is difficult to conceive why one would include so many equations in a financial model. Perhaps the model builders were caught up in the syndrome of the 1960s in which the name of the game was "How many equations are there in your linear programming model?" A 2000-equation model is not a planning model but a detailed description of the company's accounting system. For financial planning this type of detail is totally unnecessary and represents statistical overkill. In other words, the sheer size of the model may have contributed to its downfall.

Furthermore, 142 pages of printout is a lot of printout. We find it difficult to believe that management could absorb that much output. Why not concentrate on the really important output variables rather than 5200 output items? Again the size of the project must have been a factor.

If, as the author of the model implies, it really took 3.5 years before any visible results were produced, it is no wonder that the model ran into serious political difficulties. Although we are not privy to information on the internal politics of this oil company, we have been told that two other events occurred that may have been relevant. First, the protector of the model either left the company or was transferred to another position where he no longer had any responsibility for the model. When you invest 23 work-years in a financial model, you need all the protection you can get. Second, the director of the project also left the company. Maybe someday the whole story will be told—maybe not.

Case 2

Case 2 involves a large aircraft company. The director of corporate planning for the company described the use of the model as follows:

> The results of the model have been used in accessing potential cost problems associated with the development of a new commercial aircraft and the results of corrective actions taken by the division in problem areas. In addition, the model has been expanded to include probabilistic market and revenue data as well as costs, which now allows us to measure break-even uncertainty in terms of time and production units. Results from the model have been so useful that we are considering further expansion of the technique to attempt to measure the total company risk.

To the best of our knowledge this last proposed activity was never implemented. The model has not been used since 1970.

In summarizing some of the problems he faced with his planning model, the director of corporate planning for the aircraft company has indicated that (1) the model was not responsive to the needs of management and (2) it failed to inspire confidence. Some typical complaints about the model's lack of responsiveness included:

- Models take a long time to build, generally three to four times as long as promised.
- It takes a long time to incorporate a change or an improvement.
- The data necessary for the simulation are not readily available.

As to management's lack of confidence in the model:

- The model is never quite done or quite right—but it soon will be (so we are told).
- The problem I want to solve has to be translated from my terms to the model's terms.
- The model cannot be explained in understandable terms. It has to be expressed in computerese and technical jargon.

- The process we are simulating changes faster than we can change the model.
- No one can define the problem range or error in outputs.

The problems with the aircraft model are not unique. Indeed, they are typical of the problems one finds with many corporate modeling projects. Several of the problems imply ineffective project management. The project leader did not ask the "right questions" about target outputs and project deadlines. As to the difficulty in incorporating changes in the model, this problem is pretty much eliminated with special purpose planning and modeling languages.

Case 3

In 1972, a large manufacturer of computer hardware decided to embark on a project involving the use of corporate modeling to determine the effect of fourth generation computer hardware/software on corporate revenue even though fourth generation computers had not yet been designed. In other words, the company wanted to use the model to facilitate the design of its fourth generation computer line—admittedly, not an easy problem.

Led by a mathematician, the eight-member modeling team consisted of six insiders and two consultants. The fundamental hypothesis underlying the project was that what one should do is attempt to model the behavior of vice-presidents of finance of large companies, since they are the individuals who typically make the final decisions on major computer hardware/software acquisitions. This was a reasonable assumption on which to begin work on the model. Unfortunately, that was the point where good judgment ceased.

The team leader had the preconceived notion that computer acquisition decisions are based entirely on rational considerations. He further assumed that vice-presidents of finance have perfect information about the marginal benefits of alternative forms of computer hardware and software. And finally, he proposed that a very sophisticated modeling technique known as Pontryagin's maximum principle be used to model the behavior of vice-presidents of finance. Although Pontryagin's maximum principle played a useful role in the Soviet and American space programs, to the best of our knowledge it has never been used to model the behavior of vice-presidents of finance. The use of the maximum principle simply required information that was not available in this case. Furthermore, the assumptions underlying the maximum principle bore no resemblance to the situation being modeled.

The consultants on the project kept insisting that some actual computer users be interviewed to gain some empirical data on why people acquire computers. This suggestion was consistently rejected by the team leader.

The situation was a classic example of a team leader knowing too much mathematics for his own good. Furthermore, the team leader carefully shielded the modeling team from any contact whatsoever with anyone in management—particularly those individuals who were supposed to have perceived the problem in the first place. This condition alone is sufficient to guarantee disaster.

Nearly eight work-years of effort went into the project over a period of 12 months. No data were collected, no model was ever specified, no equations were estimated, and no simulations were run. The net output of the project consisted of a 45-minute flip chart presentation. There were no conclusions or policy recommendations generated by the project.

That so little output could be produced from eight work-years of effort is truly amazing. But when you consider that the definition of the project goals changed at least six times in less than six months, the results are not really surprising. The people working on the project were very bright. The politics of the project was very bad.

Case 4

In late 1974, the director of corporate planning of a manufacturing firm based in New York proposed the development of a corporate planning model. A preliminary pilot model was to be developed with the assistance of an outside consultant. The modeling gameplan called for the development of the pilot model without consulting with the vice-president of finance who was a known skeptic of the use of such models. The idea was to develop the small model, show it to the president, gain his endorsement, and then solicit the support of the vice-president of finance.

Of course, the vice-president of finance found out about it and took the position that any financial model developed for the firm should be under his direction. The company also had a director of management information systems. When he learned of the proposed corporate planning model, he suggested that corporate modeling was merely a special type of information system, and that he should be in charge of the project.

Last, but by no means least, was the director of operations research. The O.R. Department happened to be located 500 miles away from the New York corporate headquarters. The director of O.R. had previously developed five successful business planning models for five of the divisions of the New York company. These models were still in use. The director of O.R. felt that he deserved the right to develop the overall corporate model, since he had done his homework by building the five division models.

In other words, the director of corporate planning, the vice-president of finance, the director of M.I.S., and the director of O.R. were all vying for control of the proposed corporate planning model. This is an example of a model that never was. It simply could not survive the political infighting.

There are two important lessons to be learned from Case 4. First, the chief executive officer was not the problem definer in this case. Indeed, he was completely oblivious to the fact that a corporate planning model was being considered. Second, conflicts between the director of corporate planning and the vice-president of finance are common in the corporate environment. Unless the president is paying attention and insists on cooperation between the chief financial officer and the planning officer, successful corporate modeling is an impossibility.

Case 5

In early 1975, a Park Avenue conglomerate also embarked on an ill-fated corporate modeling venture similar to Case 4. The executive vice-president and the vice-president of corporate planning were the problem definers. The executive vice-president was the second ranking officer in the corporation.

A consultant was hired to design the corporate modeling gameplan. A three-stage plan was designed. First, a consolidated corporate model was proposed that would take the manually produced plans from 20 divisions as data. Second, within six months the manual division plans were to be replaced by relatively simple business planning models (financial models). Third, at the beginning of the following year an effort would be made to develop econometric marketing models and production models for each division.

Since there was no one in corporate planning with experience in computer-based modeling, it was decided that a financial analyst would be borrowed from the staff of the vice-president of finance who had some experience with financial modeling. From that point on, the project was in deep trouble.

It seemed that the vice-president of finance and the executive vice-president of this company really did not get along very well. In fact, they did not like each other. The posture of the financial vice-president was that, if there was to be a financial planning model, he was going to control it. Otherwise, he would sabotage any other attempt to develop such a model.

The unfortunate financial analyst was in the unenviable position of reporting to the vice-president of finance who determined his salary, yet he was being loaned to the vice-president of planning to work on the model. The cross-pressure on the analyst was unbelievable. The project lasted only three weeks. It was shelved when the financial analyst resigned in a state of nervous hysteria.

Once again, the chief executive officer was not informed about the proposed corporate planning model. He, therefore, had no commitment to the project. He was apparently not even aware of the conflicts between the executive vice-president and the vice-president of finance. Two years later, the company still had no computer-based planning model.

EVERY COMPANY HAS A CORPORATE PLANNING MODEL

The issue is not whether or not a particular company *should have* a corporate planning model. Every company *has* a corporate planning model. In most companies the model exists only in the head of the chief executive of the company. In other companies, the model has been described in a manual or on a sheet of paper. Still others have taken the trouble to express their corporate model in the form of a computer program. These points were first brought into focus for us on a consulting assignment with a company which we shall call the Palo Alto Corporation.

In 1973, Palo Alto was a 10-year-old, highly profitable $40 million company that had experienced a rapid growth rate. The original management who had built the company had recently sold out to a conglomerate on the East Coast. Palo Alto had a completely new top-management team. We had been brought in by the vice-president of finance to do a feasibility study to determine whether some type of corporate simulation model would be appropriate for Palo Alto.

We spent three days talking with the president, vice-president of finance, vice-president of marketing, and vice-president of the three manufacturing divisions. When we reported back to the vice-president of finance, our recommendation was "If there is any one thing Palo Alto does not need at this time, it is a computer simulation model." What we had discovered was that the company had grown so rapidly that its accounting and data-processing systems had not kept pace with the growth of the rest of the company. At all levels we found corporate management pleading for more timely, more accurate historical information. Given the deficiencies in the Palo Alto management information system, a computer model would have been viewed as a frivolous activity. Without a sound database and an adequate management information system, a computer simulation model is of limited value.

The president of Palo Alto was proposing to implement a continuous budgeting system. It was clear that he had a very definite corporate planning model in his head, but he had never taken the time to write it down on paper. Unfortunately, we found that each of the Palo Alto executives had a completely different view of continuous budgeting from that of the president. In interviewing six members of the corporate management team, we observed six different corporate planning models, that is, six different concepts of corporate planning.

We believe that our recommendations to the Palo Alto management lend themselves to generalization for almost any company which now has a computer simulation model. They are summarized as follows: First, Palo Alto should take this opportunity to design and develop a management information system suitable for satisfying its present and future information requirements. Second, Palo Alto should begin collecting the financial, marketing, and production data today which may be required in two or three years when the company decides that it does need some type of computer planning model. Third, Palo Alto should develop a *verbal* corporate planning model so that each member of the corporate management team is operating on the basis of a common conceptual gameplan. This conceptual model should take the form of a series of procedures and checklists of factors to consider in financial, marketing, and production planning. Basically, it should be the blueprint for a computer simulation model. In the short run, the Palo Alto planning model would be operated manually. Once the management information system has been brought up to an acceptable level and management has had some experience with the conceptual planning model, then some type of computer simulation model might be considered.

We believe that the aforementioned procedure for the evolution of a corporate model can be easily adapted to any firm that is considering the possibility of a computer planning model at some time in the future. In other words, plan and develop today the database and conceptual framework that will be needed in the future for a corporate planning model.

NOTE

1. Based on a paper by Thomas H. Naylor, 1975, The politics of corporate model building, which appeared in *Planning Review* (January).

11 Corporate Planning Models: Case Studies

INTRODUCTION

The concluding chapter of this book consists of five case studies describing actual experiences with specific corporate planning models.

The first case by David F. Weigel and Lucy Quintilliano describes the project plan for a relatively straightforward financial planning model developed by Hammermill Paper Company. It spells out in considerable detail the necessary activities required to implement an initial corporate planning model. The project plan includes an activity plan, a Gantt chart, and sample output reports generated by the model. The project plan described in this paper was fully implemented in 1976 and the model continues to be used as an integral part of the planning process at Hammermill.

The *New York Times* model, developed by Dr. Leonard Forman, is one of the most sophisticated planning models implemented to date. It integrates an econometric marketing model as well as a production model into a financial model. The unique feature of the model is the marketing model. It consists of a set of equations for forecasting demand for the *New York Times*. Sample equations from the econometric marketing model were included in Chapter 7.

The Dresser Industries model is one of the oldest corporate planning models currently in use at the time of this writing. It dates back to 1972. The Dresser model is an integrated planning model for one of the divisions of Dresser Industries. It features a 45-equation econometric marketing model driven by the Wharton Econometric Model of the United States and an econometric production-cost model which is unique to the field. The Dresser model has enjoyed that rare combination of excellent technical support as well as political support by top management. The Dresser Case was contributed by Charles H. Hatfield, Jr. and Bryant K. Kershaw.

The CIBA–GEIGY models developed by Dr. Friedrich Rosenkranz and his colleagues represent the most advanced collection of corporate planning models in Europe today. They embody virtually all of the technical features of corporate planning models described throughout this book. The CIBA–GEIGY models include financial models, econometric marketing models, production-distribution models, integrated models, consolidated models, optimization, risk analysis, and statistical experimental design and data analysis techniques.

The last case describes the Integrated Planning Model (IPM) developed by the Office of Power of the Tennessee Valley Authority. TVA's Office of Power is the largest electric utility in the United States. The IPM differs from the other planning models mentioned in this book in terms of the degree of detail of the model. Because it simulates the power system on an hour-by-hour basis, the IPM is more of an operational planning model than a strategic planning model. Actually the IPM is one of three computer-based planning models developed by Dr. Douglas H. Walters and R. Taber Jenkins. The other models include a highly aggregated, strategic planning model and a capital budgeting model. The latter model is used to plan specific power plants. The three TVA planning models together constitute perhaps the most advanced corporate modeling system in the United States.

Hammermill Paper Company: Project Planning for Corporate Modeling

DAVID F. WEIGEL AND LUCY QUINTILLIANO[1]

The need to plan corporate planning model projects of any appreciable size should be apparent to those engaged in planning functions. Model development represents allocation of company resources. As with any other proposed expenditure, management should be aware of what they are buying, how much it will cost, and when it will be delivered. One means of doing this is to prepare a written proposal that spells out the model's capabilities, limitations, and design concepts; the number, type and duration of assignments of people assigned to the various project activities; and other direct costs such as computer time, consulting, license fees, etc. This proposal or gameplan subsequently should be the initial framework within which the model is developed.

The following example of a planning model project gameplan was developed by Hammermill Paper Company after the Corporate Planning Department decided that they wanted to develop a model and before the project was committed to full development. The gameplan is not the first step in developing a corporate planning model. Actually it is the last step before expending time and money for the extended period of time required to develop a usable model. The model's original concept, capabilities, and limitations are shaped during preparation of the gameplan. The project is fairly well presold to planning and financial managers during the give-and-take discussions in which their modeling requirements are defined.

An essential prerequisite to planning a modeling project is the need for planning management to perceive the potential benefits of corporate models. Project planning responsibility can then be assigned to one or two people who will coordinate the involvement of model users and data suppliers. The initial activity is development of a precise as possible set of requirements. Interchange of a wide variety of ideas of what a corporate model is supposed to do can be expected. This activity itself is beneficial since it forces both users and modelers to do some hard thinking about reasonable results to expect from the model. This also forestalls the embarrassed silence that develops on opening day when some senior officer inquires whether he or she can ask the model about the effects of foreign currency fluctuations when, in fact, the model is geared to constant dollars.

Having developed modeling requirements, the next step is to specify the data input and output reporting requirements. This activity is time-consuming and tedious and may result in requirements revisions if we suddenly, or perhaps slowly, realize that some essential data are unavailable. Several possible alternatives here are to modify the requirements or to include acquisition of the missing data as a project activity. At this point a model or series of models that meet requirements and produce the desired outputs can be conceptualized.

Now that the overall task is known in a broad sense, the detailed activities can be fleshed out. The technique used to develop the gameplan was to break the total job into a series of steps or activities that could be estimated, assigned to specific people, and scheduled into a plan that could be reviewed and controlled. Elaboration is not necessary since this technique purportedly is standard practice on almost every type of project in which a specific objective is to be accomplished within a time and cost framework.

The approved gameplan should be used as the initial project control network. However, be ready for change. Priorities, concepts, and commitment of people usually can be expected to start changing simultaneously with the project start. Some of the concepts may prove unworkable and others may be much easier or harder to realize than they were estimated originally to be. Why, then, should a gameplan be developed when it may be obsolete almost before approval? The gameplan primarily gives us a solid reference point from which to make changes. Management should be kept aware of any changes to concepts and schedules; particularly since some changes may be a direct result of their actions. What, in effect, is happening is that we have an evolutionary series of gameplans over the course of the project. With a well-conceived initial project plan, the final product—the model itself—should be fairly close to the original concept. The essential point here is that change is to be expected but can be better managed with a good reference or starting point.

CORPORATE FINANCIAL PLANNING MODEL PROJECT

This report covers the requirements, preliminary design and specifications, and project plan for developing a Long-Range Financial Planning Model for the Corporate Planning Department.

Project scope Develop a Long-Range Planning Model for the Corporate Planning Department. The model should interface at a corporate level with the Financial Planning Model presently being developed by the Financial Planning and Control Department.

Requirements The Corporate Planning Department needs are discussed in the Clarifications of Capabilities memo of October 24, 1975, and are summarized as follows:

1. *Consolidation*–The model will perform a timely and accurate consolidation of division long-range financial plans.

2. *Revisions/corrections*–The model will quickly recalculate pro forma financials based on revisions or corrections to division long-range financial plans. (Technically, this is the same capability as No. 1 above, but it is a distinct application.)

3. *External factors*–The model will test the impact of various inflation and interest rates on the pro forma financials.

4. *External planning*–Pro forma financials will be automatically revised to reflect acquisitions and divestitures given financing assumptions.

5. *Downside sensitivity*–The model will calculate the pro forma financials of the company for varying degrees of divisional failure to achieve their financial goals.

6. *Strategic planning*–The model will indicate the effect on the corporate and division financials of improving a division's financial measures.

A decision to develop separate models for the Corporate Planning and the Financial Planning and Control Departments led to the interface requirement at a corporate level. At one time, we were considering a model which would serve both areas, but it was decided that the requirements were different enough to develop several models. It is desirable that the financial models be able to use the results from the long-range planning model; thus the corporate level interface.

Benefits The principal benefits from the initial model will be to provide Corporate Planning with the capability of examining a wide range of alternatives in a much shorter time span and to free planning personnel from making routine, repetitive manual calculations.

Costs   Development personnel

1200 hrs–assuming a cost of \$12/hr	\$14,400
Computer time	
Assume 200 hrs time-sharing @ \$50/hr	10,000
Estimated cost	\$24,000

Note: Some outside consulting costs will be incurred in addition to the above since we plan to use a consultant at project review points.

Project plan Development of the Corporate Financial Planning Model would be a joint Planning Department–Operations Research project with Planning handling functional design and implementation aspects and O.R. handling technical design and programming. Project administrative responsibility has not yet been determined.

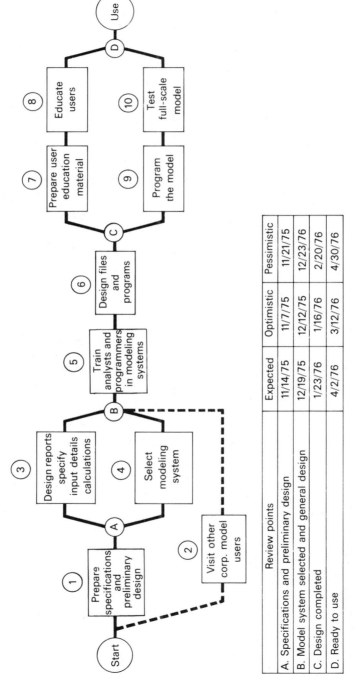

Fig. 11.1 Activity chart: corporate planning model.

Review points	Expected	Optimistic	Pessimistic
A. Specifications and preliminary design	11/14/75	11/7/75	11/21/75
B. Model system selected and general design	12/19/75	12/12/75	12/23/76
C. Design completed	1/23/76	1/16/76	2/20/76
D. Ready to use	4/2/76	3/12/76	4/30/76

Project activities and tentative schedules are shown in Fig. 11.1–Activity Chart and Fig. 11.2–Gantt chart–expected schedule.

Assuming a start date of October 20, 1975, the expected completion date would be the first week of April 1976, with a pessimistic date of late April 1976, and an optimistic date of mid-March 1976. Planned personnel assignments and expected hours and percentages of available time (not adjusted for holidays) are:

	Hrs	% Available time
Planning analyst	472	54
Programmer	412	69
O.R. analyst	332	49
	1,216	

The activity chart (Fig. 11.1) shows four review points, labeled A through D, and their approximate dates. These points afford managment an opportunity to review project progress and direction and to make changes in the direction, schedule, or number of personnel assigned.

A more complete description of project activities follows:

Project activities

1. *Prepare specification and preliminary design:*

   Assigned to LAQ and DFW
   Hrs–approximately 100

   We are currently engaged in this activity. This project plan and the description of design concepts and input and output specifications are also part of the activity. Additional time on this initial phase of the project will be spent in getting management's concurrence on the model's scope, capabilities, and limitations, and on the development schedule and personnel commitments, and in reviewing specifications and design concepts with our consultant.

2. *Visit other users of corporate models:*

   Assigned to LAQ and DFW
   Hrs–approximately 64

   This is a background activity which supplements the model design and modeling system selection activities. We have enough time allocated to visit two or three model users. Other users can be interviewed by phone. The intent here is to use the experience of others to help us to avoid pitfalls of which we are currently unaware.

3. *Design reports, specifiy input details and model calculations:*

   Assigned to LAQ
   Hrs–approximately 100

   Figure 11.1 shows the design effort divided between this effort and Activity 6:

Activity		Elapsed weeks	% Time on project	Hours required
1. Prepare specifications and preliminary design	LAQ	2	25	20
	DFW	4	50	80
2. Visits to other users of corporate models	LAQ	8	10	32
	DFW	8	10	32
3. Design reports, specify input details and model calculations	LAQ	5	50	100
4. Select modeling system	DFW	5	40	80
5. Train analysts and programmers in modeling system	LAQ	4	25	40
	SH	4	25	40
	DFW	4	25	40
6. Design remainder of system (files, programs)	LAQ	4	60	96
	SH	4	60	96
	DFW	4	25	40
7. Prepare user educational materials	LAQ	6	40	96
8. Educate users	LAQ	4	25	40
9. Program the model	SH	6	75	180
10. Test full-scale model	SH	3	80	96
	LAQ	3	40	48
	DFW	3	50	60
Project Totals	LAQ	22	54	472
	SH	15	69	412
	DFW	17	49	332
	Total			1216

Week Starting

Fig. 11.2 Gantt chart – expected schedule.

Design Remainder of System. Although this split may seem unusual, the intent is to save time by running in parallel the design activities which are not sensitive to the modeling system along with the selection of the modeling system. Detailed specification of input variables and the calculations required in modeling divisions and their consolidation into corporate, as well as the detailed design of output reports, is reasonably independent of the modeling system (e.g., FPS, SIMPLAN, etc.) which is chosen. Design and selection activities should be coordinated, however, since design requirements may exclude some systems.

4. *Select modeling system:*

Assigned to DFW
Hrs—approximately 80

This activity involves selection of the computer software upon which the model will be developed. In addition to ability to handle design requirements, other software selection criteria would include ease of learning by programmers and users, ease and flexibility of operation, cost of use, interface capabilities with databases and other models, vendor support, documentation features, and reliability. The choice here is also between higher level programming languages such as FORTRAN or BASIC and modeling systems such as SIMPLAN, CUFFS, and FPS. Packaged models are excluded due to their rigidities.

5. *Train analysts and programmers in modeling system:*

Assigned to LAQ, SH, DFW
Hrs—approximately 120

This activity's title is self-explanatory. Anyone who is likely to operate the model should at least attend the introductory sessions. The availability and scheduling of training courses may be a factor in the actual scheduling of this activity.

6. *Design remainder of system (files and program):*

Assigned to LAQ, SH, DFW
Hrs—approximately 232

This activity covers design of model aspects which are dependent on the modeling system and would include the way in which calculations and reports are grouped into programs and data arranged into files. Every modeling system has inherent features and limitations which would influence the model's detailed design. An example here would be the number of files which one program could access. The BASIC which we currently use can access at most 15 files. Since we have more than 15 divisions, this limitation would affect the way in which the consolidation model was designed.

7. *Prepare user education material:*

Assigned to LAQ
Hrs—approximately 96

This is one of the more important, but usually neglected, activities in development projects of this nature. Adequate technical documentation will result from design and programming activities, but this is not of much help to users who don't have EDP backgrounds. The intent here is to provide user guides and operating aids such that LAQ will not be the only person in Planning who can operate the model. The application manuals from this activity will provide continuity in the user area.

8. *Educate users:*

Assigned to LAQ
Hrs—approximately 40

We have allocated just about enough time here for LAQ to educate other people in Planning on the uses and limitations of the model and to explain the application guides. A project extension could be to orient divisional management in the use of the model.

9. *Program the model:*

Assigned to SH
Hrs—approximately 180

Time requirements for this activity are dependent on the modeling system selected since a learning curve is involved for new systems and languages. In general, the greater the capability and flexibility in a system, the more learning would be required. The schedule could be set up so that programming overlaps system design, that is, SH could start programming as system design segments are completed.

10. *Full-scale system test:*

Assigned to LAQ, SH, DFW
Hrs—approximately 204

Here is where we put all the pieces together and subject the model to a series of tests in which we try to determine whether the model does what it is supposed to and whether it is "robust"; that is, it doesn't give dumb answers.

Design concepts and specifications The overall design concept discussed below is shown in Fig. 11.3, Design Concept, and output reports, input details, and "What if?" capabilities are discussed in more detail in the section entitled LR Planning Model.
Model characteristics are as follows:

· "Bottom-up" planning model; starts on the division level and builds up an overall corporate picture.
· Deterministic; inputs and outputs are represented by single values rather than probability distributions.
· Modular; each operating division is represented in the model as a distinct set of accounting and financial equations or relationships. The overall corporation is also represented by a module that can stand alone; that is, it can accept inputs either from

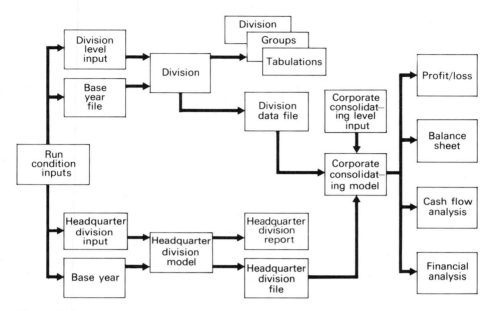

Fig. 11.3 Planning model structure.

divisional consolidation or as direct inputs. We will require a "headquarters division" with this concept.

  • Financial simulator; model is stated in terms of accounting and financial relationships.

  • Run "cases" to test sensitivity and alternatives; that is, input variables are changed systematically by the user, run through the model, and results are observed.

The modular design concept shown in Fig. 11.3 represents each division as a module and the corporation as a module. A "headquarters division" is used under this concept to carry corporate cash, debt, equity, corporate expense and miscellaneous income and serves primarily to assist in consolidating divisions into a total corporate picture. The model is tied together with its data files. Division models accept input data and produce division results that are input data to the corporate consolidation model. Some data redundancy is present in this concept since output data can be recalculated at any time as long as input data were preserved. This redundancy adds flexibility in model usage since we will be able to change selected division inputs, recalculate only those division models, and reconsolidate without recomputing all division models. The skeleton of the model is the bottom-up process in which division models are built from input data and then consolidated into corporate. Group reporting and all division tabulations are developed from division output data and are not part of the model's mainstream.

LR PLANNING MODEL

Purpose and approach   The purpose of the model is to mechanize the generation of pro forma financials to facilitate the long-range planning process. More specifically to:

· Provide a tool for timely consolidation of the division long-range plans.

· Enable timely recalculation of corporate financials given revisions to division plans.

· Project the results of strategies aimed at division and/or corporate goal achievement. These strategies can be in terms of adjustment to division pro formas, acquisition, or divestitures.

· Test the sensitivity of corporate pro forma financials to various interest rates and inflation rates.

The approach chosen to accomplish the above involves a system of models rather than one large model. There will be a *model for each operating division* which has input requirements and produces reports as well as files to be used in the subsequent consolidation model. There will be a *corporate headquarters model* which, given input specifications, calculates the accounts on the corporate books which are also required in the subsequent consolidating model. The *corporate consolidation model* then merges the operating division financials and the corporate books, performs adjustments and eliminations, and generates corporate pro forma financials.

A graphic representation of this structure of models is in Fig. 11.3 Planning Model Structure. Please clarify any questions concerning this structure before proceeding. It is essential to the understanding of the detail definition that follows.

A COMPREHENSIVE LIST OF ANTICIPATED OUTPUT REPORTS

I. Division reports[*]
   A. Financial projection summary sheet (Fig. 11.4)
      1. Profit and loss
      2. Statement of position
      3. Sources and uses[†]
      4. Ratio analysis[†]

   The above with Annual averages, Accumulations, and Average annual growth rates as indicated.

II. Group reports
   A. Same as I.A. (above)

   Note: Group summaries will be the sum of the divisions before any intragroup eliminations.

---

[*]All reference to "divisions" include wholly owned subsidiaries. All subsidiary financials will be projected as divisions; that is, all excess cash transferred to corporate–no debt outstanding or investments which represent loans to the corporation. No interest income or expense projected.

[†]These will not be generated for the "headquarters" division.

	1974	1975	1976	1977	1978	1979	1980	Average annual growth
Profit and loss								
Net sales								
Pretax profit								
Unit sales								
Position								
Current assets								
Fixed assets								
Total assets								
Working capital								
Sources and uses								Accumulated totals
Posttax profit								
Depreciation								
Decreased working capital								
Total sources								
Increased working capital								
Capital investment								
Total uses								
Net cash flow								
Ratio analysis								Annual average
Gross margin								
ROS								
ROA								
Asset turnover								
Working capital/sales								
Inventory/cost of goods								
Accounts receivable days outstanding								

Fig. 11.4 Financial projection summary. Planning unit ___

III. Division and/or group tabulations
   A. Percent total operating profits tabulated over time (Fig. 11.5)
   B. Percent total operating assets tabulated over time (Fig. 11.6)
   C. Ranking by accumulated cash usage with breakdown by sources and uses (Fig. 11.7)

IV. Corporate Level Reports
   A. Profit and loss (Fig. 11.8)
   B. Balance sheet (Fig. 11.9)
   C. Cash flow analysis (Fig. 11.10)
   D. Financial analysis (Fig. 11.11)

Input   The following detail on input requirements specifies exactly what values can be varied from one run to the next. This then indicates in what forms a condition must be expressed in order to use the model to test its impact on the corporation. As long as a

Group	1974	1975	% Corporate pretax profits 1976	1977	1978	1979	1980
A							
B							
C							
D							
E							
F							
G							
H							
I							

Fig. 11.5 Breakdown of profits.

Group	1974	1975	% Total depreciated assets 1976	1977	1978	1979	1980
A							
B							
C							
D							
E							
F							
G							
H							
I							

Fig. 11.6 Breakdown of assets.

Cash users		Cash contributors	
Group	Accumulated cash flow	Group	Accumulated cash flow
A		D	
B		E	
C		F	
		G	
		H	
		I	

Accumulated cash usage
1969–1974

Group	Average ROA	Fixed capital	Working capital	Total cash usage	% Corporate total
A					
B					
C					
D					
E					
F					
G					
H					
I					

Fig. 11.7 Net cash flow analysis.

condition or event can be expressed in terms of the input variables, the model should be helpful in analysis.

Input requirements can be categorized as follows:

Division level	Corporate consolidating input
Headquarters division level	Run condition input

I. *Division level*

Division level input is by far the most complicated—primarily because of the diversity of key operating parameters for the different businesses. Several sets of division inputs are given below—one "general" set which would suffice for any operating company, and several others more specifically tailored for particular types of businesses (paper manufacturing, merchant houses, converters, forest products). To expedite the initial model development, it is feasible that the general set of inputs be the only option available for all divisions. The more flexible models (B. through E. below), which accept the parameters most meaningful to different types of businesses, could be phased in as they are developed.

	Actual 1974	1975	Pro forma 1976	1977	1978	1979	1980	Annual growth 1976–80
Net sales								
Total division pretax earnings								
Corporate expenses								
Earnings before taxes								
Corporate taxes								
Posttax earnings								
Return on sales								
EPS (6838M shares)								
Turnover—without excess cash								
Return on assets								
with excess cash								
without excess cash								

Fig. 11.8 Pro forma statement of income.

	Actual	Pro Forma					
	1974	1975	1976	1977	1978	1979	1980
Assets							
Cash and related							
Other current							
Total current							
Investments							
Net fixed							
Total assets							
Liabilities							
Short-term debt							
Other current							
Total Current							
Long-term debt							
No. 15 P.M.							
New financing							
IRB issues							
Total long-term							
Deferred							
Total liabilities							
Equity							
Total liabilities and equity							

Fig. 11.9 Pro forma statement of position.

Note: All input alternatives assume a base year of data is on file for each division.

A. General input requirements
1. Growth rate of sales ($)
   or Growth rate of unit sales and average price[*] forecasts for each year
   or $ Sales forecasts for each year
   or Unit sales forecasts for each year and average price levels for each year
2. Growth rate of direct costs ($)
   or Direct cost $ for each year
   or Average direct cost per unit (if growth rate of unit sales or unit sales figures for each year were entered under A. 1. above)
   or Gross margin
3. Growth rate of overhead costs (excluding depreciation)
   or Overhead $ figures for each year in the planning period
4. Capital budget—budgeted $ expenditures for each year and average life of the new assets *plus* any existing assets generating sizable depreciation expense which will become fully depreciated during the planning period.

---

[*]Impact of change in mix or pricing strategy, not inflation.

	Actual	Pro forma						1975–80
	1974	1975	1976	1977	1978	1979	1980	Accumulated
Sources								
Posttax profit								
Depreciation								
Increase in deferred taxes								
Decrease in working capital								
Other								
Subtotal								
Uses								
Capital expansion								
Increased working capital								
Mandatory debt reduction								
Dividends								
Other								
Subtotal								
Net cash flow								
Known long-term borrowings								
IRB borrowing								
No. 15 financing								
Subtotal								
Funds available								

Fig. 11.10 Pro forma sources and uses.

	Actual		Pro forma					Average	Growth	Accumulation
	1974	1975	1976	1977	1978	1979	1980	1975–80	1976–80	1975–80
Size and expansion										
Sales										
Total assets										
Capital expansion										
Net worth										
Profitability										
Posttax earnings										
PS										
R.O. sales										
R.O. equity										
R.O. assets										
Asset turnover (Times)										
Flexibility										
Funded debt/ capitilization										
Unused debt capacity										
Gross cash flow										
Net cash flow										
Current ratio (Times)										

Fig. 11.11 Pro forma financial analysis.

5. Working capital as a % of Sales
   or Inventories and accounts payable as a % of Sales and accounts receivable days outstanding.

   Note: Input requirement No. 5 will eventually become optional, with functional relationships between these factors defined within the model and input of the values triggering an override option.

6. Optional—change in level of interdivisional sales (and accounts payable). Can be specified by growth rate or $ values. If not specified, continuation of base year level is assumed.

B. Paper manufacturing

   1. Paper sales (tonnage) for each year

   2. Pulp capacity (tonnage) for each year

   3. Contributed profit/ton paper for each year

   4. Average price/ton paper for each year

   5. Paper manufacturing overhead (excluding depreciation)
      Projected dollars or growth rate

   6. Contributed profit/ton market pulp for each year

   7. Pulp manufacturing overhead (excluding depreciation)
      Projected dollars or growth rate

   8. Capital budget dollars for each year and average life of assets plus any assets generating sizable depreciation expense which will become fully depreciated during the planning period.

   9. Optional—change in level of interdivisional sales (and accounts payable) can be specified as a growth rate or $ values. If not specified, continuation of base year is assumed.

C. Paper merchants (distributors in general)

   1. $ Volume for each year or growth in $ volume

   2. Gross margin (%) for each year

   3. Overhead can be broken down into fixed and variable
         Variable overhead—input a % of sales
         Fixed overhead—input a $ budget

   4. Capital budget—optional since growth can be supported by changes in fixed overhead

   5. Inventory as a % sales or of cost of sales
      or inventory turnover
      Accounts receivable days outstanding
      Interdivisional sales and purchases as % of total

      Note: All input in No. 5 above is optional. Historical values will be used if nothing else is indicated by input.

D. Converting
   1. Sales $ growth or $ amount for each year
   2. Gross margin for each year
      or Material costs as % sales and other direct as % sales
   3. Fixed costs growth rate
   4. Optional—any change in % interdivisional sales

E. Forest products
   1. Sales $ (either the $ for each year or indexed to base)
   2. Profits $ (either the $ for each year or indexed to base)
   3. Working capital/sales
      or Inventory/sales and accounts receivable days outstanding
      or Inventory/cost-of-goods-sold and accounts receivable days outstanding
      or Turnover and accounts receivable days outstanding
   4. Capital budget
   5. Interdivisional sales—% of total

F. Assumption listings generated by divisional models are narrative descriptions of the input. Also, a numerical interpretation of the input will be provided if meaningful and if this does not involve repetition of numbers generated on the output report. Any divisional input will pertain to one of the following: sales, price, direct costs, contributed profit, overhead, capital budget, and asset management. A listing of inputs for each division categorized by the affected accounts will precede the output.

II. *Headquarters Division level*

This level refers to the calculation of the corporate book entries necessary for consolidation of divisions. The operating statement consists of overhead items (G.S.&A., Interest Expense) and corporate incomes such as interest income, equity in subsidiaries and management fees. Corporate entries on the balance sheet include cash, investments, long-term debt, deferred items, and equity.

Projection of these accounts requires inputs unlike those of operating divisions. They are:

- Projected interest rates on invested funds
- G.S.&A. assumption (growth rate or values)
- Subsidiary profit assumption and management fees
- Long-term interest rate projection
- Short-term interest rate projection
- Minimum and maximum liquidity position
- Corporate accounts receivable (export corp., etc.)
- Long-term investments
- Optional—change in level of accrued expenses

- · Dividends
- · Optional—incorporate lag in dividend and tax payment
- · Assumption on changes in deferred pension fund

III. *Corporate Consolidating Level*

This is the level at which all divisions (including corporate headquarters) are added together, adjusted, eliminated and taxed to produce the total corporate after tax P/L, and the consolidated balance sheet. Most of the eliminations result directly from division calculations (interdivisional sales, etc.) or are of a special nature not predictable on a pro forma basis. The adjustments and reclassifications are just as difficult to project, but some (such as LIFO adjustments) can be of a magnitude that justifies a provision to input them directly in order to test their impact on the consolidated financials.

Input to the corporate consolidating model includes:

A. Acquisitions
  1. Pro forma financials of acquisition (using division model)
  2. Financing package for acquisition
     a. Cash—amount
     b. Stock issue—number of shares

B. Divestiture
  1. Pro forma financials of division
  2. Financing package for divestiture
     a. Stock received—balance sheet adjust.
     b. Cash—amount

C. LIFO adjustments—$ change in LIFO reserve for each year

D. Corporate tax rate for planning period or for each year

IV. *Run Condition Input*

A provision will be necessary for handling inputs which will be used in all segments of the model. Input provided for at this level will require consideration in all segments of how its impact is to be reflected in the output. The only input capability of this type provided for initially will be inflation.

The *New York Times* Newspaper Planning Model

LEONARD FORMAN[2]

INTRODUCTION

The *New York Times* model is a large-scale model that forecasts sales and earnings for the *New York Times* newspaper. Structurally, it is composed of two major blocks; a demand model and a production, cost, and revenue model. The demand model, the heart of the model, is a set of simultaneous nonlinear econometric equations that forecast physical volume, approximately 35 categories of advertising lines and ten categories of circulation. The second block is recursive and contains roughly 300 equations, some of which are stochastic behavioral equations. This block converts the volume forecasts into paging, newsprint consumption, newsprint distribution, and staffing requirements. These physical flows are then monetized, using price and wage forecasts, to produce estimates of revenue, fixed and variable costs, and operating profit. This case study summarizes the development of the model, with emphasis on the advertising and circulation model, and provides some applications of the model's use. The structure of the model is constantly evolving. Consequently, emphasis is placed on the conceptual underpinnings of the model, not on a detailed presentation of its structure.

The *New York Times* model was developed as a planning tool to evaluate the impact of changes in internal and external conditions on newspaper earnings. The approach at the *New York Times* differs from most corporate modeling efforts. In contrast to most systems, which follow a "top-down" modeling strategy, the *Times'* approach is a "bottom-up" strategy. There is no front-end corporate model. Instead, each division is modeled separately. The output from each model is then aggregated to produce a set of consolidated corporate financial reports.

A second and perhaps more interesting departure is the attempt to fully integrate the financial, production, and marketing activities of each division into a truly integrated planning model. The major effort has been at the *New York Times* newspaper which accounts for approximately one-half of corporate revenues. The newspaper model is considerably larger and more complex than other division models.

The basic assumption underlying our approach is that in the short run the state of the economy is the primary determinant of the demand for our product. Although other factors influence demand, we believe that the economy is the dominant factor. Accordingly, a significant amount of time has been spent in the construction of a marketing model, referred to as the demand model hereafter. This model, fueled by forecasts of key economic indicators, is the driving force in the newspaper model.

In what follows, no attempt is made to describe the model in all its detail. Rather, emphasis is placed on the structure of the model and the methodology followed in constructing it. The first section provides a brief overview of the model. Next, we describe its structure and the theory underlying that structure. The third section highlights the econometric methodology and discusses some of the econometric equations.

Most of the paper is devoted to the demand model which contains almost all of the econometric equations in the planning model. The concluding section describes some of the model's applications in planning and budgeting.

AN OVERVIEW

Model development at the *Times* followed a pragmatic strategy: each sector was built according to need. Initially, the most pressing problem was to produce reliable forecasts of advertising and circulation. The well-publicized problems of the New York metropolitan region necessitated a more rigorous approach to supplement the traditional sales forecasts produced by the sales staff. The decision was made to build an econometric model to forecast volume.

Normal econometric methodology was followed. However, the supreme test was its forecasting precision. If the advertising and circulation model was to be an operational tool for improving planning and short-term budgeting, forecasting accuracy was essential. The preliminary version of the demand model was completed in late 1974. Since then, the model has been used with a great deal of success for forecasting and simulation. It is an integral part of the formal planning process at the *Times*.

The second phase of the modeling project was the development of the cost and production model that, when linked to the demand model, provided a mathematical description of the newspaper's operations. The immediate problem was to eliminate many of the time-consuming manual calculations performed by the various departments in preparing the plan. The manual procedures ruled out sophisticated planning since even a single change in the underlying assumptions, either changes in exogenous variables or changes in control variables, required a great deal of effort and time to work through. Naturally, two or more efforts were in many cases impossible to handle.

The first step was the restructuring of the production and financial relationships into a systematic and internally consistent set of mathematical equations creating a working model in a reasonable period of time. Subsequent analysis revealed that many of the parametric assumptions and relationships were unsatisfactory and new relationships were developed. Some of these were stochastic.

Currently, the model contains over 300 equations. Approximately 65 are econometric equations. There are 30 exogenous variables. The model's specification produced a mixture of recursive and simultaneous linear and nonlinear difference equations. It is, however, not a finished product. Apart from the normal management of an econometric model, we are constantly respecifying parts of the model. For example, many of the production and cost econometric equations will eventually be supplemented by a more sophisticated optimization analysis. The model is constantly undergoing continuous change and refinement.

Furthermore, although model development responded to particular problems, conceptually, a unified structure was conceived prior to model construction. In Jay Forrester's terminology, this structure represented a systems view of the *New York Times* embodying "the dynamic feedbacks and linkages between information, materials, orders, people, and equipment" for all the components of the newspaper. Our modeling effort is based on the rather ambitious goal of describing total system behavior: how decisions are made in various parts of the organization and how they contribute to the total behavior of the system.

THE ELEMENTS OF A NEWSPAPER MODEL

Before describing the structure of the model, it is useful to first describe some of the salient characteristics of the newspaper industry with the emphasis on their relevance for analysis rather than on comparisons with other industries. A newspaper really produces two different products and sells them in two different markets. It sells copies to readers and space to advertisers. By itself, there is nothing unusual in this. However, for newspapers, this joint product presents unusual marketing problems. The demand for advertising space is greatly affected by the sale of copies. There is also evidence of reverse causality although the relationship is weaker. A newspaper becomes a more attractive vehicle for advertisers the larger its circulation base. Similarly, many people purchase a paper for its advertising content which provides readers with an information alternative to news content. It is even more unusual to find that the demand for space is affected by the character of the newspaper's readers. In this case, class does matter.

Conceptually, the model is based on the microeconomic theory of demand and cost modified by the peculiarities of the newspaper industry and internal financial requirements. The production function is vector-valued with output defined as the number of copies produced and the number of pages per copy.

$$Q_t = \begin{bmatrix} C_t \\ P_t \end{bmatrix} = F(K_t, L_t, TC_t), \tag{11.1}$$

where Q_t = output

C_t = copies produced

P_t = pages per copy

K_t = capital stock

L_t = labor

TC_t = technological change.

The cost equations derived from this production function differ from the traditional microeconomic approach. In order to ensure the model's acceptance and use, the cost equations were designed to be consistent with the financial and accounting conventions at the *Times*.

The model can be viewed as a rather large and sophisticated income statement or operations model. Consequently, capital stock appears only indirectly through the depreciation equations. Thus, while the fixed-variable cost specification is retained, capital stock costs do not explicitly appear.

Variable costs are defined as those costs which vary directly with paging and copies produced; newsprint and production labor costs. The number of staff working and the number of hours worked vary each day depending on paging size and copies produced. Although capital is held fixed, capital utilizaticn is not. Theoretically, depreciation is a function of capital utilization and should be treated as a variable cost. Because accounting conventions do not handle depreciation in this fashion, in the model depreciation does not vary with output.

Newsprint costs are computed by calculating the newsprint tonnage required to produce a given number of pages and copies and then multiplying by the appropriate cost per ton. There are equations for different grades of newsprint as well as equations for the many different sections of the paper.

Econometric cost equations are used to determine variable labor costs for each of the variable labor departments. While the equations differ, in general they look like:

$$LC_{it} = F_2(C_t, P_t, TC_t, W_{it}),$$ (11.2)

where LC_{it} = unit labor cost for the ith group in period t

W_{it} = the appropriate wage rate.

Changes in the production technology are rapidly making historical production and cost relationships obsolete. Eventually, these econometric cost equations will be replaced by an optimization analysis. For example, a given volume forecast of pages and copies can be produced in a variety of press configurations. Each press configuration completely determines labor requirements. Programming techniques will be used to determine the least-cost press configuration. The labor associated with this press configuration will then be monetized at the appropriate wage rates.

To complete the cost side, noncapital fixed costs are divided into labor and nonlabor fixed costs. Because the accounting system does not track these costs historically, econometric methodology is not used. Fixed labor costs are determined by equations which compute staffing requirements and wage rates in 32 different categories.

In the current version of the model, staffing requirements are determined exogenously. They are policy variables controlled by management. Research is currently underway to determine the linkages between fixed labor, output, and profitability; and formalize the decision rules management intuitively follows in determining annual fixed staffing levels. The objective is to fully endogenize these linkages.

Nonlabor fixed costs (excluding capital) are treated in a very simple way. Dollar cost for each category is increased each period by a growth factor. These costs account for a very small percentage of fixed costs.

The demand model is a simultaneous block of nonlinear econometric equations for advertising lines and copies sold (circulation). Both outputs are sold in oligopolistic markets with varying product differentiation and intense nonprice competition. Because the Sunday and daily papers are distinct products, Sunday and weekday advertising and circulation are treated separately. Conceptually, the demand for each output is treated as a function of its price, the prices of its competitors, indicators of market activity, and quality. Symbolically, the demand for circulation looks like:

$$CIRC_{ti} = F_3(p_i, p_{ji}, Prom, M_1 \ldots, M_n, Q),$$ (11.3)

where $CIRC_{ti}$ = average circulation in period t for the ith market

p_i = the unit price per copy in the ith market

p_{ji} = the price of the competitive product in the ith market

Prom = promotion expenditures

M_i = indicator of market activity

Q = quality.

The variable quality is a measure of the appeal of the paper to its readers. Potential readership depends on attitudes which in turn depend on education, household income, occupation, orientation New York City, and politics.

Similarly, the demand for advertising lines;

$$L_{ti} = F_4(p_i, p_{ji}, \text{Prom}, Q, M_1, \ldots, M_n), \tag{11.4}$$

where all variables are defined as above and L_{ti} is advertising lines for the ith category in period t. The variable Q represents the quality of a unit of linage to the advertiser as measured by the purchasing power of its readers, prestige of the newspaper, and readership. Generally, circulation can be used as a proxy variable for advertising quality. The conceptual framework for the model is summarized in Fig. 11.12. This flow diagram depicts the dollar flows between the various components of the system. The underlying physical flows are shown in Figs. 11.13 and 11.14. The solid lines in Fig. 11.12 represent dollar flows, revenues on the left and costs on the right. The broken lines portray the interaction between these dollar flows with the arrows indicating the presumed direction of the interaction. For example, expenditures for promotion are assumed to influence advertising and circulation revenues. Conversely, advertising and circulation revenues impact the dollars available for promotion expenditures. The likely natures of some of these nonlinear interactions are illustrated in Fig. 11.15.

Thus, real increases in news and editorial expenditures are likely to have a positive effect on the sale of newspapers although diminishing returns are probable. Similarly, reduced to zero revenues from paper sales would probably drop, but not to zero. The revenue loss would occur gradually, not instantaneously. The flow diagrams and graphs are conceptual simplifications of complex time-dependent interrelationships.

None of the fixed department relationships is as yet built into the model. It was suggested earlier that management has a rational belief concerning the nature of these interactions which they act on in determining staffing and expenditure levels. As the graphs in Fig. 11.15 show, these relationships can be defined mathematically and built into the model. Simulation experiments could then be performed to test the effects of various fixed department hypotheses and determine those relationships which cause simulated performance to agree with actual performance.

Shown in Fig. 11.13 is modular structure that is a convenient basis for thinking about the model although this structure does not correspond exactly to the way the system is modeled. For purposes of discussion, each of the boxes can be defined as a module. The modules are:

• *Advertising linage module.* This represents forecasts of the demand for advertising by category. Either manual forecasts by the advertising sales force or projections from the model can be used.

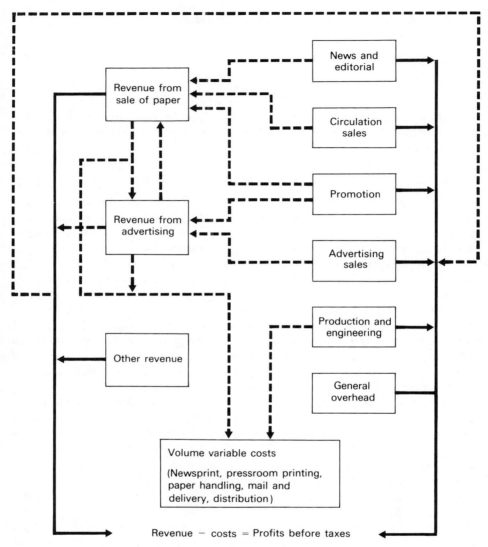

Fig. 11.12 Simulation model: conceptual framework.

· *Circulation module.* This represents the manual circulation department forecasts or the projections generated by the model.

· *Fixed department cost module.* The current exogenous staffing forecasts are used to compute fixed labor costs. Nonlabor fixed costs are computed in this module also.

· *Demand transformer module.* Given advertising lines and rates by category, this module generates new lines, paging, and advertising revenue.

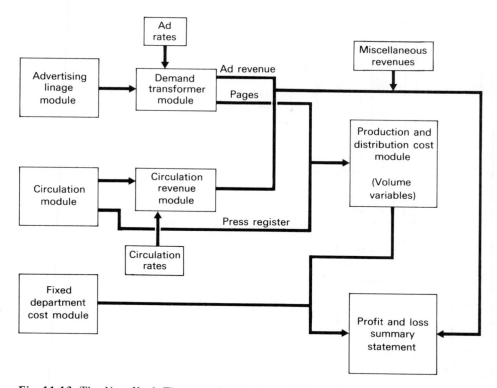

Fig. 11.13 The *New York Times* model structure.

* *Circulation revenue module.* Forecasts of circulation by region are used to generate revenue and copies produced.
* *Miscellaneous revenues.* Exogenous projections of other revenues.
* *Production and distribution cost module.* Given total pages and copies produced, this module builds up the costs of printing and distributing the paper.

A more detailed flow diagram, which corresponds more closely to the mathematical structure of the model, is shown in Fig. 11.14. This diagram details the major physical flows of the model and the financial output which results. This financial information is summarized in an income statement for management.

THE CIRCULATION AND ADVERTISING MODEL: SPECIFICATION AND ESTIMATION

Equations (11.3) and (11.4) depict the theoretical structure of the demand model. The major departures from that structure are the absence of relative prices in the advertising equations and demographic variables in the circulation equation.

Preliminary analysis indicated that within the normal range of price change there

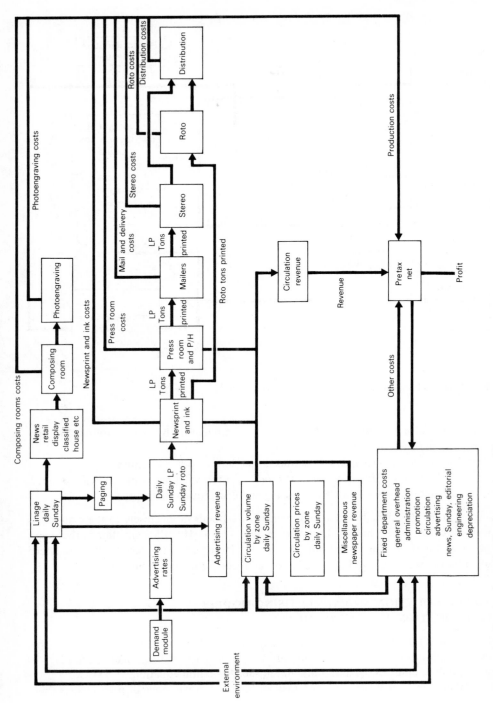

Fig. 11.14 Production–distribution cost model.

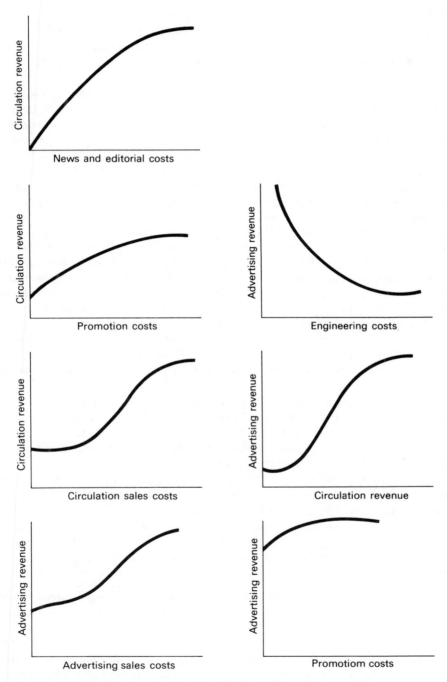

Fig. 11.15 Nonlinear relationships in the *New York Times* model.

is a high degree of price inelasticity that is consistent with the economic theory of product-differentiated markets. Competition between the *Times* and other newspapers and electronic media exists, but it is based on factors other than price. We do not mean to suggest that price changes do not affect advertising sales. They do. Price competition, however, is minimal.

Unfortunately, data problems prevented us from including the competitive factor in the model. Ideally, the market-share type of equations would be preferable. Because of data problems, however, their reliability would be suspect. In any event, changing economic conditions proved to be the major cause of cyclical swings in advertising lines.

In the circulation equations, the lack of meaningful quarterly time series demographic data prevented their inclusion as explanatory variables. There are plans to remedy this defect by linking cross-section demographic data with the available time series data.

While the extent of specification bias caused by the exclusion of relevant variables cannot be precisely determined, the nature of the New York market suggests that it is probably small. Over the last ten years, population shifts have resulted in a gradual change in the spatial distribution of our circulation sales with suburban sales increasing relative to city sales. Since these changes have not been abrupt, proxy variables that mirror these changes have been constructed and used in the circulation equations.

Another long-term problem, well documented and related indirectly to demographics, is the nationwide decline in newspaper readership. The *New York Times* is not unaffected by this trend. A number of theories purport to explain this phenomenon. It is, however, not a cyclical problem. Consequently, time trends were used to capture this process of erosion.

The quarterly fluctuations in circulation, apart from seasonal and random variation, seem to depend on price dynamics and economic changes. Circulation in each category is explained by economic indicators, advertising lines, prices, and circulation from other categories. There is considerable substitution and complementarity between various categories of circulation. For example, people who buy the daily paper tend also to purchase the Sunday paper. A weaker reverse relationship also holds. There is also some substitution between home delivery sales and newsstand sales. The equations were designed to take these relationships into account.

Advertising in each of the equations is related to various economic indicators, circulation, and the substitute–complement relationships which hold for advertising.

The parameters of the demand model were estimated according to the following methodology:

·   Preliminary analysis indicated those variables which explained quarterly fluctuations in volume. Data problems and multicollinearity eliminated some of the explanatory variables.

·   Next, the appropriate functional form for each of the equations was determined. The usual summary statistics were used in exploring various specifications. In latter versions, multiple time series techniques were used to determine dynamic lag structures.

• Each equation was then estimated by ordinary least squares. In many cases, serial correlation was present and the standard procedures were used to correct it. Unfortunately, in dynamic simulations this correction magnifies specification biases producing explosive out-of-sample forecasts. Variable adjustments to the constant term with these adjustments diminishing over time were applied. We are currently trying another technique which allows for more complex stochastic specification than the typical first-order autocorrelation adjustment. It involves applying time series techniques to the residuals from each equation. The forecast for each variable then consists of a deterministic part and a stochastic part.

• Finally, simultaneous estimation techniques were applied and the estimated model was subjected to a number of validation tests.

THE INTEGRATION OF THE MODEL INTO THE
PLANNING AND BUDGETING CYCLE: SOME APPLICATIONS

The model outlined in the preceding pages is fully integrated within the budgeting and planning cycle. Several examples will illustrate this.

The annual budget

In the fourth quarter, the newspaper prepares its annual budget for the coming year. The most important components of the budget are the volume forecasts of advertising and circulation. The advertising and circulation sales departments prepare preliminary estimates. Independently, the model produces several sets of forecasts corresponding to a most likely scenario, a more optimistic scenario, and a pessimistic scenario.

Management then reviews each set of forecasts assessing their strengths, weaknesses, and reliability. The differences are reconciled and a final set of forecasts is the result.

These forecasts are then distributed to the managers of the operating departments, and the budgeting process continues. Between the beginning and end of the budget cycle, a period of about four months, the demand model is periodically run to determine whether or not there are any departures from the original forecasts.

The procedure just outlined was followed in both the 1975 and 1976 budget cycle. The model's 1975 forecasts, produced in December 1974, were quite accurate. The forecast error for total linage was under one percent and the circulation error slightly over one percent. Individual equation errors were larger but cancelled out when aggregated.

At the end of the cycle, the full model is run and the budget is reproduced. A set of sensitivity experiments is then performed to determine the impact of volume changes and policy options in response to those changes. A set of income statements summarizes these simulations. As a result of these exercises, contingency planning is greatly facilitated.

The five-year plan

The planning and budget cycles at the *Times* overlap: the annual budget is the first year of the five-year plan. The planning cycle begins in March and ends in the early part of the fourth quarter when the budget cycle begins.

In March, a complete run of the model is produced. The volume forecasts and income statement summary are compared with the previous year's plan and the current operating goals set by management. The results of this analysis are distributed to the operating managers for comment and analysis. The advertising and circulation departments, using the model's volume forecasts as a guide, then prepare their own forecasts. This process eventually results in a set of consensus volume projections.

With this new set of volume numbers, the production-cost model is rerun and a preliminary five-year income statement is produced. If at this time the financial results still fall short of the plan's objectives, a set of action plans, strategies designed to improve performance, are developed and simulation experiments are performed to determine their impact on profits. This process continues until the five-year plan is finalized.

The model has a pivotal role in the planning process. Indeed, in the absence of a model, the planning process, in the true sense of the word, does not really exist. The manual procedures followed by the various departments prior to the model's development limited the process essentially to one pass. The model has given management the capability to explore alternative plans quickly and react promptly to changes in external conditions which cause a departure from the established plan.

New products

The cost and revenue implications of current and planned product changes have been analyzed using the simulation model. For example, responding to shifting population, special regional editions are being produced. In the 1976 plan the model was used to determine profit and loss statements for each of the new products. Following a base run, each new product change was introduced separately. In this manner, the incremental costs and revenues for each product were generated. From this information a break-even analysis could be prepared and an appropriate pricing strategy developed. This analysis provided the information management needed to determine the economic feasibility of each product, information which would not have been readily available had manual procedures been used.

CONCLUSIONS

The preceding examples document the integration of the newspaper model into the planning process at the *New York Times*. The model is used to set goals, design strategies to achieve these objectives, forecast, and monitor changes which might prevent goals from being achieved. Management uses the model and believes its output.

The model, however, is far from finished. Some of the changes that will improve the model were suggested in the preceding pages. New information and changing technology require constant modification of the model's structure. It is a living organism, constantly growing and changing. In this way we hope to ensure its continued success and usefulness to management.

Dresser Industries: The Dresser Planning Model

CHARLES H. HATFIELD, JR. AND BRYANT K. KERSHAW

INTRODUCTION

The Dresser Planning Model[3] is a large-scale econometric annual forecasting model of a major operating division of Dresser Industries. The structure follows the neoclassical economic theory of an oligopolistic firm with product differentiation. The model contains 166 behavioral equations, 441 identities and 152 exogenous variables. The specification of the model resulted in a mixture of recursive and simultaneous linear and nonlinear difference equations. The model is structured as a series of demand and cost functions. Constant dollar sales are forecast by the demand equations. An income statement is generated from the cost functions. The cost functions are derived from production functions which use output (sales in 1967$) from the demand equations. The solution is done in 1967$ and inflated to current dollars. This approach allows Dresser to track factors of production and their cost even though the model does not have a supply side.

The approach was pragmatic and focused on specific short-range (one-year) and long-range (five-year) marketing and financial problems of Dresser Industries. The model is an *operational* tool for improving the accuracy and quality of short- and long-term profit planning. The model has been completed and is now operational at the chosen division. Dresser has also modeled most of its other domestic operations at the division level.

The development was strictly an applied econometric exercise. Our foremost criterion was the logical validity of the structure of the model as viewed from the marketing viewpoint. The second criterion was the statistical and theoretical validity as assessed in the normal manner. Third was potential forecast accuracy. The following pages discuss the approach used to develop the model structure, the demand functions. This discussion is followed by an investigation of the cost functions, the econometric analysis, and the solution program. Following a section entitled Conclusions, a list of the acronyms used in this case study is given.

APPROACH

The major objective of the Dresser Planning Model was to forecast sales and earnings for a domestic division of Dresser Industries. Demand and cost functions derived from microeconomic theory were used as the basis of the model. The resulting model had to meet three objectives. The model was intended to improve the accuracy and information content of the annual and long-term profit plans. Second, it was to be a tool for management to use in evaluating alternative market strategies through simulation of the division. Third, it was a tool to be used for evaluating the Division profit plans at the corporate level. Production was divided into 15 product categories. A product category is defined as a homogenous group of products from a marketing viewpoint. (This happens to coincide with a production definition.) For purposes of this paper, these products are identified as A, B, C, . . . , O. This represents the production from three plants. All the products are basic industrial goods that go into construction and maintenance of plant, equipment, and pipelines.

The product categories were further divided into three markets; called X, Y, and Z; that is, division output is divided into 45 categories based on a market definition. Thus, the errors of aggregation for a demand relationship were minimized. The solution was done in 1967$.

The market variables used were gross sales, product–market prices in 1967$, and gross variable margin. Gross variable margin is gross sales less direct labor and materials. The acronym for gross sales is GS; for prices, PI; and for variable margin, VM. Variable names are derived based on these acronyms. For example, product B in market X for gross sales is BXGS. The acronyms are given at the end of this case study.

The financial data consist of an income statement for each product category. The items in the income statement are defined at the end of this study. Dresser has used direct costing since 1963. Data prior to 1963 were adjusted to be comparable. The items in the income statement were considered to be costs of two types of actions.

The first set of items are things management does to increase sales or reduce cost. These are market effort, engineering development, engineering support of sales, and average investment level (capital stock to an economist). In the model, these data are deflated so that they measure a level of effort. These items are exogenously determined and are used in the demand and production functions. The first set of indicators contains what are called management decision variables. Management interacts through the management decision variables to influence demand and cost.

The second set of income statement items contains what are considered to be factors of production. These include direct labor and variable overhead, direct materials, manufacturing capacity cost, and administrative and general cost. The first two are obvious. Manufacturing capacity costs include depreciation, rental, maintenance, various taxes, etc., applicable to the plant, equipment, and manufacturing function. Manufacturing capacity cost is used to measure the flow of capital services. Since most administrative and general costs (A & G) are tied to the production process, A & G is somewhat arbitrarily classified as a production input. Admittedly, some of this cost is linked to the market effort. As a consequence, market variables (marketing or engineering expense) often appear in the A & G equations. These production variables are plant-oriented.

The data collection task was tremendous. Data on all the variables mentioned were collected annually and quarterly from 1955 to 1972. Due to acquisitions, inconsistent product line data, and lack of data, the actual start dates for the various series ran from 1955 to 1963. We literally had people opening boxes in the warehouse to put the data together.

There were no industry data available. Efforts to develop series were not successful. Therefore, for relative prices and output the lowest level of industry detail contained in the Wharton Annual and Industry Forecasting Model was used. The result was mixed. For products with little product differentiation, the relative company and industries prices were significant, otherwise they were not. (Expected price elasticities for the latter items were expected to be higher.) As a result, the model understates the relative price effect between company and industry.

The model was linked to the New Wharton Annual and Industry Forecasting Model developed by Ross S. Preston at Wharton EFA. The objective was to choose variables forecasted in this model to measure Dresser market forces. These variables were used three ways. First, they were used as actual indicators; that is, the level of new housing investment is a direct indicator of how much product A goes through market X to be used in new housing construction. Second, economic variables were used as proxies for things for which we have no data and/or were not forecasted. Third, they were used to serve as indicators of economic conditions, for example, durable goods. Output is a good overall indicator of the level of economic activity in all investment goods industries. Keep in mind that all variables discussed are in 1967$.

The next step was to review each product market with experienced marketing personnel. They gave Operations Research a review of each product–market category; how the products are used, when they are used, and who uses them. The potential economic indicators and management decision variables were chosen. The statistical analysis was then begun. The equations were again reviewed after estimation.

DEMAND ANALYSIS

The products contained in the Dresser Planning Model are marketed in an industry best described as oligopolistic with product differentiation. The degree of product differentiation varies from practically none to very strong.

The price elasticities are very low in most cases. The sales are primarily to utilities. The price elasticity is lowest in those products–markets where product differentiation is highest. Prices do not even appear in many of the demand functions. (This is also due to the multicollinearity problem and the available proxy for industry price.) The demand function would be stated as:

$$Q_i = D(P_i, M_1, \ldots, M_k, E_1, \ldots, E_n, Q_1, \ldots, Q_j, \ldots, Q_m) \qquad (11.5)$$

where: Q_i = quantity demanded of the ith product–market items,

$\quad P_i$ = relative price of the ith product–market to fabricated metal prices,

$\quad M$ = the management decision variables,

$\quad E$ = economic indicator of market activity,

$\quad Q_j$ = quantity demanded of complementary products sold by Dresser in the same market where $j \neq i$.

The demand functions are developed according to this hypothesis given in Eq. (11.5). The general choice of economic and management decision variables are based on division market personnel's description of the markets.

Demand equations

The larger products in markets with stable histories give the best results as expected. Figures 11.16 through 11.21 show representative equations for major product categories in markets.

$R^2 = 93.809\%$ $\hspace{7cm}$ $\sigma = 3.582\%$

$$\frac{\text{AXGS}}{\text{AXPI}} = 2.63152 e^{-.1436155 * \text{TIME}} \text{NF}^{.5336525} \text{GPO29}^{.356440} \text{HOS}^{1.975547}$$

$\qquad$ AXPI = Product A market X price index $\hspace{4cm}$ 1967 = 1.0

$\qquad$ TIME = Time trend

$\qquad\quad$ NF = Investment, structures, nonfarm residential $\hspace{2cm}$ 1958\$

$\quad$ GPO29 = Output, fabricated metal products $\hspace{3.5cm}$ 1958\$

$\qquad\;$ HOS = Personal consumption, household operating services

Product A, market X–gross sales

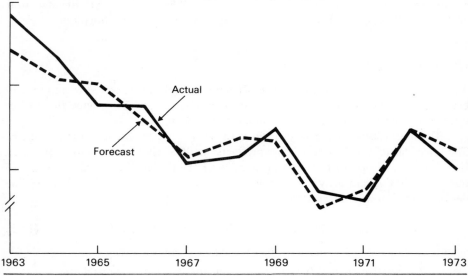

Fig. 11.16 Product A, market X gross sales (1967\$).

COST FUNCTIONS

Cost functions are used to determine the factors of production. The term cost function is used to denote cost expressed as a function of output. This is opposed to a cost equation which denotes cost in terms of input levels and imput prices. The cost function is used to determine input levels in constant dollars. A cost equation is then used

$R^2 = 96.87829\%$ $\sigma = 4.954264\%$

$$\frac{\text{AYPS}}{\text{AYPI}} = 30{,}422.57\ \text{IV27}^{.8203560}\,\text{UCCAP27}^{-.8190795}\,\text{GPO20}^{-1.023874}$$

AYPI = Product A market Y price index $1967 = 1.0$
IV27 = Investment, utilities 1958\$
UCCAP27 = User cost of capital, utilities
GPO20 = Output, rubber and miscellaneous plastic products 1958\$

Product A, market Y–gross sales

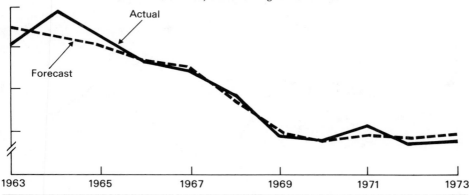

Fig. 11.17 Product A, market Y–gross sales (1967\$).

to express cost in current dollars. Each product production function is expressed as:

$$Q_i = P(\text{VLO}_i, \text{DM}_i, \text{MF}_i, \text{AG}_i, \text{INV}_i, \text{TECH}_i), \tag{11.6}$$

where: Q_i = output quantity of the ith product.

VLO_i = direct labor required for Q_i for ith product.

DM_i = direct material required for Q_i for ith product.

MF_i = manufacturing cost required for Q_i for ith product.

AG_i = administrative and general cost required for Q_i for ith product.

INV_i = total investment (capital stock) available for use in production of Q_i for ith product.

TECH_i = technological change in production process of the ith product.

All values in 1967\$.

Each product was produced in one plant only. This avoided having more than one production function for any of the products.

It is assumed that management will always expand and contract according to an expansion path. The expansion path is determined by the plant's technological con-

$$R^2 = 97.29352\% \qquad\qquad\qquad\qquad\qquad \sigma = 2.024289\%$$

$$\frac{\text{BXGS}}{\text{BXPI}} = 0.206916 \left(\frac{\text{BES}}{\text{W13}}\right)^{.4705474} \text{NF}^{.5412607}\ \text{SNF}^{1.332926}\ \text{GPO20}^{-.9914562}$$

BXPI = Product B market X price index	1967 = 1.0
BES = Product B engineering customer service	
W13 = Wage rate, fabricated metal products	1967 = 1.0
NF = Investment, structures, nonfarm residential	1958$
SNF = Stock, nonfarm residential structures	1958$
GPO20 = Output, rubber and miscellaneous plastic products	1958$

Product B, market X–gross sales

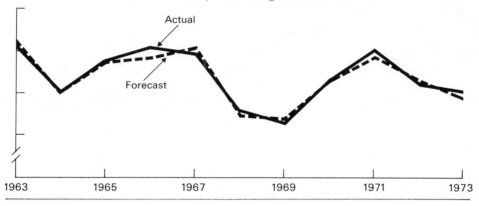

Fig. 11.18 Product B, market X–gross sales (1967$).

straints. The expansion path is defined by:

$$Q_i = E(\text{VLO}_i, \text{DM}_i, \text{MF}_i, \text{AG}_i, \text{INV}_i, \text{TECH}_i) \qquad\qquad (11.7)$$

where the variables are defined as for the production function. Since all outputs and inputs are defined in constant 1967$, these two equations can be reduced to a single cost equation in 1967$:

$$C_i = G(Q_i, \text{INV}_i, \text{TECH}_i) \qquad\qquad (11.8)$$

where $C_i = 1967\$$ vector of production cost items for the ith product. The cost equation is stated as:

$$C_i^* = \text{VLO}_i \cdot \text{PI}_{\text{VLO}} + \text{DM}_i \cdot \text{PI}_{\text{VLO}} + \text{MF}_i \cdot \text{PI}_{\text{MF}} + \text{AG}_i \cdot \text{PI}_{\text{AG}} \qquad (11.9)$$

where $\quad C_i^* =$ current $ cost of the ith product.

$\text{PI}_{\text{VLO}} =$ price index of direct labor 1967 = 1.0.

$\text{PI}_{\text{DM}} =$ price index of direct material 1967 = 1.0.

$$R^2 = 98.9415\% \qquad\qquad\qquad\qquad\qquad \sigma = 5.036099\%$$

$$\frac{DZGS}{DZPI} = 49.48484 \left(\frac{DTME}{W13}\right)^{0.4688845} e^{-0.5757387 * TIME}$$

$$\left[\left(\frac{AXGS}{AXPI}\right)_t \left(\frac{AXGS}{AXPI}\right)_{t-1}^{-0.06783384}\right]$$

$$(GPO30 + GPO31 + GPO32 + GPO33)^{0.6904410}$$

DZPI = Product D price index	1967 = 1.0
DZTME = Product D total marketing expenses	
W13 = Wage rate, fabricated metal products	1967 = 1.0
TIME = Time trend	1955 = 1.0
AXGS = Product A market X	
AXPI = Product A market X price index	
t = Time t such as 1967, 1968, etc.	
GPO30 = Output, machinery, excluding electrical	1958$
GPO31 = Output, electrical machinery	1958$
GPO32 = Output, transportation equipment excluding motor vehicles	1958$
GPO33 = Output, motor vehicles and equipment	1958$

Product D, market Z–gross sales

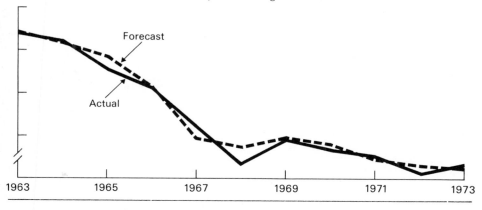

Fig. 11.19 Product D, Market Z–gross sales (1967$).

PI_{MF} = price index of manufacturing cost 1967 = 1.0.

PI_{AG} = price index of administrative and general cost 1967 = 1.0.

The specification of Eq. (11.8) is satisfactory for variable cost categories of labor (VLO) and material (DM). The VLO and DM cost functions were first solved, printed out in

$R^2 = 87.07147\%$ $\hspace{4cm}$ $\sigma = 3.460279\%$

$$\frac{GXGS}{GXPI} = 1.141837 \ IV11^{.585924} \ GPO20^{-.8023157} \left(\frac{GES + GED}{W13}\right)^{.04752923}$$

$$\times \left(\frac{FXGS}{FXPI} + \frac{HXGS}{HXPI} + \frac{IXGS}{IXPI}\right)^{.8291014}$$

GXPI	= Product G market X price index	$1967 = 1.0$
IV11	= Investment, fabricated metal products	1958$
GPO20	= Output, rubber and miscellaneous plastic products	1958$
GES	= Product G engineering customer service	
GED	= Product G engineering product development	
W13	= Wage rate, fabricated metal products	$1967 = 1.0$
FXGS	= Product F market X gross sales	
HXGS	= Product H market X gross sales	
IXGS	= Product I market X gross sales	
FXPI	= Product F market X price index	$1967 = 1.0$
HXPI	= Product H market X price index	$1967 = 1.0$
IXPI	= Product I market X price index	$1967 = 1.0$

Product G, market X–gross sales

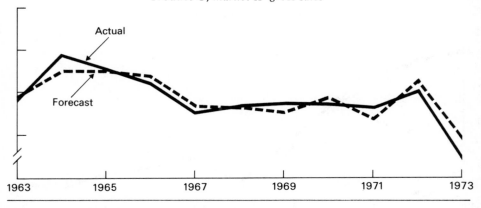

Fig. 11.20 Product G, market X–gross sales (1967$).

constant dollars, multiplied by price and printed out again. This gives management the ability to track real labor and material requirements.

The specifications of Eqs. (11.8) and (11.9) are not satisfactory for manufacturing cost (MF) and administrative and general cost (AG). The accounting system just doesn't track AG and MF costs as well as it does labor and material. Manufacturing costs and administrative and general costs are allocated costs. This makes the categories sensitive

---

$R^2 = 97.46370\%$ $\sigma = 2.112825\%$

$$\frac{\text{JYGS}}{\text{JYPI}} = 0.28376666 \ NF^{0.02166279} \ KIV27^{-1.724612} \ GPO9^{2.903913}$$

$$\text{WAT-SEW}^{0.5675896}$$

JYPI = Product J market Y price index		$1967 = 1.0$
NF = Investment, structures nonfarm residential		1958$
KIV27 = Capital stock commercial and other equipment and structures		1958$
GPO9 = Output, contract construction		1958$
WAT-SEW = Water supply systems and sewerage and waste disposal systems, contract awards		

Product J, market Y–gross sales

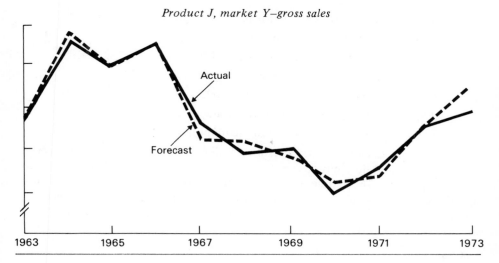

Fig. 11.21 Product J, market Y–gross sales (1967$).

to levels of production of other products in a given plant. MF contains fixed costs that are functions of plant size and are period costs. Other areas vary with levels of production. AG contains period costs as does MF. In addition, it has costs that are related to the market and engineering functions. All these elements must be taken into consideration in equation development.

Individual input cost equations for each product can be derived from the product cost equation (with the modification for MF and AG).

$$\text{VLO}_i = C_{\text{VLO}}(Q_i, \text{INV}_i, \text{TECH}_i), \tag{11.10}$$

$$\text{DM}_i = C_{\text{DM}}(Q_i, \text{INV}_i, \text{TECH}_i), \tag{11.11}$$

$$MF_i = PI_{MF}[C_{MF}(Q_i, INV_i 1, (MF_1, .. MF_{i-1}, MF_{i+1}, ..., MF_k))], \quad (11.12)$$

$$AG_i = PI_{AG}[C_{AG}(Q_i, TME_i, ES_i, ED_i, (AG_1, ..., AG_{i-1},$$

$$AG_{i+1}, ..., AG_k))], \quad (11.13)$$

where VLO_i = direct labor required for Q_i for ith product.

C_i = cost functions where i stands for VLO, DM, MF, and AG.

Q_i = output quantity = quantity demanded of product i

DM_i = direct material required for Q_i for ith product.

MF_i = manufacturing cost required for Q_i for ith product.

AG_i = administrative and general cost required for Q_i for ith product.

INV_i = total investment (capital stock) available for use in production of Q_i for ith product.

TECH = technological change in the production process of the ith product.

k = number of products produced in a given plant.

PI_{MF} = price index of manufacturing cost 1967 = 1.0.

PI_{AG} = price index of administrative and general cost 1967 = 1.0.

TME_i = total market expense of the ith product.

ES_i = engineering support of the ith product.

ED_i = engineering development of the ith product.

In the case where two or more products share facilities, their production cost becomes interdependent and this must be recognized. This was not a consideration in the demand equations. The output or sales would exhibit interdependence only near capacity levels. The cost functions are long-run functions constructed by specifying short-run functions, then shifting them through changes in the INV or capital stock variable.

Cost Equations

The cost functions for direct labor were estimated at the total product category level according to Eq. (11.6). Variable cost (VLO + DM) was estimated at the product–market level. Direct material became a residual by:

$$DM_i = \Sigma(VC_{ij}) - VLO_i, \quad (11.14)$$

where: DM_i = material required for output quantity Q_i

VC_{ij} = variable cost for ith product in jth market

VLO_i = direct labor for ith product

This approach was used because we did not have data for DM and VLO broken down to products in markets. Variable cost was available at this level. Equation (11.14) gave the ability to disaggregate variable cost, but eliminated plant scale as a variable. Investment (capital stock) was not available at this level.

Representative equations are shown in Figs. 11.22 through 11.26.

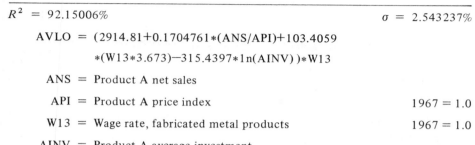

$R^2 = 92.15006\%$ $\sigma = 2.543237\%$

$$\text{AVLO} = (2914.81 + 0.1704761*(\text{ANS}/\text{API}) + 103.4059$$
$$*(\text{W13}*3.673) - 315.4397*\ln(\text{AINV}))*\text{W13}$$

ANS = Product A net sales

API = Product A price index   1967 = 1.0

W13 = Wage rate, fabricated metal products   1967 = 1.0

AINV = Product A average investment

Product A direct labor and variable overhead

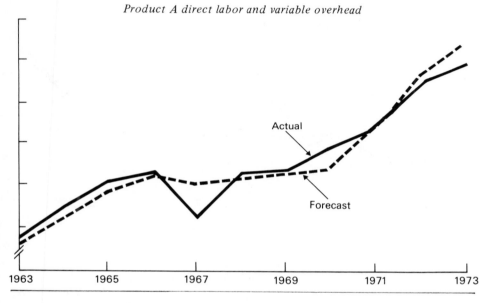

Fig. 11.22 Product A direct labor and variable overhead (current $).

ECONOMETRIC ANALYSIS

The estimation objective was purely a pragmatic one. No apprehension was felt against adding a lot of "art" to the equation estimation and specification. In deciding between alternative specifications; three factors were always considered: (1) the validity of the logic of cause and effect implied; (2) the values of the elasticities; and (3) the equation statistics, such as the *t*-statistics of coefficients and the Durbin–Watson statistic.

The number of observations available was a definite limiting factor on specifications. The data began between 1955 and 1963, depending upon the series, and went through 1972. This was more of a constraint in the demand functions than in the cost function.

$R^2 = 92.3463\%$ $\qquad\qquad\qquad\qquad\qquad\qquad\qquad\qquad$ $\sigma = 3.468602\%$

$$\frac{JVLO}{W13} = 9.31320234 * e^{.01652925 * TIME} * (JNS/JPI)^{0.8425195} * JINV^{-0.2709094}$$

TIME = Time trend

$\quad$ JNS = Product J net sales

$\quad$ JRI = Product J price index $\qquad\qquad\qquad\qquad\qquad$ 1967 = 1.0

JINV = Product J average investment

W13 = Wage rate, fabricated metal products $\qquad\qquad$ 1967 = 1.0

Product J direct labor and variable overhead

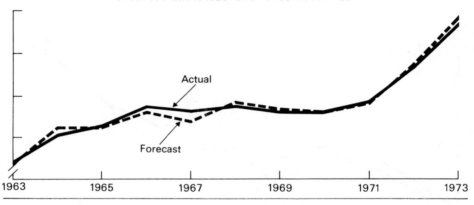

Fig. 11.23 Product J direct labor and variable overhead (1967$).

The functional form of the vast majority of the equations is nonlinear in variables. Most of these are double logarithmic (natural) functions. None is nonlinear in coefficients. The model is primarily estimated from stochastic regressors. These arise from the methods of definitions and collections of accounting data, methods of definition, and collection of national income data and the model structure.

Multicollinearity dominated the econometric analysis. Sample size was the second most important factor. The model structure was defined to minimize both effects through minimizing the number of variables necessary in each equation. Each product category and market was distinct and homogenous. The products would have only one or two general applications in their markets. They would either be repair products, consumable and/or investment items for new plant, equipment, or construction. The market could then be described with only three or four economic indicators and management decision variables. The management decision variables (market expense and engineering support of sales) were highly correlated for those products for which engineering support was important. This was resolved by treating them as one variable.

$R^2 = 98.78553\%$ $\sigma = 2.196548\%$

$$\frac{KYVC}{W13} = 2.013285 \left(\frac{KYGS}{KYPI}\right)^{0.8261461} e^{0.01487523\,TIME}$$

W13 = Wage rate, fabricated metal products   1967 = 1.0

KYGS = Product K market Y gross sales

KYPI = Product K market Y price index   1967 = 1.0

TIME = Time trend   1955 = 1

Product K market Y gross variable margin

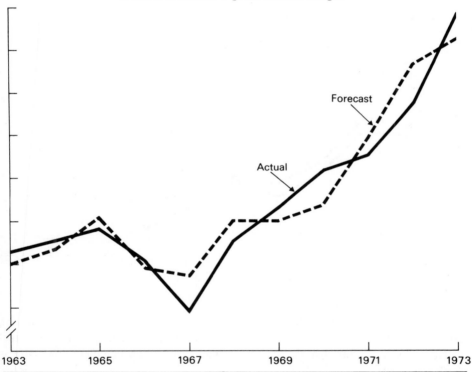

Fig. 11.24 Product K market Y variable cost (1967$).

Autocorrelation was not a significant factor. The Durbin–Watson statistics were watched closely. Autocorrelation did not cause serious problems, except in a very few cases. These were solved by using alternative specifications of the equations. The lack of a serious autocorrelation problem was attributed to three things: (1) the nature of the business, (2) the fact that it was an annual model, and (3) the lack of

$R^2 = 99.10369\%$ $\sigma = 4.2063383\%$

$$EAG = -190.1679 + .1029899*(AAG+BAG+CAG+DAG)$$
$$+15.30209*Ln(ENS)+15.41320*Ln(ETME)$$

AAG = Product A administrative and general

BAG = Product B administrative and general

CAG = Product C administrative and general

DAG = Product D administrative and general

ENS = Product E net sales

ETME = Product E total marketing expense

Product E administrative and general

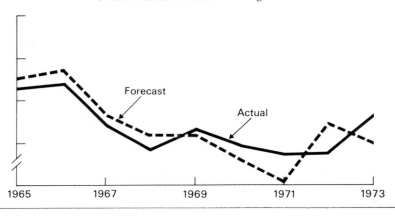

Fig. 11.25 Product E administrative and general (current $).

lagged variables. Every product–market runs through a complete manufacturing and market cycle in one year. Orders are taken in late winter and early spring, manufactured and shipped through the spring, summer, and fall. A complete new cycle is started each year.

"Errors in variables" (in an econometric sense) were both worked around and lived with. In the case where this was a problem, an instrumental variable was used; that is, another specification of the equation was used. In the case of manufacturing costs and administrative and general costs, the equations simply had to live with it. Through the estimation procedure, the value of elasticities was constantly evaluated. Alternative specifications would be tried when the coefficients acquired what we considered to be an unacceptable bias.

The stochastic effects due to the regressors being jointly determined along with regressand were evident in some cases. The structures of the model had minimized

$R^2 = 97.31861\%$ $\qquad\qquad\qquad\qquad\qquad\qquad\qquad$ $\sigma = 4.008326\%$

$$JMF = 482.0115 + JNS * .0249047 * JNS - 20.62074 * TIME$$
$$* 0.5663776 * (KMF + LMF + MMF + NMF)$$

JNS = Product J net sales

TIME = Time trend

KMF = Product K manufacturing

LMF = Product L manufacturing

MMF = Product M manufacturing

NMF = Product N manufacturing

Product J manufacturing capacity cost

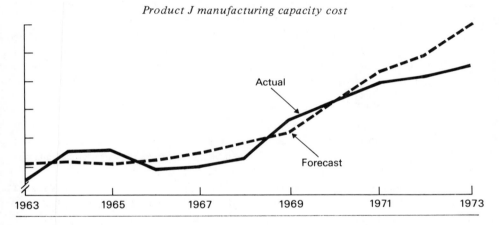

Fig. 11.26 Product J manufacturing capacity cost (current $).

the problem in the demand function but not in the cost function. Sections of the model were estimated with two-stage least squares and also the general linear model. The two-stage, least-squares advantage of consistency does not seem to help that much with our small sample sizes. It must be kept in mind that the coefficients used are manually scanned for gross bias. However, this is a point which will be watched very closely during the model update when more sample points become available.

In summary, the estimation process was determined by: (1) the logic of the cause and effect, (2) the value of the elasticities, and (3) the equation statistics such as the *t*-statistics of the coefficients and the Durbin–Watson statistics. Using the structure developed in the section entitled "Approach" and the statistical approach developed in this section, the equations needed to contain only three to five variables to achieve good specifications with respect to variables.

SOLUTION PROGRAM

The solution program generates a complete set of marketing reports and financial statements for the Division profit plan. The plan is developed by Division Management through setting various levels for the Management Decision variables, subject to the economic environment given by the economic variables. The procedure is iterative. A final solution is obtained when management is satisfied with their price structures, marketing effort, investment (capital stock), engineering effort, profit and return on investment in both the short and long runs.

Reports

The Planning Model produces two types of output. The first is the market reports which contain sales, prices, and variable margin by product and market. These reports are summed by market, plant, and division. An example is shown in Table 11.1. The second or financial report is a statement of earnings by product category. These reports are summed by plant and division. An example is shown in Table 11.2.

The market reports are stated as gross sales, etc.; whereas, the financial reports are in net terms. The market reports can be produced with current dollar or constant (1967) dollar forecasts. Both types of reports contain ten years of data. This can be any consecutive combination of actual and forecast years up to a ten-year forecast.

Programming Considerations

The program is completely user-oriented. The analyst has complete flexibility to alter assumptions, to generate reports, and to save or discard alternative solutions. The baseline case is always stored in the permanent files. A run usually consists of a series of modifications to the assumptions and a subsequent new solution.

The program has 26 options. These are all consistent in format and are as simple as possible to input (considering the complexity of the model). The analyst uses various acronyms and the solution program handles the locations, etc.

CONCLUSIONS

First, a large simulation model cannot be built without the enthusiastic support of top management. The resources required to collect the data properly are too great. Second, such a model must answer questions about alternatives in which top management is interested, that is, questions about short-term and strategic planning. The model must also have the support of the department that uses it. They must devote the time and effort to understand the structure of equations and the solution program.

The model was built according to traditional microeconomic theory. Detailed explanations of market behavior obtained from market managers and the marketing services department were translated into these terms. Statistically, this explanation fits the data very well. Historical simulations gave a mean square sales error of about five percent on all except relatively new products that have not stabilized in a market.

Earnings before taxes (EBT) estimates are small numbers when compared to sales and major cost items. Any biases built into the simulation routine will create

Table 11.1 Example market report, market X—1967 $

					(Actuals to 1973)					
	1969	1970	1971	1972	1973	1974	1975	1976	1977	1978
PRODUCT A										
SALES										
BOOKINGS										
VARIABLE MARGIN										
VARIABLE MARGIN % OF SALES										
PRICE INDEX										

Table 11.2 Example financial report, statement of earnings—product A

	1969	1970	1971	1972	(Actuals to 1973) 1973	1974	1975	1976	1977	1978
NET SALES										
STANDARD COST OF SALES										
STANDARD MATERIAL										
STANDARD DIRECT LBR/OVHD										
SUBTOTAL STANDARD COST										
VARIABLE MARGIN AT STANDARD										
% OF SALES										
DIRECT CHARGES NET VARIABLE										
MARGIN										
PRODUCT SUPPORT COST										
MANUFACTURING										
ADMINISTRATIVE AND GENERAL										
ENGINEERING—COST OF SALES										
SERVICE FEE AND OTHER										
SUBTOTAL SUPPORT										
PRODUCT MARGIN										
% OF SALES										
MARKETING EXPENSE										
% OF SALES										
DIRECT PRODUCT EARNINGS										
% OF SALES										
ENGINEERING—PRODUCT DEVELOP-										
MENT										
% OF SALES										
OTHER INCOME AND DEDUCTIONS										
EARNINGS BEFORE TAXES										
% OF SALES										
AVERAGE INVESTMENT										
% ROI										

large EBT errors. Errors in EBT forecasts by product were about ten to twelve percent. Aggregation to the division level reduced all errors considerably. Division sales errors of about two percent and Division EBT errors of seven percent are expected. This error analysis results from a 14-year simulation from 1960 to 1973.

Since this model was completed, models of the other major domestic divisions of Dresser Industries have also been implemented.

VARIABLE ACRONYMS OF DETAILED ITEMS IN THE MODEL

First and Second Characters—Products

A — Product 1
B — Product 2
C — Product 3
D — Product 4
E — Product 5
F — Product 6
G — Product 7
H — Product 8

I — Product 9
J — Product 10
K — Product 11
L — Product 12
M — Product 13
N — Product 14
O — Product 15

Third Character—Market (Not in Financial Variables)

X — First market
Z — Third market

Y — Second market

Fourth and Fifth Characters—Market Variables

GS — Gross sales
PI — Price index, 1967 = 1.0
VM — Variable margin or sales less variable cost

Third and Fifth Characters—Financial Variables

NS — Net sales
DM — Direct material
VLO — Direct labor and variable overhead
VC — Variable cost
VMS — Variable margin at standard
DC — Direct charges
NVM — Net variable margin
MF — Manufacturing cost
AG — Administrative and general expense
ES — Engineering customer service
SF — Service fee
TSC — Total support cost
PM — Product margins
AE — Advertising expense
OME — Other marketing expense

TME — Total market expense
  PE — Direct product earnings
  ED — Engineering product development
  OI — Other income and deductions
 EBT — Earnings before taxes
 INV — Average investment
 ROI — Return on investment

Corporate Planning Modeling at CIBA-GEIGY

FRIEDRICH ROSENKRANZ

HISTORICAL BACKGROUND AND PAST EXPERIENCES

Corporate modeling work within CIBA–GEIGY[4] began in 1968. Prior to the merger of the two chemical companies, CIBA and GEIGY, which took place in 1970, a great deal of time was spent on a comparison of different modeling approaches, programming languages, and systems. Two smaller corporate modeling projects were undertaken during this phase and both were abandoned before any regular and practical application was possible. However, both supplied valuable experience.

The first pilot project dealt with the description of the activities and operations of a daughter company producing electronic equipment. This firm had to cope with severe problems mainly in the production area. At times its inventory levels for finished and intermediate products were excessively high. In other periods a considerable backlog of orders was observed. Production was in batches and the process had several production stages. Since many of the intermediate products were used in several of the finished products, the description had to cope with a multiple echelon, facility, and assembly problem. The project was intended to, first, describe the operations of the firm in the areas of production, marketing, and finance, and second, to show reasons for the inventory cycles observed in order to find possible policies to smooth the whole process. The project was not initiated by the management of that particular daughter company, but by a central staff. The latter thought that it was possible to improve the quality of planning from the outside.

Since the phenomena observed at first sight seemed to resemble many of the examples originally described in Forrester's *Industrial Dynamics*, it was decided initially to try to apply an Industrial Dynamics methodology. The first model was coded using IBM's CSMP (Continuous Systems Modeling Program). At the time it became obvious that with this computer code, similar to the original DYNAMO, it was difficult to treat tables and matrices containing either measured or generated values of indexed model variables. These facilities are likely to be required for the type of problem described. The whole model was subsequently recoded in FORTRAN. It consisted of several hundred equations, some of them fairly complex, and approximately 50 of them being behavioral. Nonlinear difference equations were encountered in the production segment and equations containing stochastic disturbances in the marketing segment.

The second model concentrated on the description and simulation of the markets of one of the operating divisions, the sales of approximately 100 key products to these markets, and the flow of funds and marginal income connected with sales and distribution of the products on a worldwide basis. The project was partially carried out in parallel with the first one. It was abandoned before the construction of a production segment was begun.

As in most cases, the failures can be attributed to four interrelated shortcomings, notably:

- Inadequate project organization and management.
- Inadequate use of the available methodology.
- Inadequate data processing support.
- Incompatibilities in the firm's organization, planning, and control functions.

Certainly, in recent years, model users and model builders have accumulated considerable experience and knowledge to help prevent some of the shortcomings mentioned above. But it seems that successful model building on one level of sophistication is a dialectic process which tends to create problems on other levels. This implies that the same shortcomings have to be overcome several times.

The partial failures of the first two CIBA–GEIGY models were due mainly to the first three of the difficulties mentioned above.

Although the *Industrial Dynamics* model managed to simulate (ex post) some of the inventory cycles which had been observed in reality, it was never fully implemented. There were several distinct reasons for this result.

The analysis showed that the inventory cycles were mostly induced by fluctuations of external demand and were not internally generated—a result which could be obtained independently from the model by a careful analysis of order time series and which could not be changed by something like an adaptive marketing strategy. Still, one could imagine the descriptive power of the model being useful in production and personnel planning.

It was then realized that not only did the pattern of external demand change rapidly, but the firm itself was altering its production process and product mix. Since this first model was not built in a structured and modular fashion, it became clear that changing the very detailed model structure could not be achieved much faster than the structural changes actually occurred. Furthermore, the model variables, parameters, and equations were not always understandable to the model users.

The main reason for the failure of the second, more econometrically oriented model was the absence of user participation. After the user had roughly defined the intended use of the model, most of the data collection, model specification, and testing were carried out by the model builders. During that time the potential model users had to occupy themselves with more pressing planning work arising from changes in the planning procedure. It was not surprising in these circumstances to encounter a lack of identification of the user to the model when it came time to decide on its implementation, usage, and financing. In retrospect, one may still say that a correct methodological approach had been taken. It should also be mentioned that the project made the development of a number of modules and database utilities possible that are still used with the currently implemented systems. But the failure to close the "model manager interface" did not allow the implementation of an otherwise feasible approach.

It seems that the fourth difficulty mentioned is more likely to appear after the modeling has reached a stage in which the user employs the model and is able to discriminate its performance to approaches and methods for planning and control with which he or she has had previous experience.

General

The previously described failures at CIBA–GEIGY provided valuable experiences to the model builders with respect to the type of project management, methodology, and techniques to be employed with a corporate modeling project. At the time the first two projects had ended, an elementary, but robust and workable, first version of a corporate planning system (COMOS I) was available. With the commitment of a third user it was possible within two months to construct a sales extrapolation model for one of the operating divisions. At first it simply substituted the manual calculation of "What if?" planning alternatives, but was of immediate practical use. Also with later projects, the first objective was often merely to automate the calculation of planning alternatives which previously had taken up to several work-months for each alternative. In this initial phase, the models were able to supply the user with a great number of more timely, consistent, and accurate planning alternatives. Such a pragmatic approach, starting with straightforward, rather simple, deterministic simulations, gradually turning to more complex applications, resulted in an identification of the user with his or her models. The models which are implemented at present were coded in an extremely modular fashion in order to allow a fast and flexible generation of alternative model structures. Indeed, different "What if?" or "What to do to achieve?" types of investigations frequently require changes in the model structure and in the method of solution from one computer experiment to another.

With one exception the models that are either being implemented or constructed at CIBA–GEIGY at present should perhaps not be called corporate planning models in a strict sense, because they are either not developed far enough to describe the firm's activities equally well in the areas of finance, marketing, and production, or they were developed to solve specific planning problems in a functional or organizational area with no initial intention to describe other areas as well. However, one may observe a tendency to extend the models to areas not foreseen initially, or to close gaps between models in different areas. As a consequence, the model builder's attention has shifted lately from mainly methodological and computational problems to questions of model and database compatibility and integration as well as goal formulation.

A CIBA–GEIGY master model does not exist. Instead a family of models for different users having different objectives was constructed. An identical database design and the same methodology was used for these models and this allows their linkage and integration. Especially the corporate financial models are fully integrated into the either rolling short- or middle-range planning procedure, but they may also be used for ad hoc investigations. Some of the marketing oriented models are intended to support short- or long-range ad hoc studies, but may be also used regularly.

FINANCE

Financial corporate models have been built for the CIBA–GEIGY Corporation as a whole, for two divisions on a worldwide basis, for one group company, and one division within another group company. At present another divisional model is under construction. The corporation model has already been used for three of the yearly middle-range planning cycles whereas the other implemented models have been used for two planning cycles. Originally the models worked on a yearly time base with a time horizon of ten years. However, in most investigations only three years of this planning horizon were evaluated. Some models have also been used for short-term budgeting purposes on a quarterly time base. The corporation model is based only upon monetary values. The divisional model with one group company is largely used for income margin simulations on a quarterly basis and possesses a database disaggregated down to the level of single products with historical measurements as well as planned and budgeted values of the model variables. A combination of subjective parametrization, statistical estimation, and forecasting models are used for the latter model, whereas the other financial models are subjectively parametrized. This will probably change when more historical measurements become available.

The financial models were constructed for the central control function of the company or planning and control functions within the divisions. The divisional models are among others used to generate base plan solutions to be fed into the corporation model.

The corporation model is at present the largest and furthest developed operating financial corporate model at CIBA–GEIGY. A first version was developed with the relatively small effort of some nine work-months. Originally it was used entirely in batch operation. An extended version now used obtains its inputs and specifications of model runs in on-line time-sharing mode using a light screen. Because the corporation model is characteristic of the other financial models, we shall discuss it in the paragraphs that follow.

Objectives of the Model

The model was intended to allow simulations on the divisional, functional, group company, and corporate level. The model input and output are usually in the form of divisional contribution statements, income statements, and balance sheets of the group companies as well as of the group as a whole, and tables with financial key figures. CIBA–GEIGY is subdivided into six divisions which operate on a worldwide basis with more than 60 group companies. Because 36 planning companies have been included in the model, it was necessary for model calculations to be carried out in about 250 tables or matrices of the order 50×100. The model was conceptually understood to be a tool for middle- to long-range computerized planning, intuitive forecasting, and general exploration purposes.

More specifically the objectives of the model are:

• To aggregate the various data in order to obtain an overall view of the group, divisions, or group–companies by means of income statements, balance sheets, and financial key figures.

• To evaluate critical factors and to quantify the influence that uncertain exogenous variables, such as raw material prices, currency parities, and labor costs have on the contribution of the different organizational units or the profit of the company as a whole.

• Essentially the same analysis should be feasible with respect to decision variables of the firm, that is, to simulate the effects of quantitative and qualitative policies, such as sales prices, large investments, and acquisitions.

• The model input should be largely based on the firm's effective budgeted or planned values of the model variables. The model output should be compatible with the information needed for the firm's established planning and control procedures.

Equations

The number and type of the model equations varies from experiment to experiment. (In the case that a simulation is carried out on the level of division per group company and consequences for the group as a whole have to be shown, several thousand equations must be evaluated.) This is the case, for example, for currency simulations which take the proportion of variable product costs and inventories accruing in other currencies into account. More than 90 percent of these equations are bookkeeping identities and definitions. The rest consist of a very few behavioral equations, some technological or institutional relations, and equilibrium and boundary conditions. Nearly all the equations are linear, deterministic, and recursive.

Simulations

Three types of questions, "What if?", "What to do to achieve?" and "No External Decision" questions, have been answered with the model.

1. **"What if?" experiments**: Due to their flexibility, they are most frequently met in practice. The user of the model supplies hypothetical management decisions, externally estimated parameters or states of a firm's internal or external environment to the model which quantifies the consequences as a function of time. Pure "What if?" experiments are generally exploration experiments.

2. **"What to do to achieve?" experiments**: The user of the model supplies target values or goals for some model variables as input to the model. The latter is used as

a device to determine possible decisions or internal and external developments which lead to the preassigned targets. This type of investigation may require the use of management science methods and may in practice be more complicated to perform than a "What if?" experiment.

3. "No External Decision" experiments: Here the user does not communicate with the model. This might be the case if the model structure is completely fixed and does not reflect any decisions, as occurs if a model is run in a report generator mode, for example, for aggregations, disaggregations, or consolidations. Alternatively, decision rules might entirely be determined within the scope of a model.

Model Tests and Validation

Since no historical values of the model variables were available, there was no other alternative than to test the consistency of the model output with respect to the results of a planning alternative which previously had been calculated manually.

Implementation and Experimentation

Immediately upon the first operational version of the model being completed, it became a valuable tool for the company's annual rolling three-year planning. Whereas the users specified their hypotheses and assumptions, the necessary coding and the model runs were initially carried out by the model builders in the central operations research department and presented to the user. In order to bring the user even closer to the model and to liberate the model builders from, in principle, a largely unnecessary service function, subsequent modules were programmed that allowed changing and editing the model database as well as specifying standard model runs in on-line operations. Members of the planning and control functions were trained in the use of the model, and model builder support is necessary only for the simulation of unforeseen events and an adaption of the model to changes in the planning procedures.

PRODUCTION

The hard core of the model, which is the most advanced and ambitious module from a methodological point of view, was initially a marketing submodel which generated and aggregated market forecasts for approximately 35 product groups and 65 sales countries of one of the divisions. It was used in 1973 for the divisions' long-range planning. When the long-range production capacities of approximately ten production plants subsequently became available, attention was transferred more to a worldwide capacity analysis also taking into consideration the distribution of the product groups. More recently cost and other financial data have been collected in order to show the effects of the marketing and production areas on a financial model segment.

Objectives of the Model

1. The model should allow the generation of demand forecasts by quantity over a ten-year time horizon on the product group and country level. The product groups are detailed according to the production processes involved rather than to the chemical or physical nature of the products. Since forecasts mainly have to be made for products

defined with respect to marketing criteria, it is necessary to regroup the results in order to yield forecasts of the required product categories. This allows the consideration not only of market developments but also of changes in the product mix and in the production technology. The lifetime of the individual products typically ranges between four and ten years and so does the time required for research and the development of a new product. Hence, forecasts have to be made for as yet nonexistent products as well as technologies. The model so far is in the main descriptive using intuitively formalized estimates and guesses.

2. Based upon the forecasts and given long-range capacity figures for ten production locations, a worldwide capacity balancing has to be carried out. The model should show the time-dependent differences between anticipated sales by quantity and the available capacities taking into account consequences of changing technologies and quantitative as well as qualitative changes in the demand forecasting assumptions.

3. Based on either user supplied and subjectively estimated production–distribution preferences or on consolidated sales and cost figures, the model should allow the generation of satisficing or optimizing production and sales allocations.

4. Using local sales and cost data, the model is intended to evaluate a marginal income analysis by product-group and production as well as sales country considering the implications of product transfers, changes in prices and costs, transfer or production sites, or changes in the distribution policy.

Model Data

Most of the financial model data, such as selling prices, distribution costs, production and labor costs, are taken from the firm's financial information systems. Various levels of data aggregation have to be dealt with so that tree structures of data are of great importance. The planning and modeling system known as COMOS II includes a database and statements to deal with this situation.

Other data concerning demand forecasts and production capacities have been collected manually. The capacities are typically defined in quantity units per year, sometimes for single product groups, in other instances for sums of product groups only. In several plants, capacities depend nonlinearly on the production mix of two product groups.

For the marketing segment of the model the user supplied subjectively estimated parameters of market growth, changes in product mix or technology, and production–distribution preferences. The latter, however, were estimated on the basis of known sales-distributions and information from the firm's financial information systems.

Equations

So far deterministic model equations have been used. The nonlinearities in the capacity constraints may be simplified by using linear approximations. The capacity balancing problem may then be solved by a decomposition of the linear program into a small linear program comprising only the nonnegativity and the capacity constraints for the linearized production mix problem and into a transportation program for the remaining quantities of product groups set at any time from one production plant location to all 65 countries.

The model also attains the structure of a mathematical or goal-programming model when local cost and marginal income data are taken into consideration in order to cope with intercompany sales of intermediate products.

Model Solution and Programming

It is difficult to estimate directly the work-effort that went into the project so far, since it strongly influenced the design, the programming and the construction of COMOS I and II, from which all the other projects have profited. Indeed, all calculations could be carried out within the frame of COMOS I, which was at that time extended to incorporate the Steppingstone algorithm and the Revised Simplex algorithm. The use of COMOS, however, made it possible to implement the first two segments of the model with an effort of the order of one work-year.

Testing and Validation

Validation was limited for this model because historical values on only the three past years were available. Only a few scenarios of the demand forecasting runs had previously been calculated manually. Hence, only face validation had been carried out so far.

Implementation

The marketing segment of the model was used to generate long-range demand forecasts in simple deterministic "What if?" type of investigations. Parameters of the life cycle and the technology change forecast functions were handled as decision variables and their effect on the demand was systematically tested by the generation of deterministic response surfaces. Such results were then used as input for the capacity balancing segment of the production–distribution segment in order to show capacity bottlenecks or to optimize a solution with respect to user specified production–distribution preferences.

MARKETING

Products

With the finance- and production-oriented models little weight has been put on the estimation of model parameters and formal statistical model verification. This will probably change to some extent as more historical measurements of the model variables become available and the model describes more accurately the firm's relationship to its surroundings.

CIBA–GEIGY marketing models for two of the subsidiary companies have been developed in exactly the opposite direction. Commencing with only a few stochastic linear or nonlinear model equations, they have been supplemented by a great number of mainly deterministic equations describing the financial and production segment.

Objectives

The models were intended to serve as tools for forecasting, controlling, and budgeting sales and income margins of single or groups of consumer products over a short- to mid-term time horizon. The basic time unit of the models was typically a month or quarter. More specifically the objectives of the models were:

•   To estimate advertisement and price coefficients or elasticities and thereby to quantify the effects which the decision variables of the user have on sales and market-share of the products of product–groups.

•   To enable management to budget product sales and income margins more accurately and to generate prospective predictions of sales with given values of the decision variables.

•   To allow a comparison of historically budgeted, forecasted, and effective values of the model variables. This should give indications about the predictive performance of the models and the reason for deviations between effective and budgeted values.

It was felt that the modeling results obtained in a number of econometric investigations did not justify the use of an optimization or target approach. Therefore, the investigations carried out were, for the most part, of the "What if?" category.

Data

The database for the models contains both cross-sectional and time series data. Four kinds of data may be distinguished: (1) full sample data which are manually collected within the firm, an example being advertising expenditures measured in impulses or values; (2) data from the firm's information systems such as sales by volume and value, sales prices, and different cost elements; (3) panel data obtained from external sources describing the market-share of own and competitor products, competitors' advertising expenditures and sales; and (4) some model data, such as transformation factors between advertising impulses and expenditures, that have to be estimated subjectively by the model user.

Equations

Deterministic and stochastic linear as well as nonlinear equations have been formulated for the two models mentioned. In contrast to the models previously described, a small number of behavioral equations ($m < 30$) form the "hard core" of the model. Identities and technological and institutional equations are large in number, but are employed only to relate the stochastic sales and market-share equations to a description of income margins on an individual product or product-group basis. The models had in most cases a recursive structure. However, in a number of instances linear simultaneous model equations were also employed.

The stochastic model equations were used mainly to describe the response and carry-over effects between sales and advertising as well as competitors' policies. As a consequence, the structural equations nearly always took the form of distributed lags. Typically some 40–60 measurements of the model variables were available. With COMOS II such lag distributions are generated by prepared macroinstructions.

Estimation, Solution, and Simulation

COMOS II provides the ordinary least-squares method (OLS), the two-stage, least-squares method, and an algorithm for nonlinear estimation. In most cases OLS-estimation was and is employed. The estimated coefficients and their empirical variance–covariance matrix were then used to generate point or interval predictions, once the values of the external and decision variables had been specified. External variables were either forecast or, especially in the financial segment of the models, extrapolated or interpolated with simple interpolation and extrapolation methods available in COMOS. The solution or simulation of the models so far was straightforward because they were mostly linear and recursive. Nonlinear model equations contained only predetermined, external, and decision variables as explanatory variables.

Testing and Validation

Heavy use of statistical specification and verification testing was employed with the models mentioned. The tests available for these purposes in COMOS include the Durbin periodogram test, the Farrar–Glauber multicollinearity tests and the Cochrane–Orcutt procedure to cope with models containing predetermined variables.

Results and implementation

The models described were used for ad hoc and regular investigations. So far it was possible in about 50 percent of the investigations to obtain statistically significant results which, however, were not always found plausible and compatible with the user's *a priori* knowledge and intentions. In contrast to the other models described above, the model–manager interface was difficult to establish with the econometric models. However, certain stable modeling results have been obtained over the years. Recent field studies in which consumers were asked about their purchasing behavior have to some extent confirmed the results of the econometric analysis and have led to media–mix decisions.

PERSONNEL PLANNING

It is possible to connect a personnel planning model to the corporate financial model described above. The linkage is accomplished by feeding labor costs and sales values from the financial model into the personnel planning model which is based on different personnel categories and hierarchical grades in the planning group companies. The model has been constructed for the central management development department in cooperation with the personnel and operations research departments.

Objectives

The model is intended to serve as an instrument for long-range personnel planning on a worldwide basis. The planning horizon is up to ten years on a yearly time base. The model shows the effects of different business expansion or contraction rates, retirement and leaving rates on the demand for certain categories of employees and their age distribution. It distinguishes among approximately 700 populations which are subdivided into two hierarchical grades, fourteen geographical regions, and five types of activity.

Data

The database of the model contains data from the firm's information systems or financial models, such as age distributions, number of employees, labor costs, and sales. Other data were collected manually, examples being national pension data, death and leaving rates, and historical data on promotion and hiring. For comparison purposes, some time series on the development of the labor force and deflated sales of the main competitors were collected from published sources.

Equations

The basic model structure consists of a controlled Markov-chain as has been explicitly described by Bartholomew. Most of the equations are identities or first-order deterministic and recursive difference equations that describe the expected development of grade sizes and their variances. However, in a number of model runs they were linked to stochastic extrapolations of sales volumes.

Estimation, Solution, and Simulation

Econometric estimation methods were employed to estimate elasticities between deflated sales and the number of employees from historical data. Transition probabilities for the Markov-chain were estimated from manually collected data outside the model. Both the deterministic and stochastic model simulations involve a combination of "What if?" and "What to do to achieve?" analysis. The user formulates "What if?" hypotheses about the development of sales and/or certain goal values for certain personnel categories. The model then calculates the necessary recruitments and promotions.

Testing and Validation

The face validity of the model was established with the user. Ex ante forecasts for one year were found to be compatible with the measurements.

Results and Implementation

The model showed for several populations and areas discrepancies between personnel requirements and actual or forecasted populations. Within the planning process it will also be used in the future for ad hoc and regular investigations.

Response surfaces of the model showing important output variables, such as success rates and mean waiting times, as a function of extrapolation parameters were estimated using second-order rotatable designs.

SOFTWARE SUPPORT

The models briefly described were supported by a planning and modeling software system called COMOS (*Co*rporate *Mo*deling *S*ystem). It incorporates a standardized database, a special purpose corporate simulation language, and integrated software as well as interlanguage communication facilities. The function of these components may be seen roughly in Fig. 11.27.

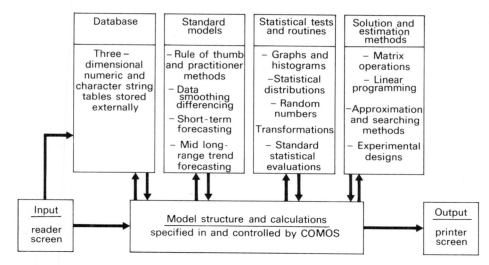

Database	Standard models	Statistical tests and routines	Solution and estimation methods
Three – dimensional numeric and character string tables stored externally	– Rule of thumb and practitioner methods – Data smoothing differencing – Short-term forecasting – Mid long-range trend forecasting	– Graphs and histograms –Statistical distributions – Random numbers Transformations – Standard statistical evaluations	– Matrix operations – Linear programming –Approximation and searching methods – Experimental designs

Input	Model structure and calculations specified in and controlled by COMOS	Output
reader screen		printer screen

Fig. 11.27 COMOS II components.

Database

Utility programs allow the generation, updating, and deletion of a model's database from card or screen input. The database consists of records of an indexed sequential file that are organized in tables. These may contain both numeric and character string data. All tables possess three dimensions. Often columns of a table contain the values of a variable in different periods. A table line item then corresponds to a specific variable. The third table dimension may then be used to store the results of different model runs or different alternatives generated in one investigation such as expected, optimistic, or pessimistic results (Fig. 11.28). Table dimensions may also be differently defined and could, for example, correspond to production locations, sales regions, and capacities.

THE COMOS LANGUAGE AND SOFTWARE

A user or model builder codes his or her model and specifies operations to be performed for different modeling steps in the free-format compiled corporate simulation language COMOS II. Earlier projects were undertaken using COMOS I, a fixed format linear interpreter. COMOS II has been developed on the basis of PL/1 and ASSEMBLER and possesses distinct compile, link, and processing steps. It allows for logical branching and repetitive evaluation of groups of statements. Aggregated commands allow direct access to the database and modeling software indicated in Fig. 11.28.

Although COMOS II also supports the construction of simple "Ad-Hoc-" and "Throw-Away-Models", notably in the financial area, it was designed primarily to support the modeling steps initially mentioned for models having a bigger database

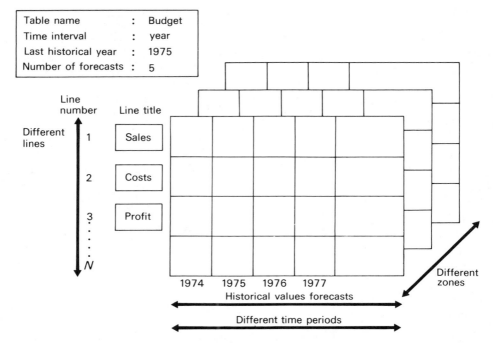

Fig. 11.28 Logical organization of COMOS database for numeric data.

and a greater number of structural equations. Typically with this type of model the specification of hypotheses and model runs is more likely to be a time-bottleneck than to be turn-around times between model runs. In a number of more recent applications, model parameters and changes to the database were specified in an interactive model using a screen-terminal. Also certain modeling results may thus be displayed. However, the steps of the model design procedure are normally carried out in batch-mode. Two points were especially emphasized during the development of the system: First, the COMOS II language should possess a number of heavily aggregated macros and statements which simultaneously reduce the number of statements to be written compared to the number to be written in a general purpose language and make the code more transparent and easier to comprehend. Because of these properties, models often become more flexible and easier to change than are models coded in a general purpose language. Second, using a CALL statement users should be able to either link fixed blocks of systems software of different degrees of sophistication or routines which they have prepared themselves in COMOS II or PL/1 directly to their COMOS model. As such, the system should support the construction of management science models "in a favorable software environment."

TYPE OF USERS

The system has been designed in such a way that users not having a background in data processing or quantitative methods may themselves specify, run, and test certain models. However, the users' backgrounds strongly determine the extent to which they are able to code a certain model and to make use of the available software. The present system is not an educational tool; that is, it cannot teach a user how to use an econometric analysis, experimental designs, or mathematical programming. But the system by its flexibility may support the instruction of users in these methods.

More technically oriented users also profit from the available software. Because the system directly allows for PL/1 subroutines, such users may, in some instances, sacrifice the transparency, flexibility, and compactness of a COMOS II calling program for a PL/1 program which allows a faster execution. Similarly, as with models and methods, it largely depends on the user and problem where the exact boundary between COMOS II and PL/1 modules is drawn.

Integrated Power System Planning Model

DOUGLAS H. WALTERS AND R. TABER JENKINS[5]

INTRODUCTION

The TVA Power Program Integrated Planning Model (IPM) is a system of computer programs and associated data files that make it possible for TVA's Power Program strategies to be tested for feasibility and for probable outcomes to be evaluated so as to facilitate the formulation of tactical plans. The purpose of the model is to support the development of a set of consistent strategic plans that properly consider market forecast, production, and financial implications. It may be of interest to discuss some of the background of the model before discussing the model itself.

Background

The need for an integrated planning model for the TVA power program has been recognized for a number of years. Individual portions of such a model had been built and were in routine use. In the spring of 1974, serious discussions began concerning a concentrated effort to develop a full model and authorization to begin construction of such a model was obtained in January, 1975. A team of ten people was assembled which included planning engineers, system analysts, an economist, and programmers. The first activities consisted of developing a conceptual design, a task which took about three months. For the most part, concepts developed in the existing programs were carried over to the IPM. In the detail design, however, it was decided to restructure

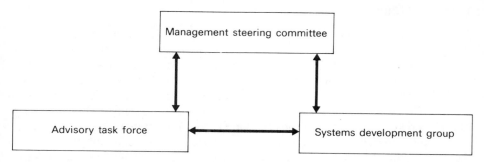

Fig. 11.29 Organizational structure for the TVA power program integrated planning model.

the coding in the existing models. Most of the detailed designs were completed by October, 1975. Coding was completed on some modules in March, 1976. Coding continued on the remaining modules and was essentially completed in December, 1976.

The organizational structure consisted of a Management Steering Committee, an Advisory Task Force, and the Systems Development Group as shown in Fig. 11.29. The Management Steering Committee, comprised of the heads of each of the involved organizations, acted as the final review group and set general policy guidelines. The Advisory Task Force included first-line managers of the different organizations that would either be the model users or would supply data to the model. They operated in a technical consultant capacity. The Systems Development Group performed the actual design development and initial testing of the model.

Overview of Strategic Planning

In order to better understand the intended use of the model, a look at a strategic planning system might be helpful. Figure 11.30 shows an integrated planning system where the first step is to review the external corporate environment. Scenarios dealing with such things as the national economy outlook, market competition, etc., are developed and expressed as exogenous variables to the system. Next, goals and objectives are established, for example, the market position amount of regional growth. These goals and objectives are then translated into strategic plans, such as product mixes, raw material and service supply strategies, and marketing programs. These plans are then tested to determine their feasibility and probable outcomes. An interactive process is established to determine if the probable outcomes would satisfy the initial goals and objectives. If not, modified or net strategic plans are developed until it is possible to arrive at a feasible set of plans. These strategic plans are then translated into tactical plans, such as how and where certain raw materials will be supplied. Detailed expansion plans and the associated capital needs are also a part of the tactical planning phase.

At this time, another interactive loop may be necessary to test feasibility and determine probable outcomes. Once the tactical plans (and ideally a set of contingency plans) are developed, the next step is to determine detailed budget items and then a

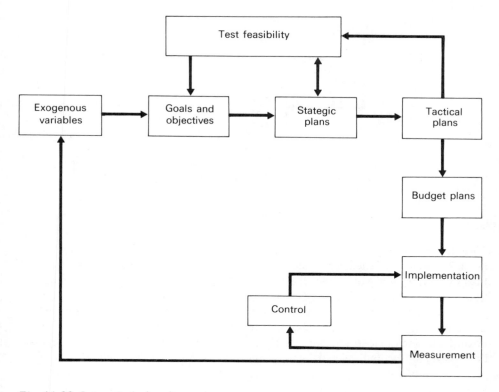

Fig. 11.30 Integrated planning system.

plan of implementation. Monitoring and a control function are necessary in any planning system in order to determine when certain areas such as raw material supplies need attention. These monitoring and control functions should be able to answer the question, "How is it going?" If deviations are severe enough, the total process may need to be repeated. As a matter of routine, the planning system would be exercised twice a year with the mid-year review being an adjustment function and the annual review being a full-scale review.

Overview of the Integrated Planning Model

In the most basic form, the IPM can be viewed as a traditional corporate model because it includes sales, production and finance. Figure 11.31 shows the Marketing Forecast that drives the Production Simulator that, in turn, is input to the Financial Simulator. The feedback is shown to depict an elasticity function. Another way of viewing the IPM is the typical input, processing, and output functions. Figure 11.32 indicates this type of division of the various modules. The input processing modules are the National Econometric Forecast, Plant Capital Cost, Fossil Fuel Unit Cost, Nuclear Fuel Component Cost, and Regional Market Forecast. These input modules are all used to

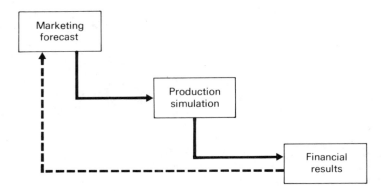

Fig. 11.31 TVA integrated planning model.

drive the processing or simulation modules which include: Nuclear Refueling and Fossil Maintenance Scheduler, System Operations, Nuclear Fuel Cost Allocator, Fossil Fuel Cost Allocator, Nonfuel Operations and Maintenance Cost, Financial, Wholesale Rate, Transmission System, and Generation System Expansion. The output modules do not provide direct input to the rest of the modules and can be viewed somewhat as report generators. These modules are Consumer Price; Environmental Accounting; Fossil Fuel Management; and Nuclear Fuel Management. Figure 11.33 is a conceptual flow diagram that indicates the interconnection of the various modules. It would probably be of value to spend some time discussing this chart and briefly indicate the function each module performs.

Flow of information is primarily from top to bottom and more or less represents the sequence in which the modules would be exercised. The initial step is to define

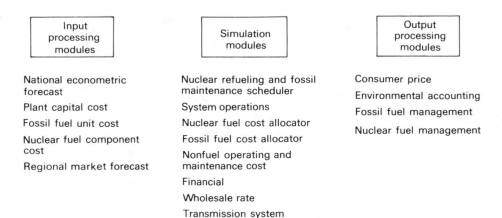

Fig. 11.32 Integrated planning model.

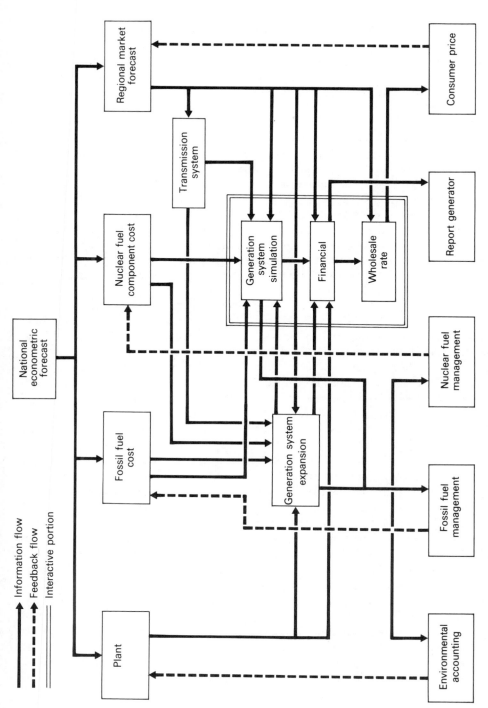

Fig. 11.33 TVA power program integrated planning model design in concept (schematic).

the base case scenario of the national economy with particular emphasis on the energy sector. This information is then used by the National Econometric forecast module which, in turn, will define some 50 indices for various commodities and also set up the references for the TVA regional energy forecast. The regional energy forecast is obtained from the Regional Market Forecast Module. Outputs from this module include an hourly load forecast, monthly energy and demand forecast, and the expected revenues based on the current rate structure. Parallel to the market forecast, three modules are used to set up base capital costs for an expansion alternative and the fossil and nuclear fuel costs. These modules are the Plant Capital Cost, Fossil Fuel Cost, and Nuclear Fuel Component Cost modules, respectively.

The Transmission System module estimates nominal losses and also certain generation constraints that would represent transmission security considerations. Once the load forecast, capital cost, fuel costs, and transmission limitations are obtained, the next step is to exercise the Generation System Expansion module. This module determines the optimal capacity expansion schedule for the time period under study from an initial list of available alternatives. After the expanded system has been established, the next activity is to simulate the expanded system in order to determine how the individual units can be expected to operate.

In order to perform this simulation, a planned maintenance and nuclear refueling schedule must be established. The system is then simulated on an hour-by-hour basis taking into account the random outages, minimum shutdown times, and other unit constraints. The resulting simulated operations are then translated into expense through the Fossil Fuel and Nuclear Fuel Cost Allocator modules and an Operating and Maintenance Cost Estimate module. The resulting operating expense, along with depreciation, interest, and other expense, is combined in the Financial module and compared with the forecasted revenue from the Regional Market Forecast module. A need for additional revenue is indicated when one or more of the financial tests are not satisfied. This additional revenue figure is then passed on to the Wholesale Rate module which will adjust the rates in order to provide the additional revenue.

Since TVA is primarily an energy wholesaler, an additional step is needed to determine the price the ultimate consumer will pay and this operation is performed in the Consumer Price module. For TVA this is considered an output module. The broken line from the Consumer Price module to the Regional Market Forecast module indicates a feedback path in the form of a price demand electricity function. This feedback is not, however, a "hard-coded" iterative loop. Other output modules are the Fossil Fuel Management and Nuclear Fuel Management modules. These are essentially macro supply-and-demand models of their respective industry sectors and, again, the broken feedback loops to their individual costing modules are included. The Environmental Accounting module reports point-source residual output from each of the plants. These outputs could be utilized by transport models to determine their ultimate impacts. If certain environmental objectives are not satisfied, modifications to the capital cost might be indicated; thus, the broken feedback line to the Plant Capital Cost module. With this overview, it would be appropriate to discuss in some detail the portions of the model that have been under active construction.

A CLOSER LOOK AT THE IPM MODEL

We will take a step-by-step look at the model beginning with the National Econometric Forecast module, then the Regional Market Forecast, the Generation System Simulation, the Financial, and finally the Wholesale Rate modules.

The National Econometric Forecast

The National Econometric Forecast module uses the Wharton Annual Model as its basic forecasting tool. The Wharton Model is a macroeconometric input/output model. The input/output matrix is 47 × 47 and the total system is represented by approximately 400 equations. Basically, the Wharton Model starts with a final demand and through the input/output matrix determines the required supply. Price adjustment, along with commodity substitution, is used to obtain an equilibrium between the final demand and supply sectors. This process of reaching an equilibrium is repeated each year to obtain a ten-year forecast. The National Econometric Forecast module projects different indices (currently 26 in number, but envisioned to exceed 100, ultimately) based on a statistical fit of the particular index to combinations of different variables derived from historical data. Then, as these variables are forecasted by the Wharton Model, the same combination of these variables is used to project the particular index. This process is repeated for each index for each year up to ten years. After ten years the variables, and hence the indices, are trended to as many years as are needed. These 26 indices, which are used by the other modules, maintain a consistency throughout the IPM and, thus, maintain consistency with the base scenario. Once the basic economic forecast is obtained, the next step is to exercise the Regional Market Forecast module.

Regional Market Forecast Module

This module forecasts the energy sales in the form of peak and energy on several different time bases for up to 50 years and is shown in Fig. 11.34. The module first determines an annual energy requirement based on an econometric approach. The annual energy forecast considers regionalized forecasted parameters such as population and labor demands. The following sectors are included: total residential, commercial, and industrial demands served by TVA distributors on a 2-digit SIC code basis category and directly served industries on a 4-digit SIC code base. Once the annual energy forecast has been completed, the monthly peak and energy forecast by both system and geographic areas within the system are obtained. This is accomplished by forecasting the directly served industries and federal monthly peak separately and then using an average load based on seasonal parameters and monthly load factors to determine the rest of the system peaks. The monthly peaks and energies are provided for the following categories: residential, distributor served commercial and industrial under 5000 Kw and over 5000 Kw, distributor total purchases, and the directly served industries and federal agencies. Along with the above peak and energy forecast, a forecast of monthly revenues by energy and demand charges is also provided. The next step is to decompose the monthly forecasts into hourly loads. Currently this step is performed using historical indices of hourly loads to monthly peaks in order to obtain

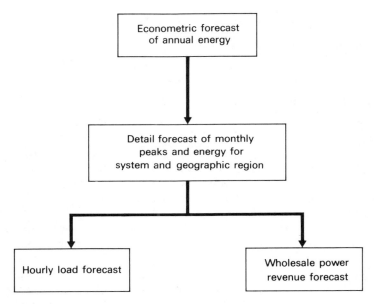

Fig. 11.34 Regional market forecast.

the hourly projections. Under development is a methodology that forecasts hourly loads based on weather data, seasonal adjustments, day of the week, hour of the day, base load, and class of customer (conceptually projected). After the market forecast is complete, the next module is the Generation System Simulation.

Generation System Simulation

This module, depicted in Figs. 11.35 and 11.36, actually consists of five submodules which are Maintenance and Refueling Scheduler, Power System Operation Simulation, Nuclear Fuel Cost Allocator, Fossil Fuel Cost Allocator, and Nonfuel Operations and Maintenance.

Each of these submodules will be addressed separately. It should be noted that an expansion schedule is assumed to be given at this point. The system expansion program has not, at this time, been interfaced into the model; therefore, its output must be input into the IPM.

Maintenance and Refueling Scheduler

The first activity in the system simulation is to determine a feasible schedule for planned outages as shown in Fig. 11.35. This schedule includes maintenance for coal-fired units and refueling of nuclear units. It is assumed that the planned nuclear maintenance will be performed during the refueling outage. The algorithm for the scheduler is a heuristic one and, basically, seeks to levelize risk (percent reserves) by scheduling unit outages during periods when loads are low. The basic time period is expressed in weeks. The generating unit maintenance requirements and constraints

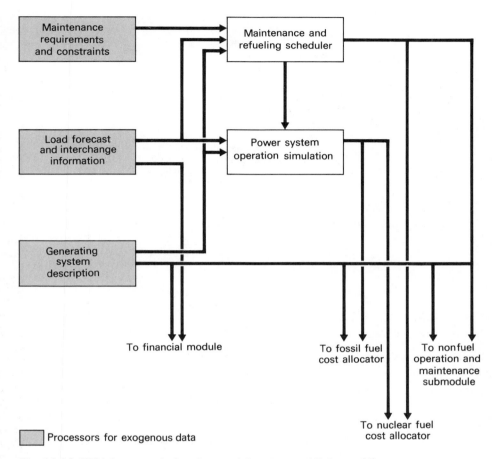

Fig. 11.35 TVA integrated planning model conceptual linkages (1).

are used to construct "windows" of sufficient frequency so that expected maintenance functions can be performed. Then the units with the most stringent requirements are scheduled first with the units having the most flexibility being scheduled last. The actual placement in the windows is determined by the amount of reserves available. The scheduler operates on a moving two-year time span with the first year being fixed once a successful schedule is obtained and the second year being flexible or "soft." The procedure is then to advance one year and the previously computed "soft" schedule is discarded and a new schedule computed using the information available about the next year. This technique allows coupling from one year to the next and is continued until the end of the planning horizon is reached. In the event a schedule cannot be obtained without violating the constraints, the constraints are relaxed on a priority basis until a schedule is obtained. These relaxed constraints are documented and the user determines if a real problem exists. The output of the scheduler is a

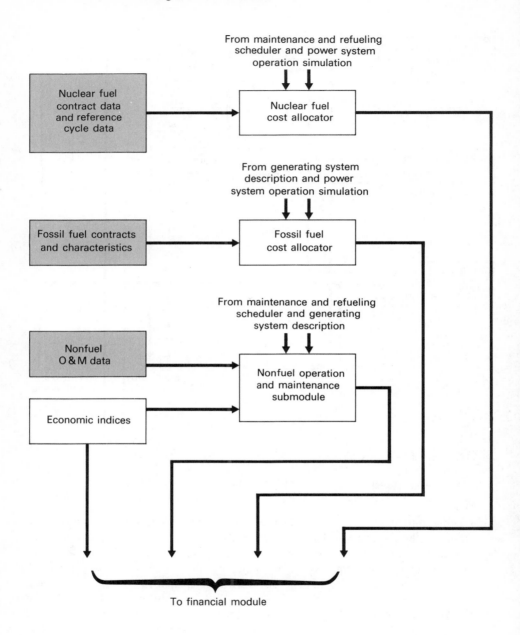

Fig. 11.36 TVA integrated planning model conceptual linkages (2).

planned outage schedule for each unit, a system reliability index for each week, a staffing and material requirements schedule, and a nuclear energy allocation schedule.

Power System Operation Simulation

The next submodule to be exercised is the Power System Operation Simulation. This submodule, as shown in Fig. 11.35, is designed to predict the response of the individual units that comprise the power system to a specific set of system loads. System constraints, such as the planned outage schedule and commitment order, as well as individual unit constraints, such as random forced outages and minimum downtimes, are represented. The simulator will handle all types of generating units including multiple pumped-storage and energy-limited units. The simulator operates on a hourly time period. The algorithm starts by considering the initial unit commitment on the basis of hydro and energy-limited plants. Once the committed units are determined, the simulator performs an economic dispatch and computes the system's incremental costs for each hour. The remaining portions of the hydro and energy-limited plants are dispatched on the basis of reducing the highest system incremental costs. After the new dispatch has been completed, new system incremental costs are calculated for those hours in which changes occurred. The next step is to dispatch the pumped-storage units on the basis of savings in system costs by recommitting and dispatching units based on a consideration of the expected system savings from generation of the pumped storage and the cost of pumpings. Reservoir constraints must be recognized during this process in that generation cannot exist with an empty reservoir nor can pumping occur with a full reservoir. The operation of the pumped-storage units is increased until no further system savings are realized. The system savings and costs, as well as individual unit operations, are determined by a stochastic energy allocation subroutine and, thus, the system costs are expected costs. The method used is a modified form of a method as developed by Baleriaux and extended in work by Booth. The last step is to compute probablistically the thermal energy production of each unit for each hour and sum the results for the week. In addition to the energy production by unit, the simulator computes the number of startups and shutdowns by unit as well as purchases of energy from other utilities and the usage of interruptible power. This information is then passed on to the rest of the submodules and to the Financial module.

Nuclear Fuel Cost Accounting

The basic function of this activity as shown in Fig. 11.36 is to convert the cost accounting data, which uses an averaging technique, into "batch" cost in a manner that properly accounts for the interest on the working capital used in manufacturing the fuel. The submodule treats the credit for discharged materials and also the condition in which the simulated extracted energy is different from the design energies. The basic steps are to first determine, batch by batch, if the simulated delivered energies are different from the design energies. If they are different, this difference is allocated among the remaining batches in the reactor unless the lead time is sufficient to modify the replacement fuel. (It should be noted that only one-fourth to one-third of the fuel is replaced during a refueling.) The cash flow is calculated for the new fuel along with the cash flow for the payments and credits for the discharged fuel. Using the cash flow associated with the batch, a unit cost of energy delivered which includes an estimate for the cost of capital is calculated. The steps above are repeated for all batches and all reactors for the period of study. The next step is to calculate the cycle unit cost considering the batch costs in relation to the batch energies produced during a given operating cycle. A cycle is the operation from startup to startup including the refueling outage occurring at the end of the cycle. The results obtained include the total nuclear fuel cash flow, monthly nuclear fuel expense, the nuclear unit cost of operation, and an updated schedule of required nuclear fuel materials and services.

Fossil Fuel Cost Allocator

The next submodule is the Fossil Fuel Cost Allocator. The Fossil Fuel Cost Allocator, shown in Fig. 11.36, develops the unit cost of fossil fuel for each fuel group at each plant. TVA's fossil-fired plants use coal as their primary fuel and oil during startup operations. The basic algorithm is an inventory accounting problem in which costs are averaged. It starts with beginning inventories and adds new deliveries and handling charges. Unit costs are calculated on an average cost per unit of heat. The simulated weekly burn from the System Operation submodule is then used to adjust the ending inventories. The process above is repeated for all periods under study for all plants. The results are the unit cost and the average heating value of fuel for each fossil-fired plant.

Nonfuel Operation and Maintenance

The final function in the Generation System Simulation module is the Nonfuel Operation and Maintenance submodule. This function, also shown in Fig. 11.36, is designed to forecast all nonfuel operating, maintenance, and transmission expenses as well as capitalized expenditures for plant upgrading. These expenses are divided into two primary categories: (1) expenses associated with planned outages and (2) expenses that occur on a regular or random basis. The expenses associated with the planned outages are computed by assigning escalated costs associated with the required resources that were obtained from the Maintenance and Refueling Scheduler. The resources are broken down into various categories of labor and materials. The rest of the expense—operating, running, and emergency outages and transmission—is computed based on historical data. Once this function is complete, the total operating and maintenance expenses, including the expense of fuel, are available so that the Financial module can be operated.

Financial Module

The Financial module, shown in Fig. 11.37, is used to analyze the simulated power system's operation in financial terms using both monthly and annual cycles. It computes the revenue requirements while considering TVA's statutory and legal requirements contained in the TVA Act, bond resolutions, and various TVA financial policies. The algorithm is used basically to compute and sum all inputted expenses along with a small margin in order to arrive at the total required revenue. This figure

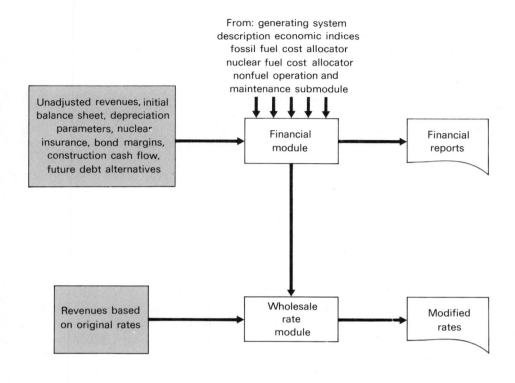

Fig. 11.37 TVA integrated planning model conceptual linkages (3).

is compared with the forecasted revenue figure from the Regional Market Forecast module. If the required revenues computed by the Financial module are greater than the forecasted revenue figure from the Regional Market Forecast model, then this information is stored. The module arrives at the required revenue figure by first computing payment in lieu of taxes based on the previous year's nonfederal revenues and also periodic payments to the United States Treasury. Interest on the outstanding debt is calculated along with the interest rate to be applied to the construction work in progress and nuclear fuel.

The next step is to calculate the construction cash flow and make the appropriate modification for projects completed during the month. This step is followed by computing the depreciation on capitalized items and then the interest and expense for nuclear fuel. After the fuel and materials expenses are obtained, three revenue bond tests are applied. There are several options available depending on the results of the bond test, but each of these yields the required revenue.

It should be noted that credit for an automatic monthly fuel adjustment is considered and these resulting revenues are added to the original forecasted revenues. Any additional revenue adjustments are then calculated. The total required capital is also computed.

If additional borrowings are required, the amount is determined and the outstanding debt is updated. The last check is on the debt ceiling and then the process starts again for the next period. The results will include annual cashflow statements, balance sheets, and such financial statistics as capital requirements and resources, investment projections, and payment in lieu of taxes. Revenue adjustments are also supplied to the Wholesale Rate module.

Wholesale Rate Module

This function, shown in Fig. 11.37, must translate the revenue adjustments determined in the Financial module to rate adjustments in both the demand charges and/or the energy charges. It should be pointed out that the basic rate structure is not modified in that the adjustments above are applied in addition to the existing wholesale rate structures. The revenues collected from the sale of electricity are from four basic categories of customers: power distributors, federal agencies, directly served industries, and other electric utilities. The power distributors purchase power under a wholesale rate, the directly served industries and federal agencies purchase power under a general power or commercial rate, and the other electric utilities are charged according to the provisions of individual contracts. Each of these rates and their constraints are recognized. Provisions are also made to consider changes in facilities' rental charges, load density credits, etc. The final results are demand and energy charge adjustments to both the wholesale rate and general or commercial power rates and a cost allocation study reflecting the relative margin of each customer class.

SUMMARY

The discussion above provides a general overview of the concepts of integrated planning for an electric utility system and the various functions involved. The testing for feasibility function was then described in terms of a model that further delineated the various tasks involved. Additional discussion was included that briefly described each of these tasks, their interactions, and the sequence in which these tasks are performed. A modular system of computer programs, their individual tasks, their methodology, and their communication links were then briefly described.

NOTES

1. David F. Weigel and Lucy Quintilliano, authors of the Hammermill case study, are, respectively, Manager of Business Systems and Corporate Planning Administrator.
2. Leonard Forman, Ph.D., author of the *New York Times* case study, is Director of Economic Research of the *New York Times*.
3. A project of this scope could not be undertaken without the enthusiastic and active support of top management and the Division personnel involved. This support

included the Corporate President; Corporate Vice-President of Planning; President of the Operating Division; Corporate Director of Management Information Services, and many operating and staff personnel throughout the company.

4. CIBA–GEIGY Corporation and Basle University/Switzerland. This paper is based on the book by Friedrich Rosenkranz entitled *An Introduction to Corporate Modeling*. Durham, North Carolina: Duke University Press, 1978.

5. The authors of this article are on the staff of the Tennessee Valley Authority, Chattanooga, Tennessee. Douglas H. Walters, Ph.D., is Supervisor of the Systems Development Staff, Division of Power Resource Planning. R. Taber Jenkins is Supervisor of the Systems Planning and Development Staff.

Appendixes

Appendix A:
SIMPLAN: A Planning and Modeling System

THOMAS H. NAYLOR, R. BRITTON MAYO, AND HORST SCHAULAND

INTRODUCTION

SIMPLAN[1] is a multipurpose planning, budgeting, and modeling system for (1) strategic, tactical, and operational planning; (2) cash management; (3) financial forecasting; (4) profit planning; (5) budgeting; (6) financial consolidation; (7) financial reporting; (8) capital investment evaluation; (9) sales forecasting and time series analysis; and (10) econometric modeling. Although SIMPLAN is extremely powerful and flexible, it can be easily mastered and put to work as a decision analysis tool by nontechnical managers, planners, and financial analysts who have had no previous experience in computer modeling.

With SIMPLAN, 16 major functions are integrated into a single planning and modeling system. These functions include:

- Database creation
- Database manipulation
- Consolidation
- Model specification
- Model changes
- Report formulation
- Report changes
- Statistical analysis

- Forecasting
- Econometrics
- Model solution
- Validation
- Policy simulation
- Report generation
- Security
- Graphical display

The aforementioned functional objectives are achieved in SIMPLAN with the aid of five completely integrated subsystems:

- Planning system
- Management information system
- Modeling system

- Forecasting system
- Econometric modeling system

The primary rationale underlying the use of SIMPLAN is that SIMPLAN enables the user to achieve significant reductions in the total cost of planning, budgeting, and modeling projects by reducing the cost of manipulating data, coding models and reports, solving models, and performing statistical and econometric forecasts and analyses. Some users have reduced their programming time by as much as 50 to 80 percent by using SIMPLAN rather than a general purpose language like FORTRAN or COBOL. In summary, SIMPLAN provides the user with a considerable amount of power and flexibility in a user-oriented environment.

APPLICATIONS

Strategic, tactical, and operational planning SIMPLAN was designed especially to facilitate such varied planning and control functions as capital budgeting, corporate strategic planning, policy simulation, cash management, tax planning, profit planning, sales forecasting, market planning, product analysis, and long-term financing. SIMPLAN models may be as simple or as complex as the functions they are designed to serve. They may be implemented independently, in combination with other models, or as modular components of an integrated corporate model.

Cash management Cash management models can assist financial managers in efforts to improve cash flow and liquidity and to maintain minimum levels of uninvested cash. With SIMPLAN, effective cash management models are easy to formulate and implement.

Financial forecasting SIMPLAN provides a flexible system which can be used to project the company's future financial condition. Pro forma income statements, balance sheets, sources-and-uses-of-funds statements, and financial ratios can be generated for any number of reporting periods. SIMPLAN can aid in evaluating past financial performance and can provide "What if?" forecasts to simulate the effects of both alternative management policies and anticipated external events on the projected financial position of the company.

Profit planning SIMPLAN is a convenient tool for developing short- and long-term profit plans, especially for companies with multiple divisions or profit centers. Division marketing and production plans are easily integrated into division financial plans and consolidated into a corporate plan. Major or minor changes to plans may be initiated at the appropriate levels and incorporated automatically into the consolidated plan.

Budgeting Multiperiod budgets, division and consolidated budgets, variance analyses, and financial forecasts are typical SIMPLAN applications. Multiple consolidations may be performed across virtually any number of divisions, departments, products, etc. Budgeting models can interact with SIMPLAN financial, forecasting, and econometric models to generate multiple contingency budgets for alternative strategies.

Financial consolidation and allocation Vertical and horizontal financial consolidations are easily accomplished with SIMPLAN for multiple regions, divisions, groups, businesses, subsidiaries, profit centers, and products. In addition, SIMPLAN models can be used to allocate burden back down to cost centers for reconsolidation at all levels.

Financial reporting SIMPLAN supports the principle that managers should have the facility to specify whatever types of reports they may desire. User-specified reports are easy to develop and easy to change and correct. Among the different types of reports that may be produced with SIMPLAN are financial statements and analyses, consolidations, financial compliance reports, budgets and variance reports, cost accounting reports, sales analyses, performance comparisons, depreciation and amortization schedules, benefit administration, and funds accounting reports.

Capital investment evaluation Capital budgeting and investment evaluation are among the more important applications of SIMPLAN. SIMPLAN models can calculate such measurements as internal rate of return, discounted cash flow, present values, and future values. Revenues, expenses, and cash flows associated with a proposed investment may be projected with such factors as depreciation, amortization, cost-of-capital, taxes and tax credits, contingent costs, and future residual values either given or based on any formula. Lease/purchase and make/buy decisions may be evaluated.

Sales forecasting and time series analysis For forecasting sales, interest rates, material supplies, factor input prices, and other key variables, SIMPLAN offers a variety of time series forecasting models. These include time trends, exponential smoothing, and adaptive forecasting. Forecasts developed by any of these methods may be incorporated directly into SIMPLAN models and reports.

Econometric modeling Sales, market share, and industry econometric models can, with SIMPLAN, be specified, estimated, validated, simulated, and linked directly to division financial and production models or corporate financial models. SIMPLAN can be used to estimate single-equation and simultaneous-equation linear and nonlinear models to simulate the effects of alternative marketing strategies and economic conditions on market share and industry demand. Direct access from SIMPLAN to all series of the NBER macroeconomic database is available on several time-sharing networks. SIMPLAN can also be modified to access other national econometric models and databases.

FUNCTIONS

SIMPLAN utilizes six basic sets of commands known as modes to implement the sixteen functions outlined in Fig. A.1. The SIMPLAN modes are listed below:

MODE	*FUNCTIONS*
DATA	1. Database creation
	2. Database maintenance
	3. Consolidation
EDIT	4. Model specification
	5. Model changes

SIMPLAN modes

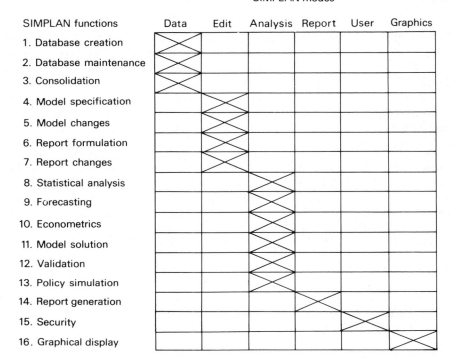

Fig. A.1 SIMPLAN functions and models.

ANALYSIS

6. Report formulation
7. Report changes
8. Statistical analysis
9. Forecasting
10. Econometrics
11. Model solution
12. Validation
13. Policy simulation

REPORT   14. Report generation

USER   15. Security

GRAPHICS   16. Graphical display

SIMPLAN modes permit the user to operate only on that information which is directly relevant to a particular function. In SIMPLAN, models, reports, and data are separate thus providing the user with a degree of flexibility which is not available in most planning and modeling systems.

Database creation SIMPLAN contains its own database system which can be used to store historical data or data generated by SIMPLAN models. Through customized interfaces SIMPLAN can also be linked to the user's database or to other external databases including national economic and financial databases. The SIMPLAN database is created by the user through Data Mode. Data may be read into the SIMPLAN database either interactively through a time-sharing terminal or, in the case of large volumes of data, through batch techniques.

Database maintenance Database maintenance functions are also performed in SIMPLAN with Data Mode. Data may be entered or deleted; values may be removed or changed; and data may be listed in Data Mode.

Consolidation Both horizontal and vertical consolidations of divisional, group, business unit, or product data can be easily implemented within Data Mode. SIMPLAN's consolidation features will be described in more detail in the section entitled "Consolidated Planning Models."

Model specification A wide variety of different types of models can be specified by the user in Edit Mode. SIMPLAN models take the form of finite difference equations. The user may specify recursive, simultaneous-equation, linear, or nonlinear models in SIMPLAN. Logical models and risk analysis models may also be specified.

Model changes Edit Mode is also used to make changes in SIMPLAN models. One of the ways in which "What if?" experiments are conducted with SIMPLAN is by changing the parameters or logical structure of SIMPLAN models through the use of the SIMPLAN editor.

Report formulation User-specified reports are also defined in Edit Mode. Basically, the philosophy of the SIMPLAN report writer is that the user should be able to have any type of report which is desired. SIMPLAN reports are quite easy to formulate even by users with no previous computer programming experience.

Report changes Changes in SIMPLAN report definitions are easily implemented within Edit Mode. Management thus has the freedom and flexibility to make frequent changes in reports or report formats without incurring substantial computer programming costs.

Statistical analysis Routine statistical analysis can be performed in Analysis Mode. Commands are available within Analysis Mode to calculate means, medians, standard deviations, correlation coefficients, partial correlation coefficients, and one-way analysis of variance. Other commands are available for doing time series forecasting and econometric modeling.

Forecasting Analysis Mode also includes a full complement of commands to do time series analysis and forecasting: exponential smoothing, linear time trends, logarithmic time trends, quadratic time trends, and adaptive forecasting.

Econometrics SIMPLAN contains a fully integrated econometric modeling capability. Within Analysis Mode it is possible to (1) *specify* an econometric model; (2) *estimate* its parameters using either ordinary least-squares or two-stage least-squares; (3) *validate* the model; and (4) conduct *policy simulation experiments* with the model.

Model solution   In Analysis Mode it is possible to solve linear, nonlinear, recursive, or simultaneous-equation models. Simultaneous models are solved using a modified version of the Gauss–Seidel method.

Validation   To validate a model by comparing results simulated by the model with actual historical data, Analysis Mode contains a VALIDATE command. The VALIDATE command computes mean percent absolute errors and Theil's inequality coefficients.

Policy simulation   Through the use of the SOLVE command in Analysis Mode, "What if?" policy simulation experiments are conducted with SIMPLAN models. The user may make alternative assumptions about policy variables or external variables which may affect the company.

Report generation   For reports which have been previously defined in Edit Mode, it is possible to generate printed output reports in Report Mode.

Security   To control who has access to SIMPLAN data, models, and reports, User Mode provides the user with an internal security system.

Graphics   The Graphics Mode of SIMPLAN provides the user with a variety of visual displays.

PLANNING SYSTEM

Although SIMPLAN embodies its own planning system, it is compatible with a number of different planning philosophies. Its planning system is equally applicable to large multidivisional companies as well as to small firms (with sales less than $10 million) in which the corporation as a whole is the only division of the company. There are two keywords in the SIMPLAN planning system—*integration* and *consolidation*; that is, at the business unit level, SIMPLAN has the ability to *integrate* financial, marketing, and production models. It also has the capability to *consolidate* business plans either horizontally or vertically.

Business Planning Models

The SIMPLAN planning system assumes that a typical corporation consists of multiple division profit centers or strategic business units. It further assumes that the corporation is decentralized and that each division has its own separate marketing, production, and financial activities. However, there is a centralized corporate financial function for the corporation as a whole. There is no centralized marketing or production activity for the corporation. Of course, SIMPLAN treats a corporation consisting of a single division as merely a special case of Fig. 2.1. In SIMPLAN, each division may be represented by a division model which consists of a front-end financial model driven by a division marketing model and a division production model. Suppose, for example, a corporation has 25 divisions. Then there would be 25 separate division models, each consisting of a separate financial, marketing, and production model. When the entire set of 25 division models is consolidated, the result is a total corporate financial model.

Financial planning models The front end of a typical SIMPLAN corporate planning model is an overall corporate financial model. The custom-designed output reports of a SIMPLAN corporate financial planning model may consist of an income statement, balance sheet, cash flow statement, and sources-and-uses-of-funds statement. In other words, SIMPLAN reports take the form of the usual financial reports which are used by the financial management of the firm. For a multidivisional company, a SIMPLAN corporate financial planning model represents the consolidation of all of the separate division financial models. Frequently, these consolidations involve complex transfers of funds among divisions and are, therefore, not merely straightforward additions.

Each division has its own financial model. Division financial models are usually quite straightforward and include a relatively small number of output variables or line items. A typical SIMPLAN division financial model might consist of an income statement model with 15 to 20 line items and an abbreviated balance sheet model with, say, 10 or 12 line items. In some corporations balance sheet information is not available at the division level. Revenue and sales forecasts may either be read into the SIMPLAN division financial model as given data or generated by a SIMPLAN marketing model. Operational and production costs associated with alternative levels of output may either be read in as given data or generated by a SIMPLAN division production model.

The SIMPLAN corporate financial model can be used to check the economic feasibility of alternative financial plans for the different divisions of the company. It may also be employed to evaluate the financial impact of alternative cash management, depreciation, capital investment, and merger–acquisition policies.

SIMPLAN also contains a number of *built-in financial functions* to facilitate the formulation of financial planning models. These include straight-line depreciation, accelerated depreciation, present value, internal rate of return, and discounted cash flow.

With SIMPLAN users have complete flexibility to specify virtually any type of financial model which they may wish. Managers with no previous training or experience with modeling or computer programming have developed financial planning models with SIMPLAN in a matter of two or three days. The important thing is for the user to understand the accounting or financial structure of the corporation which is being modeled.

Marketing planning models Each of the division models in Fig. 2.1 has its own marketing model. Marketing models are used to explain or predict sales and market share by product or major product group. With SIMPLAN, it is possible to implement two different types of marketing models: Short-term forecasting models and econometric policy simulation models. SIMPLAN contains several forecasting techniques: growth rates, time trends, exponential smoothing, and adaptive forecasting. If the user wants to simulate the effects of alternative pricing or advertising policies on sales or market share, or possibly the effects of changes in the national economy, then econometric models represent appropriate analytical tools. SIMPLAN contains a full complement of econometric modeling capabilities.

Production planning models Each division model in Fig. 2.1 also contains a production model. For given levels of output SIMPLAN production models generate operating costs and cost of goods sold. The SIMPLAN approach to production models is essentially an activity analysis approach in which the cost of operating at different levels of output is built up in terms of the resource requirements. Sales forecasts generated by marketing models provide input into SIMPLAN production models. On the other hand, production models produce much of the operating cost data which are required as input for financial models. In the case of banks and financial institutions, the term "operations model" might be a more appropriate term than "production model."

Integrated planning models One of the most powerful features of SIMPLAN is its ability to integrate financial, marketing, and production models. Model integration is easily achieved at the corporate, division, group, or business unit level.

Consolidated Planning Models

Horizontal consolidation With SIMPLAN it is possible to construct separate division planning models and to consolidate all of these division models horizontally into a consolidated corporate planning model. In other words, through the use of the SIMPLAN database system and security system, division managers may use their own models independently of other divisions or corporate management. Division managers have access to and responsibility for their own databases, models, and reports. On the other hand, corporate management may access any division model which it chooses or consolidate all of the division models into a single corporate planning model. The ADD command, which enables SIMPLAN to do horizontal consolidations, is one of the most powerful commands in SIMPLAN.

Vertical consolidation The CONSOLIDATE command of SIMPLAN consolidates vertically a hierarchy of products, business units, divisions, or groups. The combination of the ADD command and the CONSOLIDATE command provides SIMPLAN users with a broad range of consolidation features.

Multidirectional consolidation The consolidation commands and the SOLVE command make it possible to do multidirectional consolidations. With this feature it is possible to allocate overhead back down to the business unit level for reconsolidation at all levels.

Eliminations When there are transfers of funds as well as goods and services among divisions, then financial eliminations may be calculated within a SIMPLAN consolidation model.

Nonstandard chart of accounts SIMPLAN users are in no sense restricted to a standard chart of accounts. By permitting the use of a nonstandard chart of accounts, SIMPLAN consolidations offer the user a high degree of flexibility.

Postprocessing of consolidated data Postprocessing of consolidated data is another option available with SIMPLAN.

MANAGEMENT INFORMATION SYSTEM

Databases

Internal As we have previously indicated, the SIMPLAN database system permits users to create and maintain their own database as well as to link to other internal databases which may be available within the company.

External We have also previously noted that it is possible to develop interfaces between SIMPLAN and financial databases, and economic databases, and national or regional econometric models.

Database System

Records The basic unit of the information in a SIMPLAN database is the *record*. A SIMPLAN record is defined as a set of numbers associated with a particular variable such as CASH, SALES, or PRICE. A record has a name, an abbreviation, units, a security level, and values. In Fig. A.2 we have defined a record named COST OF GOODS SOLD. Its abbreviation is COG; its units are expressed in dollars, it has a security level of 1, and its values span the time period 1960 through 1980.

A SIMPLAN record normally takes the form of a time series; that is, the numbers in a record are such that the first number represents the value of the particular variable in time period 1, the second number represents the value of the variable in time period 2, etc., and the last number represents the value of the same variable in the last period of the time horizon. In our example in Fig. A.2, the first value of COG corresponds

Abbreviation COG		Record name Cost of goods sold		Units $	Security 1
File 1	File 2	File 3	File 4	File 5	File N
1965					
1980					

Fig. A.2 A SIMPLAN record.

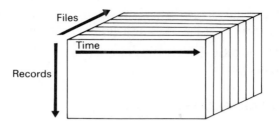

Fig. A.3 SIMPLAN database structure.

to the 1960 value, the second value is the 1961 value, etc., and the last value is the 1980 value of the record. The starting period and the number of elements in a time series are specified by the user. Time periods may be expressed as days, weeks, months, quarters, years, etc.

Files Since a record may contain more than one time series, the user must have a second index for designating a particular time series associated with a given record. This is accomplished in SIMPLAN through the use of a *file* number. Note that the term file is used in SIMPLAN to differentiate among the time series stored in a single record. In our example in Fig. A.2, the COG record contains all of the cost of goods sold data for the entire company with the values of COG associated with televisions stored in file 1, radios stored in file 2, refrigerators stored in file 3, etc.

As can be seen in Fig. A.3, every number in a SIMPLAN database can be described by three different dimensions: a record abbreviation, a file number, and a time period.

Multiple files The multiple file feature of SIMPLAN is one of SIMPLAN's most important features. Multiple files are useful in at least four ways.

First, file 1 may be used to store the database of division 1, file 2 may be used for division 2, etc. The consolidated corporate database may be stored in yet another file. Alternatively, each division's data may be maintained in a separate database. The respective divisions may be responsible for the integrity of their own databases. Yet corporate management may want to maintain a duplicate database for each division so that independent "What if?" experiments may be run by corporate management. Multiple files permit considerable flexibility and provide management with numerous options for managing the corporate and division databases.

Second, with multiple files one can maintain separate files for actual data, budgeted data, or forecast data. Likewise, one can store the results of alternative scenarios in separate files.

Third, multiple files greatly facilitate the implementation of consolidations within multiple level databases.

Fourth, multiple files can be quite useful in econometric studies involving a combination of time series and cross-section data.

Naturally, these are not the only uses for multiple files, nor is there any restriction that the other dimension of a record must be used for time series data. In fact, capitalizing on SIMPLAN's flexibility, users have applied these dimensions for other purposes.

Multiple databases Not only may SIMPLAN users use multiple files, but they may also employ multiple databases. In this instance, a file is viewed as a subset of a database and there may be more than one SIMPLAN database.

Cross-file manipulations Cross-file manipulations can be achieved within the context of a SIMPLAN model or through the use of SIMPLAN's consolidation commands.

Multiple level databases Multiple level databases are a feature of SIMPLAN which allows a hierarchic structure and direct access to all levels of information.

Multiple time periods SIMPLAN databases, models, and reports can accommodate multiple time period data, e.g., days, weeks, months, quarters, years, etc.

Independence of data, models, and reports The independence of data, models, and reports is one of the most powerful features of SIMPLAN. This feature greatly increases the flexibility and ease of use of the system.

Report Generator

User-specified reports The SIMPLAN report generator enables users to design almost any type of report they may choose. In other words, users are not restricted to a rigid report format. SIMPLAN reports are entirely user-specified. The SIMPLAN report generator is much easier to use than is FORTRAN, COBOL, PL/1, or APL. In addition to output flexibility, the SIMPLAN report generator provides for the calculation of row and column totals and subtotals, percentages, growth rates (both simple and compound), and other values. This enables users to calculate these numbers as they need them in a report rather than taking up valuable storage space to save them.

Report Mode in SIMPLAN consists of a report generator combined with a text editor. A report is specified by a "report definition" in much the same way as the logical relationships among records are described by a model. If the abbreviation of a record is used as a line item in a report definition, the name of the record will be printed, along with its units and values. Such options as the number of decimal places to be printed, formatting with dollar signs and commas, column positioning, and indentation can be specified for any portion of the report or the default values can be used. The lines below define a simple report.

```
COLUMN 55: "TOTAL      GROWTH RATE"
*COLUMNS 1970 (1971-1973) 1974 TOTAL (1-5) CGR(1,5)
*HEADER 3-4 "1970-1974"
*TABS FROM 30 BY 12
*WIDTH 10
*DECIMALS 0 0 0 2
HEADER
UNDERLINE
*INDENT 5
*FORMAT 1-3 $,F
*FORMAT 4 %PF
DIV1SALES
```

```
*FORMAT 1-3 ,
DIV2SALES
DIV3SALES
UNDERLINE
*FORMAT 1-3 $,F
*INDENT 1
TOTAL1 "TOTAL SALES"
*PAGE
```

These statements produce the report which follows.

	1970	1974	TOTAL 1970-1974	GROWTH RATE 1970-1974
SALES IN DIVISION ONE	$6,960	$9,277	$40,385	7.45%
SALES IN DIVISION TWO	840	2,400	7,598	30.01%
SALES IN DIVISION THREE	3,755	3,619	18,433	(0.92%)
TOTAL SALES	$11,555	$15,296	$66,415	7.26%

Report definition editing Edit Mode of SIMPLAN contains the facility to make changes in SIMPLAN report definitions. These changes are easily made with the SIMPLAN editor.

Graphics

The Graphics Mode of SIMPLAN permits the user to analyze relationships, patterns, and trends in data through graphical displays.

Security System

User Mode of SIMPLAN permits the user to protect the following elements in a planning and modeling system.

Individual records
Individual files
Individual models

Individual report definitions
Individual functions

MODELING SYSTEM

With the SIMPLAN modeling system it is possible for the user to specify a wide variety of financial, marketing, production, distribution investment, personnel, and forecasting models. SIMPLAN is not a model, rather it is a modeling language. SIMPLAN is designed so that management and analysts can formulate and implement their own planning models. Little or no previous experience in either modeling or computer programming is necessary for the efficient and successful utilization of the SIMPLAN language.

The basic logical structure of SIMPLAN models is that of difference equations. A SIMPLAN model consists of a set of equations and/or logical statements employing notation and symbols similar to those used in basic accounting and high school algebra. For example, in a SIMPLAN equation, +, −, *, and / denote addition, subtraction, multiplication, and division, respectively. The record abbreviation is used in a manner similar to a variable name, and the equal sign (=) is used to denote assignment in an equation. Thus, a typical line in a model might be

PROFIT = REVENUE − EXPENSE

which means for every period over which this model is run, the value of the "profit" record is to be set equal to the difference between the value of the "revenue" and "expense" records in the same period.

Recursive Models

Like most planning and modeling systems, SIMPLAN has the ability to solve causally ordered, recursive models. By placing recursive models in the correct order, it is possible to solve each equation separately in terms of given external variables, values of output variables generated in previous time periods, and values of output variables which have already been solved in earlier equations.

Simultaneous-Equation Models

SIMPLAN also has the capability to solve linear and nonlinear simultaneous-equation models as well as recursive models. Relatively few planning and modeling systems have this feature.

Logical Models

SIMPLAN contains a number of commands to facilitate logical operations. Suppose, for example, if cash balances (CASH) fall below some minimum level (MBAL), the company's line of credit may be automatically increased by the amount of cash shortfall. The SIMPLAN commands to accomplish these objectives follow.

IF CASH < MBAL

DEBT = DEBT(−1) + MBAL − CASH

CASH = MBAL

SIMPLAN includes a complete set of logical comparison operations, as well as a GO TO and an IF command.

Risk Analysis Models

SIMPLAN has a built-in function RANDOM which generates uniformly distributed pseudorandom numbers on the zero–one interval. Special functions which transform these pseudorandom numbers into specific probability distributions such as normal, exponential, binomial, triangular, Poisson, or empirical may be provided to SIMPLAN users.

Other Modeling Features

Equation-type models   The basic structure of a SIMPLAN model is the simple algebraic equation. Anyone familiar with accounting, finance, and high school algebra can develop a SIMPLAN model.

Algebraic operators SIMPLAN makes use of algebraic operators $+, -, /, *$, and $**$ to denote, respectively, addition, subtraction, division, multiplication, and exponentiation.

Storing models SIMPLAN models specified by the user can be easily stored through the use of the SAVE command. The models may then be used repeatedly when needed.

Storing results of a model Model solutions may be stored in the SIMPLAN database.

Storing equations from estimating techniques The STORE command enables the user to store equations estimated by ordinary least-squares, two-stage least-squares, and time trend forecasting techniques.

Storing projections from forecasting techniques Projections from time series forecasting techniques may also be stored automatically.

Model integration The ability to integrate financial, marketing, and production models is an important feature of SIMPLAN.

Line number independence SIMPLAN equations are independent of particular line numbers. SIMPLAN equations are also independent of the rows and columns of SIMPLAN reports.

Model editing A text editor is provided in Edit Mode which is useful in creating or modifying models. Mistakes can be corrected by specifying only the changes to be made instead of reentering the entire erroneous line. Lines can be copied from one place to another within a model, they can be resequenced, and substitutions can be made throughout the model in one operation. For example, if a model had previously used the record CASH in several equations and it was desired to use INCOME instead, all occurrences of CASH can be changed through a single command. The editor also provides for the merging of separate models and the separation of one model into several smaller ones.

SIMPLAN also contains numerous diagnostic features and guides the user through the modeling process with the aid of a substantial number of *error messages*.

FORECASTING SYSTEM

A wide variety of fully integrated forecasting methods is another important feature which differentiates SIMPLAN from other planning and modeling systems. Any data stored in the database can be easily accessed as input for all of these time series forecasting methods. The equations and parameters produced by these methods can be stored automatically; projections can be generated with a single command; and the results can be used as output using any previously established report format.

Analysis Mode includes *growth rates*; linear, quadratic, exponential, and logarithmic *time trends*; *triple exponential smoothing*; and *adaptive forecasting*.

Exponential Smoothing

Exponential smoothing is very similar in effect to a moving average forecast, since the prediction for each period is based on the values which have been encountered in previous periods. After the forecast value is generated, the discrepancy between it and the actual value is examined, and the coefficients of the estimated equation are adjusted accordingly. This process is repeated for each period over which historical data exist. Forecast values for future periods are calculated using the final coefficients derived from this process.

Time Trends

There are three commands in Analysis Mode of SIMPLAN that produce time trend forecasts: The TLINE command generates a linear trend; the TLOG command generates a semilogarithmic trend; and the TQUAD command generates a quadratic trend.

Adaptive Forecasting

The ADAPT command of SIMPLAN performs adaptive forecasting, a process in which a linear regression is refined through a weighting process. The two basic variables in an adaptive forecast are the type of pattern which is used to fit the data and the relative weight to be given to more recent data. Other options which can be specified include the time range over which forecasts are to be generated and the series into which results are to be stored in the database. Adaptive forecasting is one of the most powerful short-term forecasting techniques available.

ECONOMETRIC MODELING SYSTEM

SIMPLAN's user-oriented econometric modeling system can take much of the drudgery and mystery out of the development and implementation of econometric forecasting models. With the SIMPLAN econometric modeling system, management can easily conduct "What if?" simulation experiments to simulate the effects on sales and market share of alternative marketing strategies, as well as alternative assumptions about the behavior of competitors and the national or regional economy.

In one integrated conversational system, it is possible to specify a model, estimate the parameters of the model, validate the model, and do "What if?" policy simulation experiments with the model. With SIMPLAN, the user has the ability to move easily from each of these four steps to the next.

Specification

Linear, nonlinear, recursive, or simultaneous-equation models may be specified by the user in Analysis Mode of SIMPLAN.

Estimation

Ordinary least squares   The ESTIMATE command of SIMPLAN will produce ordinary least-squares estimates of the parameters of single equation, econometric models. It also produces a set of test statistics.

Two-stage least squares   The TSLS command produces two-stage, least-squares estimates of the parameters of a single equation in a system of simultaneous equations as well as a set of test statistics.

Nonlinear regression   Polynomials, logarithmic equations, and certain types of exponential relationships can be transformed to linear equations in SIMPLAN and estimated using either ordinary least squares or two-stage least squares.

Statistics   Both the ESTIMATE and TSLS commands also produce a comprehensive set of test statistics, including standard errors, t-statistics, F-statistics, R^2s, and Durbin–Watson statistics. Other commands are available in Analysis Mode to compute means, medians, analysis of variance, correlation coefficients, partial correlation coefficients, and residuals.

Other features   SIMPLAN contains the analytical capabilities of the X-11 variant of the Census Method II Seasonal Adjustment program. Almon lags, distributed lags, and Cochrane–Orcutt adjustments are also included in SIMPLAN.

Validation

The VALIDATE command compares simulated results with actual observed values and computes mean percent absolute errors and Theil's inequality coefficient. Model solutions are obtained using the SOLVE command and the Gauss–Seidel method.

Simulation versus actuals

Mean percent absolute errors

Theil's inequality coefficient

Policy Simulation

The SOLVE command and the Gauss–Seidel methods are also available to enable the user to conduct "What if?" policy simulation experiments.

Integrated Models

Through the use of the STORE command, econometric models which have been validated can be saved and automatically integrated into existing models. In other words, SIMPLAN's easy-to-use econometric modeling system is fully integrated into its planning and modeling systems.

National and Regional Econometric Models

As we have previously noted, SIMPLAN can be linked to national and regional econometric models and databases.

USER ORIENTATION

Free-format input   SIMPLAN accepts free-format input data. This makes the creation of a SIMPLAN database a straightforward process. Data may be entered either through a terminal interactively or through punched cards or magnetic tape.

User specified subroutines   SIMPLAN users who are familier with either PL/1 or FORTRAN may write their own PL/1 or FORTRAN subroutines which may be called and thus linked to SIMPLAN. This means that SIMPLAN is effectively an open-ended system.

Easy to use The user orientation of SIMPLAN makes it possible for users who are not trained in computer programming to learn the system within a relatively short period of time. Ease of use is perhaps SIMPLAN's most important feature.

SYSTEM AVAILABILITY

Interactive SIMPLAN was designed to be used in conversational and batch computing environments. It can be run interactively under the control of IBM's Time Sharing Option (TSO) or Conversational Monitoring System (CMS).

Batch SIMPLAN can be run effectively in a batch-computing environment. Frequently SIMPLAN users run repetitive production runs in the batch mode. However, many SIMPLAN users have used SIMPLAN effectively in batch mode for development.

Service bureaus SIMPLAN is available worldwide through seven computer service bureaus: (1) Information Services Business Division of the General Electric Company, (2) Canada Systems Group, Ltd., (3) Data Services Division of Informatics, Inc., (4) AVCO Data Services, (5) A.O. Smith Data Systems Division, (6) Martin Marietta Data Systems, and (7) McDonnell Douglas Automation Company.

In-house hardware requirements SIMPLAN is a PL/1 applications program which uses a small amount of Assembler Language for specific functions. It is designed for installation on IBM System/360 Models 50–195 and System/370 Models 138–195, IBM 3000 series, and processors such as AMDAHL and ITEL which are plug compatible with IBM operating systems. SIMPLAN runs under the control of IBM OS/MFT, OS/MVT, OS/VS1, OS/VS2, or MVS. It can also be run interactively under the control of the Time Sharing Option (TSO) or the Conversational Monitor System (CMS) available with VM/370.

In order to use all functions of SIMPLAN, a minimum region or partition of 200K under OS (576K under CMS) is needed. This requirement may be relaxed for limited applications of SIMPLAN.

In order to modify and maintain the SIMPLAN system, a PL/1 compiler and its associated libraries should be present. Either the PL/1 level F compiler, provided free of charge with OS, or the Optimizing Compiler, available as an IBM program product, can be used with SIMPLAN.

The SIMPLAN Database and Text Library reside on a direct-access device while SIMPLAN is being used. Any of the 2300- or 3300- series devices (2314, 3330, 2301, etc.) can be used for this purpose. A typical SIMPLAN Database/Text Library set will occupy approximately 1000K of auxiliary storage (4 cylinders on a normal-density 3330 disk). Approximately 5 cylinders of a 3330 are sufficient for storing the SIMPLAN Load module.

Users with smaller systems, such as the 360/40 or the 370/135, less than 512K of main memory on MFT or MVT systems, or non-OS operating systems should contact the SSI Systems Development Group to determine the feasibility of a customized SIMPLAN installation.

SUMMARY OF IMPORTANT FEATURES

Technical Features

The ten most important technical features of SIMPLAN are summarized below.

- Independence of data, models, and reports
- Flexible report generator and graphical display
- Consolidations
- Simultaneous and recursive models
- Policy simulations: "What if?"
- Econometrics and forecasting
- Econometric databases
- Integrated models
- Security
- User specified subroutines

Major Features

There are three major features which differentiate SIMPLAN from other planning, budgeting, and modeling systems: (1) power, (2) flexibility, and (3) ease of use.

Power The power of SIMPLAN is evidenced by the fact that within one fully integrated system the user has access to (1) a planning system, (2) a management information system, (3) a modeling system, (4) a forecasting system, and (5) an econometric modeling system.

Flexibility The flexibility of SIMPLAN enables the user to make changes in models, reports, or databases with little or no effort.

Ease of use Finally, the most important feature of SIMPLAN is its user orientation.

NOTE

1. SIMPLAN was developed by Social Systems, Inc., P.O. Box 2809, Chapel Hill, North Carolina, 27514. *Corporate Planning and Modeling with SIMPLAN* by R. Britton Mayo was published by Addison-Wesley in 1978.

Appendix B:
Statistical Tables

TABLE B.1 *t* VALUES

Reproduced from Table III (Distribution of *t*) on page 46 of Fisher and Yates: *Statistical Tables for Biological, Agricultural and Medical Research*, published by Longman Group Ltd., London. Previously published by Oliver Boyd, Edinburgh, and by permission of the authors and publishers.

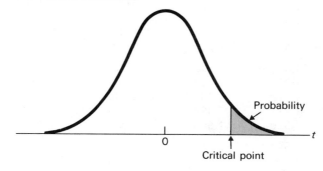

Degrees of freedom	Probability				
	.10	.05	.025	.01	.005
1	3.078	6.314	12.706	31.821	63.657
2	1.886	2.920	4.303	6.965	9.925
3	1.638	2.353	3.182	4.541	5.841
4	1.533	2.132	2.776	3.747	4.604
5	1.476	2.015	2.571	3.365	4.032

Table B.1 *Continued*

Degrees of freedom	Probability				
	.10	.05	.025	.01	.005
6	1.440	1.943	2.447	3.143	3.707
7	1.415	1.895	2.365	2.998	3.499
8	1.397	1.860	2.306	2.896	3.355
9	1.383	1.833	2.262	2.821	3.250
10	1.372	1.812	2.228	2.764	3.169
11	1.363	1.796	2.201	2.718	3.106
12	1.356	1.782	2.179	2.681	3.055
13	1.350	1.771	2.160	2.650	3.012
14	1.345	1.761	2.145	2.624	2.977
15	1.341	1.753	2.131	2.602	2.947
16	1.337	1.746	2.120	2.583	2.921
17	1.333	1.740	2.110	2.567	2.898
18	1.330	1.734	2.101	2.552	2.878
19	1.328	1.729	2.093	2.539	2.861
20	1.325	1.725	2.086	2.528	2.845
21	1.323	1.721	2.080	2.518	2.831
22	1.321	1.717	2.074	2.508	2.819
23	1.319	1.714	2.069	2.500	2.807
24	1.318	1.711	2.064	2.492	2.797
25	1.316	1.708	2.060	2.485	2.787
26	1.315	1.706	2.056	2.479	2.779
27	1.314	1.703	2.052	2.473	2.771
28	1.313	1.701	2.048	2.467	2.763
29	1.311	1.699	2.045	2.462	2.756
30	1.310	1.697	2.042	2.457	2.750
40	1.303	1.684	2.021	2.423	2.704
60	1.296	1.671	2.000	2.390	2.660
120	1.289	1.658	1.980	2.358	2.617
∞	1.282	1.645	1.960	2.326	2.576

TABLE B.2 *F* VALUES (FIVE PERCENT)

Reprinted by permission from *Statistical Methods*, 6th edition, by George W. Snedecor and William G. Cochran, © 1967 by the Iowa State University Press, Ames, Iowa.

Degrees of freedom for denominator	Degrees of freedom for numerator					
	1	2	3	4	5	6
1	161	200	216	225	230	234
2	18.51	19.00	19.16	19.25	19.30	19.33
3	10.13	9.55	9.28	9.12	9.01	8.94
4	7.71	6.94	6.59	6.39	6.26	6.16
5	6.61	5.79	5.41	5.19	5.05	4.95
6	5.99	5.14	4.76	4.53	4.39	4.28
7	5.59	4.74	4.35	4.12	3.97	3.87
8	5.32	4.46	4.07	3.84	3.69	3.58
9	5.12	4.26	3.86	3.63	3.48	3.37
10	4.96	4.10	3.71	3.48	3.33	3.22
11	4.84	3.98	3.59	3.36	3.20	3.09
12	4.75	3.89	3.49	3.26	3.11	3.00
13	4.67	3.80	3.41	3.18	3.02	2.92
14	4.60	3.74	3.34	3.11	2.96	2.85
15	4.54	3.68	3.29	3.06	2.90	2.79
16	4.49	3.63	3.24	3.01	2.85	2.74
17	4.45	3.59	3.20	2.96	2.81	2.70
18	4.41	3.55	3.16	2.93	2.77	2.66
19	4.38	3.52	3.13	2.90	2.74	2.63
20	4.35	3.49	3.10	2.87	2.71	2.60
21	4.32	3.47	3.07	2.84	2.68	2.57
22	4.30	3.44	3.05	2.82	2.66	2.55
23	4.28	3.42	3.03	2.80	2.64	2.53
24	4.26	3.40	3.01	2.78	2.62	2.51
25	4.24	3.38	2.99	2.76	2.60	2.49
26	4.22	3.37	2.89	2.74	2.59	2.47
27	4.21	3.35	2.96	2.73	2.57	2.46
28	4.20	3.34	2.95	2.71	2.56	2.44
29	4.18	3.33	2.93	2.70	2.54	2.43
30	4.17	3.32	2.92	2.69	2.53	2.43
32	4.15	3.30	2.90	2.67	2.51	2.40
34	4.13	3.28	2.88	2.65	2.49	2.38
36	4.11	3.26	2.86	2.63	2.48	2.36
38	4.10	3.25	2.85	2.62	2.46	2.35
40	4.08	3.23	2.84	2.61	2.45	2.34
42	4.07	3.22	2.83	2.59	2.44	2.32
44	4.06	3.21	2.82	2.58	2.43	2.31
46	4.05	3.20	2.81	2.57	2.42	2.30
48	4.04	3.19	2.80	2.56	2.41	2.30
50	4.03	3.18	2.79	2.56	2.40	2.29
55	4.02	3.17	2.78	2.54	2.38	2.27

Table B.2 *Continued*

Degrees of freedom for denominator	Degrees of freedom for numerator					
	1	2	3	4	5	6
60	4.00	3.15	2.76	2.52	2.37	2.25
65	3.99	3.14	2.75	2.51	2.36	2.24
70	3.98	3.13	2.74	2.50	2.35	2.32
80	3.96	3.11	2.72	2.48	2.33	2.21
100	3.94	3.09	2.70	2.46	2.30	2.19
200	3.89	3.04	2.65	2.41	2.26	2.14
400	3.86	3.02	2.62	2.39	2.23	2.12

TABLE B.3 *F* VALUES (ONE PERCENT)

Reprinted by permission from *Statistical Methods*, 6th edition, by George W. Snedecor and William G. Cochran, © 1967 by the Iowa State University Press, Ames Iowa.

Degrees of freedom for denominator	Degrees of freedom for numerator					
	1	2	3	4	5	6
1	4052	4999	5403	5625	5764	5859
2	98.49	99.01	99.17	99.25	99.30	99.33
3	34.12	30.81	29.46	28.71	28.24	27.91
4	21.20	18.00	16.69	15.98	15.52	15.21
5	16.26	13.27	12.06	11.39	10.97	10.67
6	13.74	10.92	9.78	9.15	8.75	8.47
7	12.25	9.55	8.45	7.85	7.46	7.19
8	11.26	8.65	7.59	7.01	6.63	6.37
9	10.56	8.02	6.99	6.42	6.06	5.80
10	10.04	7.56	6.55	5.99	5.64	5.39
11	9.65	7.20	6.22	5.67	5.32	5.07
12	9.33	6.93	5.95	5.41	5.06	4.82
13	9.07	6.70	5.74	5.20	4.86	4.62
14	8.86	6.51	5.56	5.03	4.69	4.46
15	8.68	6.36	5.42	4.89	4.56	4.32
16	8.53	6.23	5.29	4.77	4.44	4.20
17	8.40	6.11	5.18	4.67	4.34	4.10
18	8.28	6.01	5.09	4.58	4.25	4.01
19	8.18	5.93	5.01	4.50	4.17	3.94
20	8.10	5.85	4.94	4.43	4.10	3.87
21	8.02	5.78	4.87	4.37	4.04	3.81
22	7.94	5.72	4.82	4.41	3.99	3.76
23	7.88	5.66	4.76	4.26	3.94	3.71
24	7.82	5.61	4.72	4.22	3.90	3.67
25	7.77	5.57	4.68	4.18	3.86	3.63

Table B.3 *Continued*

Degrees of freedom for denominator	Degrees of freedom for numerator					
	1	2	3	4	5	6
26	7.72	5.53	4.64	4.14	3.82	3.59
27	7.68	5.49	4.60	4.11	3.79	3.56
28	7.64	5.45	4.57	4.07	3.76	3.53
29	7.60	5.52	4.54	4.04	3.73	3.50
30	7.56	5.39	4.51	4.02	3.70	3.47
32	7.50	5.34	4.46	3.97	3.66	3.42
34	7.44	5.29	4.42	3.93	3.61	3.38
36	7.39	5.25	4.38	3.89	3.58	3.35
38	7.35	5.21	4.34	3.86	3.54	3.32
40	7.31	5.18	4.31	3.83	3.51	3.29
42	7.27	5.15	4.29	3.80	3.49	3.26
44	7.24	5.12	4.26	3.78	3.46	3.24
46	7.21	5.10	4.24	3.76	3.44	3.22
48	7.19	5.08	4.22	3.74	3.42	3.20
50	7.17	5.06	4.20	3.72	3.41	3.18
55	7.12	5.01	4.16	3.68	3.37	3.15
60	7.08	4.98	4.13	3.65	3.34	3.12
65	7.04	4.95	4.10	3.62	3.31	3.09
70	7.01	4.92	4.08	3.60	3.29	3.07
80	6.95	4.88	4.04	3.56	3.25	3.04
100	6.90	4.82	3.98	3.51	3.20	2.99
200	6.76	4.71	3.88	3.41	3.11	2.90
400	6.70	4.66	3.83	3.36	3.06	2.85

TABLE B.4 DURBIN–WATSON VALUES

Reproduced by permission from J. Durbin and G. S. Watson, Testing for Serial Correlation in Least Squares Regression. II. Biometrika **38** (June, 1951), pp. 159–178.

Number of observations	Probability in lower tail	Number of right-hand side variables (excluding the constant)									
		1		2		3		4		5	
		D_L	D_U	D_L	D_U	D_L	D_U	D_L	D_U	D_L	D_U
	.01	.81	1.07	.70	1.25	.59	1.46	.49	1.70	.39	1.96
15	.025	.95	1.23	.83	1.40	.71	1.61	.59	1.84	.48	2.09
	.05	1.08	1.36	.95	1.54	.82	1.75	.69	1.97	.56	2.21
	.01	.95	1.15	.86	1.27	.77	1.41	.68	1.57	.60	1.74
20	.025	1.08	1.28	.99	1.41	.89	1.55	.79	1.70	.70	1.87
	.05	1.20	1.41	1.10	1.54	1.00	1.68	.90	1.83	.79	1.99
	.01	1.05	1.21	.98	1.30	.90	1.41	.83	1.52	.75	1.65
25	.025	1.18	1.34	1.10	1.43	1.02	1.54	.94	1.65	.86	1.77
	.05	1.29	1.45	1.21	1.55	1.12	1.66	1.04	1.77	.95	1.89
	.01	1.13	1.26	1.07	1.34	1.01	1.42	.94	1.51	.88	1.61
30	.025	1.25	1.38	1.18	1.46	1.12	1.54	1.05	1.63	.98	1.73
	.05	1.35	1.49	1.28	1.57	1.21	1.65	1.14	1.74	1.07	1.83
	.01	1.25	1.34	1.20	1.40	1.15	1.46	1.10	1.52	1.05	1.58
40	.025	1.35	1.45	1.30	1.51	1.25	1.57	1.20	1.63	1.15	1.69
	.05	1.44	1.54	1.39	1.60	1.34	1.66	1.29	1.72	1.23	1.79
	.01	1.32	1.40	1.28	1.45	1.24	1.49	1.20	1.54	1.16	1.59
50	.025	1.42	1.50	1.38	1.54	1.34	1.59	1.30	1.64	1.26	1.69
	.05	1.50	1.59	1.46	1.63	1.42	1.67	1.38	1.72	1.34	1.77
	.01	1.38	1.45	1.35	1.48	1.32	1.52	1.28	1.56	1.25	1.60
60	.025	1.47	1.54	1.44	1.57	1.40	1.61	1.37	1.65	1.33	1.69
	.05	1.55	1.62	1.51	1.65	1.48	1.69	1.44	1.73	1.41	1.77
	.01	1.47	1.52	1.44	1.54	1.42	1.57	1.39	1.60	1.36	1.62
80	.025	1.54	1.59	1.52	1.62	1.49	1.65	1.47	1.67	1.44	1.70
	.05	1.61	1.66	1.59	1.69	1.56	1.72	1.53	1.74	1.51	1.77
	.01	1.52	1.56	1.50	1.58	1.48	1.60	1.46	1.63	1.44	1.65
100	.025	1.59	1.63	1.57	1.65	1.55	1.67	1.53	1.70	1.51	1.72
	.05	1.65	1.69	1.63	1.72	1.61	1.74	1.59	1.76	1.57	1.78

NOTE: D_L is the lower bound and D_U is the upper bound of the range of inconclusive critical Durbin–Watson values.